GUIDE TO
BETTER CARD PLAY

The *Guide To Better Bridge* was written for the vast majority of players who are ambitious enough to improve their bidding skills beyond the basics. The *Guide To Better Card Play* is the companion volume designed to raise the playing skills for the same class of players.

It is very satisfying to be able to reach the best contract time and time again, but this will be of little avail on the scoresheet if your play lets you down. The two sections on declarer play will enable you to reap the rewards of accurate bidding.

When you are defending, not all of their contracts will be defeatable. However, you should hate it when their contract could have been beaten but you have allowed it to make. The two sections on defence will help you to wipe the smirks off their faces. If you master even half of the material in the sections on defense, you will be entering a plus score for your side far more often.

The *Guide To Better Card Play* is not a book for expert players. It does not deal with exotic and rare situations. On the contrary, it is designed to cover the fundamentals of skilful declarer play and sound defense. Its aim is to provide you with the techniques necessary to fulfil your contracts and to defeat theirs, and at the same time to emphasise the role of judgment. Bridge is not a game of rote learning. You need to know the rules, no doubt about that, but you also need the flexibility to recognise when the situation indicates a departure from the rules. The *Guide To Better Card Play* provides the rules and also the reasoning when to take a different course. The *Guide* is the farmland of technique in which the seeds of judgment are sown. Your reward will be to reap that crop.

We all like to win, and win regularly. The euphoria in winning at bridge cannot be matched and with the knowledge contained in the *Guide To Better Card Play*, you will be on the road to winning more often. Even if your efforts are not crowned with success every time, you will certainly find that success occurs with greater frequency. More importantly, you will come to recognise the distinction between bad luck and misplay or misdefense. Follow the Guide-lines and you can have faith that you have done the right thing, even if it did not work out on the actual lie of the cards. The belief that you are doing the right thing in play and defense will boost your confidence and this extra confidence will be reflected by a significant improvement in the results you have been able to manage so far.

Ron Klinger first played for Australia in 1970 when he was a member of the team that won the Far East Open Teams Championship. Since then he has competed in the world championships in 1976, 1978, 1980, 1984, 1986, 1988 and 1989. He won the Far East Open Pairs Championships in 1985 and again in 1987. In 1989, he was a member of the Australian Open Team which reached the semi-finals of the Bermuda Bowl, the world teams championship. In addition to the many state and national titles to his credit, he is an Australian Grandmaster and a World Bridge Federation International Master. He has written more than twenty bridge books, published locally and overseas. The Guide To Better Card Play has been compiled from his many successful intermediate to advanced classes conducted over the past two decades.

Other books by Ron Klinger
published by Houghton Mifflin Company

Bridge Basics
Guide to Better Bridge

By Hugh Kelsey and Ron Klinger

Instant Guide to Bridge

Standard American Edition

GUIDE TO
BETTER
CARD
PLAY

♠ ♦ ♥ ♣

RON KLINGER

*A Master Bridge Series title
in conjunction with Peter Crawley*

Houghton Mifflin Company
Boston • 1991

Copyright © 1990, 1991 by Ron Klinger

For information about permission to reproduce selections from
this book, write to Permissions, Houghton Mifflin Company,
2 Park Street, Boston, Massachusetts 02108.

Library of Congress Cataloging-in-Publication Data

Klinger, Ron.
Guide to better card play / Ron Klinger. — Standard American ed.
p.   cm.
"A Master bridge series title."
ISBN 0-395-59107-4
1. Contract bridge.   I. Title.
GV1282.3.K624   1991   91-4493
795.41′5 — dc20   CIP

Printed in the United States of America

BP 10 9 8 7 6 5 4 3 2 1

To Peter Crawley
With affection and appreciation

Acknowledgments

My thanks go to Jim Biggins and David Lilley for their helpful comments and also to Kokhan Bagchi, Peter Gill, George Havas and my wife Suzie who all gave freely of their time to proofread the manuscript. They made countless corrections and many helpful suggestions. The good bits are the product of their endeavours, but I claim sole credit for whatever errors might remain.

INTRODUCING RON KLINGER

by Alan Truscott

Look around the world of bridge in search of someone who is at the top of the tree as a player, teacher and writer and you will find perhaps half a dozen candidates. One of them, and only one, is outside North America, which is why he is not as well known as he ought to be.

His name is Ron Klinger, and his residence is in Sydney, Australia, long the home of some of the world's best players. I first met him two decades ago when I took an expert team for a Down-Under tour and encountered a young Professor of Law who was describing the play for large audiences with intelligence and wit.

Soon afterwards he abandoned academic pursuits, which may have been a loss to the Law but was certainly a gain for the bridge community. He rapidly turned himself into Australia's Mr. Bridge, the equivalent perhaps of Charles Goren in his heyday in the forties and fifties. However the parallel is inexact, for Goren had many collaborators and Klinger is a one-man band.

Like Goren, Klinger made his name to the bridge public by a string of impressive playing performances. He has lost count of the number of major titles he has won, and enumerating his international appearances is not much easier. Down-Under, as Up-Over, every expert wants to carry the flag in foreign parts and fierce selection battles occur annually.

He is almost always in the thick of it, and is the most successful player of his generation. His total international appearances may soon rival that of the legendary Tim Seres, who helped earlier Australian teams to challenge effectively at world level.

Specifically Klinger has played five times in the Far East Championships, winning the Teams in 1970 and the Pairs twice, in 1985 and 1987. On a wider scene he has played in six of the biennial Olympiads — the bridge misnomer for an Olympic — and at three consecutive ones, in 1976, 1978 and 1980, he won the Bols Brilliancy Prize: for the best-played hand in 1976, and for his bridge journalism on the other occasions. Since there are hundreds of candidates for this prize his string is not only remarkable but unique. In the Bermuda Bowl, in which the representation is by zones, the South Pacific is represented by Australia and New Zealand. In this event Klinger made his second appearance in 1989, in Perth, and the team reached the semifinals before losing to the American defending champions after a hard fight.

For occasions such as this Klinger has created his own 'Power' system, which is a clever blend of the old and the new. Most of the opening bids follow the recipe that Dr. Paul Stern devised for the Austrian team which won the first world championship, played in 1937. An updated version, 'New South Wales', was popular in Sydney with Seres and his group. Klinger has taken some elements and added hypermodern two-bids and relays, a mixture that he does not offer to his students and readers. It is reserved for his partners, who are required to have good memories.

In a 13-year stint as Editor, starting in 1972, Klinger made *Australian Bridge* one of the world's best bridge magazines. At the same time he began writing a series of successful books on the game. One of them, 100 WINNING BRIDGE TIPS, has proved very popular in the United States and as these lines are written, he is at work on a sequel. He personally published many of the original Australian editions of his books using an early desk-top publishing set-up.

He is, as I know from hearing him, a superb teacher, and regularly projects his knowledge of the game to large groups in various parts of his continent. Like all the best bridge instructors, he provides his students with prepared deals to illustrate the lesson. This involves not only careful planning but also laborious work, as I know from personal experience.

When a vivacious lady named Suzie became his bride in 1974 she immediately found that bridge would have a big impact on her life. The money in the kitty was just sufficient either to take a honeymoon or to publish his first book. (It proved a great success.) Suzie attends to all the administrative details that her husband's work entails. Their children, Ari and Keri, join in much of the family travel, and if they miss some schooling, the parents promptly turn themselves into substitute teachers.

I began by saying that Klinger is a top player, writer and teacher. But he is also a commentator, game director, editor, publisher, game inventor, group travel co-ordinator and tour guide. What else is there? Time will tell.

Alan Truscott
January 1991

CONTENTS

INTRODUCTION

The *Guide To Better Card Play* is essentially a practical book. While you will derive benefit just by reading the text, you will do far, far better if you spend time on the exercises and the revision quizzes. Always produce an answer yourself before you consult the solutions at the back of the book. It does not matter in the slightest if you make any mistakes here. The aim is to eradicate the errors when you are playing when the mistakes do cost.

You should also practise on the play hands in each chapter. If you can arrange a group of four players, you can play the hands at home by having each player sort out the appropriate hand from the lists of hands on pages 186 onwards. This way the hands can be arranged without anyone yet knowing the point of the hand. Bid the hand through — it is helpful to use written bidding — and when the auction is over, whoever is dummy should consult the relevant hand number in the text. The dummy should read out the recommended bidding. If this differs from your bidding, not to worry. Be tolerant and recognise that not everyone bids as well as you. The notes to each hand often refer to significant aspects in the bidding. Occasionally the bidding will lead to a less than ideal contract, but the contract to be played is the one in the text. If this is not the same as the one reached, you may care to replay the hand later in the contract you reached, but initially, play the recommended contract. The opening lead is made and dummy checks that it is the recommended lead. If not, replace it and make the lead suggested. The play is conducted without further reference to the text until the hand is over. Dummy can then indicate how the play should have gone if the play in the text differs from the actual play. It makes it easier if the cards are played duplicate style, keeping the cards in front of each player, so that the hand can be replayed conveniently. It also helps if everyone has their own book.

If some of the material is new to you, it will be worthwhile to read through the book again in about 3-6 months and then at regular intervals. You may always pick up something that slipped under your guard originally and refresh your memory as well. Above all, remember that bridge is a game and is meant to be enjoyed. It can and should be a lot of fun and that is how you should approach it. Who wants to play opposite a grouch? Keep your sense of perspective so that you can play the game with a smile, a chuckle and a sense of humor. I hope that you will derive as much pleasure and satisfaction from it as I have.

TO THE BRIDGE TEACHER

The *Guide To Better Card Play* is ideal for classroom use. It is set out as 4 courses of 8 lessons each. Parts 1 and 2 are suitable for Improver-Intermediate classes and Parts 3 and 4 are better for Intermediate-Advanced groups. The hands in Parts 3 and 4 are significantly tougher than the ones in Parts 1 and 2.

The bidding throughout follows Standard American principles and is compatible with 4-card majors or 5-card majors and almost all local differences. Perhaps a hand here or there might have a different opening bid because of local teaching practice. You will be aware of that and can attend to it, should the problem arise. Each chapter contains more material than you may need in the normal 2-3 hour lesson. The subject matter can be covered in less than an hour but the exercises and the play hands may be more than required. You should pick and choose the exercises which you wish to be done in class and leave the rest for the students to do at home.

It is worth spending more time on the play hands in class than on any other area because the students will derive more benefit from the play than from simply listening to a lecture, no matter how skilful and entertaining you might be. Some declarers will succeed, some will fail. Whatever happens, encourage those who fail and compliment those who make it. You can achieve more by praise and encouragement than by criticism.

It is hoped that the *Guide* will provide a useful text for your students so that they can enjoy a higher success rate. In addition, it should make the teaching and learning of card play an easier and more satisfying project.

Ron Klinger, 1991

PART 1

CONSOLIDATE YOUR

DEFENSIVE PLAY

CHAPTER 1

THE CARD TO LEAD FROM SHORT SUITS

First choose the suit to lead. This decision is covered in Chapters 3 and 4. After selecting the suit, you must play the correct card in the suit. No matter which system of leads you adopt, there is little scope for deviation from the correct systemic card. One function of the lead is to inform partner about your holding in the suit. To deviate will mislead partner. 'Short suit leads' refers to leads from doubletons or tripletons.

The **Honor Cards** are the A, K, Q, J and 10. Lower cards are called **'spot cards'**, **'pips'** or **"rags"**.

DOUBLETONS

Lead the top card. The card to lead is underlined :

A-5   **K**-J   **Q**-7   **8**-3   **3**-2

THREE-CARD SUITS

Rule 1 : With an honor and the card immediately below it, lead **TOP** of the touching cards :

K-Q-x   **Q**-J-x   **J**-10-x   **10**-9-x

K-**J**-10   **K**-**10**-9   **Q**-**10**-9   **A**-**K**-x

NOTE : From A-K-x, the ace is recommended, but the king is commonly led by many pairs.

Rule 2 : With one or two honors and no touching cards, lead the **BOTTOM** card. For example :

K-8-**2**   **Q**-10-**4**   **J**-9-**5**   **10**-6-**2**

NOTE : The 10, an honor, follows Rules 1 and 2.

EXCEPTION : From A-x-x, lead the ace in a suit contract, but bottom card at no-trumps.

Rule 3 : With no honor, lead the **MIDDLE** card. Next round, play top of the remaining doubleton.

9-6-2 : Lead the 6, play the 9 on the next round.

4-3-2 : Lead the 3, play the 4 on the next round.

8-7-6 : Lead the 7, play the 8 on the next round. For top of sequence, the sequence must contain an honor.

8-4-3 : Lead the 4, play the 8 on the next round.

This method, known as **Middle-Up-Down** or **M.U.D.** is the most popular method of leading from three cards with no honor card.

Variation : Some partnerships prefer bottom from any three cards, including three rags. Check with partner before adopting this approach.

Variation : Top-of-nothing is now a discredited method of leading from rag holdings since partner is unable to distinguish doubletons from 3-card or longer holdings. However, if your bidding has shown length in a suit (e.g. you raised partner's suit, thus promising 3-card or 4-card support), you may lead top from three or four rags. Since partner will not be misled about suit length (you cannot hold a shortage), the top card lead will deny any honor in the suit.

WHY LEAD TOP FROM DOUBLETONS?

(1) Honor Doubleton

The top card is led from holdings like A-x, K-x, Q-x, J-x and 10-x to unblock the suit and to enable partner to take as many tricks as possible in the suit.

```
            8 7 2
A 6                   K Q J 5 3
          10 9 4
```

West leads the ace and East can cash as many tricks as are available. If West leads low, the defense takes only two quick tricks in the suit. (**NOTE :** If East is on lead and leads the king, West must unblock the ace. Overtake the king with the ace and return the 6. Then East-West collect all their tricks. If East leads the king and West plays low, the defense can take only two quick tricks.)

```
           10 9 5 2
K 6                   A Q J 4 3
            8 7
```

If West leads the king and then low, East-West can take five tricks in no-trumps. If West leads low, the defense cannot take five tricks at once. In a suit contract, if West leads the king and then low to East, West is in a position to overruff South on the third round. If West leads low to East's ace and wins the second round, West is not in a position to score an overruff.

```
            8 7 2
Q 6                   K J 9 5 3
           A 10 4
```

If West leads the queen and continues, East's suit is set up whether South wins the ace at once or later. If West leads low first, South can block the East-West suit by winning the ace on the first round or by ducking the second round to West's queen.

```
        K 9 5
J 6              A Q 10 7 2
        8 4 3
```

If West leads the jack, dummy's king is trapped at once. If West leads low, declarer can play the 9. East wins but dummy's K-5 is still a stopper at no-trumps. At trumps, East could continue with the ace and give West a ruff, but jack first allows the defense to take three tricks without using one of West's trumps.

```
        4 3
10 2              K Q J 7 5
        A 9 8 6
```

If West leads the 10, East's suit sets up at no-trumps, no matter when South takes the ace. If West leads low, South can block the suit by taking the ace on the first round or by ducking the first and second rounds.

(2) Rag Doubleton

The top card from a rag doubleton is the standard way of telling partner that you have precisely two cards in the suit. When partner sees a high spot card followed by a lower spot card, partner can deduce that you have led a doubleton. In a suit contract, partner then knows that you can ruff the third round. In any contract, knowing you hold a doubleton enables partner to work out how many cards declarer holds in the suit.

WHY MIDDLE-UP-DOWN?

The purpose of middle-up-down is to distinguish 3-card holdings from doubletons. If partner sees you lead 9-then-7, partner knows you have led a doubleton. If you lead 7-then-9, partner knows you have another card in the suit . . . with 9-7 only, you would have led the 9 first.

The middle card is chosen rather than the lowest from three rags, so that the lead of the lowest card in a suit will promise an honor card in the suit led. In standard methods, there are several valuable inferences when you can tell that partner has led the highest spot card or the lowest spot card possible.

Lead of the highest top spot card is normally a singleton or a doubleton. (Exceptionally, it may be bottom from a holding like K-J-x.)

Lead of the lowest spot card promises a singleton or an honor in the suit led. (Lowest cannot be top from a doubleton or middle from M.U.D. It is either a singleton or from an honor card holding.)

High spot card followed by lower = doubleton.

Low spot card followed by higher = at least one more card in the suit led.

With M.U.D. you cannot tell the number of cards held by the leader until the second round of the suit. The first lead is bound to be ambiguous. The benefit is that top card leads and bottom card leads are clarified. Pairs who lead lowest from three rags believe it more useful to indicate the number of cards held on the *first* lead of a suit than to promise an honor (perhaps only the 10 or jack) with the bottom card lead.

WHY DO WE NOT M.U.D. WITH 10-X-X?

From 10-7-3 and equivalent holdings. the bottom card is led. The 10 will often be too valuable to discard on the second round of the suit.

```
        9 6 4
10 7 3              K Q 8 5 2
        A J
```

West leads the 3 to the queen and ace. Later, East leads the king. West plays the 7 and keeps the 10 to capture the 9 in dummy. West has led 3-then-7 so that East can work out that West has the 10 left.

If West leads the 7 first — queen — ace, what does West play when East later cashes the king? If West drops the 10 to follow through with middle-up, the 9 in dummy is high, so that is out, but if West plays 7-then-3, East will read the lead as a doubleton.

```
        9 5 4
10 7 3              A K 8 6 2
        Q J
```

West leads the 3 to the king and drops the 7 under the ace. West's 3-then-7 lets East know that the missing card in the suit is with West. If West wrongly leads the 7 first, which card does West play when East takes the ace on the next trick? To drop the 10 would set up dummy's 9. However, if West drops the 3, West has led 7-then-3 and East may be deceived into thinking West can ruff the third round of the suit. A third round of the suit could be fatal for the defense.

```
        Q J
10 5 2              K 8 7 6 4
        A 9 3
```

West leads the 2 to the queen, king, ace. When the jack is played later, West follows with the 5 and East knows West has another card in the suit. The same follows if East ducks the first round and plays the king next time. However, if West leads the 5 first, he has to play the 2 next time as he cannot afford the 10. 5-then-2 shows a doubleton and East may now abandon the suit, fearing South has the strength.

NOTE: If West wrongly leads the 10 (the dreaded top-of-nothing) in any of the above layouts, this will create an extra trick for declarer.

THE LEAD OF THE 9

The 9 lead in standard methods will always be a singleton or a doubleton (with one rare exception). The 9 cannot be M.U.D since if the 9 is 'middle', the 'up' card would be an honor and we never play Middle-Up-Down from a suit including an honor. *The rare exception?* From K-J-9, the standard lead is also the 9.

Where the 8 is led and the 9 is visible, the same inference applies. The 8 will be a singleton or a doubleton. Since the 9 is visible, the 8 cannot be a Middle-Up-Down lead, for again the 'up' card would be an honor. *Rare exceptions :* The 8 is also the standard lead from K-J-8, K-10-8 and Q-10-8.

The same inferences apply if the 7 is led with the 8 and 9 visible, or the 6 is led with the 7, 8, 9 visible.

THE CORRECT LEAD FROM A-X-X

In no-trumps, lead the bottom card.

	6 4	
A 5 2		K J 10 7 3
	Q 9 8	

West leads the 2, East takes the king and returns the jack. South scores no tricks. However, if West leads the ace first, South makes a trick with the queen.

	7 3	
A 6 4		Q J 10 9 5
	K 8 2	

West leads the 4, East plays the 9 and South takes the king. (If South ducks, South makes no trick.) Now if either East or West gain the lead, the defense can take four tricks. However, if West leads the ace first, South can hold up the king till the third round. Now West cannot return East's suit later.

In a trump contract, the danger of a singleton makes it superior to lead the ace first.

	7	
A 6 4		Q J 10 9 5 3
	K 8 2	

In a suit contract, West leads the ace. The defense takes one trick and so does declarer. If West leads low, declarer takes a trick but the defense has none.

	6	
A 5 4		K 10 9 8 3 2
	Q J 7	

In a suit contract, West leads the ace. The defense takes a trick and declarer cannot score a trick without conceding a trick to East. If West leads low to the king, declarer can later lead the queen and score a trick without losing a second trick.

EXERCISE ON THE CORRECT LEAD FROM A SHORT SUIT

A. In standard methods, which is the correct card to lead from each of these holdings in a no-trumps contract?

1.	6 4	**11.**	J 10 9	**21.**	Q J	**31.**	K Q	**41.**	A K
2.	9 2	**12.**	J 10 8	**22.**	Q 10	**32.**	K J	**42.**	A 10
3.	8 7	**13.**	J 10 2	**23.**	Q 6	**33.**	K 7	**43.**	A 4
4.	6 3 2	**14.**	J 9 8	**24.**	Q J 10	**34.**	K J 2	**44.**	A 9 3
5.	9 8 7	**15.**	J 9 4	**25.**	Q J 5	**35.**	K J 10	**45.**	A 8 7
6.	8 5 3	**16.**	J 7 5	**26.**	Q 9 4	**36.**	K 10 8	**46.**	A 10 2
7.	10 9	**17.**	J 3 2	**27.**	Q 9 8	**37.**	K 10 9	**47.**	A 10 9
8.	10 6	**18.**	J 10	**28.**	Q 10 2	**38.**	K Q 3	**48.**	A K Q
9.	10 9 2	**19.**	J 9	**29.**	Q 10 9	**39.**	K 9 8	**49.**	A K 4
10.	10 8 2	**20.**	J 3	**30.**	Q 4 3	**40.**	K 7 4	**50.**	A J 10

B. If the contract were trumps, which, if any, of the above answers would change?

C. In each of the following questions, you are given the dummy, East's cards and West's lead. What can East tell about West's holding in the suit from the card West has led?

1.	**NORTH**		**2.**	**NORTH**		**3.**	**NORTH**	
	J 6 5			K 9 6			J 10 9	
WEST		**EAST**	**WEST**		**EAST**	**WEST**		**EAST**
Lead : Q		K 10 8 3 2	Lead : 8		A Q J 5 2	Lead : 7		A K 8 6 3

4.	**NORTH**		**5.**	**NORTH**		**6.**	**NORTH**	
	7 6 4			10 7			A Q J 8 3	
WEST		**EAST**	**WEST**		**EAST**	**WEST**		**EAST**
Lead : 10		A K 9 5 3	Lead : 2		A K J 6 4	Lead : 4		K 10 7 2

PLAY HANDS BASED ON SHORT SUIT LEADS

Hand 1 : Dealer North : Nil vulnerable

NORTH
- ♠ Q 10 9
- ♡ 10 7 5 2
- ◇ K
- ♣ A K Q J 3

WEST	EAST
♠ 8 4	♠ A K J 7 2
♡ J 8 6	♡ 3
◇ J 10 9 7 2	◇ Q 6 5 4
♣ 8 6 4	♣ 9 7 2

SOUTH
- ♠ 6 5 3
- ♡ A K Q 9 4
- ◇ A 8 3
- ♣ 10 5

WEST	NORTH	EAST	SOUTH
	1♣	1♠	2♡
Pass	4♡	All pass	

Lead : ♠8. Partner's suit. Top from a doubleton.

Play : East wins the first spade (jack over dummy's 9 or 10) and cashes ♠ K. Noting West's high-then-low lead, East knows that South holds the last spade. East cashes the ♠ A and West should discourage a diamond switch. In standard methods the ◇ 2 discard would be suitable : lowest discard = "I do not want this suit."

As a club switch is futile and West has rejected diamonds, East should continue with a fourth spade. This creates a trump trick for West by promoting the jack. If South ruffs low or discards, West ruffs with the jack. If South ruffs high, West discards and the ♡J becomes high later.

Notes : (1) From West's *eight* of spades lead — top spot card — East knew at trick 1 that West held a singleton or a doubleton spade.
(2) If East switches to clubs, diamonds or a trump at trick 4, South wins, draws trumps and has 10 tricks.
(3) South's best chance — not successful — when the fourth spade is led is to ruff high and then cash two top trumps, hoping the ♡J falls singleton or doubleton.
(4) If East fails to overcall, West might lead ◇ J. Dummy wins, trumps are drawn, South's spades are discarded on dummy's clubs and South makes 13 tricks!
(5) If West held ♠ 84 ♡ 864 ◇ A10972 ♣ 864, and South had ♠ 653 ♡ AKQJ9 ◇ J83 ♣ 105, a fourth spade would be disastrous. After trumps are drawn, the clubs allow the diamonds to be pitched. With those cards, West could signal on the third spade for a diamond switch. In standard methods, the ◇ 10 asks partner to play a diamond. Without West's signal, East cannot be sure whether to play the fourth spade or try for a diamond trick. Best of all, West should ruff the third spade and cash ◇ A. Do not ask partner to do something you can do yourself.

Hand 2 : Dealer East : N-S vulnerable

NORTH
- ♠ 4 3
- ♡ Q 7 2
- ◇ 8 7 6 5 2
- ♣ 10 9 8

WEST	EAST
♠ K Q J 10 7	♠ A 8 6 2
♡ 9 4 3	♡ 10 5
◇ J 4	◇ K Q 10 9 3
♣ Q J 7	♣ A K

SOUTH
- ♠ 9 5
- ♡ A K J 8 6
- ◇ A
- ♣ 6 5 4 3 2

WEST	NORTH	EAST	SOUTH
		1◇	1♡
1♠	Pass	3♠	Pass
4♠	Pass	Pass	Pass

Lead : ♡2. Partner's suit. Bottom card from three to an honor. On a club lead, declarer can make 11 tricks easily.

Play : The defense can defeat 4♠. Win ♡K, cash ◇ A and *lead a low heart to North's queen*. North returns a diamond for South to ruff. This is a tough defense but South can work it out. North's lead of the TWO of hearts is from an honour or a singleton. The only honour not visible is the queen. Two hearts + ◇ A = 3 tricks, not enough to defeat the contract. The diamond ruff is needed to defeat 4♠. To score the diamond ruff, South must cash ◇ A at trick 2 to create the void and then put partner on lead. The only hope for that is in hearts. So, ♡K, ◇ A, low heart catering for ♡Q or a singleton heart with North, diamond ruff. One down.

Notes : (1) If South cashes ♡A at trick 2 or 3, the defense fails.
(2) If North's lead were a singleton, the defense would be just as effective : ♡K, ◇ A, low heart ruffed by North, diamond ruffed by South.
(3) The defense cannot defeat 4♠ if North leads the *queen* of hearts. That removes North's vital entry. It is usually an error to lead top of partner's suit from K-x-x, Q-x-x, J-x-x or 10-x-x. Lead top only from a doubleton or from a sequence holding.

Hand 3 : Dealer South : E-W vulnerable

          NORTH
          ♠ 6
          ♡ A K Q 7 5
          ◊ Q J 5
          ♣ Q 9 4 2

WEST   **EAST**
♠ J 2   ♠ A K Q 10 9 7 5 4
♡ J 10 9   ♡ 4 2
◊ A K 10 9 3   ◊ 4
♣ 8 7 3   ♣ K 10

          SOUTH
          ♠ 8 3
          ♡ 8 6 3
          ◊ 8 7 6 2
          ♣ A J 6 5

WEST	NORTH	EAST	SOUTH
			Pass
Pass	1♡	4♠	All pass

Lead : ♡6. Partner's suit. M.U.D. with 3 rags.

Play : North wins with the ♡Q (defenders win tricks with the cheapest card possible) and cashes ♡K. On the second heart South follows with the 8. With eight hearts gone, North deduces that South has the last heart. With a doubleton, South would play 8-then-6. As South played 6-then-8, South has another heart. Since a third round of hearts is futile and diamonds cannot provide two more tricks, North should switch to clubs. The correct card is the ♣2, normal fourth highest. East's best hope is to try the ♣K, hoping North has ♣A. South wins and another club means one off.

Notes : (1) A strong pre-empt of 4♡/4♠ (up to about 15 HCP) is all right after partner has passed or RHO has opened. With chances for slam remote, pre-emption is more attractive.

(2) If South leads the ace of clubs (dreadful), 4♠ makes.
(3) If South leads ♡6 but carelessly plays the ♡3 on the second round of hearts, North may believe South began with a doubleton heart and try to cash a third heart. Disaster.
(4) It would not be correct for North to switch at trick 2. South might have led a singleton or a doubleton.
(5) If North does try to cash a third heart, East can score 11 tricks : ruff the third heart high, cash ♠A, then ◊A and a low diamond ruffed, spade to the jack, ◊K (discarding a club) and as the ◊Q-J have fallen, the ◊10 allows a second club discard.
(6) If South led ♡8, the out-of-fashion top-of-nothing or unsound top-of-partner's-suit, North could not tell whether the 8-then-6 was a doubleton or not.

Hand 4 : Dealer West : Both vulnerable

          NORTH
          ♠ A K Q 9 6
          ♡ J 3 2
          ◊ 7 6
          ♣ 10 8 2

WEST   **EAST**
♠ 5 2   ♠ 4 3
♡ A K Q 7 5   ♡ 10 4
◊ 5 4 3 2   ◊ 10 9 8
♣ A Q   ♣ J 9 6 5 4 3

          SOUTH
          ♠ J 10 8 7
          ♡ 9 8 6
          ◊ A K Q J
          ♣ K 7

WEST	NORTH	EAST	SOUTH
1♡	1♠	Pass	3♠
Pass	Pass	Pass	

Lead : ♡10. Partner's suit. Top from a doubleton.

Play : West wins the first trick with the ♡Q (cheapest card). West knows that North has ♡J (the 10 lead denied the jack) and that East has a singleton or doubleton heart. With the 9 in dummy, East's 10 could not be from a sequence. West cashes the ♡K and learns that East began with 10-4 doubleton and that North holds the missing heart.

It is tempting to cash the ♡A but a count of tricks will set West on the right path. To defeat 3♠, five tricks are needed, three tricks from hearts and *two* from clubs. However, to score two club tricks, the club lead must come from East (or North). To give East the lead for the club switch, West continues with a low heart at trick 3, forcing East to ruff. East leads ♣5, normal fourth highest, one off.

Notes : (1) West should not be fooled if North drops the ♡J on the first or second lead of hearts. The lead of the 10 coupled with the 9 in dummy marks East with the short hearts. *Trust partner, not the opposition.*
(2) If West wins ♡A at trick 3 and plays a fourth heart, hoping to promote a trump trick for East, declarer scores 10 tricks (discard a club and ruff in dummy, draw trumps and discard the other clubs on the diamonds).
(3) If West muffs the defense, playing ♡Q, ♡K and ♡A, East can save the day. East should ruff the third heart, even though it is a winner, and lead a club. East can find this play by focussing also on the tricks needed. After three hearts, the other two tricks must come from clubs. Partner figures to hold ♣A for the opening bid (and if North has it, there is nothing to be done). The only chance for *two* club tricks is if East leads clubs and West has the A-Q. In order to play clubs, East must take the lead now (last chance) by ruffing partner's heart.

CHAPTER 2

THE CARD TO LEAD FROM LONG SUITS

The basic approach to long suits (four or more cards) is to lead fourth-highest unless the suit contains a sequence (when you lead top of the sequence). Where a suit contains a sequence including at least one honor, make the sequence lead, not fourth-highest. However, there is more to it than just that.

SEQUENCE LEADS

Solid sequence = three touching cards. Lead top card from each of these holdings:

K-Q-J-x   Q-J-10-x   J-10-9-x   10-9-8-x

For top card lead, the sequence must include at least one honor.

Near sequence = two touching cards, then a gap of just one card. Lead top card from these holdings:

K-Q-10-x   Q-J-9-x   J-10-8-x   10-9-7-x

For top card lead, the near sequence must include at least one honor.

Interior sequence = honor card, then a gap, then another honor card and the card immediately below it. Lead top of the touching cards from these interior sequences:

K-J-10-x   K-10-9-x   Q-10-9-x

To qualify for an interior sequence lead, the top of the touching cards must be an honor. Where the interior sequence suit contains the ace (A-Q-J-x, A-J-10-x or A-10-9-x), the interior lead (Q, J, 10) is made at no-trumps only. In a trump contract, avoid leading these suits if possible, but if you must lead such a suit, lead the ace, not a lower one.

The above leads apply whether the suit is three cards, four cards or longer.

FOUR OR MORE WITH NO SEQUENCE

From a 4-card or longer suit with no sequence lead, lead fourth-highest, except from four rags.

FROM FOUR RAGS

It is best to restrict fourth-highest leads to show length (from a 5-card or longer suit) or strength (at least one honor card in the suit if it is a 4-card suit). With four rags, *second-highest* is recommended (similar to the M.U.D. lead from three rags). By so doing, you can deduce that partner's lead of the lowest card possible promises an honor (or is a singleton — but any card could be a singleton).

LEADS AGAINST NO-TRUMPS VERSUS LEADS AGAINST SUIT CONTRACTS

The strategy will vary according to the contract, but once you have chosen the suit to lead, *the card* to lead against no-trumps is the same as the card to lead against a suit contract, with three exceptions:

(1) Suits headed by A-K (A-K-x-x or longer)

Against no-trumps, lead fourth-highest.

Against suit contracts, lead the king (or ace).

(2) Suits headed by K-Q (K-Q-x-x or longer)

Against no-trumps, lead fourth-highest.

Against suit contracts, lead the king.

(3) Suits headed by the ace (A-x-x-x or longer)

Against no-trumps, lead fourth-highest.

Against suit contracts, lead the ace. However, this is not an attractive lead. Try to find some other suit for your opening lead.

In no-trumps, you hope to set up the long cards in your suit. Your high cards will take tricks later anyway because it is no-trumps. In a suit contract, you aim to cash tricks. A shortage in dummy or in declarer's hand may mean you do not score your high cards if you lead a low one initially. For example:

J 7

A K 5 3 2   9 8 4

Q 10 6

In no-trumps, you lead fourth-highest and declarer wins the trick. If you or partner gain the lead later, you can cash four tricks in the suit. In a trump contract, cash the ace and king. You score two tricks and declarer one. If you lead low in a trump contract, declarer still has one trick, but you score only one trick instead of two as North can ruff the third round.

Note also in the above layout the benefit of leading a low card in no-trumps rather than king, ace and another. If you lead a low card initially, it does not matter whether *you* gain the lead later or partner. In either case, you can cash four tricks. However, if you lead king, ace and another, you set up two extra winners, but now you must gain the lead. If partner has the lead later, partner has no cards left in the suit to return. Leading low initially will usually leave partner with a card to return to you.

Another reason to choose the low card lead from A-K-x-x-x in no-trumps is this layout :

```
            9 6 5
A K 4 3 2            Q 7
            J 10 8
```

If West leads low, East wins and returns the suit. The defense cashes five tricks. If West leads the king or ace first, then a problem arises. A low card at trick 2 leaves East on lead and the suit is blocked. Cashing the second honor crashes East's queen and gives declarer an unnecessary trick.

WHY LEAD TOP OF SEQUENCE?

```
            9 8 5
K Q J 10            6 4 2
            A 7 3
```

West can lead any card to dislodge the ace. It is immaterial *to West* whether the K, Q, J or 10 is led. The purpose of top-of-sequence is to let partner know your holding. When the king lead forces the ace, East knows the location of the queen.

```
            7 5 2
Lead : Q            A 8 6 4 3
```

West leads the queen, denying the king. As East knows that South has the king, East should play the ace. South's king might be singleton.

```
            K 5 2
J 10 9 6            A 8 3
            Q 7 4
```

West leads the jack, denying the queen, and dummy plays low. East knows that South holds the queen. East plays low, preserving the ace to capture the king later. If East plays the ace at once, declarer makes *two* tricks. If East keeps the ace to take the king, declarer scores only one trick.

The lead of an honor card denies the next higher honor.

A queen lead denies the king.

A jack lead denies the queen.

A ten lead denies the jack.

Exception : If the partnership leads the king from A-K-x and longer holdings, the king lead would not deny the ace. The king lead would then promise one of the touching honors, either A-K-x or K-Q-x or longer suits. Where the partnership has agreed to lead the ace first from A-K-x or longer, the king lead denies the ace (except for A-K doubleton).

ACE OR KING FROM A-K-X OR LONGER?

The king is commonly led from A-K-suits but many pairs prefer to lead the ace. There is not much to choose between the methods and both can lead to ambiguous situations.

Leading king from A-K-x and from K-Q-x creates an ambiguity unless the ace or queen is visible to partner.

A-K DOUBLETON

If the king is led from A-K-x, A-K-x-x and the like in your partnership against trump contracts, lead the ace from A-K-doubleton, and the king next. Partner's reaction on seeing the ace will be, "Ah, no king." When the king appears at trick 2, partner should realise that the lead was A-K doubleton.

If the ace is your partnership's lead from A-K-x, A-K-x-x and the like against trump contracts, then from A-K doubleton, lead the king first, ace next. On seeing the king, partner assumes 'no ace'. When the ace appears at trick 2, the reason for departing from the normal order is A-K doubleton.

When the A-K doubleton is revealed, partner should signal on the second round the suit in which an entry is held :

HIGH CARD = HIGH SUIT

LOWEST CARD = LOW SUIT

Suit preference signals are covered in Chapter 20.

Pairs that lead the ace from A-K-x and so on will do this only at trick 1. If you switch to an A-K-x or longer suit later in the play, lead the king. There is much less risk of an ambiguity later. Switching to an ace will normally deny holding the king in the suit. Switching to an ace and following up with the king shows ace-king doubleton and on the king, partner will give a suit-preference signal (high card/high suit, low card/low suit) to show which suit to lead next.

WHY LEAD FOURTH-HIGHEST?

The main function of fourth-highest is to let partner know how many cards you hold in the suit led.

Top-of-sequence shows the high cards held.

Fourth-highest shows the number of cards held.

```
          NORTH
           8 6
WEST                EAST
Lead : 2            A 5 4
```

When the 2 is led, if this is fourth-highest, West cannot hold a fifth card in the suit. There is nothing lower than a two (despite Charlie Brown's lament, "I feel lower than the 2 of clubs."). Therefore West has four cards and as East can see five others, South holds four cards in the suit.

When partner's lead is the lowest card, partner cannot hold more than a 4-card suit.

If partner leads the 2, partner cannot hold more than four cards in this suit. If partner leads the 3 and the 2 is visible, partner cannot have more than a 4-card suit. Once you know the number of cards in the opening leader's suit, add that to your cards and the cards in dummy in that suit, deduct from 13 and the answer is the number of cards held by declarer in that suit.

<pre>
          NORTH
          J 6 2
WEST   EAST
Lead : 4   A 5 3
</pre>

West leads the 4. East, seeing the 3 and the 2, knows West has led bottom card. Therefore West has a 4-card suit and by deduction, South has three.

When partner's lead is known to be the second lowest card, partner may hold a 4-card suit or a 5-card suit. When partner's lead is the third lowest possible card, partner may hold a 4-card, 5-card or 6-card suit.

<pre>
          NORTH
          8 6
WEST   EAST
Lead : 3   A 7 5
</pre>

West leads the 3 and the 2 is not visible. West has led second lowest and may have a 4-card or 5-card suit. When East plays the ace, East will note the card played by South. If South drops the 2, East knows that West has led bottom card and so began with a 4-card suit. If South drops a high card, East may conclude that the 2 is with West and that West began with a 5-card suit. Of course, South may also be foxing by withholding the 2. This is sound deceptive strategy by declarer.

RULE OF 11

The fourth-highest lead allows both third player and declarer to apply the Rule of 11 :

Subtract the card led from 11. The answer = the number of cards higher than the card led in the other three hands (dummy, 3rd hand and declarer).

<pre>
          NORTH
          A J 8
WEST   EAST
Lead : 6   K 9 3
</pre>

West leads the 6. Assuming the 6 is fourth-highest, $11 - 6 = 5$. Dummy, East and South therefore hold five cards higher than the 6. Yet East can see five cards higher than the 6 (three in dummy and two in hand). If the 8 is played from dummy, East should play the 9, not the king. The full layout :

<pre>
                A J 8
   Q 10 7 6 2   K 9 3
                5 4
</pre>

After the 6 lead and 8 from dummy, if East plays the king, declarer makes two tricks in the suit. If East plays the 9, it wins and declarer makes only one trick in the suit. After the 9 wins, East should return the king (top from remaining doubleton) to help set up West's suit. If South is able to beat the 9, this does not mean the Rule of 11 has failed. It means that West has not led fourth-highest.

The Rule of 11 is almost never useful when partner leads the 2 or the 3. There are too many higher cards missing for any helpful inference. It is useful only occasionally when a higher fourth-highest card is led (such as the 4, 5, 6 or 7). Still, you should do your sums and apply it each time so that you do benefit from those occasions when it does provide valuable information.

EXERCISE ON THE CORRECT LEAD FROM A LONG SUIT

A. In standard methods, which is the correct card to lead from each of these holdings in a no-trumps contract?

1. 8 6 4 3	11. J 8 6 4	21. Q J 8 5	31. K J 9 4 3	41. A Q 10 9 8
2. 8 6 4 3 2	12. J 9 8 7	22. Q J 10 3	32. K J 10 4 3	42. A Q J 6 5
3. 9 8 7 6	13. J 10 5 2	23. Q J 9 8 7	33. K Q 6 5 3	43. A Q 7 4 2
4. 9 8 7 6 5	14. J 10 8 4	24. Q J 7 6 5 2	34. K Q 10 3 2	44. A K 5 3
5. 6 5 3 2	15. J 10 9 3	25. Q 9 8 7 4	35. K Q J 4 3	45. A K 9 8 7
6. 10 7 5 2	16. Q 7 5 3	26. K 8 5 2	36. A 8 7 4	46. A K J 7 3
7. 10 9 8 5	17. Q 10 8 4	27. K 9 8 7 3	37. A 10 7 5	47. A K Q 5
8. 10 9 7 5	18. Q 10 9 4	28. K 10 8 3 2	38. A 10 9 5	48. A 9 8 7 4 2
9. 10 9 6 5	19. Q J 6 2	29. K 10 9 3 2	39. A J 9 6	49. A J 9 8 7
10. 10 6 5 4 3 2	20. Q J 9 5	30. K J 7 5 2	40. A J 10 6	50. A K 10 9 8

B. If the contract were trumps, which, if any, of the above answers would change?

PLAY HANDS BASED ON LONG SUIT LEADS

Hand 5 : Dealer North : N-S vulnerable

NORTH
♠ 9 2
♡ Q J 10 7 6
◇ A Q 10 4 3
♣ K

WEST
♠ A K J 10 8 7 4
♡ K
◇ K 7 5
♣ J 2

EAST
♠ Q
♡ 8 5 4
◇ 9 8 6 2
♣ A Q 10 9 8

SOUTH
♠ 6 5 3
♡ A 9 3 2
◇ J
♣ 7 6 5 4 3

WEST	NORTH	EAST	SOUTH
	1♡	Pass	2♡
4♠	Pass	Pass	Pass

Lead : ♡Q. Normal. With any other suit led, 4♠ makes.

Play : South should take the ♡Q with the ace. West is marked with the king of hearts and South cannot make more tricks by playing low at trick 1. If North has led from a 5-card suit, West has the ♡K singleton. If South plays low, West scores an undeserved trick with the king and South never makes the ♡A. In fact, if South fails to play the ace of hearts at trick 1, West can win 13 tricks!. After ♡A, South should switch to ◇J. South knows that West would ruff a heart continuation. West would win 12 tricks if South plays a heart at trick 2.

Reading North for the ◇A, West should duck the ◇J. North should overtake with the ◇Q, cash the ◇A and when South shows out, the diamond ruff defeats the contract.

Notes : (1) East is too weak to overcall 2♣.
(2) A 4♡ or 4♠ pre-empt is acceptable even with 14-15 HCP after an opponent has opened the bidding. Where both opponents have bid, your chances for a slam are too remote to reject these pre-emptive game bids.
(3) North should not bid 5♡, particularly at this vulnerability. There is no need to sacrifice if you can defeat their contract. If you have reasonable defensive prospects, choose to defend rather than sacrifice.
(4) West should duck the ◇J. As North opened, the ◇A is marked with North after South won the ♡A.
(5) When South switches to the ◇J and West ducks, if North also ducks, the ◇J holds the trick. As South is unable to play a second diamond, West can discard the diamonds on dummy's clubs after drawing trumps.
(6) On seeing ◇J from partner, North should read it as a singleton or a doubleton. It cannot be a sequence lead as North holds the ◇10. As the ◇J might well be a singleton, North must overtake with the ◇Q. To overtake cannot cost if South started with two diamonds and is essential if South has a switched to a singleton.

Hand 6 : Dealer East : E-W vulnerable

NORTH
♠ K 5 3
♡ K Q J 10 7 2
◇ K 2
♣ Q 7

WEST
♠ J 10 7
♡ 9 5 3
◇ A 7 5 4
♣ 8 6 5

EAST
♠ A Q 8 6
♡ 8 4
◇ Q J 9 8 3
♣ 10 3

SOUTH
♠ 9 4 2
♡ A 6
◇ 10 6
♣ A K J 9 4 2

WEST	NORTH	EAST	SOUTH
		Pass	1♣
Pass	1♡	Pass	2♣
Pass	4♡	All pass	

Lead : ◇Q. Top of near sequence. On any lead but a diamond, 4♡ makes with overtricks.

Play : West should win trick 1 with ◇A. (If not, declarer makes 12 tricks.) West should switch to ♠J. This allows the defense to cash three spade tricks to defeat the contract.

Notes: (1) 3NT might succeed but it is a riskier contract than 4♡. 3NT by South could be defeated on the ♠J lead.
(2) The ◇Q lead denied the king. When West plays ◇A and the ◇K does not fall, West knows that North still has the ◇K. As there is only one more diamond in dummy, the defense cannot come to a second diamond trick and a diamond continuation would be futile. If West plays a diamond at trick 2, North can make 12 tricks.
(3) If West switches to the ♠7 at trick 2 instead of the ♠J (an error — from J-10-x, the jack is led), North can duck this. North will then make 4♡ as the defense can take only two spade tricks. The ♠J may also be necessary from J-x-x if three spade tricks are needed urgently. Interchange the ♠6 and the ♠10 and West must switch to the *jack* of spades at trick 2 to defeat the contract.
(4) Note how the lead of the *queen* of diamonds made the defense straightforward for West.

Hand 7 : Dealer South : Both vulnerable

NORTH
- ♠ J 8 7 4
- ♡ A K
- ◇ 9 3
- ♣ K Q 10 9 4

WEST	EAST
♠ 6	♠ 9 3 2
♡ 10 8	♡ 9 6 5 4 3 2
◇ Q J 10 6 2	◇ A K 7
♣ 8 7 6 5 2	♣ A

SOUTH
- ♠ A K Q 10 5
- ♡ Q J 7
- ◇ 8 5 4
- ♣ J 3

WEST	NORTH	EAST	SOUTH
			1♠
Pass	3♠	Pass	4♠
Pass	Pass	Pass	

Lead : ◇ Q. Not the ♡ 10 : prefer a sequence to a doubleton lead. Not the ♣ 5 : prefer a suit with three honors to a suit with none.

Play : East should overtake the ◇ Q with the king, cash the ♣ A to create the void and return the ◇ 7. West wins and leads a club for East to ruff.

Notes : (1) If North-South are using limit raises, North would respond 2♣ and raise South's 2♠ rebid to game. If North does bid 2♣, East should not bid 2♡. Do not overcall on poor suits. (2) If West leads the ♡ 10, South can make 11 tricks : win ♡ A, cash ♠ A, ♠ K, heart to the king, spade to the queen, cash ♡ Q and discard one diamond from dummy, then lead the ♣ J and continue clubs.

(3) East knows from the *queen* of diamonds lead that West has the *jack* of diamonds as well and can thus plan the above defense. With 11 HCP in hand, 13 in dummy and 3 with West via the ◇ Q-J, East can tell that West cannot hold any useful high cards outside diamonds. As there are only two diamond winners and the ♣ A in top cards, the fourth trick must come via a ruff.
(4) If East ducks the ◇ Q lead, 4♠ cannot be defeated. West now has no entry to give East the club ruff.

Hand 8 : Dealer West : Nil vulnerable

NORTH
- ♠ 9 8 7 3 2
- ♡ 7 5 2
- ◇ A K
- ♣ 10 9 7

WEST	EAST
♠ K Q J	♠ 10 6 5
♡ A 9 6	♡ K Q J 10 4 3
◇ Q 7 5	◇ 9 6 2
♣ K Q 8 4	♣ A

SOUTH
- ♠ A 4
- ♡ 8
- ◇ J 10 8 4 3
- ♣ J 6 5 3 2

WEST	NORTH	EAST	SOUTH
1NT	Pass	4♡	All pass

Lead : ◇ J. Top of near sequence. Not ♠ A : an ace lead is unappealing and ace-doubleton with only a singleton trump is a huge gamble. Not ♡ 8 : a singleton trump is not recommended. Not ♣ 3 : prefer a suit with two honors to a suit with only one.

Play : North wins the *ace* of diamonds at trick one and plays the *king* of diamonds at trick 2. This order of play shows A-K doubleton. With A-K-x or longer, you would win the king first, not the ace. On the second round, South signals with the *ten* of diamonds to indicate the entry is in spades (high card/high suit, trumps excluded). If North reads the message correctly, North will switch to a spade. South wins ♠ A and returns a diamond for North to ruff. One off.

Notes : (1) As it happens, East-West can make 3NT but that is hard to judge in the auction. Most partnerships would reach 4♡ which would make on many occasions where 3NT would fail.

(2) On a club lead, East can make eleven tricks. Win ♣ A, ♡ K, ♡ Q, heart to the ace and use the ♣ K-Q to discard two diamonds.
(3) On ♠ A lead, declarer can make 4♡ even if South switches to a diamond. South no longer has an entry to give North the diamond ruff.
(4) It is not relevant to this deal, but declarer should play low from dummy on the ◇ J lead. The ◇ Q cannot win and playing it will not promote any other card. Therefore play low and hope North has to play an honor.
(5) After ◇ A-K, North cannot tell whether to return a spade or a club without South's assistance. If South held the ♣ A instead of the ♠ A, South would play the *three* of diamonds (lowest card = lowest suit).
(6) If South fails to signal correctly or North fails to read the message of the ◇ 10, North may fail to find the switch to spades. If so, declarer would succeed.
(7) If West happened to be declarer in 4♡ after a transfer sequence, North would lead ace-then-king of diamonds to show the doubleton. South would again signal with the highest diamond on the second round to show the entry in the high suit.

CHAPTER 3

OPENING LEADS IN NO-TRUMPS

Playing no-trumps, declarer will usually tackle the best suit, the partnership's longest suit. What is good for declarer holds true for the defenders. *It is usually best to lead the partnership's longest combined suit.*

BLIND LEADS

Where the bidding has been uninformative, such as 1NT : 3NT, you have only your own cards as evidence of the partnership's longest suit. Here you lead 'fourth-highest of your longest and strongest' except when your long suit has some sequence holding from which you lead top-of-sequence (see Chapter 2).

A 5-card or 6-card suit is an attractive lead, but *a 4-card suit with only one honor is not appealing.* Avoid, if possible, leads from suits such as J-x-x-x, Q-x-x-x or K-x-x-x. A second honor in these suits would make them more attractive but A-Q-x-x or K-J-x-x is also a risky start. Where the 4-card suit has two *touching* honors, such as Q-J-x-x or J-10-x-x, the lead has more promise and less risk. A 4-card suit including a 3-card sequence is highly attractive. A solid holding like K-Q-J-x or Q-J-10-x is even more attractive than a weak 5-card holding like J-x-x-x-x.

With equally long suits, prefer the suit with more honors. Prefer to lead from Q-J-x-x-x than from K-x-x-x-x. Prefer a solid sequence to a near sequence.

♠ A 9 7 4 2   With two long suits, one headed
♡ K 8 6 3 2   by the ace and one headed by a
♢ 5 3   lower honor, prefer to lead the suit
♣ 6   which does not have the ace. Here
lead the ♡3 rather than the ♠4. The reason is that if you manage to set up the hearts, the ♠A is your entry to the heart winners. If you lead a spade and set up the spade suit, the ♡K may not be an entry.

INFORMED LEADS

The bidding can be most revealing and is almost always relevant when choosing your opening lead.

(1) LEAD PARTNER'S SUIT

If partner has shown length in a suit, prefer to lead partner's suit. As partner has bid, that is evidence for that suit being the partnership's longest suit. The *card* to lead in partner's suit is standard : see Chapters 1 and 2. Partner's bid encourages you to choose that suit. It does not affect the card to lead.

When should you avoid leading partner's suit?

(a) When partner's suit bid was artificial or semi-artificial, lead your own 5-card or longer suit. In many systems, the 1♣ opening may be a shortish suit with no lead-directing suggestion even as regards length. In Precision and other big club systems, the 1♢ opening does not promise length in diamonds.

However, if you have no good suit of your own, stick to leading partner's suit. The fact that partner has opened a dubious club does not mean that partner does not have club length.

(b) Prefer to lead your own long suit if the suit is an attractive one *and* you have entries in the outside suits. Particularly if you hold a singleton in partner's suit, prefer your own suit *if you possess entries.* However, if your suit is not exciting, lead partner's. If you do not have any entries, lead partner's suit. There is no point setting up your suit if you have no entry to cash the winners later. Be like declarer. Declarer would not set up a suit if there were no entries to reach the established winners. Neither should you.

The fact that you have a singleton in partner's suit is not enough reason to avoid it. The fact that they have bid no-trumps over partner's bid is not enough reason to avoid it. You must have a strong alternative : a decent suit *plus* entries.

Some players avoid partner's suit just because declarer has bid no-trumps over partner. This is not logical. The fact that declarer bid no-trumps over partner's suit means only that declarer has one or two stoppers in that suit. Your job is to eliminate those stoppers and set up partner's length. If you do not lead the suit, declarer will still have the stoppers later. For example :

```
              8 6 4
    3 2                 K J 10 7 5
              A Q 9
```

South bid no-trumps over East's suit bid. South has two winners and two stoppers in East's suit. South will always have those winners whether West leads this suit or another. As long as East has length in the suit, West should normally lead it. If the suit is not led, East will not come to the tricks after the first two which Lady Luck has given South.

(2) AVOID THEIR SUITS

If an opponent has shown length in your long suit, do not lead this suit. The evidence is overwhelming that this is not your partnership's longest combined suit. A convenient club or a doubtful diamond need not dissuade you from that suit, but if they are known to hold four or more cards in a suit, try some other suit.

WHICH SUIT DO YOU TRY IF YOUR LONG SUIT IS OUT?

(a) Prefer an unbid major to an unbid minor. With length in a major, the opponents usually bid the suit to try for a major suit contract. Their failure to bid a major suggests that they do not have it. It follows that partner may have length in that suit. However, opponents have no qualms about ignoring a minor and therefore they may have length in an unbid minor.

(b) Prefer a 3-card suit to a doubleton. If your lead does connect with partner's suit, the more cards you have in the suit, the better your chances of setting up partner's long cards in the suit.

(c) Prefer the stronger of equal length suits. From Q-x-x and x-x-x, prefer to lead bottom from the Q-x-x. If you do hit partner's long suit, such as K-J-x-x-x, your Q-x-x will be far more helpful than x-x-x. (However, at duplicate pairs Q-x-x is much riskier and may give declarer an overtrick. At teams or rubber bridge where your aim is to defeat their contract, Q-x-x gives you a better chance. At pairs, defeating the contract is not always the primary consideration and holding declarer to the minimum number of (over)tricks is vital. At pairs, avoid risky starts such as three or four cards with just one honor.)

WHEN CAN YOU LEAD THEIR SUIT?

With a 4-card sequence such as K-Q-J-10-x or Q-J-10-9-x, your suit is stronger than their suit. With such strength, it is sensible to lead a suit they have bid.

If you decide to lead their suit when you have only a 3-card sequence such as Q-J-10-x-x or J-10-9-x-x, choose fourth-highest and not top of your sequence. For the lead to work, partner will need to hold a useful card and leading top may block the suit.

5 2

Q J 10 6 3   K 4

A 9 8 7

If West leads the 6, East plays the king and four tricks are set up for West. If West leads the queen, then if East plays the king to unblock, South scores a second trick and if East plays low, declarer can block the suit by taking the ace on the first round or by ducking twice.

K 4

Q J 10 6 3   9 2

A 8 7 5

If West leads the 6, declarer can only score two tricks and the suit will not be blocked for the defense. If West leads the queen, declarer can take the king and the defense will be stymied on the next round: if the 9 is led or West leads low to the 9, declarer can duck and the defense cannot continue the suit; if West leads the jack later, this crashes East's 9 and enables declarer to win the ace and score a third trick.

K 7 2

J 10 9 4 3   Q

A 8 6 5

If West leads the 4, declarer scores only two tricks. If West leads the jack, declarer can play low in dummy and when East plays the queen, South takes the ace and knows the position. South can set up a third trick by leading towards dummy. If West plays low, South can finesse the 7 and if West plays an honor, the king takes and South's pips are worth an extra trick.

If leading their suit with a 3-card sequence, it does not matter whether the suit was bid on your left or on your right. Fourth-highest works best most of the time.

A 10 8 7

K Q J 4 2   9 5

6 3

If West leads the king first, declarer can score two tricks. If declarer ducks the first round and West plays low next, declarer will put in dummy's ten. However, if West leads the 4 at trick 1, almost every declarer would play low from dummy. East then scores the 9 and returns the suit, setting up West's length.

If fourth-highest is so successful here, why lead top of sequence? Because it is only when an opponent is *known* to have length in the suit that top from a 3-card sequence is not best. Top of sequence usually is best and prevents declarer winning a trick cheaply.

7 5 2

K Q J 6 3   9 8 4

A 10

If West leads an honor, South makes only one trick. If West leads fourth-highest, South scores two tricks and thus has a second stopper.

7 5 2

Q J 10 8 4   6 3

A K 9

If West leads top of sequence, South makes only two tricks. If West leads low, South scores the 9, too.

(3) LEAD-DIRECTING DOUBLES

(a) A double of an artificial bid asks you to lead that suit.

WEST	NORTH	EAST	SOUTH
1NT	Pass	2♣	Double

2♣ was Stayman, an artificial bid. South's double asks for a club lead. Similarly, if East replied 2◇, 2♡ or 2♠, a transfer bid, double would ask for the lead of the suit bid.

WEST	NORTH	EAST	SOUTH
. . .	. . .	. . .	. . .
4NT	Pass	5♡	Double

Given that 5♡, the answer to Blackwood, is artificial and is not their trump suit, South's double asks for a heart lead.

WEST	NORTH	EAST	SOUTH
1♡	1♠	2♣	Pass
2◇	Pass	2♠	Double

2♠ is an artificial bid, usually asking for a stopper in spades for no-trumps. South's double asks for a spade lead. It will often be based on a holding such as A-x, K-x or Q-x in partner's suit (not enough to raise but keen to have that lead).

(b) A double of 3NT asks for a specific lead.

1. If you have bid a suit, lead your suit.

2. If partner has bid a suit, lead partner's suit.

3. If both you and partner have bid a suit, lead your own suit. Without the double, it is assumed you would have led partner's suit (the normal courteous move).

4. If neither you nor partner has bid, lead dummy's first bid suit.

WEST	NORTH	EAST	SOUTH
1♣	Pass	2NT	Pass
3NT	Double	All pass	

North's double calls for a club lead.

WEST	NORTH	EAST	SOUTH
1♣	Pass	1♠	Pass
1NT	Pass	3NT	Double
Pass	Pass	Pass	

South's double calls for a spade lead.

5. If no suit has been bid (e.g. 1NT : 3NT), some pairs play that a double asks for a specific suit, e.g. spades. The double of 3NT in such an auction is so rare that it costs nothing to use the double for this purpose. A holding such as ♠ K-Q-J-x-x plus an ace is suitable. However, make sure this has been discussed before springing it on your partner.

(4) LEADS AFTER PRE-EMPTS

After auctions like 3♣ : 3NT or 3◇ : 3NT, dummy's long suit usually provides enough tricks for declarer to succeed. Unless your tricks come quickly, they are not coming at all. In these cases, it often pays you to start a short strong suit rather than a longer weaker suit. Unless you have dummy's pre-empt suit well held, choose to lead holdings like A-K-x or K-Q-x rather than poor suits like J-x-x-x-x or Q-x-x-x-x.

(5) LEADS AGAINST NO-TRUMP SLAMS

Against 3NT or no-trump partscores, it is normal to lead your long suit. You need your length tricks for the five or more tricks to defeat their contract. Against 6NT, you need only two tricks and against 7NT only one trick is required. Your long suit is not necessarily the most appealing. Your priorities against 6NT or 7NT are in this order :

1. Lead a 3-card or longer sequence.

2. Avoid leading any suit which has an honor card. Prefer a passive lead from a suit of rag cards.

If they are in 7NT and you hold 4-5 points, partner probably has nothing. If they are in 6NT and you hold 7 or more points, partner is likely to have nothing. If you lead from a suit with an honor card, it may well cost you a trick. Choose a valueless suit and wait for the tricks to come to you.

(6) RETURNING PARTNER'S LEAD

If you win partner's opening lead or win a trick later, it is normal to return partner's suit, unless it is clearly futile or you have a superior choice. When you are returning partner's suit, the card to return is specified:

1. 1 card left : No choice.
2. 2 cards left : Lead top of the remaining doubleton.
3. 3 cards left : Return bottom card, your original fourth-highest, unless there is a risk of blocking the suit. With Q-J-x, J-10-x or 10-9-x left, return the top of touching cards in order not to block the suit.

```
              6 4
K 9 8 5 2              A J 10 3
              Q 7
```

West leads the 5 to the ace. If East returns the 3, the defense can take only four tricks. On the jack return, the defense can come to five tricks.

```
              7 5
A 8 6 4 2              K 10 9 3
              Q J
```

Remaining holdings like 9-8-x, 10-8-x or J-9-x may also block the suit. Even though it may be ambiguous for partner, return the top from these holdings if the danger of a blockage exists.

                    10 5   K 5
         Q 7 6 4 2   K 9 8 3   A 7 6 4 2   Q 10 8 3
                    A J   J 9

West leads the 4 to the king and ace. If East gains the lead, return the 9, not the 3. The 3 holds the defense to three tricks in the suit. On the 9 return, the defense can take four tricks.

                    8 6
         K 7 5 3 2   A J 9 4
                    Q 10

West leads the 3 to the ace. If East returns the 4, four tricks is the limit. On the jack return, the defense can take five tricks.

West leads the 4 and South misguesses, playing low from dummy, and East wins with the queen. If East returns the 3, the defense can take only four tricks. If East unblocks by returning the 10, the first five tricks go to the defense.

These unblocking moves are not required if partner has only four cards in the suit, but if partner may have five or more, be ready to unblock when necessary.

4. 4 or more cards left : Return the card that was originally fourth highest (or top of touching honours).

EXERCISE ON OPENING LEADS AGAINST NO-TRUMPS

A. In each of the following questions, you are given the dummy, East's cards and West's lead. East plays the top card and wins the first trick. Which card should East return?

1.	NORTH		2.	NORTH		3.	NORTH	
	8 6			9 6			J 7	
WEST		EAST	WEST		EAST	WEST		EAST
Lead : J		K 7 2	Lead : 3		K J 5	Lead : 3		K 10 8 4

4.	NORTH		5.	NORTH		6.	NORTH	
	9 7 3			8 6			8 6	
WEST		EAST	WEST		EAST	WEST		EAST
Lead : 5		K 8 4 2	Lead : 4		K 10 9 3	Lead : 4		A Q J 2

B. For each of the following questions you are given the West cards on lead against a no-trumps contract.
(i) What should West lead if the bidding has been 1NT : 3NT?
(ii) What should West lead after each of the auctions given?

1. ♠ 7 5 2	a. SOUTH	WEST	NORTH	EAST	b. SOUTH	WEST	NORTH	EAST
♡ 8 7		Pass	1♢	Pass		Pass	Pass	1♡
♢ A J 10 9 4	1NT	Pass	3♢	Pass	1NT	Pass	Pass	Pass
♣ 9 8 5	3NT	Pass	Pass	Pass				

2. ♠ Q J 9 8 2	a. SOUTH	WEST	NORTH	EAST	b. SOUTH	WEST	NORTH	EAST
♡ Q 4	1♠	Pass	2♡	Pass	1NT	Pass	2♣	Pass
♢ J 10 3 2	2NT	Pass	3NT	All pass	2♡	Pass	3NT	All pass
♣ 9 8								

3. ♠ 6 3 2	a. SOUTH	WEST	NORTH	EAST	b. SOUTH	WEST	NORTH	EAST
♡ K 9 7 5 3	1NT	Pass	3♡	Pass	2NT	Pass	3♠	Pass
♢ Q 10 7	3NT	Pass	Pass	Pass	4♠	Pass	4NT	Pass
♣ J 8					5♡	Pass	6NT	All pass

4. ♠ Q 10 9 8 2	a. SOUTH	WEST	NORTH	EAST	b. SOUTH	WEST	NORTH	EAST
♡ J 8 3		Pass	1♠	Pass		Pass	1♣	Pass
♢ J 7 3 2	2♢	Pass	3♢	Pass	1NT	Pass	2NT	Pass
♣ 4	3NT	Pass	Pass	Pass	3NT	Pass	Pass	Dble //

5. ♠ J 10 9 8 6	a. SOUTH	WEST	NORTH	EAST	b. SOUTH	WEST	NORTH	EAST
♡ 7		Pass	1♢	1♡		Pass	3♣	Pass
♢ A Q 10	2♢	Pass	2♡*	Pass	3NT	Pass	Pass	Pass
♣ 7 4 3 2	2NT	Pass	3NT	All pass				
	*Asking for a stopper in hearts							

PLAY HANDS BASED ON LEADS AGAINST NO-TRUMPS

Hand 9 : Dealer North : E-W vulnerable

	WEST	NORTH	EAST	SOUTH
		3♢	Pass	3NT
	Pass	Pass	Pass	

```
            NORTH
            ♠ 8 3
            ♡ 7 6
            ♢ A Q J 7 6 5 2
            ♣ J 3
WEST                    EAST
♠ J 6 5 4 2            ♠ Q 9 7
♡ A K 5               ♡ 10 8 4 3 2
♢ 8                    ♢ K 4
♣ Q 7 5 4             ♣ 10 9 8
            SOUTH
            ♠ A K 10
            ♡ Q J 9
            ♢ 10 9 3
            ♣ A K 6 2
```

Lead: ♡ K (or ace). Against a pre-empt, prefer a strong short suit to a weakish long suit. On a spade or a club lead, South wins, takes the diamond finesse and makes at least ten tricks.

Play : East encourages the lead (♡ 8 — standard high signal). West continues with ♡ A (or king) and a third heart. South wins and leads the ♢ 10, finessing. When the finesse loses, East cashes two more hearts for one down.

Notes: (1) 3NT over a minor pre-empt shows a strong, balanced hand with the missing suits held. 3NT is far better than 5♢ and makes on a black suit lead. On a heart lead, it succeeds if hearts are 4-4 or the ♢ K is onside.
(2) If East disliked hearts and discouraged the heart lead, West would still be able to switch to a black suit at trick 2.
(3) The normal play is to take the diamond finesse, particularly as North has no outside entry. If West is known or expected to hold the remaining hearts, the diamond finesse is vital to keep West off lead. However, if declarer reads the position that East has the remaining hearts, it is slightly superior to reject the diamond finesse. Playing ♢ A is a safety play guarding against the danger hand East holding ♢ K singleton. It will allow 3NT to make if West has ♢ K doubleton or East has the ♢ K singleton. Nevertheless, this play could cost the contract if West holds all three missing diamonds : West would hold off on the second diamond. After the third diamond, declarer would have to hope that West has the ♣ Q and that the ♣ J is an entry to dummy.

Hand 10 : Dealer East : Both vulnerable

	WEST	NORTH	EAST	SOUTH
			Pass	1♡
	1NT	Double	All pass	Pass

```
            NORTH
            ♠ A Q 6 2
            ♡ 10 4 3
            ♢ K 8 3
            ♣ 7 6 3
WEST                    EAST
♠ K 10 7              ♠ 9 8 5 4
♡ A 9 8               ♡ Q 6
♢ A Q J 5            ♢ 10 7 4 2
♣ Q J 5              ♣ 10 8 4
            SOUTH
            ♠ J 3
            ♡ K J 7 5 2
            ♢ 9 6
            ♣ A K 9 2
```

Lead : ♡ 3. Partner's suit. Bottom from three to an honor.

Play : If dummy plays the queen, South covers with the king, else South plays the jack. West wins and leads ♢ A, ♢ Q, hoping to use dummy's ♢ 10 as an entry for a possible spade finesse later. North wins ♢ K. If the ♡ Q was played at trick 1, North can continue with ♡ 10 and another heart. If trick 1 was 6 — J — A, North plays ♡ 4 — Q — K. South should then cash ♣ K to show South's entry before playing the third heart. North wins ♡ 10 and leads a club to South. After two hearts, South shifts to the ♠ J. The defense takes 2 spades, 4 hearts, 1 diamond, 2 clubs, +800.

Notes: (1) The double of 1NT is for penalties, *not a negative double.* Double the 1NT overcall when your side holds more than 20 HCP (unless you have great support for partner and want to try for game).
(2) South knows that North began with 10-x-x or 10-x-x-x (or a singleton, which is not likely). North's *three* of hearts, the lowest, promises an honor. Since West presumably holds the ace for the 1NT bid, North has the 10.
(3) If trick 1 goes ♡ 3 — Q — K — low, South can cash the ♣ K (to show the entry) before continuing hearts.
(4) If trick 1 goes ♡ 3 — 6 — jack — low, South continues with ♡ K. If West plays low again, South should then cash the ♣ K before playing the third heart. If West takes the second heart, North must not unblock the ♡ 10. When North later cashes ♡ 10, South plays the *two*, showing the entry is in clubs (lowest card = low suit).
(5) **NOTE** that if North's initial lead is the *ten* of hearts (error), declarer can score an extra trick. After ♡ 10 — *queen* — king — ace, declarer's 9-8 are sure to produce a second heart trick. From 10-x-x, the standard lead (and working out best most of the time) is the low card. Do not squander the honor.

Hand 11 : Dealer South : Nil vulnerable

NORTH
- ♠ A K J 2
- ♡ J 8
- ◇ K Q 8 4
- ♣ Q 10 7

WEST
- ♠ 10 9 7
- ♡ 9 7
- ◇ A 7 6 5 2
- ♣ A 9 4

EAST
- ♠ 8 6 5
- ♡ K 10 6 4 3
- ◇ - - -
- ♣ K 8 6 3 2

SOUTH
- ♠ Q 4 3
- ♡ A Q 5 2
- ◇ J 10 9 3
- ♣ J 5

WEST	NORTH	EAST	SOUTH
			Pass
Pass	1NT	Pass	2♣
Pass	2♠	Pass	3NT
Pass	Pass	Pass	

Lead : ♣3. Had the bidding been 1NT : 3NT, East would lead the ♡4 (prefer the major to the minor) but declarer makes 3NT with ease here on a heart lead.. On this auction, South's 2♣ was exploring a major suit contract. As spades were rejected, logically South will turn up with four hearts. As it it undesirable to lead a suit in which the opposition hold length, East should choose the club lead.

Play : After ♣A, West returns the ♣9, top from a remaining doubleton. East should recognise that North began with three clubs and therefore has a stopper (the ♣9 denies the 10 or higher). *East should duck the second club.* When declarer plays diamonds, West wins ◇A and returns a third club. East cashes out the clubs.

Notes : (1) With a 4-card major and game values, South should explore the possible heart fit via 2♣ Stayman.
(2) If declarer cleverly plays the *queen* of clubs at trick 2, pretending to hold Q-7 doubleton, East should read the position and still duck. As West's *nine* denies the 10, North still has the 10. *Trust partner, not declarer.*
(3) If declarer were tackling A-x-x opposite K-x-x-x-x, the natural play is to duck one round. When East leads to the ace and ducks the second round, the defense is doing exactly what declarer would do.
(4) If North cashes spades before touching diamonds, East should throw a heart on the fourth spade, not a club.

Hand 12 : Dealer West : N-S vulnerable

NORTH
- ♠ 10
- ♡ 10 5 4 2
- ◇ A J 9 5
- ♣ K 7 4 2

WEST
- ♠ A K 9 4
- ♡ J 9 7
- ◇ 8 7
- ♣ Q 9 6 3

EAST
- ♠ 8 6 5
- ♡ A K Q 6
- ◇ Q 10
- ♣ A J 10 8

SOUTH
- ♠ Q J 7 3 2
- ♡ 8 3
- ◇ K 6 4 3 2
- ♣ 5

WEST	NORTH	EAST	SOUTH
Pass	Pass	1NT	Pass
2♣	Pass	2♡	Pass
3NT	Pass	Pass	Pass

Lead : ◇3. On most auctions, South would lead a spade (prefer a major to a minor and prefer a suit with two honors to a suit with only one). However, as West's bidding implies spades, South should not choose the suit where an opponent holds length.

Play : North wins the ace of diamonds and should return the *jack* of diamonds to unblock the suit. Trick 2 is ◇J − Q − K − 8. North wins the third diamond with the 9 and returns the ◇5 which South must overtake with the ◇6 to cash the fifth diamond.

Notes : (1) With four spades and enough for game, West uses 2♣ Stayman. When East does not show spades at once, West rebids 3NT. East would bid 4♠ over 3NT with both majors. West's bidding — Stayman and then reject hearts to rebid in no-trumps — implies four spades. (If in doubt, ask for an explanation.) 4♡ is superior but very hard to reach.
(2) On any lead but a diamond, 3NT will succeed. Declarer takes repeated club finesses for 4 clubs, 4 hearts and 2 spades. The technique for the clubs is to run the 9 first, then run the queen, then low to the A-J.
(3) If North wins ◇A and returns ◇5, the diamonds are blocked. The defense then can take only four diamond tricks and this allows declarer to make 3NT.
(4) North must not play the ◇J at trick 1. When dummy has only low cards, play third hand high. To do otherwise is the error known as 'finessing against partner'. If North plays the ◇J, East wins ◇Q and can come to eleven tricks.
(5) After ◇A, then ◇J to the king, South should return the ◇2 at trick 3, not the 6 of diamonds which would again block the suit.
(6) After ◇A, ◇J to the king, ◇2 to the 9, South must overtake ◇5 with the 6 at trick 4. Otherwise North is left on lead with no more diamonds.

CHAPTER 4

OPENING LEADS IN SUIT CONTRACTS

(1) PREFER A SUIT BID BY PARTNER

If partner has shown values in a suit, it is normal to lead that suit. It enables you to cash the tricks available in that suit or at least avoid giving away tricks in another suit.

You may choose a suit other than partner's if:

(a) You hold a suit headed by A-K or K-Q-J. *OR—*

(b) You and partner have ten cards between you in partner's suit so that there is at most one trick available in that suit. *OR—*

(c) You have a singleton to lead plus control of trumps (such as A-x, A-x-x or K-x-x). You plan to lead the singleton, gain the lead in trumps and then lead partner's suit as the entry for partner to give you the ruff. *OR—*

(d) You hold A-Q-x or A-Q-x-x in partner's suit and it is not certain that partner holds the king. If partner has overcalled and you hold the A-Q in partner's suit, it is a virtual certainty that partner has the king. However, an opening bid or a response to an opening bid does not promise a strong suit. The situation could be :

```
                8 6
  A Q 5 4                J 10 9 7 2
                K 3

                OR

                J 6
  A Q 7                  10 8 5 4 3 2
                K 9
```

In either case, if West leads the suit, South receives an undeserved trick. You should be almost as reluctant to lead from an A-Q holding in partner's suit as from an unbid suit headed by the A-Q.

(2) AVOID SUITS BID BY THE OPPOSITION

It is very risky to lead a side suit bid by declarer. It is rarely attractive to lead a suit bid by dummy. If the opponents have bid all the suits genuinely, it may be best to lead a trump. If this is out of the question, prefer a suit bid by dummy to a suit bid by declarer. If dummy has bid two suits, prefer the second suit.

You may lead a suit bid by the opposition if —

(a) It is a singleton and the other conditions for a singleton lead are right (see later). Where dummy has shown a long suit, the lead of that suit generally indicates a singleton.

(b) You have a powerful holding in their suit, such as A-K-Q or K-Q-J-10 or Q-J-10-9. Weaker or lower holdings are not appealing.

It is not attractive to lead a doubleton in dummy's long suit. Firstly, it takes three rounds before you can ruff and by then your trumps have usually been drawn. Secondly, it often traps an honor held by partner.

```
                A J 10 6 2
  8 3                     Q 9 5
                K 7 4
```

If West leads the suit, declarer has no loser.

```
                A Q 7 4 2
  9 3                     J 8 6 5
                K 10
```

If West leads the suit, declarer can score five tricks in the suit without any risk.

NOTE : The 'lead-through-strength' principle does not apply to the opening lead and does not apply to a *long* suit in dummy.

(c) Partner is likely to be short in their suit and you are able to give partner a ruff. A mere suspicion or hope that partner has a shortage is not enough to justify leading their suit. There must be strong evidence that partner is the one that is short, not declarer.

If the opponents have bid and raised a suit, they will normally hold at least eight cards between them. If you hold four cards in that suit, partner figures to have a singleton. If you have five cards in that suit, partner is probably void. As long as you can give partner the ruff before trumps are drawn (e.g. you have A-x-x-x in the suit where partner is short or you hold the ace of trumps so that partner's trumps cannot be drawn), leading this suit is a good move.

WEST	NORTH	EAST	SOUTH
	1♡	Pass	2♣
Pass	3♣	Pass	4♡
Pass	Pass	Pass	

North-South probably have at least eight clubs. If East has four or more clubs, West will be short.

(3) IT IS NORMAL TO LEAD AN UNBID SUIT IF PARTNER HAS NOT BID

Where dummy has shown a 5-card or longer suit and you are not particularly strong in that suit, it is usually vital to lead an unbid suit. Do not lead the long suit in dummy and do not lead trumps. For example :

NORTH	SOUTH	
1♠	2♡	South will have five or more hearts. Lead a club or a diamond.
3♠	4♠	

NORTH	SOUTH	
1♢	1♡	North has at least five diamonds and, on this sequence, probably six. Lead a club or a spade.
2♢	3♡	
4♡	**Pass**	

Declarer's usual strategy when dummy has a long suit is to draw trumps and use the long suit in dummy to discard losers in the other suits. If you lead trumps, you are helping declarer's task. If you lead dummy's long suit, you are helping declarer. Choose an unbid suit. It is usually essential that you come to your tricks in the unbid suits before declarer can discard the losers there.

Frequently you may have to choose between unbid suits.

(A) GREAT SUITS TO LEAD

(1) A 3-card or longer sequence : Suits headed by K-Q-J, Q-J-10, J-10-9 or 10-9-8 make excellent leads because they establish tricks for your side without the risk of losing a trick with the lead.

(2) A suit headed by the A-K : The advantage of a suit like A-K-x-x-x is that you will (almost always) win the first trick. You can study dummy, note partner's signal and then decide whether to continue with that suit or switch. If you decide to switch, your lead has not yet set up winners for declarer in that suit. That is the difference between leading an A-K suit (great) and leading an ace-high suit without the king (poor). When you lead an ace, you also see dummy and partner's signal, but you have given up control of the suit and often set up winners for declarer instead of for your side.

(3) Lead a singleton : A singleton lead is often best. It is particularly attractive when you hold a very weak hand and worthless trumps. The aim of a singleton lead is, of course, to score ruffs. For that, partner needs entries to return the suit for you to ruff. If it is clear from the bidding and your own HCP that partner can scarcely hold an ace or a king, you are wasting your time with a singleton lead. For example, if they bid

1♠ : 3♠, 4♠ . . . and you hold 13 points, forget a singleton lead. How will partner ever obtain the lead?

Likewise, if your trumps are strong, a singleton lead is not useful. With Q-J-10-9 in trumps, you have two trump tricks by strength. You do not need to ruff in order to score those tricks.

Singleton leads from weak hands are very appealing if your trump holding is A-x, A-x-x or K-x-x. With these holdings, your trumps cannot be drawn quickly. With two or three worthless trumps, you may find that declarer wins your singleton and draws trumps. Result : You have probably wasted your lead (and may have helped declarer avoid a loser in the suit led).

A singleton in dummy's suit or declarer's side suit has a secondary danger. It may alert declarer to the bad break and cause declarer to draw trumps at once. On the other hand, if you lead some other suit, declarer may not suspect a bad break. Declarer may then lead dummy's suit, hoping for a quick discard, and, hey presto, you score your ruff. *Chances are you are more likely to score your ruff by not leading a singleton in dummy's suit or declarer's side suit.*

Where you have a choice of great leads :

● Prefer a high solid sequence (K-Q-J or Q-J-10) to an A-K suit (except perhaps against a slam).

● Prefer a sequence to a singleton.

● Prefer an A-K suit to a singleton. You can still switch to your singleton at trick 2.

However, a singleton ace is usually a very fine lead, as long as partner is likely to have an entry. You lead the ace and judge from dummy, the bidding, your cards . . . where partner's entry lies. If partner can read the ace lead as a singleton, partner may be able to signal the suit in which the entry lies.

(B) AVOID THE ABYSMAL LEADS IF YOU HAVE NO GREAT LEAD

When you have an obviously good lead, your first problem is over. Most of the time you will not have a great lead available. With other holdings, try to eliminate those with a very high risk factor. The riskiest leads are an ace-high suit (no king), leading a doubleton honor or a singleton trump or leading a 3-card or 4-card suit with only one honor.

Any of these leads might be best on any given hand. That is what makes the opening lead so tough. However, they should be avoided because in the long run they are more likely to cost your side tricks than gain tricks for you.

The worst leads, in order of horror, are :

(1) DO NOT LEAD AN ACE-HIGH SUIT

Ace plus king : Yes

Ace and no king : No

However, if you must lead a suit headed by the ace, lead the ace, not a low card. For example :

```
              8
A J 6 4 2         Q 10 9 5
            K 7 3
```

If West does not lead this suit, declarer can never score a trick with the king. If West must lead the suit, take your ace. Then West scores one trick and declarer makes one trick with the king. However, if West leads low, disobeying the rule 'Never lead away from an ace in a trump contract', South scores one trick with the king but West never makes a trick.

Rule 1 : Do not lead from an ace-high suit in a trump contract.

Rule 2 : If you break Rule 1, lead the ace.

These two rules apply only at trick 1. Later in the defense it may be vital to switch to an ace-high suit and even to lead a low card when you hold the ace.

The usual calamity of leading aces is that you set up winners for declarer. If the declarer side is the stronger, declarer or dummy is much more likely to hold the king or queen than partner is. Leading the ace will often set up winners for declarer.

```
             7 4 2
A 8 5 3            Q J 10 6
             K 9
```

If West leads the ace, West wins a trick and South makes the king. If West leaves the suit alone, South can never score the king.

```
             7 4 2
A 10 5 3          K J 6
             Q 9 8
```

If West leads the ace, South can score a trick with the queen. If West avoids this suit, South cannot make a trick here.

```
             K 7 5
A 9 2             J 10 8 3
             Q 6 4
```

With king plus queen, declarer is bound to win one trick. If West leads the ace, declarer has two winners. If West stays off the suit, declarer can make only the one trick available.

The best value for an ace is to capture a high card. When you lead the ace, it is not likely that you will capture any useful high card.

Leading an ace may be reasonable against a slam or where declarer started with a pre-emptive opening. As a pre-emptor is unlikely to hold the king in the suit led, the ace lead is less likely to cost. An ace is also a good start if partner figures to be short in that suit.

Where you hold four or five trumps, a sound strategy is to force declarer to ruff and reduce declarer's trump length. Your best chance is to lead your long suit and if this suit is headed by the ace, go ahead and lead the ace. The forcing defense is covered in Chapter 18.

(2) DO NOT LEAD K-X, Q-X OR J-X IN AN UNBID SUIT. EVEN 10-X IS RISKY.

A doubleton honor in partner's suit is a great start, but in an unbid suit it can often be fatal.

```
             Q J 7
K 4               9 8 6 2
             A 10 5 3
```

If declarer plays this suit, declarer loses a trick. If West leads the king, declarer has no loser.

```
             8 7 4
Q 5               A 9 6 2
             K J 10 3
```

If declarer tackles this suit, declarer will usually lose two tricks, finessing the jack first and losing to the queen. If West leads the queen, the queen will not score a trick and declarer loses only one trick.

```
             Q 10 9
J 7               K 6 5 4
             A 8 3 2
```

If declarer has to play this suit, declarer must lose one trick. If West leads the jack, the queen covers and declarer loses no tricks.

```
             Q 7 2
10 5              A J 8 4 3
             K 9 6
```

Left alone, declarer can make only one trick with the king and queen. However, if West leads the 10, South can make two tricks : cover the 10 with the queen, taken by the ace, and later finesse the 9. The lead of the 10 has set up for declarer a finessing position which declarer could not have managed without help.

For similar reasons, it is very risky to lead a singleton king. You may make a trick with it if you do not lead it. If you lead it and the opponents have the ace, you have lost any chance of scoring a trick with it. A singleton queen lead is moderately risky. A singleton jack also has some risk but if the other conditions for a singleton lead are right, you should chance it.

(3) DO NOT LEAD A SINGLETON TRUMP

Where you have a singleton trump, partner often has three or four trumps. Your singleton trump lead will often destroy partner's trump trick(s).

```
          A 7 6 3
   5                Q 10 4
          K J 9 8 2
```

With nine trumps, declarer will usually play ace and king and East then scores the queen. If West leads the trump, the defence scores no tricks.

```
          A 4 3
   6                J 10 5 2
          K Q 9 8 7
```

If declarer starts this suit, playing ace then king or king then ace, East makes one trick. If West leads the trump, it goes low from dummy — 10 — king. Now, a trump to the ace reveals the position and East's J-5 can be finessed.

```
          8 7 6 2
   3                Q J 4
          A K 10 9 5
```

Declarer would normally lead the ace and then is bound to lose a trick. If West leads the trump, it goes low from dummy, jack or queen from East and South wins. Suspecting that West would not lead from J-x or Q-x in trumps, South may well cross to dummy and lead a trump, finessing the 10. East's probable trump winner has been eliminated by West's inferior lead.

Nevertheless, when the circumstances are right, a singleton trump lead may be obligatory or highly desirable.

(a) If partner passes your takeout double at the 1-level, lead a trump. This trump lead is mandatory, even with a singleton.

(b) If partner passes your takeout double at the 2-level, lead a singleton trump if you have no great lead.

(c) Lead a singleton trump if they are sacrificing and you have no great alternative lead.

(d) Lead a singleton trump if the opposition have bid to a high level with about 20 HCP or less. How can they hope to win so many tricks with so little in high card strength? Only by ruffing. How can you reduce their ruffing potential? By leading trumps early and often, even starting with a singleton trump.

However, these situations are exceptions to the rule and the principle remains that it is usually best to avoid leading a singleton trump.

(4) DO NOT LEAD FROM A SUIT WHICH HAS ONLY ONE HONOR

Suits such as J-x-x, J-x-x-x, Q-x-x, Q-x-x-x, K-x-x or K-x-x-x are often poor beginnings.

```
          K 10 3
   J 6 2             Q 8 5 4
          A 9 7
```

Declarer has two tricks and cannot score a third trick if tackling this suit. However, if either defender leads the suit, declarer can score *three* tricks. If West leads the 2, it goes — 3 — queen — ace, and declarer can finesse the 10 later. If East starts with the 4, it goes 7 — jack — king and the A-9 tenace allows declarer to finesse against East's queen later.

```
          8 6 2
   K 7 5             J 10 9 4
          A Q 3
```

If West leads the suit, South wins two tricks. If West avoids this suit, declarer can score only the ace, with the queen finesse losing.

If you have to lead from suits with only one honor:

● **It is safer to lead from a king than a queen.**

● **It is safer to lead from a queen than a jack.**

WEST	West	North	East	South
♠ K	Pass	Pass	Pass	1♠
♡ J 7 6 2	Pass	3♠	Pass	4♠
◇ Q 8 4 3	Pass	Pass	Pass	
♣ K 7 5 2		What should West lead?		

On the above auction, the king of spades would be the worst lead. No choice is attractive but following the above priorities (lead from a king rather than a queen, lead from a queen rather than a jack), West's best choice is the 2 of clubs.

(C) IN-BETWEEN LEADS – NOT GREAT, NOT ABYSMAL

If you have no great lead and you have eliminated any abysmal lead and you are still left with a choice of leads in unbid suits, these guidelines could help:

● Prefer a near-sequence to an interior sequence.

● Prefer a suit with two honors to a suit with one honor.

● Prefer a suit with touching honors to a suit with broken honors. K-Q-x-x or Q-J-x-x is usually superior to K-J-x-x or Q-10-x-x.

● Prefer a suit with no honors to a suit with only one honor.

● A rag doubleton is appealing with a weak hand.

The logic here is the same as for a singleton lead. The weaker the hand, the more attractive it is to start with a doubleton. The weaker your hand, the better the chance of partner having the entries needed to give you ruffs. The stronger your hand, the less likely it is that partner has entries and the less attractive the doubleton lead becomes.

● With no attractive lead, there is nothing wrong with leading from three or four rags in an unbid suit or from two or three rag trumps.

TRUMP LEADS

When dummy has not indicated a long suit which is likely to give declarer discards and dummy has shown trump support, a trump lead may be best if your trump holding is safe to lead. Reasonably safe are x-x, x-x-x, A-x (lead the ace), A-x-x (lead low) or K-x-x. Four or five rags are also fine if you hold no long suit with which you are likely to force declarer to ruff. Dangerous trump leads are from K-x, Q-x, J-x, 10-x, Q-x-x, J-x-x, 10-x-x, K-Q-x or A-J-x.

LEAD A TRUMP IF :

(a) Declarer has shown a two-suiter and dummy has shown a preference (such as 1♠ : 1NT, 2♡ : Pass) and you are strong in declarer's other suit. Similarly, if the unusual 2NT has been used and declarer has chosen one of the minors, lead a trump if you are strong in the other minor. Declarer often has only two or three trumps in this situation and will plan to ruff out the other minor if you do not reduce or eliminate the ruffs.

(b) Declarer or dummy is known to hold a 4-4-4-1 pattern so that their value lies in ruffing and there is no long suit which threatens to give declarer discards.

(c) Each opponent bid a suit and they have ended in their third suit. This usually indicates a crossruff since dummy is probably short in declarer's first suit and declarer is likely to be short in dummy's first suit. The best way to counter a crossruff is to lead trumps at every opportunity.

(d) Your side has clearly more points than their side. If they expect to make more tricks than their high card values indicate, they must be bidding on good shape and expect to come to extra tricks by ruffing frequently. By leading trumps you cut down their trumping power.

(e) No other lead is attractive and dummy has not shown a useful long suit. It is usually safer to lead from rag trumps than to break open other dangerous holdings like doubleton honors or one-honor suits.

DO NOT LEAD A TRUMP IF :

(a) Dummy has not shown any support for declarer. For example, after 1♠ : 2◇ , 4♠ ... there is no basis for a trump lead. If you do lead a trump in this case, dummy may have a singleton or a void in trumps and your lead could neatly trap partner's potential winner.

(b) Dummy has shown a useful long suit. Lead one of the unbid suits before declarer can discard losers in these suits on dummy's long suit.

(c) Your trump is a singleton. See page 27.

(d) You have four or more strong trumps. Prefer to lead your long suit and try to force declarer to ruff, thus causing declarer to lose control of the trump suit (see Chapter 18).

(e) You have a dangerous trump holding and to lead a trump is very likely to cost you a trick or destroy a possible winner in partner's hand.

WHICH TRUMP DO YOU LEAD?

The standard approach is to lead top from two touching honors doubleton (J-10, 10-9 are fine but avoid K-Q or Q-J doubleton), top from a 3-card sequence (K-Q-J, Q-J-10), bottom from an even number of trumps and middle-down-up with three or five trumps. From J-10-x, the bottom card is led:

A 9 5 2

J 10 3   **Q**

K 8 7 6 4

If West leads low, the defense takes the trick to which it is entitled. If West leads the jack, declarer can play low from dummy. After capturing the jack and queen, declarer can finesse against West's 10-3 and the defense takes no tricks.

Bottom card is led from a two or four trumps to inform partner of the number of trumps held and to retain the higher trump in case a possibility to overruff arises. Playing high-low in trumps (middle-down) shows another trump, again enabling partner to count the trump suit and to let partner know you have another trump with which to ruff, if that is relevant.

OPENING LEADS AGAINST SUIT SLAMS

(A) AGAINST A GRAND SLAM

Lead a solid sequence. If that is not possible, lead a trump (but still avoid a singleton trump — partner could have Q-x-x, J-x-x-x or J-10-x-x). Against a grand slam, you should lead as safely as possible and the trump suit is the area least likely for your side to have a trick. If a trump lead is out, avoid leading from any suit with just one honor or broken honors. Prefer a long rag suit to a short rag suit.

(B) AGAINST A SMALL SLAM

1. Choose a sequence or an A-K suit if available. From an A-K suit lead the ace even if you normally lead the king from A-K suits.

2. Lead a singleton if partner might hold that ace or the ace of trumps. If you have an ace or they are known to hold all four aces, a singleton lead will almost never work and may well cost.

3. Avoid a trump lead unless you have broken honor holdings in the other suits.

4. Prefer an unbid suit, especially if headed by K-Q or Q-J.

5. With a likely winner in trumps or in a long suit held by the opposition, aim to set up a second trick by leading from a K-high or Q-high suit, or cash an ace.

6. Cashing an ace against a small slam is quite often right, far more often than at lower levels. Cash an ace if you have a sure or probable trump winner or you are confident you can give partner a ruff in that suit or partner might hold the king in that suit. Refrain from leading an ace in a suit bid by the opponents unless partner is marked with a void or singleton in that suit.

LEAD-DIRECTING DOUBLES

1. The double of an artificial bid asks partner to lead that suit (see page 21).

2. The double of a slam by a player not on lead is called a **Lightner Double** and asks for a specific lead:

(a) Do *not* lead a suit bid by your side.

(b) Do *not* lead an unbid suit.

(c) Do *not* lead a trump.

(d) *Do* lead dummy's first bid suit.

The Lightner Double (named after Theodore Lightner) asks for an unusual lead. A suit bid by your side, an unbid suit or a trump is not unusual. A suit bid by the opposition is an unusual lead. With a choice of such suits, lead the first suit bid by dummy. The Lightner Double is often based on a void in the suit requested. Where dummy has not bid a suit, the Lightner Double asks you to find partner's void (usually opposite your longest suit).

None of the above applies if their slam is a sacrifice. The double of a slam sacrifice is for penalties, not Lightner, not lead-directing. Make your normal lead.

The corollary of Lightner Double principles is that you should not double a slam if that asks for a specific lead and you do not want that lead. If you need partner's normal lead to defeat the slam, do not double.

OTHER SYSTEMS OF LEADS

There are systems of leads just as there are systems of bidding. You may come across these popular but non-standard methods.

RUSINOW LEADS OR UNDERLEADING

Underleading honors is a method which requires you to lead second card from sequence holdings :

The king from A-K-x-x holdings in suit contracts or from A-K-Q or A-K-J suits.

The queen from K-Q-x-x holdings in suit contracts or K-Q-J or K-Q-10 suits.

The jack from Q-J sequence combinations.

The 10 from J-10 sequence combinations.

The 9 from 10-9 sequence combinations.

The correct Rusinow card to lead is underlined :

K-J-10-5   Q-J-9-6   J-10-7   Q-10-9-8

This solves the problem of the ace from A-K or king from A-K suits. The ace lead denies the king (except for ace-then-king which shows A-K doubleton). It eliminates the king from A-K-x-x or king from K-Q-x-x ambiguity. The king lead denies the queen.

A fringe benefit of the method is that it can reveal K-Q doubleton. From K-Q-x and longer suits (where standard leaders start with the king), the Rusinow lead is the queen. From K-Q doubleton, standard leaders still start with the king. The Rusinow lead is the king followed by the queen. This departure from the normal queen-first indicates that the holding is precisely K-Q doubleton (like A-then-K from A-K doubleton).

However, the 9 lead in Rusinow is ambiguous. In standard methods, the 9 lead is a singleton or a doubleton (or K-J-9). The 9 lead cannot be a legitimate fourth-highest because when it is fourth-highest, there are three higher honors. With three honors, lead top of the touching honors, using standard leads.

The Rusinow 9 lead may be a singleton or doubleton or from a 10-9 sequence (10-9-8-x) or from an interior sequence (K-10-9-7-3).

With two touching honors doubleton, the higher honor is led (Q-J, J-10, 10-9). This can also lead to an ambiguity. The queen lead might be from K-Q-x or longer or from Q-J doubleton. The jack lead might be from Q-J sequences or from J-10 doubleton and the 10 lead might be from J-10 sequences or 10-9 doubleton. Nevertheless, Rusinow leads are a very efficient way of treating honor card leads.

When leading partner's bid suit, the Rusinow lead is abandoned (except for king from A-K-x and longer). Lead top of touching honors in partner's suit.

THIRDS AND FIFTHS

Playing thirds and fifths, the third-highest card is led from 3-card and 4-card suits and the fifth-highest card from 5-card and longer suits. This is in contrast to the standard fourth-highest from long suits.

The method is popular with those experts who believe that the benefit (knowing the *number* of cards held by the leader) outweighs the loss (being unable to distinguish between a lead from rags or a lead from an honor — the 2 is led from 6-5-2 and from K-5-2 — the 4 is led from 8-6-4-2 and from K-10-4-2).

If playing thirds and fifths, the card to lead is underlined :

8-7-<u>6</u>   J-9-<u>3</u>   10-8-<u>2</u>   J-8-<u>6</u>-2   9-7-<u>3</u>-2
10-8-<u>5</u>-2   K-8-6-3-<u>2</u>   Q-9-7-5-<u>4</u>-2   8-7-6-4-<u>2</u>

If playing against a pair using thirds and fifths, the Rule of 10 applies to a fifth-highest lead and the Rule of 12 applies to third-highest leads. These rules operate like the Rule of 11 (see page 15).

Thirds and fifths is a recommended method for a regular, serious partnership. Greater ambiguity exists with standard fourth-highest and M.U.D.

EXERCISE ON OPENING LEADS AGAINST SUIT CONTRACTS

For each of the following questions you are given the West cards on lead against a trump contract.

(i) What should West lead if the bidding has been 1♠ : 3♠, 4♠ ?

(ii) What should West lead after each of the auctions given?

1. ♠ A J 2
   ♡ J 7
   ◇ 9 7 4 3
   ♣ A 8 5 2

a. SOUTH	WEST	NORTH	EAST	b. SOUTH	WEST	NORTH	EAST
1♠	Pass	2◇	Pass		Pass	1NT	2♡
2♠	Pass	4♠	All pass	4♠	Pass	Pass	Pass

2. ♠ K 2
   ♡ J 8 4 3
   ◇ K 8 3
   ♣ A 9 6 4

a. SOUTH	WEST	NORTH	EAST	b. SOUTH	WEST	NORTH	EAST
1♠	Pass	2♣	Pass	1♡	Pass	2♣	Pass
3♣	Pass	4♠	All pass	2♠	Pass	3♡	Pass
				4♡	Pass	Pass	Pass

3. ♠ 8 3
   ♡ 9
   ◇ K J 7 5 2
   ♣ Q 9 8 4 3

a. SOUTH	WEST	NORTH	EAST	b. SOUTH	WEST	NORTH	EAST
1♣	Pass	1♠	Pass	1♡	Pass	2♣	Pass
2♣	Pass	Pass	Pass	3♣	Pass	4♡	All pass

4. ♠ A Q 8
   ♡ 8 3 2
   ◇ Q J 7 2
   ♣ 8 4 3

a. SOUTH	WEST	NORTH	EAST	b. SOUTH	WEST	NORTH	EAST
1♠	Pass	1NT	Pass	1♣	Pass	1◇	Pass
2♡	Pass	Pass	Pass	1♡	Pass	2♡	Pass
				3♡	Pass	Pass	Pass

5. ♠ K J 6
   ♡ A 9 7 5
   ◇ 2
   ♣ K Q 7 5 4

a. SOUTH	WEST	NORTH	EAST	b. SOUTH	WEST	NORTH	EAST
1◇	Dble	Pass	Pass	3♡	Pass	Pass	Pass
Pass							

6. ♠ 9 8
   ♡ A J 6 4
   ◇ K 7 6 3
   ♣ 8 7 3

a. SOUTH	WEST	NORTH	EAST	b. SOUTH	WEST	NORTH	EAST
	Pass	1♣	Pass	1♠	Pass	1NT	Pass
1♠	Pass	3♣	Pass	2♡	Pass	2♠	All pass
3♠	Pass	4♠	All pass				

7. ♠ A 8
   ♡ 7
   ◇ K 8 7 2
   ♣ 9 7 6 4 3 2

a. SOUTH	WEST	NORTH	EAST	b. SOUTH	WEST	NORTH	EAST
1♠	Pass	3♠	Pass	1♠	Pass	3◇	Pass
4NT	Pass	5♡	Pass	4◇	Pass	4NT	Pass
6♠	Pass	Pass	Pass	5♡	Pass	6♠	All pass

8. ♠ K 2
   ♡ 8 6
   ◇ Q J 10 7
   ♣ 9 8 6 4 2

a. SOUTH	WEST	NORTH	EAST	b. SOUTH	WEST	NORTH	EAST
		1♣	Pass			1♣	Pass
2♠	Pass	3♠	Pass	4NT	Pass	5♡	Pass
4NT	Pass	5♡	Dble	6♠	Pass	Pass	Dble
6♠	Pass	Pass	Pass	Pass	Pass	Pass	

PLAY HANDS ON LEADS AGAINST SUIT CONTRACTS

Hand 13 : Dealer North : Both vulnerable

NORTH
♠ 10 8 3
♡ A Q 8 7
♢ 8 3
♣ Q 9 3 2

WEST
♠ A Q 9 6 2
♡ 6 4
♢ Q J 7
♣ J 8 4

EAST
♠ 7 5
♡ K 2
♢ 10 9 6 5 4 2
♣ 10 7 6

SOUTH
♠ K J 4
♡ J 10 9 5 3
♢ A K
♣ A K 5

WEST	NORTH	EAST	SOUTH
	Pass	Pass	1♡
1♠	2♡	Pass	4♡
Pass	Pass	Pass	

Lead: ♢ Q. The spade lead is unappealing and so is J-x-x in clubs. Either a trump or a diamond lead is reasonable. The Q-J-x is less risky and on most hands will be more productive than a trump lead.

Play: Declarer wins as East discourages. If South now takes the heart finesse, East wins ♡ K and switches to ♠7. West wins, cashes a second spade and plays a third spade, ruffed by East. One down.

Notes: (1) The correct play is to reject the heart finesse. Win ♢ A, lead ♡ J and when West plays low, win the ♡ A. Lead a second heart, drawing trumps. The spade ruff has vanished. South can deduce from West's 1♠ overcall that West began with five or six spades to the A-Q and that East is therefore short in spades. South can afford to lose two spades and the ♡ K, but not the spade ruff.

(2) Even though not intending to finesse in hearts, South should lead the *jack*. Many a West with K-x will cover an honor. Result : no heart loser. However, West would not play the king if South leads a low heart.
(3) If East began with K-x-x, declarer can always be defeated.
(4) 3NT can be defeated on the normal low spade lead.
(5) If South does take the heart finesse, it would be an error for East to return a diamond. In a suit contract, the Q lead denies the K and A. Therefore South holds ♢ A-K and with only two diamonds in dummy, a diamond return is futile. To defeat 4♡, three more tricks are needed. There are no more heart tricks or diamond tricks. (It is highly unlikely that the ♢ Q lead was a singleton.) Clubs cannot yield enough tricks (with ♣ A-K-x, West would have led a club, not the ♢ Q). Even if West had not bid, the spade switch is best.

Hand 14 : Dealer East : Nil vulnerable

NORTH
♠ 9 2
♡ A 7 6 5
♢ K 10 5 2
♣ 7 6 4

WEST
♠ A J 10 8 7 3
♡ K 10 2
♢ J 9
♣ 10 3

EAST
♠ K Q 6
♡ 8 4
♢ A 7
♣ A Q J 9 8 2

SOUTH
♠ 5 4
♡ Q J 9 3
♢ Q 8 6 4 3
♣ K 5

WEST	NORTH	EAST	SOUTH
		1♣	Pass
1♠	Pass	3♣	Pass
3♠	Pass	4♠	All pass

Lead: ♢ 2. As dummy has shown a long strong suit, North should not make a passive lead. Do not lead a trump, do not lead a club. When choosing between A-x-x-x and K-x-x-x, lead from the K-suit.

Play: Declarer should win ♢ A, play ♠ K and a spade to the ace. The ♣ 10 is run when North plays low. South wins ♣ K and should switch to ♡ Q. The defense takes 2 hearts, 1 diamond and 1 club.

Notes: (1) After East's jump to 3♣, any action by West below game is forcing.
(2) If West ducks in dummy at trick 1, South wins ♢ Q and switches to ♡ Q. However, West should realise that North would have led the K from ♢ K-Q-x-x. Thus, the ♢ 2 lead marks South with one top diamond at least and it cannot gain to duck at trick 1.

(3) West keeps a top spade in dummy as an entry later to the clubs, if necessary. As dummy has the ♠ Q as an entry, there is no point in South ducking the first round of clubs.
(4) After winning ♣ K, South could cash the ♢ Q before switching to the ♡ Q. A low diamond, however, is fatal — North wins and the defense can no longer collect two heart tricks.
(5) If North led a heart at trick 1, this would give West the ♡ K and the defense cannot collect two heart tricks.
(6) If a club is led at trick 1, West should win ♣ A (the lead may well be a singleton), draw trumps and then set up clubs. No diamond trick for the defense. The same applies after a trump lead (draw trumps, set up clubs).

Hand 15 : Dealer South : N–S vulnerable

WEST	NORTH	EAST	SOUTH
			1NT
Pass	4♡	All pass	

NORTH
♠ K 9
♡ Q J 9 8 6 4 2
♢ 9 5
♣ K 10

WEST
♠ Q 6 4 3
♡ 10 7
♢ A Q 8 3
♣ 5 4 3

EAST
♠ J 7 2
♡ 5 3
♢ 7 6 4 2
♣ A Q 9 2

SOUTH
♠ A 10 8 5
♡ A K
♢ K J 10
♣ J 8 7 6

Lead : ♢ 6. As there is no evidence on the bidding that dummy has a long suit, there is no urgency to find an attacking lead from a dangerous holding. The club lead is worst and the spade lead is also abysmal. Both the heart and the diamond are passive leads. The trump is riskier with the suit bid only by North.

Play : ♢ 6 — M.U.D. from three or four rags — J — Q wins. Then ♢ A : East plays the 7. If East played low on the second diamond, West might read it as a doubleton and play a third diamond. This would allow North to throw a club. After East's ♢ 6-then-7, West sees that a third diamond is futile. The natural switch is to clubs, dummy's weaker suit. East cashes two clubs, one off.

Notes : (1) On ♡ 3 lead (bottom from two trumps) the contract could also be defeated, taking 2 clubs and 2 diamonds later.
(2) The ♣ A or a low club lead allows North to make the ♣ K and so the contract.
(3) A low spade lead can give North 11 tricks ! ♠ 2 : 5 — Q — K. Then, ♠ 9 : 7 — 8 — 3; ♡ A; ♡ K; ♠ A, discarding a minor loser, and when the ♠ J drops, the ♠ 10 is high for a second minor suit discard.
(4) If South is declarer in 4♡ after a transfer sequence, West should lead the ♣ 4 or, second choice, a trump. Both defeat the contract. The ♢ A lead gives South the ♢ K, while the ♠ 3 lead is also fatal : ♠ 3 : 9 — J — A; spade to the king; heart to the ace; ♠ 10 : Q — ruffed (if West fails to cover, a minor suit loser is discarded from dummy). Next a heart to the king draws the trumps and the ♠ 8 is high, allowing a minor suit discard from dummy. Note how dangerous it can be to lead from J-x-x, J-x-x-x, Q-x-x or Q-x-x-x.
(5) 3NT is on for North-South but that is impossible to judge in the auction. Most pairs would play in 4♡.

Hand 16 : Dealer West : E–W vulnerable

WEST	NORTH	EAST	SOUTH
Pass	Pass	1♡	1♠
2♡	2♠	4♡	All pass

NORTH
♠ J 7 4
♡ 6 3 2
♢ A 10 7 4 3 2
♣ 8

WEST
♠ K 10 3 2
♡ 10 7 5 4
♢ 9 6
♣ Q 7 4

EAST
♠ 6
♡ A K J 9 8
♢ K 8
♣ K J 10 6 5

SOUTH
♠ A Q 9 8 5
♡ Q
♢ Q J 5
♣ A 9 3 2

Lead : ♢ Q. The ♣ A is abysmal and despite North's spade support, the ♠ A is a poor choice. North's raise does not promise the king. The ♢ Q is the only lead that is not repulsive.

Play : The ♢ Q is taken by North's ace. As the ♢ Q denies the king and the ♢ K does not drop, North knows that a diamond return is futile. North should switch to the ♣ 8, won by the ace. The club return is ruffed; spade to the ace, club ruffed. Down two.

Notes : (1) West and North are just good enough to raise. With only five losers and strong suits, East is worth 4♡.
(2) 4♠ is a good sacrifice if 4♡ is on. As 4♡ can be defeated without too much difficulty, 4♠ is foolish. With so many defensive values, South should defend, and if South chooses to defend, North should not overrule that decision.
(3) On ♢ Q to the ace and a diamond back, 4♡ makes.
(4) On ♠ A lead, the contract can be beaten but only by one trick. The ♠ A is valuable as an entry for the second club ruff. ♠ A and a second spade allows 4♡ home. The defense has to find the club ruff for success.
(5) The ♡ Q lead allows 4♡ home. Declarer wins, draws trumps and sets up the clubs, losing just three aces.
(6) If North ducks the ♢ Q lead, again 4♡ will make.
(7) If North takes the ♢ Q with the ace and returns a spade, South wins the ace and then has to find ♣ A and a second club for North to ruff to defeat the contract. It is far easier for North to find the club shift than South. As North needs to find three tricks after the ♢ A, the spade return is futile. East is marked with a singleton or void in spades and the defense cannot collect more than one trick in spades.

CHAPTER 5

CARD COMBINATIONS IN DEFENSE

PART 1 : PLAY BY THIRD HAND

A. Dummy has no significant high cards :

1. Third hand will usually play high.

	Dummy	
	7 6 5	
3 led		A J 8
	Play the ace.	

	Dummy	
	7 6 5	
3 led		K J 10 8
	Play the king.	

2. But with equally high cards, play the cheapest of the touching cards.

	Dummy	
	6 5 2	
4 led		K Q J 7
	Play the jack.	

	Dummy	
	8 7 3	
4 led		A K 5
	Play the king.	

	Dummy	
	6 5 4	
3 led		Q J 9 8
	Play the jack.	

It follows from Rule 2 that the card played when playing third hand high denies the next lower card. As you play the cheapest of touching high cards when playing third hand high, the ace denies the king, the king denies the queen, the queen denies the jack, the jack denies the ten, the ten denies the nine, and so on. By applying this principle, the opening leader can frequently place the location of the key honors.

EXERCISE

(a)

	Dummy	
	4 2	
You		Partner's
J 8 6 5 3		play : 10
	Declarer plays the K.	

You lead the 5.
1. Who has the ace?　2. The queen?　3. The 9?

(b)

	Dummy	
	7 5 2	
You		Partner's
K 9 6 3		play : J
	Declarer plays the Q.	

You lead the 3.　1. Who has the ace?　2. The 10?

3. Rules 1 and 2 apply just the same if dummy has the ace but declarer plays low from dummy.

(c)

	Dummy	
	A 6 4	
You		Partner's
Q 8 5 3 2		play : J
	Declarer plays the K.	

You lead the 3, low from dummy, jack from partner and declarer wins the king. Who has the 10?

(d)

	Dummy	
	A 6 4	
You		Partner's
K 8 5 3 2		play : J
	Declarer plays the Q.	

You lead the 3, low from dummy, jack from partner and declarer wins the queen. Who has the 10?

4. If dummy plays high and you are unable to beat dummy's card, the card you play is a signal to partner (see Chapter 6).

5. If partner leads an honor and you hold an honor doubleton, you should normally play your honor to unblock, unless you can see that this gives declarer an extra trick.

	Dummy	
	6 4 2	
Q led		K 9
	Play the king.	

	Dummy	
	10 4 2	
Q led		K 5
	Play the 5.	

To play the king here would allow declarer to make an extra trick with the ten if the layout is like this:

	10 4 2	
Q J 9 8		K 5
	A 7 6 3	

To unblock with an honor doubleton may also be necessary if dummy wins the trick.

Dummy
A 5 3

Q J 10 8 2   **K 4**

9 7 6

West leads the queen and dummy's ace is played. East should play the king. Playing low blocks the suit.

6. If partner leads an honor and you hold three or more cards in the suit :

a. With a higher, non-touching honor, play third-hand-high if dummy has only low cards.

Dummy
6 2

A J 10 9 4   **K 5 3**

Q 8 7

In a no-trumps contract, West leads the jack. East should play the king. If South has A-Q it will not cost to play the king and if West has led from an interior sequence, the king prevents declarer winning an undeserved trick with the queen.

b. With two touching honors in a 3-card suit, be prepared to unblock your honors.

Dummy
7 6

Q J 9 8 2   **A K 4**

10 5 3

West leads the queen in a no-trumps contract. If East plays low, the suit is blocked and there are only three immediate tricks for East-West. East should play the king, then ace (unblocking) and continue the suit, giving East-West five immediate tricks.

Dummy
A 6 3

J 10 9 5 4   **K Q 7**

8 2

In no-trumps, West leads the jack and dummy's ace is played. If East plays low, the defense can take only two further tricks in this suit when they regain the lead as East's K-Q blocks the suit. East should unblock, playing the king under the ace.

c. Where third hand has no honor card in the suit led, third hand's play on is a signal, often a discouraging signal. This applies whether partner's honor card lead is captured or whether it holds the trick. Where third hand has three or more cards including an honor touching the honor led by partner, third hand gives a signal, usually an encouraging signal.

A 7 2

Q J 10 6 3   **K 8 4**

9 5

West leads the queen. Whether dummy plays low or the ace, East should play the 8, an encouraging signal. If dummy plays low and West continues with the jack, East should unblock the king on this round.

B. Dummy has one or more honors

1. If you have dummy's honor 'surrounded' and declarer plays low from dummy, play the card below dummy's honor.

'Surrounded' means you hold the card immediately above dummy's and the card immediately below dummy's relevant high card.

	Dummy	
Partner's	**K 6 5**	**You**
lead : 3		**A Q 7**

If dummy plays low, play the queen, not the ace. Obvious, of course, but the principle applies to lower holdings as well.

	Dummy	
Partner's	**Q 7 6**	**You**
lead : 3		**A K J 4**

If dummy plays low, play the jack.

	Dummy	
Partner's	**A J 5**	**You**
lead : 3		**Q 10 6 2**

If dummy plays low, play the 10, not the queen.

2. With dummy's card surrounded and touching cards immediately below dummy's honor, play the cheapest of these touching cards.

	Dummy	
	K 6 5	
4 led		**A Q J 9**

If dummy plays low, win with the jack, not queen.

	Dummy	
	Q 8 7 3	
4 led		**A K J 10 9**

If dummy plays low, win with the 9.

	Dummy	
	A 10 6	
5 led		**J 9 8 2**

You have dummy's 10 surrounded. If dummy plays low, play the 8, not the 9 and definitely not the jack.

3. Where you have dummy's high card 'nearly surrounded' (that is, your surrounding cards are within one card of the card touching dummy's honor), it is still usually best to play your lower surrounding card, not the higher one. This succeeds most of the time.

EXERCISE

In each of these cases, West leads the 3 and dummy plays low. Which card should East play?

1.
	Dummy
	Q 7 6
3 led	K 10 4

2.
	Dummy
	Q 7 6
3 led	A J 4

3.
	Dummy
	Q 7 6
3 led	A 10 5

4.
	Dummy
	A J 5
3 led	K 10 7

5.
	Dummy
	A J 5
3 led	Q 9 7

6.
	Dummy
	A Q 6
3 led	K 10 4

7.
	Dummy
	A 10 6
3 led	J 8 5

8.
	Dummy
	A 10 6
3 led	Q 9 5

9.
	Dummy
	K 10 5
3 led	Q 9 4

10.
	Dummy
	A 10 5
3 led	J 8 7 6

4. Where either 'surrounding' card is two or more cards away from the card touching dummy's honor, play your higher honor, unless it is clear that this cannot gain.

	Dummy
	A J 4
3 led	K 7 5

If dummy plays low, play your king. The 7 is too far away from the jack to be useful as a surround card.

	Dummy
	A 10 4
3 led	J 7 5

If this is a trump contract and dummy plays low, play your 7, not the jack. Partner will not hold K-Q (partner would have led the king), so that playing the jack cannot gain. Your best chance is to hope partner has led from Q-9-8-3 or K-9-8-3. If so, playing low holds declarer to two tricks but playing the jack allows declarer to make three tricks.

EXERCISE

1. a.
	Dummy
	A 8 3
J 6 5 4 2	9 played

You lead the 4, 3 from dummy and partner's 9 is taken by declarer's king. What is the layout of this suit? 1. Who has the queen? 2. The 7? 3. The 10?

b.
	Dummy
	10 6 5
Q 8 4 3 2	J played

You lead the 3, 5 from dummy and partner's J is taken by the ace. 1. Who has the king? 2. The 9?

c.
	Dummy
	K 8 6 3
Q 10 4 2	7 played

The 2 is led, 3 from dummy, 7 from East and South wins the 9. 1. Who has the A? 2. Jack? 3. The 5?

2. IS IT SAFE? In no-trumps, you often have to decide whether it is safe to continue the suit led or whether you have to wait for partner to come in and lead the suit back to you. Try these situations.

a.
	Dummy
	7 6 3
K 10 5 4 2	9 played

You lead the 4 and East's 9 is taken by the queen. Is it safe to continue this suit later?

b.
	Dummy
	10 5 3
Q 7 6 4 2	9 played

You lead the 4 and East's 9 is taken by the king. Is it safe to continue this suit later?

c.
	Dummy
	A 10 2
Q 7 6 5 3	9 played

You lead the 5, 2 from dummy and East's 9 is taken by the king. Is it safe to continue this suit later?

PART 2 : PLAY BY SECOND HAND

A. Declarer leads a low card towards dummy and second hand could win the trick.

Win the trick if :

(a) It is the setting trick (unless you are sure to beat the contract anyway and you may make more tricks by playing low). To forego the setting trick, you have to be absolutely certain that declarer cannot succeed.

(b) You have enough tricks in addition to this trick to defeat the contract, with the same proviso as in (a).

(c) You need to obtain the lead to make a vital switch, to set up extra tricks or to preserve an entry for partner.

(d) Partner cannot possibly win the trick and declarer will not make fewer tricks if you play low. Some of these positions may be difficult to judge.

(e) To make sure of winning a trick that you may otherwise not win. These situations are also not always clearcut. However, if dummy has a doubleton honor and you have the higher touching honor, it often pays you to take your trick.

Dummy
Q 5

K 8 7 2

If South leads low towards the queen, West should normally take the king. If South has A-x-x, South will make two tricks anyway, but if West does not take the king, West may make no tricks.

Dummy
J 7 2

Q 6 5

If South leads low towards the J, West should normally take the queen. This could be wrong, but if South has A-K-x-x, this is West's only chance to take a trick. If South has K-x-x, West will win the queen and partner will still make the ace later. If West plays low, the jack will force the ace and West may not make the queen later. However, if South has A-10-x, West would do better by playing low. Unless declarer's holding is known, you will not always do the right thing here.

Second player should play low if this may produce extra tricks for the defence, for example if dummy has split honors and playing low puts declarer to a guess.

Dummy
K J 6

A 7 3

If declarer leads low towards dummy, it will usually be best for West to play low. Declarer will often finesse the jack and partner will score the queen.

However, West ought to take the ace if declarer cannot misguess the position. For example, if West is marked on the bidding with the ace, it may pay West to make sure of the trick by taking the ace. Again, if declarer is known to be leading a singleton towards dummy and cannot obtain a useful discard by finessing the jack, West should make sure of a trick by taking the ace.

Dummy
Q 10 3

K 8 5 2

If declarer leads low towards dummy or cashes the ace followed by low towards dummy, it may pay West to play low smoothly. If West does not give away the fact that the king is held, declarer will often finesse the 10, allowing East to win with the jack.

This is an equivalent position :

Dummy
J 9 3

Q 7 5 4

If declarer leads low towards dummy, West may do best by playing low. Declarer is quite likely to finesse the 9, allowing East to win with the 10.

If second hand holds the ace and dummy has the king, it is usually best to play low as long as you are confident of making your ace later. The exception is when dummy or declarer has a running side suit which will allow declarer to discard losers later.

Dummy
K 7 3

A 8 5 4   J 10 6
Q 9 2

If South leads low towards dummy and West plays the ace, South makes two tricks. If West plays low, South makes only one trick.

If second hand has the ace and dummy's honor is the queen or lower, second hand usually does best by playing low. Either partner will be able to beat dummy's honor or declarer has the other honors which you can capture later.

Dummy
J 7 3

A 8 5 4

If South leads low towards dummy, West should usually play low. If partner cannot beat the jack, South has the K-Q and you can capture one of these later. Again the danger sign is where there is a running side suit which will give declarer discards if you do not take your ace now.

B. Declarer leads a low card *towards* dummy and second hand *cannot* win the trick.

It is usually best to play low if you cannot beat the highest card in dummy in the suit led. There is almost never an advantage to play a high card to force out a high card from dummy. Most of the time declarer will play dummy's high card anyway.

Dummy
A Q 8 6 2

K 5

If declarer plays a low card towards dummy, West gains no benefit by putting in the king.

Dummy
K 10 3

J 7 4

If declarer leads low towards dummy, West gains no benefit by playing the jack. Likewise, if West had Q-x-x, it would be an error to insert the queen.

Dummy
A K 10 4

Q J 5

If declarer leads a low card towards dummy, West should play low. Playing the jack or the queen cannot gain. However, if second hand has two touching honors and dummy has only one higher honor, West can insert an honor to make sure of one trick.

Dummy
K 10 3

Q J 4 2   8 7 6

A 9 5

If South leads low towards dummy, West can play the jack or queen to ensure one trick. If West plays low, South might put in the 10.

Dummy
K 6 3

Q J 4 2   A 8 7

10 9 5

If South leads the 5 towards dummy, West should play low. The king will be played from dummy, East will win and the defence has three tricks and declarer has none. . If West plays the jack on the 5, declarer comes to one trick later.

Dummy
Q 9 2

J 10 5

If declarer leads low towards dummy, West might play the jack or the 10 to ensure a second trick if East has the king or ace. Although unlikely, declarer might put in the 9 and score an extra trick.

C. Declarer leads a low card *from* dummy and second hand could win the trick.

Second hand should win the trick under the same conditions as when declarer leads low *towards* dummy (see Section A). However, if there is no such compelling reason to play high, second hand should usually play low if holding only one top honor. Declarer may have a guess-finesse position and by playing low, second hand puts declarer to the guess.

However, where a singleton is led from dummy in a trump contract and second player holds the ace, it is usually best to take your ace. If you are sure to make your ace later anyway or you hope that by playing low you will cause declarer to misguess a finesse, you might chance playing low on the singleton.

Also, if dummy has the ace and a low card is led away from the ace, second player with king doubleton should usually play the king. With K-x-x or longer, second hand should often play the king as well, unless you are confident that you can make the king later. It is true that playing low may cause declarer to misguess a Q-10-x finesse position, but playing low may also result in your not scoring the king at all.

D. Declarer leads a low card *from* dummy and second player does *not* hold the highest card in the suit led.

If second player holds only one honor card in the suit and it is not the top card, there is little to be gained by playing the honor. Play low.

If second player has two honors in the suit led from dummy, it will still usually be best to play low. Declarer may take a deep finesse and lose an extra trick.

Dummy
7 6 2

10 8 5 3   K Q 4

A J 9

If a low card is led from dummy and East plays low, declarer will almost always finesse the 9 and make only one trick. If second player plays the king or queen, declarer can work out the position, win the ace, cross to dummy and lead low towards the jack to score a second trick. However, if East needs only one trick from this suit to defeat the contract, East should play an honor to establish that trick.

Where second player has a sequence of three or more honors, it will usually be best to play one of these high cards to ensure building up as many tricks in the suit as possible. Most top players play top from a sequence in second seat, just like top of a sequence when leading, to clarify the position for partner.

PART 3 : WHEN TO COVER AN HONOR WITH AN HONOR

When declarer leads an honor card and second player has a higher honor card, it may be correct to 'cover', that is, to play the higher honor.

Example 1   **Dummy**
                       A Q 10 5 3
K 7   9 8 4 2
                       J 6

If South leads the jack, West should play the king. If West plays low, South can duck in dummy, play a second round and make five tricks with this suit. If West plays the king on the jack, declarer makes at best four tricks.

However, it may be wrong to 'cover'.

Example 2   **Dummy**
                       Q J 10 9
83   K 7 4 2
                       A 6 5

If the queen is led from dummy, East should play low and continue to play low when the jack and the 10 are led. If East plays the king on an early round, declarer has four winners in this suit. If East plays low each time, declarer can win only three tricks.

When should you cover and when should you duck?

1. Do not cover if this will promote tricks only for declarer.

This happens commonly at trick 1, particularly in a suit contract where partner is known not to hold the ace or any other top honor. In example 2 above, if West leads the 8, East knows this is West's highest spot card and that therefore the ace must be with South. There is no holding of A-8-x or longer where the 8 is the correct lead. Given that South is known to hold the ace, East can tell that playing the king cannot provide a trick for the defence. South would simply capture the king and dummy's cards are all high. Since playing the king cannot gain, East should play low.

These are similar positions :

                       Dummy
                       J 10 9 5
82   Q 6 4 3
                       A K 7

West leads the 8 and declarer plays the jack from dummy. If East plays the queen, declarer has four tricks. If East plays low, declarer has only three tricks. Again, East can tell from the lead that West cannot hold the ace or king. There is no holding of A-8-x or K-8-x or longer where the 8 is the correct lead.

                       K J 10 9 7
6   Q 5 4 3 2
                       A 8

West leads the 6 and declarer plays the jack from dummy. East should play low. If East plays the queen, declarer has 5 tricks. If East plays low, declarer can come to no more than four tricks.

Note that in the above cases it was wrong to play third-hand-high and wrong to cover-an-honor-with-an-honor. If it cannot gain a trick for your side, if it helps only declarer, do not squander the honor.

2. Where a sequence is led, do not cover until the last of the touching cards is led.

                       Dummy
                       J 10 2
K 9 3   Q 8 4
                       A 7 6 5

If declarer leads the jack from dummy, East should duck. Dummy has touching honors and East should cover only when the last of these touching honors is led. If the jack is led and East covers, declarer wins and leads low towards dummy's 10-2, losing only one trick in the suit. If the jack is led and East plays low, West can beat the jack. If East later covers the lead of the 10, declarer has two losers in the suit.

3. If declarer leads an honor from hand, assume that declarer has a touching honor in hand and do not cover unless you are sure that it will gain your side a trick.

                       Dummy
                       A 7 6 5
Q 4 3   2
                       K J 10 9 8

With 9 trumps, declarer will usually play for the drop, but with this layout declarer loses nothing by leading the jack first. If West covers, declarer has no loser in the suit. West should play low smoothly. Declarer then is likely to go up with dummy's ace, intending to play for the drop as usual.

                       Dummy
                       K 7 3 2
J 6 4   Q 5
                       A 10 9 8

Declarer cannot escape a loser in this suit against normal defense. However, South can afford to lead the 10 from hand. If West falls from grace and covers with the jack, the king wins and the defense makes no tricks. With a solid interior sequence, it costs declarer nothing to try such ploys. The defenders must be alert to avoid giving declarer undeserved extra tricks.

4. If declarer is tackling a long suit, often the trump suit, it will not gain you to cover if partner is known to hold a void or a singleton in the suit (unless covering definitely creates an extra trick for *your* hand).

<pre>
          Dummy
          J 5 3
A   K Q 7
          10 9 8 6 4 2
</pre>

South, having bid and rebid this suit, leads the jack from dummy. If East covers, the three tricks for the defense are telescoped into two.

<pre>
          Dummy
          Q 7 4 2
A   K 8 5
          J 10 9 6 3
</pre>

South, having opened this 5-card major, leads the queen from dummy. If East covers with the king, two tricks are transformed into one. Note that it costs declarer nothing to try to lure East into such an error.

To create a trick for partner by covering an honor, partner normally needs to hold at least three cards in the suit. If partner is marked with a doubleton or shorter, it rarely pays you to cover.

5. Do not cover if you have greater length than third hand, as your honor cannot be captured.

<pre>
          Dummy
          A 7 2
K 8 5 3   4
          Q J 10 9 6
</pre>

If South leads the queen, West should play low. If South then leads the jack, West should play low again. West has more cards than dummy's A-x-x so that the king cannot be captured. If West plays the king early. South makes five tricks. If West withholds the king, South can win only four tricks.

<pre>
          Dummy
          A K 4
Q 7 5 2   6
          J 10 9 8 3
</pre>

If South leads the jack, West should play low. Dummy has fewer cards than West so that the queen cannot be captured. If West plays the queen on the jack, South makes five tricks. If West ducks, South can come to four tricks at most.

6. If you are not covering, try to play your cards as smoothly as possible. If you fumble or hesitate, you are giving away valuable information to declarer that you hold an honor.

Try to plan these situations in advance. If dummy has an honor which you could cover, decide early whether you intend to cover if the honor is led. Then you will be ready to play low without a trance when the honor is led if that is your decision. It is more difficult when the honor is led from declarer's hand, but prepare yourself also for these positions if you can.

7. Do cover if partner might have length in this suit and you may build up extra tricks for partner by covering.

<pre>
          Dummy
          A 10 8 4 2
K 6   Q 9 5
          J 7 3
</pre>

If South leads the jack, West should cover with the king. If West plays low on the jack, declarer can let the jack run and will lose only one trick in this suit. If West covers the jack, dummy's ace can win but East then has Q-9 over dummy's 10 and will make two tricks. Covering the jack promotes East's 9.

EXERCISE

In each of these cases, North opened with 1NT and South responded 4♠.

1.
<pre>
          Dummy
          ♠ Q 6 2
                     East
                     ♠ K 7 3
</pre>
The queen is led from dummy. Should East cover?

2.
<pre>
          Dummy
          ♠ A 8
West
♠ Q J 5
</pre>
South leads the 10 from hand. Should West cover?

3.
<pre>
          Dummy
          ♠ K 8 2
West
♠ J 6 5
</pre>
South leads the 10 from hand. Should West cover?

4.
<pre>
          Dummy
          ♠ J 6 5 3
                     East
                     ♠ Q 8
</pre>
The jack is led from dummy. Should East cover?

5.
<pre>
          Dummy
          ♠ Q 9 4 2
                     East
                     ♠ K 10
</pre>
The queen is led from dummy. Should East cover?

PLAY HANDS ON DEFENSIVE CARD COMBINATIONS

Hand 17 : Dealer North : Nil vulnerable

WEST	NORTH	EAST	SOUTH
	Pass	Pass	1NT
Pass	3NT	All pass	

NORTH
- ♠ A J 5
- ♡ K 6 2
- ◇ K 7 4 3
- ♣ 8 6 2

WEST
- ♠ Q 8 7 6 2
- ♡ A 7 5 3
- ◇ Q 10
- ♣ 9 4

EAST
- ♠ K 10 3
- ♡ 9 8
- ◇ J 8 6 2
- ♣ J 10 7 5

SOUTH
- ♠ 9 4
- ♡ Q J 10 4
- ◇ A 9 5
- ♣ A K Q 3

Lead : ♠6. Long suit. Fourth-highest. Normal.

Play : Declarer should play low in dummy and East should play the 10, winning, and continue with ♠K. Declarer ducks but East perseveres with a third spade to knock out the ace. When hearts are played, West wins and cashes two more spades. One off.

Notes : (1) With A-J-x opposite 9-x or 9-x-x, the better chance is to play low from dummy if a low card is led. This scores two tricks for you if the opening lead is from a suit headed by K-10 or Q-10. The same applies when dummy has A-J-9 opposite junk. On a low card lead, the percentage play is to finesse the 9, not the J. Similarly if dummy has J-9-x opposite your A-x or A-x-x, on a low card lead, you should play the 9 from dummy, rather than the J. This scores a second trick twice as often as playing the jack.

(2) If declarer does play the jack (wrongly) from dummy, East wins the king and should return the 10. If East returns the 3, South's 9 forces West's queen. Declarer could now take the ace while East's 10 blocks the suit.

(3) Likewise, if declarer plays low from dummy and East wins with the 10, East must continue with the king. If East returns the 3 and declarer wins with the ace, the spades are again blocked.

(4) If declarer plays low from dummy and East wins with the king, declarer makes 3NT easily. Not only does declarer have a second trick in spades, but West's spades cannot be set up before the ♡A is knocked out.

(5) 3NT is a sound contract. It would make if spades were not led, if West's spade lead were from K-10 or Q-10 or if East held the ♡A (in which case declarer's hold up with the ♠A cuts East off from West's spades).

Hand 18 : Dealer East : N-S vulnerable

WEST	NORTH	EAST	SOUTH
		1♣	Pass
1♡	1♠	Pass	2♠
4♡	Pass	Pass	Pass

NORTH
- ♠ K Q 10 9 5
- ♡ K
- ◇ Q 8 7 6 2
- ♣ 10 5

WEST
- ♠ 3
- ♡ A 9 8 7 5 4 3
- ◇ 10 4
- ♣ A 6 3

EAST
- ♠ 8 7 4
- ♡ J 2
- ◇ A K 3
- ♣ K J 8 4 2

SOUTH
- ♠ A J 6 2
- ♡ Q 10 6
- ◇ J 9 5
- ♣ Q 9 7

Lead : ♠K. Normal near-sequence lead.

Play : South should encourage and North continues spades, ruffed by West. West's best chance is to cross to dummy's ◇A and lead the jack of hearts. South should duck this and the jack is taken by the king. North plays a third spade ruffed by West. The ♡A is cashed, followed by a diamond to the king and a diamond ruff. Then a trump is led to South's queen. South exits with a spade, ruffed by declarer who tries ♣A and a club to the jack. When the club finesse loses, the contract is one down.

Notes : (1) West is too strong to bid 4♡ over 1♣. Over 2♠, 3♡, non-forcing, would be timid. East's pass over 1♠ shows a minimum opening without heart support.

(2) Crossing to the ◇A to lead the jack of hearts is far better than laying down the ♡A. Playing the ace creates two losers whenever the suit is 3-1. Crossing to dummy and leading the jack caters for a legitimate trump position: singleton 10 with North and K-Q-6 with South. In that case to lay down the ace gives South two tricks, but leading the jack pins the 10 and holds the defense to one trump trick only. In addition, leading the jack may tempt a defender to err : if South slips up and covers the jack of hearts with the queen, declarer takes the ace. When the king drops, there is only one trump loser. South should not cover the jack as North cannot hold length in trumps.

(3) Declarer's line (eliminating diamonds and throwing South in with ♡Q) would succeed if South began with 3 spades, 3 hearts, 3 diamonds and 4 clubs. If the throw-in does not work, declarer can try the club finesse later.

Hand 19 : Dealer South : E-W vulnerable

NORTH
♠ K J 10 9 2
♡ A 7 3
♢ A J
♣ 6 4 2

WEST
♠ 7
♡ 10 6 5
♢ 10 9 8 6 5 2
♣ A 7 3

EAST
♠ Q 8 5
♡ K Q J 8
♢ Q 7 4
♣ 10 9 5

SOUTH
♠ A 6 4 3
♡ 9 4 2
♢ K 3
♣ K Q J 8

WEST	NORTH	EAST	SOUTH
			1♣
Pass	1♠	Pass	2♠
Pass	4♠	All pass	

Lead : ♡K. Normal top of sequence.

Play: Faced with two losers in hearts and one in clubs, declarer must avoid losing a trick in trumps. The standard play with 9 trumps missing just the queen is to play for the drop. Here if declarer plays ♠ A-K, declarer fails by one trick. Because declarer holds the 10-9 as well as the ♠ J, declarer can afford to lead the ♠ J when starting trumps. If East covers with the queen, declarer has avoided the spade loser and makes the contract. If East plays low smoothly, declarer can still make the standard play, up with the ace and back to the king. This wins if spades are 2-2 or the ♠ Q is singleton. If East does play low smoothly and declarer does play for the drop, declarer fails but that is expected here when trumps do not break.

Notes: (1) There is a slight risk in ducking the first heart (West might ruff the second heart, play a club to East's ace and ruff another heart), but there may be a very tangible benefit. If hearts are 5-2, North could win the second heart, draw trumps and tackle clubs. If clubs are 3-3 and the ♣ A is with the player short in hearts, declarer would be able to discard a heart loser on the thirteenth club. This benefit outweighs the risk of a 6-1 break in hearts, so North should duck the first heart. On the actual hand, North does not benefit from this play. (2) If East trances, fumbles, hesitates . . . when North leads the ♠ J and gives away the location of the ♠ Q, declarer could let the jack run if East finally follows low. East should follow low smoothly with Q-x-x or longer in trumps: it cannot gain to cover with the queen as West cannot hold length in trumps. N.B. It would be grossly improper and a breach of the Laws of Bridge for East to fumble and hesitate *deliberately* without the queen *with the intention of deceiving declarer.*

Hand 20 : Dealer West : Both vulnerable

NORTH
♠ J 9 4
♡ 10 9 5
♢ Q 8 7 3
♣ 4 3 2

WEST
♠ 5 2
♡ K Q 6
♢ J 5 4 2
♣ Q 10 9 6

EAST
♠ A K 10
♡ A J 7 2
♢ 10 9
♣ A J 8 7

SOUTH
♠ Q 8 7 6 3
♡ 8 4 3
♢ A K 6
♣ K 5

WEST	NORTH	EAST	SOUTH
Pass	Pass	1NT	Pass
2NT	Pass	3NT	All pass

Lead : ♠6. Normal fourth-highest from the long suit.

Play: North plays the jack of spades and East wins with the ace. Declarer should cross to dummy with a heart and lead the ♣ Q, finessing when North plays low. South wins the ♣ K and should switch to the ◇ K. North encourages with the ◇ 8 and South continues with ace and another diamond. North wins two more diamonds to defeat 3NT by one trick.

Notes: (1) If South wins the ♣ K and continues with a second spade, 3NT makes with an overtrick. Even if the position in spades were not clear, it would be sound technique to cash the ◇ K to obtain a signal from North. If North discouraged diamonds, South could proceed with whatever other defense seemed best. (2) In fact the spade position should be clear to South. North's ♠ J is third-hand-high and thus denies the ♠ A and ♠ K. In addition, as third hand plays the lower of touching high cards, the card played by third-hand-high denies the next lower card. Thus, North's ♠ J denies the ♠ 10 and declarer is therefore marked with ♠ A-K-10. To play a second spade from the South seat will give declarer an unearned third trick in spades. In addition, holding 12 HCP, South can deduce that North cannot hold more than a queen in addition to the ♠ J played. Dummy has 8 points, declarer has 17 or 18 and South has 12. That leaves at most 3 HCP for North. The only hope left is to find North with the queen of diamonds together with four diamonds. Accordingly, South must switch to the king of diamonds and continue with the diamonds on receiving North's encouraging signal.

CHAPTER 6

SIGNALLING ON PARTNER'S LEAD

If partner leads low and dummy plays low, third hand plays high. This is *not* a signal. When partner leads high or dummy plays high so that third hand cannot win or try to win the trick, this is the moment for third hand to signal. The standard approach is to signal whether you like the suit led or whether you prefer a switch. In standard methods :

High card = Please continue this suit.

Lowest card = Please switch to another suit.

High-then-low = Please play a third round.

These signals are not used by the player leading, only by the player in third seat.

You should obey partner's signal unless you *know* that it is correct to disobey.

In a trump contract, if partner leads an ace or a king, you should signal high-then-low with a doubleton if you want partner to continue so that you can ruff the third round. However, if you are unable to ruff or do not wish to ruff or you prefer a switch, do not play an automatic high-low with a doubleton. High-then-low asks partner to continue. If you do not want partner to continue, play low-high, even with a doubleton.

When you ask for a switch, you cannot indicate which suit you want. Partner has to work it out from the bidding, the cards in dummy and the cards in hand.

You want a switch : Play your lowest card.

You do not want a switch : Do not play lowest.

If you play bottom from three or four rags, partner will (should) switch. If you feel it is better for partner to continue the suit led rather than break open a new suit, do not play your lowest. Even if partner's lead has not worked out well, it may be better to stick with that than to create a further loss with another suit.

When you play a middling card, partner will not be able to read it as your lowest. You can follow with a higher card on the second round, low-then-high, saying, "I am not interested in a third round." High-then-low says, "Play the third round, please."

For example, suppose partner leads the ace and you have 8-6-5-2. Play the 6 if you are not keen on a switch and play the 8 next if you are not interested in a third round. If you would rather have a third round of the suit than a switch, start with the 6 and follow with the 5 or the 2. Do not confuse this with M.U.D.

although the order of playing the cards is similar. M.U.D. is a method of *leading* a suit. It is not a signal. Signals are in third seat and you may choose to signal in the same order, but that is just a coincidence.

NON-STANDARD METHODS

1. REVERSE SIGNALS

In this method, lowest is encouraging, high asks for a switch and low-then-high asks for a third round (exactly the opposite of standard methods). This is a sound alternative approach preferred by many experts.

The standard high-encouraging is chosen for newer players who are more likely to notice a high spot card and read the correct message from it. New players tend not to notice low spot cards until they have had quite some experience. To make an impact, therefore, high-then-low may catch their attention.

At top level, reverse signals are superior because you are not squandering a high card when you wish the suit continued. If you have no interest in the suit led, you can usually afford to signal with a high card to show no interest.

2. COUNT SIGNALS ONLY

In this method, when third player is not playing third-hand-high, third player 'gives count', that is, indicates the number of cards held in the suit led :

Bottom card = Odd number of cards in suit led.

High card = Even number of cards in suit led.

From this signal, partner can deduce the number of cards held by third hand and from this, the number of cards held by declarer in the suit led.

This is a mechanical method which replaces judgment with rote. It is decidedly inferior in many layouts and is not useful in deciding whether third player wants a switch or a continuation.

3. REVERSE COUNT SIGNALS ONLY

Again, third player signals only the number of cards held, but the method is the opposite of above :

Bottom card = Even number of cards in suit led.

High card = Odd number of cards in suit led.

This is a better way of giving count since the top card of a doubleton is not wasted in a signal. Other than that, it is still a mechanical method which places no value on judgment or co-operation.

EXERCISE ON SIGNALLING

A. Assuming you are using standard high encouraging and low discouraging signals, work out the card with which to signal in each of these situations.

1.
NORTH
♠ A 5
♡ J 5 3
◊ K 9 4 2
♣ Q 10 9 3

    EAST
    ♠ Q 8 4
    ♡ 10 6 4 2
    ◊ J 10 8 3
    ♣ K J

SOUTH	NORTH
1NT	3NT
Pass	

West leads ♠ J, low from dummy. Which card should East play?

2.
NORTH
♠ A 6 2
♡ Q J 10 3
◊ 7 4 2
♣ Q 8 5

    EAST
    ♠ Q 8 4
    ♡ 9 7 4
    ◊ 10 5
    ♣ A K J 3 2

SOUTH	NORTH
1◊	1♡
1NT	Pass

West leads ♠ J, low from dummy. Which card should East play?

3.
NORTH
♠ A Q 5
♡ 5 4
◊ K 8 6 3
♣ Q 7 5 2

    EAST
    ♠ J 7 4
    ♡ 9 7 2
    ◊ J 7 4 2
    ♣ A 8 3

SOUTH	NORTH
1NT	3NT
Pass	

West leads the queen of hearts. Which card should East play?

4.
NORTH
♠ 9 8
♡ J 7 5 3
◊ J 10 6 3
♣ A Q 3

    EAST
    ♠ 7 6 4
    ♡ Q 10 9
    ◊ Q 7 2
    ♣ K J 8 2

SOUTH	NORTH
1♡	2♡
4♡	Pass

West leads ◊ K, (K from A-K). Which card should East play?

5.
NORTH
♠ Q 8 7 5
♡ Q 4 3 2
◊ K 9
♣ J 5 2

    EAST
    ♠ 6 3
    ♡ 9 7 5
    ◊ J 10 8 2
    ♣ Q 8 7 3

SOUTH	NORTH
1♡	2♡
4♡	Pass

West leads ♠ K, (K from A-K). Which card should East play?

6.
NORTH
♠ 9 8 7 5 3
♡ K 9
◊ K 3
♣ A Q 6 5

    EAST
    ♠ 2
    ♡ A Q 8 6 2
    ◊ 10 7 6 5 2
    ♣ 8 3

SOUTH	NORTH
1♠	3♠
4♠	Pass

West leads ♣ 10, ace from dummy. Which club should East play?

7.
    NORTH
    ♠ J 10 8 3
    ♡ Q 6 3
    ◊ Q 9
    ♣ Q 9 7 2
WEST
♠ 9 6 2
♡ 9 7 5 2
◊ 8 7 5 2
♣ A K

SOUTH	NORTH
1♠	2♠
4♠	Pass

West leads the ♣ A, then ♣ K, to show the A-K doubleton. East follows 3-then-5, South 4-then-8. What next?

8.
    NORTH
    ♠ A J 8 3
    ♡ J 8 7
    ◊ A 9 3
    ♣ A Q 2
WEST
♠ 6 2
♡ A K 6 4
◊ J 7 5
♣ K 8 4 3

NORTH	SOUTH
1NT	4♠
Pass	

West leads ♡ K. East plays the two. What should West play at trick 2?

9.
    NORTH
    ♠ 9
    ♡ A 4 3 2
    ◊ A J 10 9 8
    ♣ A 9 3
WEST
♠ Q 7 6 2
♡ 10 5
◊ 7 6 2
♣ J 8 4 2

West	North	East	South
	1◊	1♡	1♠
Pass	2◊	Pass	4♠ //

West leads ♡ 10, won by dummy's ace. East plays the 7 and South the 6. The ♠ 9 is led, 3 from East, 5 from South and West wins ♠ Q. What next?

B. If East-West are using reverse signals, which card would East or West play in each of the above situations?

PLAY HANDS FOR SIGNALLING ON PARTNER'S LEAD

Hand 21 : Dealer North : N-S vulnerable

NORTH
♠ 8 7
♡ 9 7 4 3
◇ A Q
♣ J 7 6 4 3

WEST
♠ A K J 9 3
♡ Q
◇ 7 5 4 2
♣ A 10 9

EAST
♠ 10 4
♡ 10 8 5
◇ 10 9 8 6 3
♣ 8 5 2

SOUTH
♠ Q 6 5 2
♡ A K J 6 2
◇ K J
♣ K Q

WEST	NORTH	EAST	SOUTH
	Pass	Pass	1♡
1♠	2♡	Pass	4♡
Pass	Pass	Pass	

Lead : ♠K (or ace). No other suit has any appeal.

Play : East should signal West to continues spades by playing the *ten* of spades. East wants a spade continuation in order to ruff the third round. West continues with the ace of spades (or king) and East's 10-then-4 high-low signal requests West to play a third round of the suit. Even though dummy can ruff, West should trust partner and play the third spade. East would not play 10-then-4 if East did not want that third round played. East overruffs dummy on the third spade and the natural return is a club. West wins and a fourth round of spades ruffed by East produces two off.

Notes : (1) 4♡ is a sensible contract. Interchange the ♡9 and ♡10 and 4♡ can be made. 3NT could be defeated on a spade lead.
(2) If East plays 4-then-10 in spades, asking West not to play a third spade, and West switches, 4♡ can be made.
(3) In view of dummy's diamond holding, it is obvious that East should return a club, not a diamond, at trick 4. If this were not clearcut for East (swap the king and ace of diamonds), East should study the card led by West at trick 3. West's lead of the *three* of spades for East to ruff would ask East to return a club. When giving partner a ruff, lowest card asks for the low suit back. Hence the ♠3, the lowest spade, would ask East to return a club. West would return a high spade (jack or 9) if West wanted the higher suit, diamonds, returned.

Hand 22 : Dealer East : Nil vulnerable

NORTH
♠ 9 8 7
♡ K 5
◇ K 10 9 8
♣ A K 4 3

WEST
♠ Q 4 2
♡ 9 2
◇ A Q J 6 5 4 2
♣ 7

EAST
♠ A 6 5
♡ J 10 8 7 4
◇ 7
♣ Q J 8 5

SOUTH
♠ K J 10 3
♡ A Q 6 3
◇ 3
♣ 10 9 6 2

WEST	NORTH	EAST	SOUTH
		Pass	Pass
3◇	Pass	Pass	Double (1)
Pass	Pass	Pass	

(1) Takeout double

Lead : ♣K (or ace). A top club is easily the most attractive start, enabling you to see dummy and partner's signal. On that basis, you can then decide whether to continue clubs or find a switch.

Play : South plays the *two* of clubs, asking North to switch : lowest card on partner's lead is a signal saying, "Please do not continue this suit." North could choose a spade or a heart switch but the spade is superior. Prefer not to switch to dummy's long suit. On the ♠8 (M.U.D.) switch, declarer plays low in dummy and South wins with ♠K, marking West with the ♠Q. South returns the ♠J, won by declarer who starts on trumps. The defence should score 1 spade, 2 hearts, 2 diamonds and 1 club, +300 for two off.

Notes : (1) After West's pre-empt, North is too weak to take action. South is worth a takeout double in the pass-out seat. Since East is a passed hand and West has pre-empted, North has to hold reasonable strength.
(2) If South had not been a passed hand, North might have tried 3NT at this vulnerability. However, opposite a passed hand, the penalty pass is clearly superior, since 3NT is unlikely to be a good bet.
(3) 3NT by North-South might well fail. On a diamond lead to the ace and a club switch or a heart switch, declarer is hard pressed to find more than eight tricks in no-trumps.
(4) If North leads the ♣K and continues with ♣A, West can make 3◇ doubled : ruff the ♣A, cross to ♠A, cash the ♣Q-J, discarding two hearts and then lead a spade. West loses just 1 spade, 2 diamonds and 1 club.
(5) If North switches to ♡K, South discourages with ♡3, asking North to switch again, clearly to spades.
(6) If South leads a third heart, West should ruff low, not with an honor, else West may lose an extra trick.

Hand 23 : Dealer South : Both vulnerable

NORTH
♠ 3 2
♡ 6 4
♢ Q 9 6 2
♣ Q 10 9 4 3

WEST
♠ J 7 6 5
♡ A K Q J 3
♢ 8 5 3
♣ A

EAST
♠ A K 10 9 8
♡ 9 7
♢ J 10 4
♣ K 6 5

SOUTH
♠ Q 4
♡ 10 8 5 2
♢ A K 7
♣ J 8 7 2

WEST	NORTH	EAST	SOUTH
			Pass
1♡	Pass	1♠	Pass
3♠	Pass	4♠	All pass

Lead: ♢ K (or ace). Clearcut. It is hard to do better than an A-K suit and here nothing else is even remotely attractive.

Play: North encourages with the *nine* of diamonds rather than the six. With a choice of encouraging cards, choose the highest you can afford (and the highest from touching cards... the 9-signal denies the 10). South cashes the ♢ A (or king), North following with the *two*, and leads a third diamond taken by North's queen. North continues with the thirteenth diamond, promoting South's ♠ Q to become the setting trick.

Notes : (1) East-West can make 3NT, but that is hard to judge in the auction. 4♠ is the contract that almost all pairs would reach.
(2) On a non-diamond lead, declarer can make thirteen tricks by the normal spade play, ace and king, playing for the queen to drop, and discarding the diamond losers on the hearts.
(3) On the second diamond, North should drop the 2, not the 6. While 9-then-6 is also high-low, the 2 has the advantage that if partner missed seeing your first card, the 2 will confirm that you have played high-low. Whatever your first card, the 2 is the completion of a high-low signal. With the 6, partner may not be sure of your signal if partner failed to notice your first card. *And partners are fallible!*
(4) After three rounds of diamonds, it should be clear to North that a heart or a club switch would be futile. If South has a certain trump trick, it does not matter what North plays at trick 4, but the thirteenth diamond may create a trump trick where there wasn't one. North does not know that the thirteenth diamond will promote the extra trick but North can deduce that nothing else will work.

Hand 24 : Dealer West : Nil vulnerable

NORTH
♠ Q 5
♡ A Q J 7 6
♢ 4 3
♣ K Q J 10

WEST
♠ 10 7 3 2
♡ 3 2
♢ K 9 8 7 6
♣ 7 2

EAST
♠ A K 9 8
♡ 5 4
♢ J 10 5 2
♣ A 9 4

SOUTH
♠ J 6 4
♡ K 10 9 8
♢ A Q
♣ 8 6 5 3

WEST	NORTH	EAST	SOUTH
Pass	1♡	Double	2NT (1)
Pass	4♡	All pass	

(1) 2NT over double = support for opener and 10 HCP or more.

Lead : ♠ K (or ace). Obvious choice.

Play: On the ♠ K, West should discourage by playing the *two* of spades. East should obey the request for a switch and lead the ♢ 2. Declarer finesses the ♢ Q, losing to West's king. West returns a club to East's ace and East cashes the top spade for one down.

Notes: (1) Note the use of 2NT to show a strong high-card raise over the takeout double. A jump to 3♡ would imply good shape but deny as much as 10 HCP. Redouble in the modern style would indicate 10 HCP or more but denies support for opener's suit. The function of the redouble is to indicate a misfit and enlist partner's co-operation in seeking a penalty double in a context where the opening side holds the greater strength.
(2) If East cashes the second spade at trick 2, declarer will succeed. The ♠ J is now high and if a diamond is led, declarer will take the ace, rejecting the finesse, draw trumps ending in the South hand and play the ♠ J to discard the diamond loser. It is often a fatal tendency for a defender after winning the ♠ K to think, "Oh well, I may as well cash the ace also . . ." Disaster.
(3) On some occasions it may pay North to drop the ♠ Q at trick one, trying to suggest a singleton and have East discontinue the suit led. This does not apply here as North would love to have spades continued.
(4) If East switches to a trump, declarer succeeds by drawing trumps and conceding ♠ Q to set up the ♠ J.
(5) If East switches to ♣ A at trick 2 (a riskier switch than the diamond), West will again discourage, playing the *two* of clubs. Then East should find the diamond switch.

CHAPTER 7

DISCARDS AND SIGNALS

To discard on the run of declarer's or dummy's long suit is a tough task. Consider these guidelines :

1. KEEP LENGTH WITH DUMMY

If dummy holds four cards in a suit and you also have four in that suit, keep the same length as dummy if you can beat one of dummy's cards.

```
        Dummy
        A K Q 4
J 10 8          7 5 3 2
        9 6
```

South has three tricks in dummy. If East discards one of the seemingly useless cards, declarer has four tricks in dummy, for the 4 will become the thirteenth if East comes down to three cards. However, if dummy held A-K-Q-9, East could throw one or more as East cannot beat any of dummy's cards.

```
        Dummy
        K J 8 2
Q 10            9 7 4 3
        A 6 5
```

South has three tricks as the queen falls on the second round. If East discards a card, declarer can score four tricks.

```
        Dummy
        K 8 7 4 2
J 10            Q 9 5 3
        A 6
```

Declarer can set up one extra trick by playing ace, king, ruff, cross to dummy and ruff again. As long as there is another entry to dummy, declarer can cash the established winner. If East discards a card in this suit, declarer can set up two extra tricks via ace, king and ruff, and needs one less entry to dummy as well.

2. KEEP LENGTH WITH DECLARER

If the bidding has revealed a 4-card or 5-card suit with declarer, do not discard from that suit if you also hold four cards until declarer comes down to fewer than four cards.

```
        6 2
J 9 8           10 7 4 3
        A K Q 5
```

South has bid this suit and has three tricks. If East discards a card, South has four winners.

3. TRY TO KEEP AT LEAST ONE CARD IN PARTNER'S SUIT SO THAT YOU CAN RETURN PARTNER'S LEAD

If you are likely to obtain the lead only once, try to keep at least one card in partner's suit. However, if it is highly unlikely that you will obtain the lead at all, it is better to discard all your cards in partner's suit so that partner can place the rest with declarer. In most cases, it is also more important to keep length with dummy or keep length with declarer.

4. If none of the above apply, watch declarer's discards. You can usually afford to throw the same suit that declarer is discarding.

5. If declarer could ruff a suit in dummy but instead leads out trumps after all trumps have been drawn, you can discard the suit which declarer could have ruffed in dummy.

6. Make a mental note when declarer shows out of a suit. You can discard that suit unless you need to keep length with dummy.

SIGNALLING WITH YOUR DISCARD

Standard discard signals are :

Lowest discard = Not interested in this suit.

High discard = Interested in this suit.

High-then-low discard = Please play this suit.

These signals apply both at no-trumps and for suit contracts. In a suit contract you may be able to signal high in the suit that you want, but in no-trumps you usually cannot afford to discard the suit you want. In no-trumps it is far more common to discard lowest in the suit(s) that you do not want.

NON-STANDARD SIGNALS WHEN DISCARDING

1. Reverse Signals : The opposite of standard signals, i.e. high discard = not interested in this suit, lowest card discard = "Please play this suit." This is superior to standard methods since it does not require you to play a high card in the suit you do want, and you can usually afford to discard a high card in a suit you do not want.

2. Suit Preference Discards :

Message 1 : "I do not want the suit I am discarding."

Message 2 : (a) High card = Play the higher of the outside suits.

(b) Lowest card = Play the lower outside suit.

There are only two suits in contention. The suit to which you are not following is obviously excluded and the suit you are discarding is excluded (message 1). This method is also often called McKenney Discards or Lavinthal Discards after the inventors of the method. For further information on suit preference signals and secondary signals, see Chapter 20.

3. Odd-Even Discards

In this signalling method, you must note whether partner discarded an odd card or an even card.

Odd card discard = "Please play this suit."

Even card discard :
1. I do not want the suit which I am discarding.
2. (a) High even discard = Please play the higher outside suit.
(b) Low even discard = Lower outside suit, please.

Odd-even discards give you a wide range of discard choices and are recommended, but only for regular and experienced partnerships. (See Chapter 20.)

EXERCISE ON DISCARDING

A. Assuming you are using standard high encouraging and low discouraging signals when discarding, which card should you discard in each of these situations.

1.
NORTH
♠ 8 6 3
♡ Q 9 5
♢ K J 10 8 4
♣ 7 6

EAST
♠ A Q 9 2
♡ 10 7 4 3 2
♢ 9 3
♣ 10 5

South opens 2NT and North raises to 3NT.

West leads ♣3 and your 10 is won by declarer's ace. Declarer continues with the ♢ Q, which wins, a diamond to dummy's king and then the ♢ J. Your discard on the third diamond?

2.
NORTH
♠ Q 9 8
♡ K J
♢ J 7 4 3
♣ J 10 7 5

EAST
♠ 7 6 5 4
♡ 8 6 5 2
♢ 10 8
♣ A 9 4

South opens 1♠, West doubles and North's 2♠ ends the auction.

West leads the ace of diamonds and continues with the king and queen of diamonds. Which card do you play on the third round of diamonds?

3.
NORTH
♠ 10 9 3 2
♡ J 5 4
♢ K J 3
♣ Q J 5

EAST
♠ 7
♡ 8 2
♢ 10 9 8 7 6
♣ A 6 4 3 2

South opens 1♠ and rebids 4♠ over North's 2♠ raise.

West leads the ace of hearts, East playing the 8. West continues with the king of hearts, followed by the queen of hearts. Which card should East play on the third heart?

4.
NORTH
♠ 10 5 4 3
♡ 9 8 6
♢ K Q 10
♣ Q J 8

WEST
♠ J 9 2
♡ Q
♢ 8 6 3 2
♣ 10 6 5 4 3

South opens 1♠, North raises to 2♠ and East intervenes with 3♡. South's 4♠ ends the auction.

West leads the queen of hearts, East overtaking with the king. East continues with the ♡10 and ♡J. What should West play on the second heart and on the third heart?

5.
NORTH
♠ 10 3 2
♡ A Q J 3
♢ K 7
♣ J 7 5 3

WEST
♠ 7 6 4
♡ 10 8 5 4 2
♢ 10
♣ A Q 9 2

East opens with a pre-emptive 3 ♢. South bids 3♠ and North's raise to 4♠ ends the auction.

West leads ♢ 10, low from dummy and East wins with the jack. East continues with the ace of diamonds. Which card should West play on the ace of diamonds?

6.
NORTH
♠ 10 3 2
♡ A Q J 3
♢ K 7
♣ J 7 5 3

WEST
♠ J 6 4
♡ K 10 9 7 2
♢ 10
♣ A 9 6 4

East opens with a pre-emptive 3 ♢. South bids 3♠ and North's raise to 4♠ ends the auction.

West leads ♢ 10, low from dummy and East wins with the jack. East continues with the ace of diamonds. Which card should West play on the ace of diamonds?

B. If East-West are using odd-even discards, which card should East or West play in each of the above situations?

PLAY HANDS ON DISCARDS AND SIGNALS

Hand 25 : Dealer North : E-W vulnerable

NORTH
♠ A J
♡ 9 7 3
◇ A K 8 4
♣ K Q 7 6

WEST
♠ 9 8 5 3 2
♡ A K J 10
◇ 10 9 7 2
♣ - - -

EAST
♠ 7 6 4
♡ 8 4 2
◇ 6 5
♣ A 9 8 5 4

SOUTH
♠ K Q 10
♡ Q 6 5
◇ Q J 3
♣ J 10 3 2

WEST	NORTH	EAST	SOUTH
	1NT	Pass	3NT
Pass	Pass	Pass	

Lead : ♣5. No reason to depart from the normal long suit lead.

Play : North should win the lead and return a club. After trick 1, North has only eight tricks on top and needs a second club trick for the contract. East should win the ♣ A at trick 2 and switch to hearts, West having signalled for the switch at tricks 1 and 2. West is able to cash four heart tricks to defeat the contract.

Notes : (1) If North cashes the diamonds and spades before playing the second round of clubs, North makes the defense transparent to East. If you need to steal a trick to land the contract, try to steal it early before the defense can tell where your values lie.
(2) If East ducks the second club, do not pursue clubs. Leave well enough alone and cash four diamonds and three spades to secure your contract. If you play a third club, East may wake up.
(3) East should appreciate there is no point in ducking the second club. East cannot cut declarer off from the club tricks and declarer will not allow East's clubs to set up. In addition, the danger that the second club will be declarer's ninth trick is a very real threat. As ducking cannot gain, win ♣ A and find the right switch.
(4) Using standard signals, West should discard the ◇ 2 on the club lead (red on black to attract partner's attention). The ◇ 2 says "I do not like diamonds." On the second round of clubs, West should discard the ♠ 2 : "I do not like spades either." East has no trouble (hopefully) deducing that the switch must be to hearts.
(5) It would be a serious error for West to discard the ♡ J or ♡ 10 to ask for the heart lead. All the hearts are needed to defeat the contract. Do not signal with a card that is needed as a winner.
(6) Reverse signals : Discard ◇ 10 and ♠ 9. Suit Preference Discards : discard ♠ 9 (not spades, want higher of other two suits) or ◇ 2 (not diamonds, want lower of other two). Odd-evens : ♠ 8 or ◇ 2 carry the same message.

Hand 26 : Dealer East : Both vulnerable

NORTH
♠ 8 7 4 3 2
♡ K Q 8 7
◇ 8 6
♣ 10 5

WEST
♠ Q J 9
♡ 6 5 4 3
◇ J 10 9 5 4
♣ 7

EAST
♠ A K 10
♡ J 10 9
◇ K Q 7
♣ A K Q 9

SOUTH
♠ 6 5
♡ A 2
◇ A 3 2
♣ J 8 6 4 3 2

WEST	NORTH	EAST	SOUTH
		2NT	Pass
3♣	Pass	3◇	Pass
3NT	Pass	Pass	Pass

Lead : ♣4. With outside entries, it is natural to lead the long suit.

Play : North plays the 10 of clubs and East wins the ace. East should continue with the ◇ K and ◇ Q, South ducking. South wins the third diamond on which North signals no interest in spades. South needs to find the switch to the ♡ A, North encouraging, and a second heart won by North. Two more hearts defeat 3NT.

Notes : (1) Better to explore hearts via 3♣ Stayman than diamonds via 3◇ . With no major fit, choose 3NT. 5◇ has no chance.
(2) Needing three diamond tricks, East should tackle diamonds at once and not start cashing clubs or spades.
(3) If the ◇ A is taken on the first or second round of diamonds, North has no chance to signal. South should hold off in diamonds, firstly, to try to cut East off from dummy (perhaps there is no entry), and secondly, to obtain a signal from North.
(4) North's ♣10 at trick 1 denied the A, K, Q and 9. South should realise that a club continuation is futile.
(5) In standard methods, North's signal on the third diamond is the ♠2, showing no interest in spades. South has to deduce that the heart switch is needed. North cannot spare any of the hearts for a signal. (Reverse signals : North plays the ♠8, discouraging spades. Suit Preference Discards or odd-even signals : North discards the ♠8, discouraging spades and asking for the higher remaining suit, i.e. hearts.)

Hand 27 : Dealer South : Nil vulnerable

```
              NORTH
              ♠ 9 5 4 3
              ♡ 4 2
              ◇ K Q J
              ♣ A Q 8 6
WEST                      EAST
♠ K Q J 10 7 6            ♠ 8
♡ A 8 6                   ♡ J 10 9 3
◇ 4 3                     ◇ 9 8 6 2
♣ J 2                     ♣ 10 7 5 4
              SOUTH
              ♠ A 2
              ♡ K Q 7 5
              ◇ A 10 7 5
              ♣ K 9 3
```

WEST	NORTH	EAST	SOUTH
			1NT
Pass	2♣	Pass	2♡
Pass	3NT	All pass	

Lead : ♠ K. Clearcut.

Play: South should duck the first spade and win the next, as East discards a diamond. South has eight tricks and the ninth can come from a favourable break in clubs or by setting up a heart trick. It is too risky to try hearts first. It may pay declarer to run four diamond tricks first and force some discards from the defenders. On the third diamond West discards the ♡8 and on the fourth diamond the ♡6. East should discard a heart on the fourth diamond and retain all four clubs. Declarer now cashes the ♣K and dummy's ♣A-Q. When clubs do not break, declarer tries a heart but West wins ♡A and cashes the spades for one down.

Notes : (1) With sound defensive chances, West should pass, but if West did bid 2♠ over 1NT, North should simply bid 3NT. *After a 1NT opening only,* responder's 3NT does not promise a stopper in a suit overcalled by second player.

(2) If South tackles the clubs before playing four rounds of diamonds, the defenders have no chance to misdefend. It often pays declarer to run a long solid suit early to force the defenders to make some discards. Discarding is a difficult area of defense and many defenders will discard incorrectly if you give them the chance.

(3) If East discards a club at any stage, declarer will succeed as dummy's clubs will then be good for four tricks. When choosing a discard, follow the principle 'keep length with dummy' as long as possible (unless all of dummy's cards are higher than yours). When West signals high-low in hearts, East has no trouble in letting a heart go, but even without that signal, East should know to keep clubs and let a heart go. If South has the top hearts, 3NT cannot be defeated. 'Keep length with dummy' will solve many of your discarding dilemmas.

Hand 28 : Dealer West : N-S vulnerable

```
              NORTH
              ♠ K 4 2
              ♡ 10
              ◇ 10 7 2
              ♣ K 10 7 5 4 3
WEST                      EAST
♠ A Q J 10               ♠ 9 8 5 3
♡ 5 4 3 2                ♡ 9 8
◇ K 8 5                  ◇ A Q J 4 3
♣ A Q                    ♣ J 8
              SOUTH
              ♠ 7 6
              ♡ A K Q J 7 6
              ◇ 9 6
              ♣ 9 6 2
```

WEST	NORTH	EAST	SOUTH
1NT	Pass	2♣	2♡
2♠	Pass	4♠	All pass

Lead: ♡ 10. Even without partner's bid, this would be the most attractive start.

Play: South wins the ♡J and cashes another heart. On the second heart, North should signal for a club switch. If South obeys and plays a club, declarer will fail. Declarer takes the club finesse and North collects the ♣K now and the ♠K later.

Notes: (1) Even though the spade suit is weak, East's best route is the Stayman sequence. 4♠ is superior to 3NT. In 3NT, even if North leads a club initially, there is still time for the heart switch when North comes in with the ♠K.

(2) West's trumps are too weak to double 2♡ (which makes easily), and so West bids 2♠. With no major, West would pass 2♡.

(3) If North fails to signal for the club switch or South ignores North's club request and plays a third heart, 4♠ can succeed. Declarer will be able to draw trumps and discard the club loser and the other heart loser on dummy's diamonds. The defense will collect only 2 hearts and 1 spade. The defense will not come to the king of clubs.

(4) If North held ♠ J-x-x and the ♣ A, North would discourage a club shift by discarding the lowest club at trick 2. South would then play a third heart allowing North to ruff with the ♠ J and cash the ♣ A for one down. The lowest club does not deny values in clubs. It simply says, "Do not play a club now." *A signal is used to tell partner what to do rather than what you hold.* Without North's signal, it is not clear to South whether to switch to clubs at trick 3 or whether to play North to ruff higher than dummy.

CHAPTER 8

SPECIAL SIGNALLING TECHNIQUES

SUIT PREFERENCE SIGNALS AT TRICK 1

If it is absolutely obvious that you cannot possibly want a continuation of the suit led, your signals change meaning and suit preference signals are used :

High card = Switch to the higher suit.

Lowest card = Switch to the lower suit.

The trump suit is excluded. There are only two relevant suits since the position arises only when you cannot want a continuation of the suit led.

The situation is very rare and does not normally apply just because dummy has a singleton. In a trump contract, if partner leads dummy's singleton, a high card (encouraging) signal says, "It is safe to continue this suit. I would sooner you played this suit than switch to something else." To ask for a switch, you can simply play a discouraging signal.

The most important case for a suit preference signal at trick 1 is when partner has led a short suit and needs to know your entry in order to obtain a ruff. If partner has led an obvious singleton and there is no value in your playing third-hand-high, then give a suit preference signal. If partner's lead is a singleton, it is obviously pointless to encourage partner to continue that suit or to discourage it. Similarly, if partner leads A-then-K to show A-K doubleton, you give a suit preference signal *on the second round* to indicate your entry : High card = high suit, Lowest card = low suit. On the first lead of A-K doubleton, you will have given an encouraging or discouraging signal. Only when the second round is played will you realise it is A-K doubleton. At that point you give a suit preference signal which overrides the signal on the first round.

HONOR CARD SIGNALS

One does not squander a potential trick with a signal, so that you signal with an honor card only when you can afford to do so. Normally this arises when you have a sequence headed by an honor.

When Following Suit : An honor card signal when following suit denies the next higher honor. A jack signal denies the queen, a queen signal denies the king, and so on. If you can afford to signal with the jack, you could afford to signal with the queen if you held it as well.

Dummy
A

K 8 6 4 3   J played

West leads the 4 and East plays the jack under dummy's ace. If the jack is not a singleton, East will have the 10 as well. West can also tell that South holds the queen. The jack aims to tell West that it is safe to continue the suit if West has the queen, and warns West that cashing the king will set up declarer's queen.

The Q Signal on the A or K

Dummy
8 3

A K 7 5   Q played

When West leads a top card and East drops the queen, it is either a singleton or promises possession of the jack. The purpose of this queen signal is to inform partner that it is safe to play a low card next if partner wants you on lead. Either you will ruff (if the queen was singleton) or you will win with the jack. This message that it is safe to lead low at trick 2 is so important that we do not play the Q under the ace (or king) from queen-doubleton (except, of course, queen-jack-doubleton).

It is normal to drop the jack from jack-doubleton to signal a doubleton and a desire to ruff, but do not drop the queen from Q-doubleton. *The queen promises either a singleton or a Q-J combination.*

Honor Card Discards

An honor card discard is an encouraging signal and promises a sequence of honors. Thus, an ace discard will normally promise K-Q-J as well. How could you afford to pitch the ace otherwise? Any honor discard denies the next higher honor. If you can afford to throw that honor, you could afford to throw the next higher one also. Thus, a queen discard promises the jack and ten but denies the king.

Dummy
8 3

K 7 2   Q discard

East's queen discard lets West know that it is safe to lead the king or to lead low from the king. It also lets West know that it is safe to discard the king and lower cards if the problem is which suit to pitch and which suit to hold.

Dummy

8 3

A 7 2   **Q discard**

East's queen discard denies the king. When on lead, West should not cash the ace but try to find East's entry. East can then lead through and trap South's king.

Discarding an ace promises possession of all the relevant high cards in that suit. It not only tells partner what to lead but lets partner know what to do in the 'what-do-I-keep, what-do-I-discard' position. The same applies when partner discards the currently highest card in a suit when there are still other cards around in that suit. To be able to afford that, partner must hold the next highest cards in that suit.

TAKING CONTROL OF THE DEFENSE

(1) Ace doubleton on partner's king lead.

When partner leads the king and you hold ace-doubleton, overtake with your ace and return your low card to show the doubleton. In no-trumps, you should overtake to avoid blocking the suit.

                    8 7

K Q J 5 4 2   **A 3**

                    10 9 6

Against 3NT, West leads the king. If East plays low, the suit yields only two tricks. If East correctly overtakes the king with the ace and returns the suit, East-West collect six tricks.

You may overtake in order to score a ruff.

                    8 6 5

K Q 7 4 2   **A 3**

                    J 10 9

In a suit contract, West leads the king. If East

plays low, there are only two tricks for the defense unless West has an entry. If East overtakes the king with the ace and returns the suit, West can win with the queen and play a third round for East to ruff.

(2) Overtake the king with the ace to clarify the defense for partner.

                    ♠ 6 4

♠ K led   **♠ A 7 3 2**

                    ♦ A

West leads the ♠ K against 4♡. East overtakes with the ♠ A, cashes the singleton ◊ A to create the void and returns a spade in order to get a ruff.

                    ◊ 6 4

                    ♣ Q 7 5

◊ K led   **◊ A 7 3 2**

                    ♣ A K J

West leads ◊ K against 2♠. East overtakes with the ◊ A, cashes the ♣ K to show where the tricks are coming from and returns a diamond. On winning the second diamond, West knows to play a club.

(3) Ruff partner's winner or overtake the king with the ace to shift to a more promising suit.

                    ◊ 6

                    ♣ 8 6 5

◊ K led   **◊ A J 8 2**

                    ♣ Q J 10 4

West leads the ◊ K against 4♠. With only a singleton in dummy, East may well overtake to switch to the ♣ Q. On other layouts, East may choose to overtake in order to switch to a singleton. East may also decide to overtake and switch to a trump to reduce the number of diamond ruffs in dummy.

EXERCISE ON SPECIAL SIGNALLING TECHNIQUES

1.
NORTH
♠ 8 6 3 2
♡ 5
◊ 8 4 3
♣ K Q J 10 4

WEST
♠ A 5
♡ 9 7 4 3 2
◊ 9 7 6 5 2
♣ 3

East opened 1♡, South bid 1♠ and after a competitive auction, South is in 4♠ doubled. West leads ♣3. Dummy's king wins and East plays the 2. A trump is led from dummy, East plays the 9, South the king and West wins with the ace. How should West continue?

2.
NORTH
♠ Q 6 4
♡ A J 3 2
◊ A K Q 10
♣ 7 4

EAST
♠ A 9 5
♡ 9 8 6 5
◊ 2
♣ A K Q 8 3

North opened 1NT and South's 4♠ ended the auction. West leads the jack of clubs. How should East plan the defense. Which four tricks does East hope to take?

3.
NORTH
♠ K Q J 2
♡ A K Q 10
◊ 8 6
♣ J 9 7

EAST
♠ 7
♡ 8 7 2
◊ Q J 10 4 2
♣ 8 6 4 3

West opened 1♣, North doubled and South ended in 4♠. West leads the king of diamonds. Which card should East play on that? How does East expect the defense to go?

PLAY HANDS ON SPECIAL SIGNALLING TECHNIQUES

Hand 29 : Dealer North : Both vulnerable

WEST	NORTH	EAST	SOUTH
	1♡	Pass	1♠
Dble	2♠	Pass	4♠
Pass	Pass	Pass	

NORTH
♠ K J 7 6
♡ A K J 6 5
◇ 10 3
♣ 7 2

WEST
♠ 8
♡ 10 9 7
◇ A K 8 4 2
♣ A Q 8 3

EAST
♠ 4 3
♡ 4 3 2
◇ Q J 9 7
♣ 10 9 5 4

SOUTH
♠ A Q 10 9 5 2
♡ Q 8
◇ 6 5
♣ K J 6

Lead : ◇ K (or ace). Clearcut.

Play : On the top diamond lead, East should signal with the *queen* of diamonds. This promises either a singleton queen or the jack as well as the queen. In either case, it lets partner know that it is safe to underlead the king. At trick 2, West leads a low diamond. East wins with the jack and switches to the 10 of clubs. West collects two club tricks to defeat the contract by one trick.

Notes : (1) Double by West has a greater chance of finding a fit than a 2 ◇ overcall.
(2) If West cashes king and ace of diamonds, 4♠ cannot be defeated. In fact, West would have to cash ♣ A at trick 3 to hold South to ten tricks. On a major suit lead, South has an easy road to eleven tricks.

(3) If East fails to signal with the *queen* of diamonds at trick 1, it is very difficult for West to find the winning defense. It is true that West *might* find it if East plays an encouraging 9 of diamonds, but the queen makes West's task much easier. Part of your duty as a defender is to simplify partner's problems. A key maxim for successful defense, although cynical, is "If you give partner the chance to find the wrong play, partner will find it." The more often you clarify the defense for partner, the more often you will defeat contracts that can be defeated.

Hand 30 : Dealer East : Nil vulnerable

WEST	NORTH	EAST	SOUTH
		1♠	Pass
3♠	Pass	4♠	All pass

NORTH
♠ 9
♡ A Q 10 7 5
◇ 9 8 5 4 2
♣ 6 3

WEST
♠ 10 6 4 3 2
♡ K 3
◇ K 7
♣ A Q 5 2

EAST
♠ Q J 8 7 5
♡ J 9
◇ A 10 6
♣ K J 4

SOUTH
♠ A K
♡ 8 6 4 2
◇ Q J 3
♣ 10 9 8 7

Lead : ♣10. Prefer the longer sequence, despite the stronger 2-card diamond sequence. The shorter the sequence, the greater the risk.

Play : Declarer should win with dummy's ace of clubs and lead a trump. On the ace of clubs, North should discourage with the ♣3. When South wins the ♠ K, South should continue with the ♠ A. The purpose is to obtain a signal from partner whether to switch to hearts or to diamonds. On the ♠ A North signals a desire for hearts and the heart shift breaks the contract.

Notes : (1) If East-West are using limit raises, West would respond 2♣ and rebid 4♠ over East's minimum 2♠ rebid.
(2) In order to mask the strength in clubs, declarer should win the first trick with the ♣ A, not with the Q, K or J. The ◇ K is available later as an entry to dummy after the clubs are unblocked.

(3) On the ♣ A, it would be an error for North to signal encouragement with the 6 of clubs. One does not high-low *automatically* with a doubleton. The function of the high-low is to signal partner to continue the suit led. Encourage with a doubleton when you wish to ruff the third round. With no prospect of a ruff, the ♣6 can mislead partner who may read you for the ♣ K and continue with clubs upon winning the ♠ K. If South does play another club upon winning the spade, declarer can succeed by discarding a heart on the queen of clubs.
(4) After winning the ♠ K, South should appreciate that it cannot cost to cash the ♠ A as well in order to receive that vital signal from partner. Without the signal, the correct switch is guesswork.
(5) If South wins ♠ K and plays a club or a diamond next, declarer must not play another spade. That would give the defense a second chance to find the right shift. With just one top trump out, leave it out. Play ♣ K, ♣ J, cross to the ◇ K and discard a heart loser on the ♣ Q. East has to play one round of trumps to eliminate the low trump, but if the defense does not play the second trump, there is no need for declarer to knock out the top trump.

Hand 31 : Dealer South : N-S vulnerable

```
            NORTH
            ♠ A K Q J 10
            ♡ J 6 3
            ◇ Q J 10
            ♣ 10 6
WEST                    EAST
♠ 2                    ♠ 8 7
♡ A K Q 8 7 5          ♡ 10 2
◇ A 7 2                ◇ K 9 6 4 3
♣ 7 5 4                ♣ 9 8 3 2
            SOUTH
            ♠ 9 6 5 4 3
            ♡ 9 4
            ◇ 8 5
            ♣ A K Q J
```

WEST	NORTH	EAST	SOUTH
			Pass
1♡	1♠	Pass	3♠
Pass	4♠	All pass	

Lead : ♡10. Partner's suit. Top card from doubleton.

Play : West should win with the ♡ Q (defenders win with the cheapest card possible) and cash ♡ K. East's 10-then-2 indicates a doubleton lead so that West knows declarer holds another heart. It is tempting to lead a third heart to allow East to ruff higher than dummy. Before doing so, West should cash the ◇ A, on which East signals encouragement with the ◇ 9. West should obey East's signal and play a diamond. East wins ◇ K to put the contract down.

Notes : (1) The jump raise of an overcall is not forcing. It indicates good support and a 7-loser hand. With a maximum overcall and 7 losers also, North accepts the game invitation. West should certainly not bid again at the 3-level or higher.

(2) If West plays a third heart at trick 3, the contract will make. East is unable to ruff higher than dummy. Declarer ruffs the heart, draws trumps and discards two diamonds on the clubs, losing 2 hearts and 1 diamond.

(3) The object of cashing ◇ A at trick 3 is to receive a signal from partner. If partner has the ◇ K and is unable to ruff higher than dummy, partner will encourage diamonds. West will then continue diamonds. If partner does not have the ◇ K and can ruff higher than dummy, partner will discourage diamonds. West will then switch back to hearts.

(4) There is a further benefit to cashing ◇ A even if the heart ruff follows at trick 4. Partner cannot misguess which suit to return after taking the ruff. Even when the return is obvious, partners are prone to getting it wrong.

Hand 32 : Dealer West : E-W vulnerable

```
            NORTH
            ♠ 7 3
            ♡ 7 5
            ◇ 9 7 5
            ♣ K Q 10 9 5 3
WEST                    EAST
♠ A K 10 9 2           ♠ Q 8 6 5
♡ A K J               ♡ Q 6 4 3
◇ 8 4 2               ◇ Q 6 3
♣ 6 4                 ♣ 8 7
            SOUTH
            ♠ J 4
            ♡ 10 9 8 2
            ◇ A K J 10
            ♣ A J 2
```

WEST	NORTH	EAST	SOUTH
1♠	Pass	2♠	Dble
Pass	3♣	3♠	All pass

Lead : ♣ K. A near sequence is more appealing than a doubleton.

Play : South should overtake the ♣ K with the ace, cash the ◇ K to show North the correct switch and then return the ♣ 2. North wins the club and plays a diamond. South takes two more diamond tricks to defeat 3♠ by one trick.

Notes : (1) It is sound competitive strategy to push above their suit at the 3-level when you have little defense in their suit and your side holds about half the HCP and 9 trumps or more. In fact, 3♣ cannot be defeated. It would be unsound for North-South to compete to the 4-level with only part-score values.

(2) If South merely discourages the club lead at trick 1 by playing the ♣ 2, North may not be sure whether to switch to hearts or diamonds. The heart switch may appeal to North since South's double implies hearts and North has only a doubleton there. If North were to switch to hearts, declarer can make 3♠ : win ♡ A, cash ♠ A and ♠ K (keeping the ♠ Q as an entry to dummy), cash ♡ K and ♡ J, cross to ♠ Q and discard a diamond loser on the ♡ Q. As you are following suit, the ♣ 2 does not operate as a suit-preference signal : the ♣ 2 simply discourages clubs and leaves it to North to deduce whether to switch to hearts or diamonds. When partner leads the first round of a suit, your primary signals in standard methods are high encourage, low discourage. Suit preference signals on partner's lead are used only in clearly defined positions.

(3) If South encourages clubs by playing the ♣ J and North plays a low club to South's ace, the contract can no longer be defeated. To beat 3♠, North has to lead a diamond to give South three diamond tricks.

(4) If South were to overtake the ♣ K with the ace and return the ♣ 2 at once (without playing the ◇ K first), this would imply a doubleton club and a desire to ruff the third round of clubs.

REVISION TEST ON PART 1

The material in Chapters 1-8 will help you answer these questions. If you experience difficulty in producing the correct answers, it will pay you to read these chapters again.

A. Which is the correct card to lead from each of these holdings in no-trumps?

1. K 8 3	**6.** K Q 8 2	**11.** A K 7 4 2
2. 10 9 5	**7.** K 10 9 8	**12.** K J 10 9 4
3. A 9 8	**8.** J 10 5 3	**13.** Q 9 8 7 6
4. 8 6 5	**9.** 8 6 4 3	**14.** A 9 7 3 2
5. Q 10 4	**10.** Q J 9 6	**15.** 10 9 5 3 2

B. Which, if any, of the answers to A. would change if the lead were against a trump contract?

C. What is your opening lead in these cases?

WEST
♠ K 7 6
♡ Q J 10 9
♢ J 6 5 3 2
♣ 8

a. The bidding has been 1NT by South, 3NT by North. What should West lead?

b. What should West lead from the same hand after this auction?

SOUTH	WEST	NORTH	EAST
	Pass	1♡	Pass
1NT	Pass	3♣	Pass
3NT	Pass	Pass	Pass

c. And what should West lead after this auction?

SOUTH	WEST	NORTH	EAST
1♢	Pass	2♣	Pass
2♢	Pass	2♡	Pass
2NT	Pass	3♢	Pass
3NT	Pass	Pass	Pass

D. What should West lead after these auctions?

WEST
♠ K 6 2
♡ 8 6 3
♢ J 7 3 2
♣ Q 8 4

a.	SOUTH	NORTH
		1♢
	2♡	3♡
	4NT	5♡
	5NT	6♢
	7♡	Pass

b.	SOUTH	NORTH	**c.**	SOUTH	NORTH
	1♡	2♡		1NT	4NT
	2NT	3♡		6NT	Pass
	Pass				

E.
               Dummy
               9 6 3
    A J 5 4 2

In no-trumps West leads the 4, East plays the 8 and South wins with the king. What is the complete layout? 1. Who has the Q?   2. The 10?   3. The 7?

F.
               Dummy
               8 7 2

West leads the 4 and dummy plays the 2. Which card should East play from each of these holdings?

1. Q 10 9 5	**11.** A Q 6
2. Q J 9 5	**12.** A K J 6
3. K Q 6	**13.** A 10 5 3
4. K Q J 6	**14.** K J 10 3
5. A J 9 5	**15.** A K Q 5
6. A K	**16.** K Q J 10 6
7. A K 5	**17.** J 9 5 3
8. 10 9 6	**18.** J 10 5 3
9. 10 9 5	**19.** J 10 9 3
10. K J 5	**20.** A K Q J 3

G.
               Dummy
               Q 7 5

West leads the 4 and the 5 is played from dummy. Which card should East play from these holdings?

1. K 10 6 2	**9.** A K 3
2. K 3 2	**10.** A K J 3
3. K J 10 6	**11.** A K J 10 3
4. 9 6 2	**12.** K 10 9 3
5. 9 8 6 2	**13.** K 10 9 8
6. A 6 2	**14.** J 10 2
7. A J 8	**15.** 10 9 8 2
8. A J 10 9	**16.** 10 9 8 6

H.
               Dummy
               7 2

After an auction of 1NT : 3NT, West leads the queen and dummy plays low. Which card should East play from :

1. A 5?   **2.** A K 5?   **3.** A K 8 5?   **4.** K 5?   **5.** K 9 8 2?

I.
               Dummy
               A J 6

West leads the 4 and the 6 is played from dummy. Which card should East play from these holdings?

1. K 10 2?   **2.** K Q 2?   **3.** K Q 10 9 5?   **4.** Q 9 7 2?

J.
               Dummy
               K Q 10 9 7
                      EAST
                      J 6 5 4 2

West leads the 8, 10 from dummy. Which card should East play?

PART 2

CONSOLIDATE YOUR

DECLARER PLAY

CHAPTER 9

SETTING UP A LONG SUIT (1)

With many card combinations it is possible to establish extra winners by eliminating the opponents' cards in that suit. Honor cards which are not winners can become promoted in situations like these :

                    A 10 7 2
     9 8 6 5 3   K Q J
                      4

Play the ace, ruff a low card, back to dummy via another suit, ruff a low card. With tge K-Q-J falling in three rounds (a lucky position), the 10 is now high. Cross back to dummy and cash the 19. If no honor falls when you play the ace, the 10 cannot legitimately be established as a winner with the above North-South cards.

                    A J 7 3
     10 9 8 6 2   K Q 4
                      5

Play the ace and ruff a low card, back to dummy and ruff another low card. If the king and queen have dropped, the jack is now high. Note that you cannot gain an extra trick if you lead the jack and ruff it. If no honor falls when you ruff the first time, the jack v ill not legitimately score a trick.

                    A 9 5 3
     8 7 6 2   Q J 10
                    K 4

Cash the king anc ace and ruff dummy's low card on the third round. If the Q, J and 10 have all fallen, the 9 is high (a very lucky outcome on these cards).

Where you have no high card to promote, you may still set up extra winners if you or dummy hold greater length than the opponents.

Dummy   A 7 4 2   Dummy   A 7 4 2

You   5   You   5 3

You have the ace, but you cannot create any extra tricks with either of the above holdings. At least one opponent holds as many cards as dummy.

                Dummy   A 7 6 4 2

                You   5

The opponents hold 7 cards. If these divide 4-3, you can make the ace plus one extra trick. The rule is:

Your length minus their length = Extra tricks possible.

Here dummy's length is 5, with a 4-3 division, their length is 4, so $5 - 4 = 1$. To score that extra trick: play the ace; ruff a low card; *cross to dummy;* ruff a low card; *cross to dummy;* ruff a low card; *cross to dummy after drawing trumps* and cash the last card in the suit. The last card will be a winner if the suit broke 4-3. If the suit divides 5-2 or worse, you cannot genuinely set up an extra trick. (You may succeed in such a case if the opponents unwisely discard from this suit — see page 46 : *Keep length with dummy.*)

Note that to succeed you had to *cross to dummy* three times, so that dummy needed *three entries.*

Dummy   A 7 6 4 3 2

You   5

How many tricks can you score with this holding in addition to the ace?

Take dummy's length. Subtract their length. The answer is the number of additional tricks you can set up.

A. The suit divides 3-3 :

Dummy's length (6) minus their length (3) = 3.

                    A 7 6 4 3 2
     Q 10 9   K J 8
                      5

Play the ace and ruff a low card; *cross to dummy* and ruff a low card. With a 3-3 split, dummy's three remaining cards are high; draw trumps and *cross to dummy* to cash your three winners.

B. The suit divides 4-2 :

Dummy's length (6) minus their length (4) = 2.

                    A 7 6 4 3 2
     Q 10   K J 9 8
                      5

Play the ace and ruff a low card; *cross to dummy,* ruff a low card; *cross to dummy,* ruff a low card; draw trumps; *cross to dummy* and cash two winners. Extra entries to dummy required = 3 (plus no overruff).

C. The suit divides 5-1 :

$6 - 5 = 1$. One extra trick can be established, provided that you have sufficient entries to dummy.

$$
\begin{array}{ccc}
 & \textbf{A 7 6 4 3 2} & \\
\textbf{K} & & \textbf{Q J 10 9 8} \\
 & \textbf{5} &
\end{array}
$$

Play the ace; ruff; *cross to dummy;* ruff; *cross to dummy;* ruff; *cross to dummy;* ruff; draw any remaining trumps; *cross to dummy* and cash one winner. Extra entries needed : 4. You also need plenty of trumps and no overruff by West.

Similarly :

$$
\begin{array}{c}
\textbf{A 7 4 3 2} \\
\textbf{K 5}
\end{array}
$$

In addition to the ace and king, two extra tricks can be set up if the suit divides 3-3 ($5 - 3 = 2$). Cash the king and ace and ruff the third round; if the suit did split 3-3, dummy's last two cards are winners. You need one more entry to dummy to reach those winners.

One extra trick can be set up if the suit splits 4-2 ($5 - 4 = 1$). Cash the king and ace; ruff; cross to dummy; ruff; dummy's last card is high. Draw any outstanding low trumps before crossing to dummy to cash the established winner. Two extra entries to dummy are needed, one to ruff the fourth round of the suit and one to re-enter to cash the winner.

Where a trick has to be lost in the suit anyway, it is often a good strategy to lose that trick early. This often saves you an entry to dummy.

$$
\begin{array}{ccc}
 & \textbf{A 7 4 2} & \\
\textbf{Q 8 6} & & \textbf{J 10 9} \\
 & \textbf{K 5 3} &
\end{array}
$$

As the suit divides 3-3, an extra trick is possible ($4 - 3 = 1$). You could play king, ace and give up the third round. With the 3-3 break, dummy's 13th card is a winner but you need an entry in another suit to reach that winner. Since you have to lose a trick anyway, it is better to duck a round at once (play low from both hands) or cash the king first and then duck one round. You can now enter dummy on the third round by using dummy's ace and do not need an entry in an outside suit.

$$
\begin{array}{ccc}
 & \textbf{A 8 5 3 2} & \\
\textbf{Q 9} & & \textbf{J 10 7} \\
 & \textbf{K 6 4} &
\end{array}
$$

With a 3-2 break, you can set up two extra tricks ($5 - 3 = 2$). You could play king, ace and lose the third round. Dummy has two winners and you will need an entry elsewhere to reach those winners.

It is superior to duck the first round of the suit or cash the king and duck the second round of the suit. Now dummy's ace is the entry to reach the established winners and you do not need an outside entry.

$$
\begin{array}{ccc}
 & \textbf{A 8 5 3 2} & \\
\textbf{J 10 9 7} & & \textbf{Q} \\
 & \textbf{K 6 4} &
\end{array}
$$

With the suit breaking 4-1, you can set up only one extra trick ($5 - 4 = 1$). You could play king, ace and give up the third round. You then need two entries to dummy, one to ruff the fourth round and one to re-enter to cash the winner. It is better to duck one round at once or cash the king and duck the second round. Later you can play the ace on the third round and ruff the fourth round. Now you need only one extra entry to dummy to reach the winner.

$$
\begin{array}{c}
\textbf{A 9 5 3 2} \\
\textbf{6 4}
\end{array}
$$

You could cash the ace and then give up the second round. However, whether the suit breaks 3-3 or 4-2, it is better to duck the first round. Later cash the ace and ruff the next round. Whatever the break, this approach needs one less entry to dummy.

Where you hold no high card winner at all in the suit, you may still be able to set up extra tricks.

$$
\begin{array}{ccc}
 & \textbf{8 6 5 4 2} & \\
\textbf{Q J 9} & & \textbf{A K 10 3} \\
 & \textbf{7} &
\end{array}
$$

If the suit breaks 4-3, you can set up one extra trick ($5 - 4 = 1$). Give up a trick to make yourself void. Then, *cross to dummy;* ruff; *cross to dummy;* ruff; *cross to dummy;* ruff the fourth round, leaving the last card in dummy as a winner; draw any missing low trumps; *cross to dummy* and cash the last card. To produce the extra trick, you need four entries to dummy.

$$
\begin{array}{c}
\textbf{7 6 5 4 3 2} \\
\textbf{9}
\end{array}
$$

Give up a trick to create the void. Then, *cross to dummy;* ruff; *cross to dummy;* ruff, etc. If the suit splits 3-3 ($6 - 3 = 3$), three extra tricks are available (and dummy needs three entries). If the break is 4-2 ($6 - 4 = 2$), two extra tricks can be set up but four entries to dummy will be needed.

Because these plays often require many entries to the hand with the long suit, it is a common strategy not to draw all their trumps at once but to use the trump suit itself for the required entries. This is illustrated in the hands that follow.

PLAY HANDS ON SETTING UP A LONG SUIT (1)

Hand 33 : Dealer North : Nil vulnerable

NORTH
♠ Q 7 5
♡ 4
♢ A K Q 9 5 2
♣ Q J 10

WEST
♠ A J 6 4 2
♡ K 10 8
♢ 8 4
♣ A 5 3

EAST
♠ 9
♡ A Q J 9 7 5 2
♢ J 6
♣ 9 7 2

SOUTH
♠ K 10 8 3
♡ 6 3
♢ 10 7 3
♣ K 8 6 4

WEST	NORTH	EAST	SOUTH
	1♢	3♡	Pass
4♡	Pass	Pass	Pass

Lead : ♢ 3. Bottom from three cards to an honor. Do *not* play middle-up-down when holding the 10.

Play : North wins ♢ Q (a defender wins with the cheapest card possible) and cashes the ♢ K. As South has played low-high, indicating more than a doubleton, North sees that a diamond continuation is futile. The natural switch is to clubs, dummy's weaker and shorter holding. The ♣ Q switch is won by the ace, as South encourages with the ♣ 8. After ♣ A, declarer continues with ♠ A; ruff a low spade; heart to dummy's 8; ruff a low spade; heart to dummy's 10; ruff a low spade. Dummy's ♠ J is now a winner. Cross to the ♡ K and cash the ♠ J, discarding a club. 10 tricks.

Notes : (1) With better than three tricks for partner, it is reasonable to raise a non-vulnerable pre-empt to game. In addition to three sure tricks, West has potential for a diamond ruff and potential to set up spade tricks.
(2) After winning the ♣ A, East can see four losers (2 diamonds, 2 clubs). There are nine winners (7 hearts, 2 aces). By far the best chance for the extra trick is via the spade suit by setting up the fifth spade as a trick.
(3) It would be an error to draw trumps before tackling spades. Even one round of trumps eliminates one vital entry to dummy. You can then set up the ♠ J as a winner but cannot return to dummy to cash it.
(4) If North's three spades had included the king and queen (e.g. K-Q-5), declarer could score 11 tricks: win ♣ A; ♠ A; ruff a *low* spade (Q falls); heart to the 8; ruff a *low* spade (K falls); heart to the 10 drawing the last trump; cash ♠ J and discard a club; cash dummy's fifth spade and discard the other club.

Hand 34 : Dealer East : N-S vulnerable

NORTH
♠ A K Q 9 3 2
♡ 6 2
♢ J 10 9
♣ A Q

WEST
♠ 5 4
♡ J 9 7 5
♢ 7 5
♣ 10 8 7 6 5

EAST
♠ 7 6
♡ Q 10
♢ A K 8 4 3
♣ K J 9 2

SOUTH
♠ J 10 8
♡ A K 8 4 3
♢ Q 6 2
♣ 4 3

WEST	NORTH	EAST	SOUTH
		1♢	1♡
Pass	2♠	Pass	4♠
Pass	Pass	Pass	

Lead : Top diamond. Normal, attractive start.

Play : East cashes the top diamonds, West signalling high-low asking East to continue with a third round. West ruffs the third diamond and switches to the 6 of clubs. Declarer should win the ♣ A, rejecting the club finesse; cash one top trump; then play off the ♡ A, ♡ K and ruff a heart *high*; cross to the ♠ 10; ruff a heart; cross to the ♠ J and cash dummy's fifth heart to discard the ♣ Q. 10 tricks.

Notes : (1) North's jump to 2♠ is forcing, showing 16 points or more and at least a 5-card suit. Many partnerships play that a change-of-suit is not forcing after a 1-level overcall.
(2) 3NT would be easier but that is very hard to judge.
(3) It would be an error to finesse the ♣ Q at trick 4. The ♣ K is marked with East : only 14 HCP are missing and East opened the bidding. Without ♣ K, East would have opened with only 11 HCP, possible but unlikely. Even if there had been no opening bid, the club finesse is only a 50% line, while setting up the hearts works if hearts are 3-3 (36%) or 4-2 (48%), an 84% chance. Even if North held a singleton heart, setting up the fifth heart is better than the 50% chance of a successful finesse.
(4) After taking ♣ A, it would be an error to draw two rounds of trumps. When hearts are 4-2, dummy is one entry short to reach the established heart winner.
(5) It would be an error to ruff the third round of hearts with a low trump. This runs the unnecessary risk of an overruff by East who could then cash the ♣ K for two down. *When you can afford it, ruff high.*

Hand 35 : Dealer South : E-W vulnerable

NORTH
- ♠ 7
- ♡ A Q 6
- ◇ K 9 8
- ♣ A 7 6 5 4 3

WEST
- ♠ K J 9 6 4
- ♡ J 8 2
- ◇ 7
- ♣ K Q J 9

EAST
- ♠ A Q 8 5 3 2
- ♡ K 10 7 5 3
- ◇ - - -
- ♣ 10 2

SOUTH
- ♠ 10
- ♡ 9 4
- ◇ A Q J 10 6 5 4 3 2
- ♣ 8

WEST	NORTH	EAST	SOUTH
			5 ◇
Pass	6 ◇	All pass	

Lead : ♣ K. As it happens, the spade lead collects one trick for the defense, but West cannot tell that and the ♣ K lead is normal.

Play : The best chance is to ruff out the club suit. Win ♣ A; ruff a club *high*; diamond to the 8; ruff a club; diamond to the 9; ruff a club. The last two clubs are winners. Cross to the ◇ K or ♡ A; cash the two clubs, discarding a spade and a heart. 13 tricks.

Notes : (1) Not vulnerable, a pre-emptor may bid for three tricks more than the number of playing tricks held. South is worth 8 tricks in diamonds and therefore should choose 5 ◇. Any less would be an underbid, causing North to misassess the combined values.
(2) North has three sure tricks (◇ K and 2 aces), enough for 5 ◇ opposite eight playing tricks. With excellent potential for a fourth trick (spade ruff *or* heart finesse *or* set up the clubs), North has enough to justify 6 ◇. 7 ◇ is out: it pays to assume the pre-emptor has no significant high cards outside the suit opened, so that it is overwhelmingly likely that the ace of spades is missing.
(3) Neither West nor East has the values to bid at this level, notwithstanding that 6 ♠ is a good sacrifice, even at this vulnerability.
(4) South should not play a trump at trick 2. This could cost the contract if clubs were 5-1. If there were a 5-1 club break, declarer could still succeed on this lead by tackling the clubs at once.
(5) It would be an error to take the heart finesse. This is a 50% chance only. After the ♣ A wins, playing to set up clubs is 100% certain to work even against the worst break in clubs.

Hand 36 : Dealer West : Both vulnerable

NORTH
- ♠ J 10 2
- ♡ 8 6 5
- ◇ A K 8 6 3
- ♣ 7 2

WEST
- ♠ A 6 3
- ♡ A Q J 10 7 2
- ◇ Q 7
- ♣ 10 3

EAST
- ♠ 9 5 4
- ♡ K 9 3
- ◇ J 2
- ♣ A K 6 5 4

SOUTH
- ♠ K Q 8 7
- ♡ 4
- ◇ 10 9 5 4
- ♣ Q J 9 8

WEST	NORTH	EAST	SOUTH
1 ♡	Pass	2 ♣	Pass
2 ♡	Pass	3 ♡	Pass
4 ♡	Pass	Pass	Pass

Lead : Top diamonds. Normal attractive start.

Play : North cashes two top diamonds. South plays a discouraging signal on the first diamond but should play the ◇ 10 on the next diamond as a suit preference signal for spades (high card = high suit). Even without this assistance, North has a natural shift to the jack of spades. South plays the 8 as an encouraging signal. West should win the ace and continue via ace of clubs, king of clubs and a third club, ruffed *high*. After a low trump to dummy's 9, ruff another club *high*, establishing dummy's last club as a winner. Cash a top trump from hand and then lead a trump to dummy's king to draw all the trumps. One spade is discarded on the fifth club. Making 10 tricks.

Notes : (1) It would be an error to draw trumps. You could afford to draw one round of trumps with a top trump from the West hand but two rounds of trumps would be fatal. You could still set up a club winner but dummy would be one entry short to cash the club.
(2) Declarer must take care to ruff the third club high. If not, North overruffs and two spades are cashed. Down two.
(3) After ♣ A, ♣ K, club ruff, heart to the 9 and a club ruff, it is vital to draw all the missing trumps before attempting to cash dummy's club winner. If declarer simply plays a heart to the king at that stage, there will still be one trump left out. This will ruff the club winner and cost the contract.
(4) If clubs were 3-3, you could make 11 tricks : ♣ A, ♣ K, club ruff high; then ♡ A, ♡ Q, a heart to the king, and the two club winners allow both spades to be discarded. That is why there is no benefit in holding off with the ace of spades at trick 3.

CHAPTER 10
CARD COMBINATIONS FOR DECLARER (1)

1. Cashing out a suit — High card from shortage

When you have winners in dummy and winners in your own hand, play your winners first from the hand with shorter length. The rule is 'High-from-shortage-first, low-from-length-first'. Follow this principle and you always finish in the hand containing the suit length. This rule will ensure you do not block a suit, do not end up in the wrong hand and generally make as many tricks as possible.

EXERCISE A : In which order should you play your winners with these combinations?

1.	K 7	2.	K 7 3 2	3.	A K Q J 6
	A Q 5		A Q 5		10 4

4.	Q 5	5.	A Q 5 2	6.	A K Q 6
	A K J 2		K J 8		J 3

You might break the high-from-shortage rule if you need an urgent entry in the hand with the length and you have an outside entry in that hand so that you can return later to cash your extra winner(s). For example :

WEST	EAST
♠ A Q 8 6 4	♠ J 10 9 2
♡ A 8 3	♡ 5 4
◇ A K	◇ J 6
♣ A K 8	♣ Q J 10 9 3

West plays 6♠ on a heart lead. The best chance for success is to lead the ♣8 to dummy, blocking the clubs, and take the spade finesse. You cannot afford to follow the high-from-shortage rule here. If the ♠K is onside and trumps are 2-2 or 3-1, draw trumps, unblock the clubs and return to dummy via a trump. You discard two heart losers on the clubs.

When you have the same number of cards in dummy and your hand, with winners in both hands, take your tricks in whichever order suits you.

2. Knocking out an ace — High-from-shortage

When you have the high cards in a suit but the ace is missing, you use the high-from-shortage rule when playing an honor card to knock out the ace. Again, this makes sure you do not block the suit and prevents you from ending in the wrong hand.

EXERCISE B : In which order should you play these combinations when knocking out the ace?

1.	K Q 7 6	2.	J 10 7 3 2	3.	Q J 6
	J 10 2		K Q 5		K 10 4 3

4.	J 5	5.	Q J 5 2	6.	K Q J 6
	K Q 7		K 10 8		10 3

7.	Q 6	8.	K J 7 4	9.	Q 10 3 2
	K J 10 2		Q 10 5		K J 5

Again, you might break this rule if you need to set up an entry urgently in the hand with the length. With the same number of cards in each hand, lead from either hand to knock out the ace, as it suits you.

3. Overtaking to avoid blocking a suit

With a solid suit and high cards in both hands, it may be necessary to overtake a winning card in order to gain entry to the other hand. Follow the high-from-shortage rule and overtake when the last card is played from the shorter length.

EXERCISE C : In which order should you play your winners with these combinations?

1.	A Q J	2.	Q 10 5 2	3.	A Q
	K 10 9 4 2		A K J		K J 4

4.	K Q	5.	A K 6 5 2	6.	A 10 7 6
	A J 10		Q J 10		K Q J

7.	K J	8.	K J 5 2	9.	A J
	A Q 10		A Q 10		K Q 10

4. Leading towards honors

Holding honor cards but not a solid sequence, it is best to lead towards the honor cards with which you hope to win. Do not lead an honor card itself if you do not have a solid sequence. Arrange the play so that the honor card is played third on the trick.

A.   **Dummy**
                          7 6 5 2
      10 9 8 3   **A**
                          K Q J 4

South should not lead an honor from hand.

B.

                    Dummy
                    7 6 5 2
        3   A 10 9 8
                    K Q J 4

Best is to cross to dummy and lead from dummy towards your honors. If the suit divides 3-2, the error of leading an honor from hand would not cost. In A, leading from dummy gives declarer three tricks when the singleton ace appears. In B, if declarer is able to lead from dummy three times, declarer can again score three tricks. In either case, leading an honor from hand holds declarer to just two tricks.

                    Dummy
                    K Q 7 3
        A J 9   10
                    8 6 5 4 2

Declarer should lead low from hand towards the K-Q in dummy. If West plays the ace, you naturally play low. If West plays low, play the king. If it wins, return to hand via another suit and lead from hand again, so that the queen is played in *third* seat if West follows low. Leading from dummy will give the defence two tricks if West started with A-J-10, A-J-9 or A-10-9, while leading twice from hand towards dummy restricts West to just one trick. Likewise, leading an honor from dummy first gives the defense two tricks if West has ace singleton and East has J-10-9. Leading from hand again gives them one trick only.

                    Dummy
                    Q J 4

                    K 7 3 2

If dummy or declarer had the 10 instead of a low card, it would be correct to lead the Q or J initially. Without the 10, 'lead-towards-honors' means you should lead low from hand towards dummy, playing an honor if West follows low. If the honor wins, come to hand via another suit and again lead low towards the remaining honor in dummy. You gain when West has ace singleton and also in this layout :

                    Q J 4
        A 6   10 9 8 5
                    K 7 3 2

If the Q or J is led first, West captures it and you make only two tricks. Leading low from hand twice results in West's ace capturing only low cards and you win three tricks. Whenever you have a 4-3 fit with the K, Q and J, lead twice towards the hand which contains two honors (provided you have enough entries for this).

1. K Q 7 2	**2.** K Q 7	**3.** Q 4 3 2
J 6 5	J 6 5 2	K J 5

4. Q J 4	**5.** J 4	**6.** J 4
A 5 3 2	A K 3 2	A Q 3 2

5. Unblocking a suit

When you are planning to cash all the cards in a suit, notice what will happen when you play the last card from the short hand. It is vital that the long hand is able to win the trick when the last card is played from the short hand.

                    Dummy
                    K 9 5 2

                    A Q 6 4 3

After cashing the A, K, Q, which card will be left in dummy? If it is the 9, you are unable to overtake it. The 9 would block the suit and you would need an extra entry to cash the fifth card in your hand. The solution is to play the 9 (unblock) on the second or third round of the suit. Then you can win the fourth round and continue the suit. Similarly—

                    Dummy
                    K 9 8 2

                    A Q 5 4 3

What will you have left in dummy after you cash the A, K, Q? If it is the 8 or 9, the suit is blocked. To avoid this problem, play the 8 and 9 on the early rounds and keep the 2 in dummy for the fourth round. The last card from the short hand must be lower than a card in the long hand to allow re-entry.

                    Dummy
                    A 7 6 4 3 2
        J 8   Q 10
                    K 9 5

Suppose you need six tricks from this suit and dummy has no other entry. You need a 2-2 break but you also must take care not to block the suit. After you play the A and K and the suit does break 2-2, which card will you have left in hand? It had better not be the 9 or you will not be able to look partner in the eye. The last card in the short hand must be lower than a card in the long hand. Get rid of that 9. Cash the king, then lead the 9 to the ace and continue with the 5, overtaking with dummy's 6 or 7.

6. Retaining the tenace

When you have winners in dummy and in your own hand, the order in which you cash your winners may be important. If you have a highish card, almost but not quite a winner, plus a winning card in the same hand, you have a combination which may be useful for a finesse. A tenace is a split-honor holding where an opponent holds the missing high card(s).

Dummy
A J 6 4 2

K 8 7 5 3

Dummy's ace-jack combination is a tenace. With a winner in each hand plus a tenace combination, **play the winner first from the hand that does not contain the tenace.**

In the above layout, cash the king first. If both opponents follow, draw the last card. However, if East shows out, West began with Q-10-9 and you have dummy's A-J intact to take advantage of the finessing position that has presented itself. (If *East* began with Q-10-9, you cannot escape a loser.)

Whenever you have winners in both hands, check to see which hand contains a card nearest to winning rank. Treat that as your tenace and cash first the winners from the other hand.

Dummy
K 10 5 3

A Q 6 2

The 10 is nearest to a winner, therefore cash the ace and queen first, retaining the K-10 tenace. If the suit splits 3-2, your precaution was unnecessary. However, if West began with J-x-x-x, cashing the A-Q first saves a trick. On the second round East shows out and you can then take the marked finesse of the 10. (If *East* began with J-x-x-x, a loser is inevitable.)

Dummy
K Q 5 3

A 9 6 2

The 9 is nearest to a winning card. Therefore, treat that as the tenace and cash the K-Q first. If the break is 3-2, there are no losers. If the suit splits 4-1, the correct approach also avoids a loser whenever West started with singleton 10 or singleton J. On the king, West's honor falls. On the queen, West shows out and with the A-9 tenace left, you are able to take advantage of the marked finesse against East's remaining honor.

7. Retaining the tenace when knocking out an ace

The same principle applies when you have the top honors bar the ace. Check which hand has a card nearest to one of the top honors and play the honors from the other hand first.

Dummy
Q 9 5 2

K J 4 3

If the suit divides 3-2, you lose only the ace. As the 9 is nearest to an honor, retain the Q-9 tenace till last. Play the honors from the other hand first. After the king and jack, if East began with a singleton, East shows out on the second round. You have the Q-9 left to finesse against West's 10.

If you have enough entries, it may be useful to lead twice from dummy towards your K-J-x-x. If East began with A-10-x-x, you may be able to take your tricks and engineer an endplay to avoid giving East two tricks.

8. Keeping a suit fluid

Where you have high cards in dummy and in your own hand, good technique in playing your high cards will allow you entries to either hand in that suit.

Dummy
Q 5 4 2
J 9   **10 6**
A K 8 7 3

If you cash the ace and lead the 3 to the queen, you have no further entry to dummy in this suit. It costs nothing to manage your entries more adroitly. If you cash the ace and king, you have two entries to dummy and one to your own hand. If you cash the ace and lead the 8 to the queen, you have one entry to dummy and two to your own hand.

K 8 6 4
A 3   **5 2**
Q J 10 9 7

In knocking out the ace, if you lead the 7 to the king, you have no further entries to dummy in this suit. If however you lead the queen first and the jack next, you have two entries to dummy and one entry to hand. If you prefer two entries to hand, retain the 7 and lead a high card to the king, low back to a high card in hand. Then you have two high card entries in hand if you wish and you can also lead the 7 to dummy's 8 if you need an entry to dummy.

9. Finessing for the king

Finessing is the best chance to avoid a loser in a suit where the king is missing (unless you have 11 or 12 cards). To finesse may not be the best approach: perhaps the bidding has revealed that the finesse cannot work or is unlikely to work; perhaps the correct play of the complete hand requires that you forego the finesse.

However, even where the finesse is the right play, there are techniques to finessing for the king. In order to finesse you need a tenace or a sequence of honors.

A Q 7 6 4

9 8 5 3 2

Dummy's A-Q tenace provides a finessing position. The best chance not to lose a trick is to lead low from hand and play the queen if West plays low. Playing the ace avoids a loser only if East has the king singleton. Finessing the queen avoids a loser if East has the 10 singleton or the jack singleton (when West holds K-J or K-10). The finesse is thus twice as good a play as playing the ace.

A 8 7 6 4

Q 9 5 3 2

Here there is no tenace and no touching honors. The only legitimate chance to avoid a loser is to cash the ace and hope the king is singleton. This is not a great chance but it is the only one. The trap to avoid is leading the queen. This has zero chance. If East has the king, the queen loses. If West has the king, West can cover the queen with the king and after the ace wins, *their* jack or *their* 10 will be high. No matter where the king is, leading the queen loses *because you do not hold the jack.*

A 8 7 6 4

Q J 5 3 2

Here you hold the queen and jack, touching honors. Now a finesse is again a genuine play. Lead the queen from hand: if West covers with king, it is *your* jack that is high. If West plays low, let the queen run: you win if West began with K-10, K-9 or K-singleton.

With 9 cards, similar principles apply:

A Q 7 4

8 6 5 3 2

Lead low from hand and finesse the queen. You escape a loser if West began with king-doubleton.

A 8 7 4

K   **J 10 9**

Q 6 5 3 2

The correct play is to cash the ace. You have no tenace and no touching honors. You cannot avoid a loser but you can limit your losers to one. In the above case, leading the ace drops the king and East makes just one trick. If you lead the queen, it goes queen — king — ace and East scores two tricks. Playing ace first and leading low towards the queen also holds the losers to one if East began with K-J-x or K-10-9. Again, leading the queen would give East two tricks.

As a general guide, do not lead an honor for a finesse unless you have a touching honor in the same hand as the honor card you are leading.

This does not cover every case but it will stop you making a no-win play in most positions.

A Q 7 2

J 6 5 4 3

Lead low from hand and finesse the queen. Do not lead the jack first (since you do not hold the touching 10). Leading the jack gives East a trick if the layout looks like this:

A Q 7 2

K   **10 9 8**

J 6 5 4 3

Lead the jack and it goes jack — king — ace. After the queen is played, East's 10 is high. Lead low first and you still have the jack to capture East's 10 later.

A Q 7 2

J 10 6 4 3

Here you can afford to lead the jack. You may always lead an honor for a finesse if second player's covering promotes your other high cards into winners. Here, if West covers the jack even with king singleton, it is *your* queen and *your* 10 that are now high. Before leading an honor for a finesse, check that you will be the one to benefit if second player covers with a singleton honor.

With only eight cards between you and dummy, it is even more important not to lead an honor initially unless you have touching honors in the same hand.

A Q 4 3

J 6 5 2

Start by leading low to the queen. Do not lead the jack as you do not have the 10.

```
            A Q 6 2
K 9                      10 8 7
            J 5 4 3
```

The correct play to avoid losing a trick with this combination is to lead low to the queen and then cash the ace. You avoid a loser only when West started with K-x. The trap to avoid is leading the jack first. This loses a trick on every layout against accurate defense. If East has the king, the finesse loses and if West has the king, West covers the jack. In the above layout, East's 10 then becomes a winner on the third round. Leading the jack is an S.I.W. — a self-inflicted wound. Low to the queen then cash the ace scores all the tricks. Leading the jack loses a trick.

After playing low to the queen which scores, cash the ace. Do *not* return to hand and lead the jack. Again that would cost you a trick: the jack is covered by the king and *their* ten becomes high.

```
            A Q 6 3
            J 10 5 2
```

Where you have eight cards with two touching honors opposite the tenace, the best play (if you have adequate entries) is to lead low to the queen first. If the queen wins, come to hand and then lead the jack: now if West covers with the king, it is *your* 10 that is good after the ace captures the king. You can afford to lead the jack because you hold the touching honor. The position is the same if you interchange either of declarer's honors with the queen in dummy.

If you are short of entries, you may need to lead the jack on the first round, but if you can afford to lead low first time, it is superior to do so.

```
            A Q 6 3
K                        9 8 7 4
            J 10 5 2
```

In this layout, if you lead low, you will capture West's singleton king, thus losing no tricks. Lead an honor on the first round and a singleton king with West costs you a trick. If you have only two honors left after you capture the king, East's 9-8-7 gives the defense a trick. If West began with K-x or K-x-x, you will still be able to avoid a loser by leading low to the queen, then returning to hand via another suit and leading an honor *on the second round.*

Where you have 5, 6, 7 or 8 cards including the A, Q, J, 10 and 9, it is always safe to lead an honor card for a first round finesse. If the honor is covered, all your other top cards become winners.

10. Finessing for the Q : the 8-ever, 9-never rule.

Where you have the A, K and J between the two hands (with a tenace so that a finesse is available), the 8-ever, 9-never rule means that with 8 cards it is a better chance to finesse for the queen, while with 9 cards it is a better chance to 'play for the drop' (cash the ace and king and hope the queen falls).

The 8-ever, 9-never principle applies when the queen is missing, *not when the king is the missing honor.* See the preceding section when the king is missing. The rule is also only a guideline and there may be many other considerations. For example, maybe you cannot afford to let one particular opponent obtain the lead; perhaps the play of the whole hand means you cannot afford to lose the lead just yet so that a finesse would be too risky; perhaps you know the location of the queen from the bidding.

If you know who has the queen, aim to capture it. Take a finesse or play for the drop, as applicable, regardless of the number of cards you hold.

```
            A 7 3 2
8                        Q 10 6
            K J 9 5 4
```

With no knowledge as to the location of the queen, cash ace and king and hope for the best. If the bidding indicates that East must hold the queen or is highly likely to hold it, cash the ace and finesse the jack. Do not follow any rule blindly. Do not let a rule deflect you from sensible bridge logic.

```
            A K J 3
10 8 4                   Q 9
            7 6 5 2
```

Without knowing who has the queen, the best chance for no loser is to finesse for the queen. That would lose in the above layout. Tough luck. However, if you know that East is certain or very likely to hold the queen because of the bidding, do not be bound by any rule. Play the ace and king and hope that the queen drops. If your judgement is correct that the queen is with East, the finesse is bound to fail. It is foolish to take a finesse that must lose. Knowing the queen is with East, you know that the finesse play has no chance. Play the ace and king and hope for the best. If the finesse has no chance, you may as well adopt a line that has some hope. If East began with Q-x-x, then nothing would have worked and if West had the queen after all, you need to do some more work on your card reading.

Do not take a finesse which you know will lose.
Do not obey a rule just for the sake of obeying.

Where you have 10 cards missing the queen, cash one top honor first. If the suit divides 2-1, you can draw the remaining card on the second round. If the suit divides 3-0, you will be able to finesse against the queen if it is at all capturable by following the 'retain-your-tenace' rule (see No. 6, page 56).

K 8 6 3 2

--- **Q 10 9**

A J 7 5 4

Cash the king first, retaining your A-J tenace. When East turns up with Q-10-9, you can finesse against the queen on the next round. Had you cashed the ace first, you would be saddled with a loser. If West started with Q-10-9, you always have a loser, no matter how you play. Cater for the problems you can handle, not those which inevitably lead to a loss. Good advice for life, good advice for bridge.

With 9 cards missing the queen, cash the ace and king unless you have a sound reason for another line. It normally makes little difference which you cash first if they are in opposite hands. Nevertheless, if a tenace situation exists, it is better to cash first the honor opposite the tenace (retain the tenace). If a really bad break occurs, you may still be able to avoid a loser.

K 6 5 3 2

--- **Q 10 8 4**

A J 9 7

With this combination, you normally do not intend to finesse. Still, cash the king first and leave your tenace holding intact. If both follow, play to the ace and hope. If West shows out on the first round, you can now take advantage of the tenace. Lead low and capture East's card as cheaply as possible. Return to dummy in another suit and repeat the finesse. Note that if you had cashed the ace first, you would have had a loser.

When you hold 8 cards, your plan is to finesse unless you have a strong reason to avoid the normal play. Even so, it is usually best to cash one top honor first just in case the queen is singleton. **When finessing for the queen, finesse on the second round.**

A K J 4

8 5 3 2

Cash the ace first. This saves a trick if East has the queen singleton. If the queen does not drop, come to hand in another suit and lead low to the jack.

K 7 2

A J 5 4 3

Play the king first (saving a trick if the queen is singleton), then finesse the jack *on the second round.*

The 8-ever, 9-never principle can also be used where you hold the king, queen and ten with the ace and the jack missing.

Q 5 3 2

K 10 7 6 4

The best chance (if you have no clues about the division of this suit or the location of the ace and jack) is to lead low from hand towards the queen. On the next round, play the king. With four cards missing, it is marginally superior to play for the jack to drop.

Q 5 3 2

K 10 6 4

With only eight cards, the jack is unlikely to fall in two rounds. Lead low to the queen first (keeping the tenace intact). Whether the queen wins or loses, lead low from dummy next time and finesse the 10 if East plays low.

These combinations are played in the same way as K-x-x-x opposite A-J-x-x(-x) because the combinations are the same except that each honor card has dropped by one rank. As always, your knowledge of the location of the cards may indicate that the standard line is not best on any given hand.

Where the jack is not part of a tenace, **do not lead the jack unless you have the 10 touching.**

J 7 3 2

10 9 8 **Q 6**

A K 5 4

The only legitimate chance for no loser is to cash the king and ace. If the queen drops, as above, the jack can capture the 10. If you lead the jack, you lose when West wins with the queen and you lose when East has the queen and covers the jack. West's 10 will then be the top trump on the third round.

J 10 3 2

A K 5 4

This time you have the jack *and* 10 touching. Cash the ace first (in case the queen is singleton). If the queen has not dropped, cross to dummy in another suit and lead the jack: if East covers, your 10 becomes high. If East plays low, let the jack run.

PLAY HANDS ON CARD COMBINATIONS FOR DECLARER (1)

Hand 37 : Dealer North : N-S vulnerable

NORTH
♠ J 9 8 4 2
♡ A 9 4 2
♢ Q 10
♣ 10 6

WEST
♠ A 3
♡ K Q J 6
♢ A 8 3
♣ A K 5 4

EAST
♠ Q 7
♡ 7 3
♢ K 7 6 5 4 2
♣ 8 3 2

SOUTH
♠ K 10 6 5
♡ 10 8 5
♢ J 9
♣ Q J 9 7

WEST	NORTH	EAST	SOUTH
	Pass	Pass	Pass
2NT	Pass	3NT	All pass

Lead : ♠4. Normal fourth highest from the long suit.

Play : Hoping North holds the ♠K, declarer should play the queen from dummy. South covers with the king. If declarer ducks, South returns the 5 of spades. After winning ♠A, West should tackle the diamonds. With the spades wide open, West cannot afford to let the opposition in and must hope for a 2-2 break in diamonds : cash ♢A, then lead the *eight* of diamonds (unblocking) to the king. The diamonds do break 2-2, so play off the rest of dummy's diamonds followed by the ♣A-K : 9 tricks.

Notes : (1) East should stick with no-trumps and not introduce the diamonds over 2NT. 3NT will succeed more often than 5♢.
(2) If declarer plays hearts after winning ♠A, North wins ♡A and cashes the spades. South should unblock ♠10 under the jack.
(3) If declarer fails to unblock the 8 of diamonds, e.g. ♢A and then ♢3 to the king, or ♢3 to the king and then back to the ace, declarer is restricted to three diamond tricks and 3NT can then be defeated. Declarer has to realise that with spades wide open, six diamond tricks have to be run. To do that, *dummy* has to win the *third* round of diamonds, so West must not retain the 8.
(4) If the ♠Q had won the first trick, so that a spade stopper is still held, the correct play in diamonds would be to cash the ace and then duck the second round. This would cater for the more likely 3-1 break. With stoppers still held in all suits and only five diamond tricks needed, it would be sensible to duck a diamond (even at pairs).

Hand 38 : Dealer East : E-W vulnerable

NORTH
♠ J 10 7 6
♡ 4 2
♢ Q 7
♣ K Q 6 4 3

WEST
♠ A 9 3
♡ Q 9
♢ A 10 5 4 2
♣ 10 8 7

EAST
♠ 8 5 4 2
♡ K 10 8 6 5
♢ J 9 8
♣ J

SOUTH
♠ K Q
♡ A J 7 3
♢ K 6 3
♣ A 9 5 2

WEST	NORTH	EAST	SOUTH
		Pass	1NT
Pass	2♣	Pass	2♡
Pass	2NT	Pass	3NT
Pass	Pass	Pass	

Lead : ♢4. Normal fourth highest of long suit.

Play : With Q-x in dummy opposite K-x-x, declarer should play the queen at trick 1. When the queen holds the trick, declarer can count 7 tricks and needs to set up some spade winners. At trick 2, declarer should lead a spade to the king. If West takes this, cash the ♠Q on regaining the lead, then cash the clubs followed by dummy's spades and the ♡A. If West ducks the first spade, South should lead the ♠Q. If West ducks again, cross to the ♣K and lead the ♠J. With the ♠A with West, declarer is safe for 10 tricks.

Notes : (1) North should explore the spade game via 2♣ Stayman. With no spade fit revealed, invite game in no-trumps.
(2) With a good holding (K-Q) in responder's major and 17 points, South accepts the invitation.
(3) If declarer fails to play the ♢Q from dummy at trick 1, West's diamonds will be set up. When West comes in with the ♠A, West can cash out the remaining diamonds for one down.
(4) If declarer cashes out the clubs after winning the ♢Q, dummy has no entry to reach the spade winners later. Declarer must set up the spade winners and unblock the suit while dummy still has an entry. If it turns out that East holds the ♠A and returns a diamond, declarer can still succeed if the diamonds were 4-4 originally. If East has the ♠A and West has enough diamonds to defeat 3NT, tough luck.
(5) When cashing the clubs, declarer should unblock the ♣9 or discard a club on the spades. If not, the fourth round of clubs will be won in hand and declarer will be unable to reach the fifth club winner in dummy.

Hand 39 : Dealer South : Both vulnerable

NORTH
♠ K Q J 9 8 7 5
♡ A
♢ 5
♣ K 7 5 3

WEST
♠ 10 6
♡ 10 8 7 5
♢ Q 8 7 3 2
♣ J 10

EAST
♠ A 3
♡ 9 4 3 2
♢ J 10 9 4
♣ A Q 9

SOUTH
♠ 4 2
♡ K Q J 6
♢ A K 6
♣ 8 6 4 2

WEST	NORTH	EAST	SOUTH
			1♣
Pass	2♠	Pass	2NT
Pass	4NT	Pass	5♢
Pass	5♠	All pass	

Lead : ♢ J. Top of sequence is the most attractive start.

Play: North wins in dummy and should continue with the other top diamond on which the ace of hearts is discarded (jettison play). The K-Q-J of hearts follow, on which North discards three clubs. Only then is a trump led to the king and ace. On regaining the lead, North draws trumps and makes 11 tricks, losing 1 spade and 1 club.

Notes: (1) North is justified in making a jump shift with a self-sufficient suit and only four losers. If North bid 1♠ initially, it would still be necessary to check on aces after South rebids 1 NT.
(2) Even after the jump shift to 2♠, North should ask for aces over South's 2NT. A 4♠ rebid does not do justice to this powerhouse.
(3) South needs very little to make 6♠ an excellent slam. Most opening hands with two aces will give North good chances. For example, if South has ♠ 4 2 ♡ Q 7 5 2 ♢ A 8 4 ♣ A Q 6 2, 6♠ is likely to succeed and even with that minimum opening, the ♡ Q is wasted.
(4) If East were to lead a heart or ace and another spade, declarer should win ♡ A, cross to ♢ A and discard all four clubs on the ♢ K and the ♡ K-Q-J.
(5) The jettison play is superior to any other line, even in 4♠. To win the ♢ A, cash ♢ K and lead a trump is futile, while winning ♢ A, cashing ♢ K to discard a club and then leading a club to the king is hopeless in 5♠ and only a 50% chance even in 4♠.

Hand 40 : Dealer West : E-W vulnerable

NORTH
♠ 9 8 5
♡ A J 10 6
♢ Q 10
♣ J 5 3 2

WEST
♠ A Q 6 4
♡ 8 7
♢ J 6 3 2
♣ Q 6 4

EAST
♠ J 7 3 2
♡ Q 4
♢ A K 5 4
♣ A K 8

SOUTH
♠ K 10
♡ K 9 5 3 2
♢ 9 8 7
♣ 10 9 7

WEST	NORTH	EAST	SOUTH
Pass	Pass	1NT	Pass
2♣	Pass	2♠	Pass
4♠	Pass	Pass	Pass

Lead : ♣10. Neither major is attractive. The near-sequence in clubs appeals more than the rags in diamonds.

Play : Declarer should win in hand and tackle the spades. The correct play is to lead a low spade to the queen. When the queen wins, continue with the ♠ A. When the king drops, draw the last trump with the ♠ J. The correct play in the diamond suit is to cash the ace and king. As it happens the ♢ Q drops, so that the ♢ J draws the last diamond and declarer loses just two hearts, making 11 tricks.

Notes: (1) 3NT would be defeated on a heart lead (North wins ♡ A and continues with ♡ J). Responder should Stayman to explore a safer major suit game. In spades, West is worth 10 points and bids 4♠. If East did not show a spade suit, West would rebid 2NT.
(2) It would be an error to lead the ♠ J on the first round of spades. With only an 8-card suit, do not lead an honor card for a finesse unless you hold the card below it or you have a sequence of honors between you and dummy. If the ♠ J is led and South covers with the king, declarer has created a spade loser.
(3) After a low spade to the queen wins, it would be an error to return to hand to lead the ♠ J, since you do not hold the 10. If you did that, the ♠ K covers the jack and North's ♠ 9 is set up as a winner on the third round. The only legitimate chance for no loser with J-x-x-x opposite A-Q-x-x is to find K-doubleton onside.
(4) Similarly, do not lead the ♢ J for a finesse on the first or second round of diamonds, since you lack the 10. To play J-x-x-x opposite A-K-x-x for no losers, the only genuine chance is to play the A-K and hope the queen drops.

CHAPTER 11

DOUBLE FINESSES
Card Combinations Where Two Or Three Critical Cards Are Missing

There are several card combinations where more than one finesse is available within the same suit. Declarer may need to choose which finesse to take first. The standard technique to make the most tricks possible needs to be learnt. Later it will become necessary to judge when to depart from the standard technique on a particular hand.

1. The A-K-10 combination

With 8 cards or fewer where your aim is to lose no tricks: Lead low towards the A-K-10 and finesse the 10 if second player plays low.

A K 10
5 4 3

The chance for three tricks with this combination is only 25% and the recommended play works only when both honors are with West. This is a far better chance than any other play.

Dummy
A K 10 2
Q J 7   **9 8 6**
5 4 3

If you cannot afford to lose a trick, lead low towards dummy and play the 10 if West plays the 7. If West plays the jack or queen, win in dummy, return to hand in another suit and lead low towards A-10-2. If West plays low, finesse the 10.

However, if your object is to win only three tricks and you can afford one loser, it is better to cash the ace and king.

A K 10 2
Q 7 6   **J 9 8**
5 4 3

After ace and king, if no honor has dropped, play a third round and hope for a 3-3 break.

A K 10 2
Q 9 7 6   **J 8**
5 4 3

After ace and king, if an honor has dropped over the A-K-10, come to hand in another suit and lead

towards dummy's 10-2. This scores three tricks whenever the suit is 3-3 or when West began with Q-x-x-x or J-x-x-x. Note that finessing the 10 yields only two tricks on this layout.

When you hold 9 cards in the suit:

A K 10 3
Q 4   **J 9**
8 7 6 5 2

Cash the ace. If no honor drops, continue with the king. If the suit is 2-2, you have no loser.

A K 10 3
J   **Q 9 4**
8 7 6 5 2

If you cash the ace and an honor drops 'under' the A-K-10, continue with the king. You cannot capture J-x-x or Q-x-x sitting over the A-K-10.

A K 10 3
Q 9 4   **J**
J 9 4   **Q**
9 4   **Q J**
8 7 6 5 2

If you play the ace and an honor card drops 'over' the A-K-10, play that honor to be a singleton. Return to hand in another suit and lead towards the K-10-x, finessing the 10 when second player lays low. There are two combinations where the honor is singleton and finessing the 10 produces no loser. In only one case, the rarer Q-J doubleton, the finesse of the 10 loses a trick that might have been saved. Take the line with the greater winning chance. You need a powerful reason to play against a line that has a significantly superior chance.

When you hold 10 cards in the suit: Cash the ace. If the suit breaks 2-1 (78% of the time) you have no loser. If it breaks 3-0 (22%), you will lose a trick.

2. The A-Q-10 combination

With 8 cards or fewer: For no losers or for the maximum number of tricks, finesse the 10 first. If that wins or the 10 loses to the jack, finesse the queen later.

```
              A Q 10
    K J 7               9 8 5 2
              6 4 3
```

Lead low towards dummy and play the 10 if West plays low. Return to hand and lead low, finessing the queen if West does not play the king. You score three tricks whenever West has the king and jack. If you lead low and play the queen when West follows with the 7, you score only two tricks. Your best chance for three tricks is to finesse the 10 first.

```
              A Q 10
    K 7 2               J 9 8 5
              6 4 3
```

Lead low towards dummy and finesse the 10, losing the jack. Later lead from hand and finesse the queen. You score two tricks, the maximum possible when East holds one of the honors.

```
              A Q 10
    J 7 2               K 9 8 5
              6 4 3
```

Lead low towards dummy and finesse the 10. This loses to the king but it gives you two tricks, the maximum possible when East holds one honor.

Other considerations may make it desirable to finesse the queen first. If you need only two tricks and cannot afford to lose one, finesse the queen, not the 10. If you can afford a loser but need to keep East off lead, it may be necessary to finesse the queen first.

```
              A Q 10
    K 9 5                J 8 6
              7 4 3 2
```

If you need three tricks but cannot afford East to gain the lead, start by playing low towards dummy and finesse the queen. (Note that finessing the 10 allows East in.) Return to hand in another suit and lead low : if West plays the king, duck in dummy, but if West plays low, take your ace and play a third round. This will not work on all layouts but is your best chance for three tricks without letting East in.

With 9 or 10 cards: Finesse the queen first, not the 10 (assuming you have no knowledge about the location of the missing honors).

```
              A Q 10 6
    K 9                  J 2
              8 7 5 4 3
```

Lead low and finesse the queen. When no honor drops, continue with the ace. Note that finessing the 10 loses a trick.

```
              A Q 10 6
    K 9 2                 J
              8 7 5 4 3
```

Lead low and finesse the queen. When the jack drops, it is almost sure to be singleton. Return to hand in another suit, lead low towards dummy and finesse the 10. Note that finessing the 10 on the first round loses a trick.

If the finesse of the queen loses, should you play the ace next or finesse the 10? There is very little in it, but the odds slightly favour cashing the ace on the second round. You win when the suit breaks 2-2 but you lose when the layout is like this :

```
              A Q 10 6
    J 9 2                 K
              8 7 5 4 3
```

If you can afford to lose a trick, playing the ace first is a safety play (see Chapter 26) and gains a trick when the king is singleton offside.

```
              A Q 10 5 3
              8 7 6 4 2
```

Lead low and finesse the queen. This is the best chance for no loser.

3. The A-J-10 combination

The best chance to lose just one trick is to take two finesses : lead low to the jack first. If this loses, lead low towards the A-10 next, finessing the 10 if second player plays low. Even with 10 cards in the two hands, it is superior to finesse first rather than play the ace first.

```
              A J 10 4 3
    K Q 9                ---
              8 7 6 5 2
```

Lead low and finesse the jack if West plays low. If East were to win this, the ace would capture the remaining honor. Leading low to the jack saves a trick when West holds K-Q-9. Laying down the ace would give West two tricks.

Where you hold 9 cards, playing the ace first is only slightly inferior to the double finesse and should be adopted if there are entry problems which make it awkward to take two finesses.

With 6, 7 or 8 cards, finessing twice is the best chance to maximise your tricks.

```
              A J 10
              8 4 3
```

Lead low and finesse the jack. Assuming this loses, later lead low towards dummy and finesse the 10. The chance for a second trick is about 75%.

```
                 A J 10
       K 9 2                Q 7 6 5
       Q 9 2                K 7 6 5
       K Q 2                9 7 6 5
       9 6 2                K Q 7 5
                 8 4 3
```

In three of the four positions for the king and queen, the double finesse produces two tricks. Only when both honors sit over the A-J-10 will you lose two tricks.

4. The A-J-9 combination

Should you finesse the 9 first or the jack first?

```
a.                 A J 9
       K 10 7 3               Q 8 4
                   6 5 2
-------------------------------------------------
b.                 A J 9
       Q 10 7 3               K 8 4
                   6 5 2
-------------------------------------------------
c.                 A J 9
       K Q 7 3                10 8 4
                   6 5 2
-------------------------------------------------
d.                 A J 9
       10 7 4 3               K Q 8
                   6 5 2
```

The best chance for two tricks is to lead low towards dummy and finesse the 9. If this loses to the king or queen with East (situations a and b above), return to hand later and lead low, finessing the jack. You will score two tricks in layouts a and b and lose in c if West plays low. Finessing the jack first loses two tricks in a and b and scores two tricks only in c. Finessing the 9 is thus twice as likely to work as finessing the jack on the first round. Neither finesse avoids two losers in position d.

5. The K-Q-10 combination

With 10 cards, lead low to the king first. You will know the layout of the missing cards after this trick.

With 9 cards, lead low to the king first.

```
                 K Q 10 4
       A J 6                9
                 8 7 5 3 2
```

If the king wins, come to hand and lead low towards the Q-10. This holds the losers to one trick whenever this is possible. If the king loses to the ace, cash the queen next and hope the jack falls.

With fewer than 9 cards, lead low towards the honors and play the king if second hand plays low.

```
                 K Q 10
       J 4 3                A 9 7 6
                 8 6 5
```

If the king loses to the ace, you later lead from hand and finesse the 10. This scores two tricks if the position is as above.

If the king wins, you return to hand and lead low towards the Q-10. If second player plays low again, you have a problem: do you finesse the 10 or do you rise with the queen this time? If the ace is over the K-Q-10, it is good strategy for fourth player not to take the ace on the first round. It is clear that this sets up a finessing position with the Q-10. Thus, when the king holds on the first round, it does not mean the ace is necessarily on your left.

If the bidding indicates which opponent is likely to hold the ace, your task is easier.

```
                 K Q 10
       ??                    ??
                 6 5 4 3
```

You lead low to the king which wins. You return to hand and lead low. West follows low... Now what?

If you place the ace with West, rise with the queen. If the ace figures to be with East, finesse the 10. If the bidding has given no indication, the best shot is finesse the 10 on the second round.

```
                 K Q 10 7 3 2
                 4
```

If you can take only one finesse, either because you have only one card as above or only one entry, it is better to finesse the 10 on the first round to try to win the maximum number of tricks.

6. The K-J-x combination

```
                 K J 4
       ??                    ??
                 5 2
```

If you need only one trick, lead low towards the K-J-x and guess whether to finesse the jack or the king. If the bidding suggests the ace is on your left, play the king. If the ace is more likely to be with East, finesse the jack. Place the ace with the opponent who has shown more points in the bidding. If there are no clues from the bidding, you will just have to guess well.

If you are playing for the maximum number of tricks, finesse the jack on the first round.

K J 7

4 3 2

Lead low and finesse the jack. If this loses to the queen, come to hand later and lead low towards the king. You score a trick if West has the ace.

If the jack forced out the ace on the first round, you have a trick with the king. If the jack won on the first round, come to hand and lead to the king. You will score two tricks if West began with the ace and queen.

7. The K-10-9 combination

<pre>
            K 10 9
J 8 7 3   A Q 5
            6 4 2
</pre>

The best chance for one trick is to lead low from hand and finesse dummy's 9. Assuming this loses to the queen or jack, come to hand later and lead towards dummy's K-10, finesssing the 10 if West plays low. This line produces one trick 75% of the time, whenever West has Q, the J or the Q and J. Leading low to the king works only 50% of the time.

8. The Q-J-x and Q-10-x combinations

<pre>
            Q J 6
K 9 2   A 10 7 4
            8 5 3
</pre>

Lead low towards the Q-J-x and play the queen if West plays low. If this loses to East, play from hand later towards the J-x. Play the jack if West plays low. You score one trick 75% of the time, when West has the A, the K or the A and K.

<pre>
            Q 10 6
A J 7   K 9 4 3
            8 5 2
</pre>

Lead low from hand and finesse dummy's 10 if West plays low. If the 10 forces the king or ace from East, play from hand later towards dummy's Q-x. Play the queen if West plays low. You will score one trick if West holds K-and-J or A-and-J in the suit.

<pre>
            Q 10 9
J 7 4 3   A K 8
            6 5 2
</pre>

Where your holding is as strong as Q-10-9, lead low from hand and finesse dummy's 9 if West plays low. If this is taken by East's ace or king, play from hand later and finesse dummy's 10 if West plays low. You will score one trick if the jack is onside, regardless of the location of the ace and king.

NOTES

(1) Your card reading may indicate the location of the missing honors and that may influence you to play the above combinations in a different way. The recommended lines apply if you have no indication where the missing cards are.

(2) Where you are following the recommended line, do not lose your nerve. If the correct play is to finesse on the second round, take the finesse on the second round. The given lines may not always work but they work more often than other lines. Steel yourself and follow them through.

(3) The play of the above combinations refers to the suit in isolation. The play of a complete hand may require a different treatment of these combinations. Your decision may be affected by the number of tricks needed and whether you can afford to allow a particular opponent to gain the lead.

Knowing the correct way to handle various suit combinations is called 'technique' and it is a vital part of your bridge education. Knowing when to depart from the 'normal' play is called 'judgment'.

Here is a case in point :

NORTH
♠ A 6 4
♡ A Q J
♢ J 7 4 2
♣ 6 4 2

SOUTH
♠ 5 3 2
♡ K 9 8
♢ A K Q
♣ K 10 9 3

South is in 3 NT and West leads the king of spades. East shows out on the second round of spades. You have eight tricks and the ninth can come only from clubs. The best play for one trick is to finesse the 10 and later finesse the 9. Here this would be suicidal, as West has enough spades to take you two off if West gains the lead. Unblock your diamonds. cross to the hearts, cash the ♢ J and then lead a club to your king. If East has the ace, you make your game. Playing the king gives West only one chance to gain the lead. Finessing the 10 gives West three chances.

The same logic applies if South's clubs are K-J-x-x. Since you need only one club trick and you cannot afford to allow West in, you must play a club to your king, not to the jack. Low to the jack gives West two possible entries with the queen and the ace, playing to the king gives West only one chance to gain the lead.

PLAY HANDS ON DOUBLE FINESSES

Hand 41 : Dealer North : E-W vulnerable

WEST	NORTH	EAST	SOUTH
	1NT	Pass	2♣
Pass	2♠	Pass	4♠
Pass	Pass	Pass	

NORTH
♠ 8 7 4 3
♡ A 9
♢ A Q 3
♣ A K 5 2

WEST
♠ J 9
♡ K 8 3 2
♢ 10 9 8 5
♣ Q 10 9

EAST
♠ K 6 2
♡ Q J 10 6 5
♢ 7 6 2
♣ J 8

SOUTH
♠ A Q 10 5
♡ 7 4
♢ K J 4
♣ 7 6 4 3

Lead : ♡ Q. Normal top of sequence.

Play : North can see that there is an inevitable loser in hearts and one or two losers in clubs. North must play the spades for the maximum number of tricks. Win the ace of hearts and play a spade towards dummy, inserting the 10 when East plays low and losing to the jack. After regaining the lead, North leads a spade from hand and finesses the queen when East plays low. This finesse works and the last trump is drawn. When the clubs turn out to be 3-2, you set up the fourth club as a winner and lose 1 spade, 1 heart and 1 club.

Notes : (1) A heart lead would defeat 3NT. Even with a stopper in every suit, 3NT can be risky when holding a short suit. Therefore, with game-invitational values or better and a 4-card major, check via Stayman whether a 4-4 major fit exists. If so, choose the major suit game. If not, revert to no-trumps.

(2) As the cards lie, it would work to finesse the queen of spades first, but this could be an error. If it turned out that clubs were 4-1, so that there were two club losers, it would be vital not to lose a spade trick. The only hope for no spade loser is if both spade honors are with East and the 10 of spades is finessed on the first round of spades. This does not harm you if it turns out later that clubs were 3-2 after all.

(3) Do not falter and lose your nerve when it comes to taking the second spade finesse. Trust your knowledge of the best line of play and follow it through. If it turns out that West began with K-J doubleton in spades (so that playing the ace on the second round would have worked), this does not mean that your line of play was incorrect. It just means that it did not work this time although it will work more often in the long run than any other line. Consider it a temporary setback on the road to long-term success.

Hand 42 : Dealer East : Both vulnerable

WEST	NORTH	EAST	SOUTH
		1NT	Pass
3NT	Pass	Pass	Pass

NORTH
♠ J 6
♡ J 8 5 2
♢ Q 9 6 5
♣ K 9 2

WEST
♠ A 7 4
♡ 7 3
♢ 8 7 4
♣ A J 10 6 3

EAST
♠ K 9 3
♡ A Q 6 4
♢ A K 3 2
♣ 8 5

SOUTH
♠ Q 10 8 5 2
♡ K 10 9
♢ J 10
♣ Q 7 4

Lead : ♠5. Normal fourth highest of long suit.

Play : Win the king of spades and lead a club to the 10. North wins the king and returns a spade. On this round declarer could hold up and win the ace on the next round. A diamond to the ace is followed by a second club finesse, low to dummy's jack. When the second club finesse wins, declarer cashes the clubs and makes 2 spades, 1 heart, 2 diamonds and 4 clubs : 9 tricks.

Notes : (1) With 9 HCP and a 5-card suit, West is worth 3NT. A 2NT response would be too timid.

(2) East should not hold up on the first round of spades. A switch to hearts could be unwelcome.

(3) Do not win the first spade with dummy's ace. You want to be in hand to take the club finesse. In addition, if you do win ♠A and come to hand with a diamond to take the club finesse, the defense can thwart your plans by ducking the first club.

(4) After the second club finesse works and you have your four club tricks, do not take the heart finesse. You do not need the heart finesse for your contract. The heart finesse goes into the danger hand and if the heart finesse loses, South might be able to cash enough spades to defeat you.

Hand 43 : Dealer South : Nil vulnerable

NORTH
♠ A J 6 4
♡ 8 6 4
◇ K 9 5
♣ 7 6 3

WEST
♠ Q 10 9
♡ A K Q
◇ 8 6 3 2
♣ A K 9

EAST
♠ 7 5 3
♡ 10 9
◇ A Q 10 7 4
♣ J 5 4

SOUTH
♠ K 8 2
♡ J 7 5 3 2
◇ J
♣ Q 10 8 2

WEST	NORTH	EAST	SOUTH
			Pass
1NT	Pass	2NT	Pass
3NT	Pass	Pass	Pass

Lead: ♠4. Not wonderful but nothing else is appealing either. With no long suit and no 4-card suit with a sequence, prefer an unbid major to an unbid minor.

Play: South wins the king and returns the 8 of spades (top from the remaining doubleton). North wins and cashes two more spades. When declarer regains the lead, declarer must win the rest of the tricks. This entails losing no trick in diamonds. The best chance with nine cards and an A-Q-10 combination is to finesse the queen, not the 10. When declarer leads low to the queen, the finesse works and South drops the jack, obviously a singleton. Return to hand in another suit and repeat the diamond finesse. This brings in the game.

Notes: (1) With 7 HCP and a 5-card suit, East is worth 2NT. It would be wimpish to pass and futile to introduce the diamonds. With a balanced hand, a long minor and prospects for game but not slam, stick with no-trumps.
(2) There is no reason to depart from the normal best play with this diamond combination. Finessing the queen works if North holds K-x or K-x-x. Have no regrets if you take the correct play and it does not work (and certainly never criticise partner's play if an inferior line would have worked).

Hand 44 : Dealer West : N-S vulnerable

NORTH
♠ A Q 10 4
♡ A K 5 2
◇ Q J
♣ 4 3 2

WEST
♠ K J 6
♡ J 10 3
◇ 10 8 6
♣ A K 10 6

EAST
♠ 8
♡ 9 8 7 6
◇ 7 5 4 3 2
♣ Q 9 8

SOUTH
♠ 9 7 5 3 2
♡ Q 4
◇ A K 9
♣ J 7 5

WEST	NORTH	EAST	SOUTH
1♣	Double	Pass	2♠
Pass	4♠	All pass	

Lead: ♣K (or ace). An A-K suit is attractive in a trump contract.

Play: West cashes the two top clubs and East signals high-low to continue clubs. East wins the third club with the queen. East switches to diamonds. South wins and must lose no more tricks. South leads a spade and finesses dummy's 10 when West plays low. After the 10 wins, come to hand with the queen of hearts and lead another spade, finessing the queen when West plays the jack. Draw the last trump and claim 10 tricks.

Notes: (1) With both majors, North should double despite the poor diamond holding. 1NT with no club stopper cannot be recommended and even with a club stopper, double would be preferable when both majors are held. As partner will reply with a major as first choice, it is worth doubling and risking a diamond reply.
(2) With 10 points, South is too strong for 1♠ and should jump to 2♠. A 1♠ reply might be based on no points at all. A jump to 3♠ to show 10-12 points and a *five*-card suit is a sensible approach.
(3) Without a club lead, declarer could discard a club loser from either hand.
(4) Contrast declarer's play on this hand with the recommended play on Deal 43. There the diamond holding was equivalent to the spade holding here. Yet on 43, the correct play was to finesse the queen on the first round, while here the winning line is to finesse the 10. How can you account for this different approach?

This is the difference between technique and judgment. The correct technique with this holding is to finesse the queen, as in 43. However, the bidding on this deal should make declarer judge that West has both the king and jack and therefore the finesse of the 10 first is indicated. North-South have 26 HCP, so that East-West began with 14 HCP. After trick 3, East has turned up with the queen of clubs, 2 points, and so all the remaining high cards should be with West to justify the opening bid in first seat. Play an opening bid to have 12 HCP or more in normal circumstances, especially if the opening hand is balanced (which is indicated after it turns out that West started with only four clubs – if West is 4-4-4-1, declarer is bound to fail).

CHAPTER 12

DECLARER'S PLAY AT TRICK ONE

As declarer, you are often confronted with the problem whether to play high from dummy at trick 1 or whether to play low and let the lead run to your hand. There are many combinations which can be learnt by rote. Unfortunately there are very few general principles in this area.

Many combinations exist which look similar, yet the correct play differs. A slight variation in suit lengths or the position of honors can change the best play. Try to learn as many of the following combinations as possible and then test yourself again and again on the exercises until you are confident in this area. The play is given at no-trumps and is the same at a trump contract unless stated otherwise.

A. Dummy has king-doubleton

Dummy's cards are at the top, your cards are below and the card led in each case is the 3. Which card should you play from dummy?

1. K 6	2. K 6	3. K 6	4. K 6
7 5 4	10 5 4	J 5 4	J 4

5. K 6	6. K 6	7. K 6	8. K 6
Q 5 4	Q 10 4	A 10 4	A J 4

Answers :

1. K 6
**   7 5 4**
Play the king. You score a trick if West has the ace. In a trump contract the ace should be with East. Play low and hope East plays the ace. If West is a weak player and might lead away from an ace, play the king.

2. K 6
**   10 5 4**
Play the king. You make one trick if West has the ace. In a trump contract East figures to have the ace — play low.

3. K 6
**   J 5 4**
Play low from dummy. This play guarantees one trick no matter where the ace and the queen are.

a.
```
              K 6
A Q 8 3 2              10 9 7
              J 5 4
```
----

b.
```
               K 6
A 10 8 3 2             Q 9 7
               J 5 4
```

c.
```
               K 6
Q 10 8 3 2            A 9 7
               J 5 4
```
----

d.
```
               K 6
10 8 7 3 2           A Q 9
               J 5 4
```

Playing the king from dummy will yield a trick for you in a, b and d. Playing low from dummy produces a trick for you in every case.

4. K 6
**   J 4**
Play low from dummy. It is a guess in no-trumps whether to play the king or whether to play low, but you may as well play low. With a choice of two suits, West would be less likely to lead from the suit with the ace. In a suit contract, it is clearcut to play low as the ace is almost certainly with East.

5. K 6
**   Q 5 4**
Play the king. You have one trick whatever you do. If the king loses to the ace, it is normally best to duck the next round at no-trumps (hold-up play). If the king wins, West is marked with the ace on a layout like this:

```
              K 6
A J 9 3 2             10 8 7
              Q 5 4
```

You have Q-5 left which is a stopper if West gains the lead. Try to develop any extra tricks needed without allowing East to gain the lead.

In a trump contract, East figures to have the ace, so that you may as well play low from dummy. Some Easts might play the ace and give you two tricks.

6. K 6
**   Q 10 4**
Play low. You have one trick for sure. Playing low guarantees two tricks wherever the ace and the jack are. If East plays the ace, your king and queen are high; if East plays low, your 10 wins and the K + Q will yield a second trick; if East plays the jack, your queen wins and your K + 10 will produce a second trick.

RULE 1 : If dummy holds an honor and declarer holds honor + 10, play low from dummy and let the lead come round to your honor-10. This either guarantees an extra trick or is your best chance for an extra trick.

7. **K 6**
A 10 4
Play low (Rule 1). You have two tricks already. You will score a third trick if West has led from a Q-J suit.

8. **K 6**
A J 4
Play low. This guarantees three tricks. If East plays low, you win the jack; if East plays the queen, you win the ace and your K + J are both winners.

B. Dummy has three or more cards including the king

West leads the 3. Which card do you play from dummy?

9. K 6 5	**10.** K J 6	**11.** K 10 5	**12.** K 10 5
Q 4	10 5 4	A 9 4	A 8 4

13. K 10 9	**14.** K 7 6	**15.** K J 5	**16.** K Q 6
A 5 4	5 4	A 6 4	A 10 5 4

RULE 2: If it is correct to play low from dummy with honor doubleton, it is correct to play low from dummy where dummy has honor to three or longer.

For example, in 3, 4, 5, 6, 7, 8, if dummy has three or more cards including the king, playing low is still correct.

9. **K 6 5**
Q 4
Play low from dummy. If West has the ace, you score two tricks. Same applies with Q-x-x or longer in hand.

10. **K J 6**
10 5 4
Play low. This guarantees two tricks if West has led from the queen. Without the 10 in hand, play the jack from dummy.

11. **K 10 5**
A 9 4
Play low. You have two tricks. If West has led from the queen or jack, you can make three tricks. If East plays low, your 9 is the third trick. If East plays an honor, win the ace and sooner or later you can finesse dummy's 10. This will be your third trick if West has the other honor. The same applies if you hold A-9 doubleton and need a third trick.

12. **K 10 5**
A 8 4
Play low. You have two tricks. If West has led from a Q-9 suit or from a J-9 suit, you can score three tricks.

K 10 5
J 9 7 3 2   **Q 6**
A 8 4

West leads the 3, the 5 from dummy: if East plays low, your 8 is the third trick; if East plays the queen, you win the ace and sooner or later you can finesse dummy's 10 for the third trick.

13. **K 10 9**
A 5 4
Play the 9 (or 10). You have two tricks. If the 9 wins, you have three tricks. If East plays an honor, take it with your ace. Sooner or later you can finesse dummy's 10. This will give you a third trick if West has the other honor.

14. **K 7 6**
5 4
Play low in no-trumps unless you need this trick urgently. If West has the ace, you can still score your king later. By playing low East wins the trick and the K-7 in dummy is still a stopper with East on lead.

If you do need to win this trick urgently, play the king (but only at no-trumps) and hope West has led from the ace. In a suit contract, play low. The ace is almost certainly with East, so that you cannot gain a trick by putting up the king.

The same applies in a suit contract if West leads the queen or jack and you have K-x-x or longer in dummy and nothing of value in hand. Play low from dummy. The ace is on your right and you cannot gain by losing your king to the ace. Playing low could gain if the layout is something like these:

K 7 6
Q J 10 9 8 3   **A 2**
5 4

By playing low twice from dummy, the king can be set up as a winner. If you play the king on West's queen lead, you score no tricks. The more cards you hold, the better the chance that the ace will be short.

K 7 6 4
Q J 10 9 5   **A**
8 3 2

The queen is led. If you play the king, you have no tricks. Play low and the king does become a trick.

15. **K J 5**
A 6 4
Play the jack. You have two tricks. Playing the jack scores a third trick if West has the queen. If East has the queen, you were not due for a third trick anyway. You could delay the jack finesse by playing low from dummy, winning your ace and finessing the jack later, when it suits you. The advantage of finessing now is that if the queen covers, you do not lose the lead. However, playing low may work if East plays the queen anyway or has queen singleton, or if you need two entries to dummy in this suit later. If you play the jack and the queen covers, it could be prudent to duck as a hold-up play.

16. **K Q 6**
A 10 5 4
Play low (Rule 1). You have three winners. This guarantees you four tricks whatever East plays.

RULE 3 : Where you have equivalent (touching) cards in dummy and in hand, the correct play is the same if those cards are interchanged.

For example, what is the correct play from dummy for each of these holdings if West leads the 3?

17.	Q 6	18.	Q 6	19.	A 6
	K 5 4		K 10 4		K 10 4

20.	A 6	21.	Q 6 5	22.	K 10 6
	K J 4		K 4		J 5 4

23.	K 9 5	24.	A 10 5	25.	A 10 9
	A 10 4		K 8 4		K 5 4

26.	A J 5	27.	A Q 6	28.	A K 6
	K 6 4		K 10 5 4		Q 10 5 4

Answers :

17. Queen in no-trumps, low in suit — same as 5.
18. Play low — same as 6.
19. Play low — same as 7.
20. Play low — same as 8.
21. Play low — same as 9.
22. Play low — same as 10.
23. Play low — same as 11.
24. Play low — same as 12.
25. Play the 9 — same as 13.
26. Play the jack — same as 15.
27. Play low — same as 16.
28. Play low — same as 16.

C. Dummy has the queen and no higher honor

West leads the 3. Which card should you play from dummy?

29.	Q 5	30.	Q 5	31.	Q 6 5
	A 4		A 6 4		A 7 4

32.	Q 6	33.	Q 6	34.	Q 6 5
	A J 4		A 10 4		A 10 4

35.	Q 5	36.	Q 6 5	37.	Q 6
	A 9 4		A 9 4		J 5 4

38.	Q 10 4	39.	Q 10 6	40.	Q 10
	K 6		A 5		A 5 4

Answers :

29. Play the queen. You score a second trick if West holds the king.

30. Play the queen. Same as for 29.

31. **Q 6 5**
A 7 4 *Play the queen if you need a second trick quickly* (the queen will win if West has the king). Play low if there is no urgency for a second trick. After the ace wins, you still have the Q-6 stopper in dummy. You will score a second trick later if West holds the king.

32. **Q 6**
A J 4 Play the queen. You have two tricks anyway. If the queen is covered by the king, you score only two tricks. However, if West has the king, the queen wins and your A-J operates as a further double stopper if West gains the lead. If West does lead the suit again (West may be unable to tell whether you started with A-J-x or with A-x-x), you end up with three tricks in the suit. With A-J left, you will try to develop *extra* tricks in other suits by keeping East off lead.

33. **Q 6**
A 10 4 Play low. You have one sure trick and by playing low you *guarantee* a second trick. If East plays low, your 10 is the second trick; if East plays the king, your Q is high (whether you take your ace or whether you elect to hold up); if East plays the jack, win your ace — now your Q opposite the 10-4 will produce another trick.

34. **Q 6 5**
A 10 4 Play low — same as 33. **Rule 2 :** If low from Q-x was correct, the best play is the same with Q-x-x or longer.

35. **Q 5**
A 9 4 Play the queen. You started with one trick. Your best chance for a second trick is if West has the king. If you play low and East plays the 10 or J, you cannot score a second trick.

36. **Q 6 5**
A 9 4 If you need a second trick at once, play the queen and hope West has the king. However, the normal move is to play low and capture East's card. Dummy's Q-6 is still protected and you can make a second trick later if West has the king. You also score a second trick if West has led from the J-10 in a position like this :

```
              Q 6 5
J 10 7 3                K 8 2
              A 9 4
```

West leads the 3 and the 5 is played from dummy. Whatever East plays, you make two tricks. Note also that if West leads the jack in this layout, you can acquire a double stopper by playing low from both hands. Then, if West continues with the 10, cover with the queen (promoting your 9) and if West continues with a low card, play low from dummy.

37. **Q 6**
J 5 4 Play low. You began with no trick, but playing low guarantees you one trick whatever East plays.

Q 6

K 9 7 3 2   A 10 8

J 5 4

If you play the queen (wrongly), you normally end up with no tricks, as in the above layout. Note that if dummy has Q-x-x or Q-x-x-x or longer, it is still correct to play low (Rule 2).

38. Q 10 4   Play the 10. You began with one
    K 6   trick. This produces two tricks if West holds the jack or the ace.

39. Q 10 6   Play the 10. You started with one
    A 5   trick. This produces a second trick if West holds the jack or the king. In addition, if the 10 forces the king, you can hold up with the queen later. If West has K + J and your 10 wins, West may fear to lead the suit later in case this gives you an extra trick.

40. Q 10   It is a guess whether to play the Q
    A 5 4   or the 10. If you can tell that West has precisely a 4-card suit, a strong player is more reluctant to lead from J-x-x-x than K-x-x-x, so play the queen. In a trump contract, a weaker player is less likely to lead from the king, so play the 10.

D. Dummy has the jack

West leads the 3. Which card should you play from dummy?

41.	**J 5**	**42.**	**J 5**
	A K 4		**A 7 6**

43.	**J 5**	**44.**	**J 5 4**
	A 10 6		**A 9 6**

41. J 5   Play the jack. You have two
    A K 4   tricks. The jack will be your third trick if West has the queen. The jack is also the correct card with J-x-x opposite A-K-x.

42. J 5   Play the jack. You have one trick.
    A 7 6   The only chance for a second trick here is if West has K + Q, for example, if West has led from K-Q-8-3-2. Even with A-9-x in hand opposite J-x, the jack is the card to play.

43. J 5   Play low. You have one trick.
    A 10 6 Playing low *guarantees* a second trick. If East plays low, you score the 10. If East plays an honor, capture it so that your J opposite 10-x produces another trick against their remaining honor. Note that if dummy has J-x-x or J-x-x-x or longer, playing low is still correct opposite A-10 or A-10-x or longer (Rule 2).

44. J 5 4   Play low. You have one trick. Your
    A 9 6   best chance for a second trick is if West began with K-10 or Q-10.

J 5 4

Q 10 7 3   K 8 2

A 9 6

West leads the 3, dummy's 4 is played. If East plays the 8, you make the 9. If East plays the king, take it and dummy's J-x over West's queen will become a second trick later.

J 9 4

A 6 5

When the 9 is in dummy and West leads low, the approach is similar. Play dummy's 9. Again, if West has Q-10 or K-10 in the suit led, you can score two tricks. The 9 will force East's honor which you can capture. Dummy's remaining J-x over West's honor can produce a second trick later. (With J-9 *doubleton* in dummy opposite A-x-x, play the jack, not the 9.)

E. Dummy has the 10

West leads the 3. Which card should you play from dummy?

45.	**10 5**	**46.**	**10 5**
	A K 6		**A Q 6**

47.	**10 5**	**48.**	**10 5**
	K Q 6		**K J 6**

45. 10 5   Play the 10. You have two tricks.
    A K 6   Your 10 will be a third trick if West has led from the Q-J.

Note the play with 10-x(-x) opposite A-K-9 :

10 5

Q 8 7 3 2   J 6 4

A K 9

West leads the 3. Even though the 10 and 9 are equals, play the 10. If you play low and East plays the jack, West will know that you hold the 9. With J-9-x, East would play the 9 if dummy plays low. If you play the 10 and East covers with the jack, West cannot tell who has the 9. Try to keep East off lead as you develop extra tricks and if West comes in and leads the suit again, you score a third trick.

46. 10 5   Play the 10. You have two tricks
    A Q 6   after the lead. If West has led from a K-J suit, the 10 will win. Your A-Q is then a double stopper against West. You will try to develop extra tricks without letting East in, if possible.

```
              10 5
K 8 7 3 2              J 6 4
              A Q 9
```

West leads the 3. Even though the 10 and 9 are equals, play the 10. If you play low and East plays the jack, West knows you hold the 9 (as in 45 on page 77). If you play the 10, covered by the jack, West cannot tell who has the 9. After you win the queen, try to keep East off lead. If West gets in and leads the suit again, you score a third trick with the 9. The same applies if dummy has 10-x-x.

47. 10 5 Play the 10. You have one trick.
K Q 6 You can score a second trick if West has the jack or East has the ace. This applies also if dummy has 10-x-x. With 10-9-x opposite K-Q-x, play the 10 or 9 if West leads low. This guarantees a second trick.

48. 10 5 Play low. You have one trick. By
K J 6 playing low you will score a second trick if East plays the queen.

```
              10 5
A 9 8 3 2              Q 7 4
              K J 6
```

West leads the 3, low from dummy, queen from East, taken by the king and declarer has a second trick later. However, had the 10 been played from dummy and covered by the queen, declarer can be held to just one trick. Likewise, it is correct to play low from 10-x-x opposite K-J-x (Rule 2).

F. Dummy has the ace

West leads the 3. Which card should you play from dummy?

49.	A 8	50.	A K 4
	Q 6 5		J 5
51.	A Q 4	52.	A Q 4
	J 5		10 5
53.	A J 4	54.	A J 4
	K 10 6		K 9 6
55.	A 10 4	56.	A K 10 4
	J 6		9 5

49. A 8 Play low. You have one trick. By
Q 6 5 playing low you guarantee a second trick, no matter who has the king.

50. A K 4 Play low. You have two tricks.
J 5 The jack will be a third trick if West has the queen. In a suit contract, you might wish to play high in dummy rather than risk losing a trick. However, if you need an extra trick or can afford a loser, you may still decide to play low.

51. A Q 4 Play low. You have two tricks. If
J 5 West has the king, you will score three tricks. Your jack will win now and sooner or later you can finesse dummy's queen.

52. A Q 4 Play low. You have one trick. The
10 5 best chance for extra tricks is to play low from dummy.

```
              A Q 4
K J 7 3 2              9 8 6
              10 5
```

If West has the K + J, you score three tricks. West leads the 3, you duck in dummy and win the 10. Later you can finesse dummy's queen.

```
              A Q 4
K 9 7 3 2              J 8 6
              10 5
```

West leads the 3, low in dummy and East wins the jack. Later you finesse the queen to score two tricks.

```
              A Q 4
J 9 7 3 2              K 8 6
              10 5
```

West leads the 3, low from dummy and East wins the king. Dummy has two winners. Note that playing the queen at trick 1 restricts you to one trick.

```
              A Q 4
9 8 6 3 2              K J 8
              10 5
```

West leads the 3, low from dummy and East wins the jack. With East holding both the king and jack, you cannot score two tricks. However, when East wins the jack, East cannot continue the suit. Dummy's A-Q is a double stopper against East. Had you played the queen from dummy, East could win the king and continue with the jack to force out the ace and thus set up West's suit.

A Q 4 In a trump contract if you need *two* tricks
10 5 from this suit *and cannot afford to lose a trick,* finesse the queen instead of playing low. That is your best chance for two tricks *without losing a trick.*

53. A J 4 Play low or play the jack. This
K 10 6 *guarantees* you a third trick in the suit no matter who has the queen.

54. **A J 4** Play low. You have two tricks.
K 9 6 Playing low will gain a third trick unless East has the queen and the 10. If East plays low, your 9 wins. If East plays the Q, you take it and dummy's cards are high. If East plays the 10, take it and finesse dummy's jack later. If West has the queen, you have your third trick later.

55. **A 10 4** Play low. You have one trick.
J 6 The best chance for a second trick is to play low and hope West has one honor. If West has K + Q, your jack is your second trick. If East plays an honor, you can finesse later against the other honor with West. If dummy has plenty of entries, you can play low from hand. The advantage of keeping the jack concealed is that East might return the suit for you. If you unblock the jack, East might make a damaging switch. However, if dummy is short of entries you may have to unblock your jack so that you can lead low to the 10 later.

56. **A K 10 4** Play low in no-trumps. You
9 5 have two tricks. If West has both the Q + J, you have a third trick.

A K 10 4
Q 8 7 3 2   **J 6**
9 5

West leads the 3, low from dummy and East wins. Later you can finesse dummy's 10 for a third trick if West has the other honor.

In a trump contract, you would normally win in dummy to avoid any loser in this suit. However, if you can afford a loser and wish to play for a third trick, play low from dummy. If East wins, you can try a finesse of dummy's 10 later.

G. West leads an honor

West leads the king. Do you take the ace or duck with these holdings?

| **57.** **J 6 4** | **58.** **J 6 4** |
| **A 5 2** | **A 10 2** |

| **59.** **8 6** | **60.** **A 2** |
| **A J 2** | **J 10 3** |

57. **J 6 4** Capture the king. West's king lead
A 5 2 signifies the queen as well. Dummy's J-6 over West's queen operates as a second stopper and will be a second trick later. It is true that if you duck and West leads the suit again, you also have your second trick. However, if West does not play the suit again (and East no doubt will make a discouraging signal), you will score just one trick instead of two.

58. **J 6 4** Capture the king. Your J-6 and
A 10 2 10-2 will produce a second trick later as only the queen is outstanding.

59. **8 6**
K Q 10 9 7   **5 4 3**
A J 2

Play low from hand if you can afford West to switch. This duck with A-J-x after West leads the king (or queen) is known as the 'Bath Coup'. Your remaining A-J is a double stopper against West. If West continues the suit, you have two tricks. If West switches, you have retained a stopper in the suit. However, if a switch is even more dangerous to you, capture the king and then try to keep East off lead (as a lead by East through your remaining J-x could be disastrous).

60. **A 2** Capture the king. Your remaining
J 10 3 J-10 guarantees you a second trick, as the ace and king have gone.

61. **K 10 4** If West leads the queen, play low
A 6 3 from dummy and capture it in hand. You began with only two tricks but West's lead has given you a third trick, assuming the lead is from a Q-J suit. You can score a third trick by finessing dummy's 10 when it suits you. With K-10-x in dummy and A-x in hand, you can likewise score a third trick if West leads the queen from a Q-J sequence. In a trump contract, the third trick may provide a useful discard.

62. **K 6** If West leads the queen (or jack),
10 9 4 cover the honor with your king. This will provide one trick. Either the king will win or, if East captures the king, your 10-9 will yield a trick later against their remaining honor.

63. **Q 9 4** If West leads the jack (from some
A 6 2 J-10 sequence), cover with the queen. Either the queen wins or if East covers with the king, you capture it and your 9-4 over West's presumed 10 is a second trick later.

64. **Q 4** If West leads the jack, cover
A 9 8 with the queen. This guarantees a second trick. Either the queen wins or, if East covers, capture the king, leaving you with 9-8 which will set up a trick later against their 10.

H. West leads a suit bid by East

When West leads a suit bid by East, you can frequently diagnose the location of the critical cards. An honor lead denies the next higher honor and a 9 lead denies the 10 or a higher honor (normally).

65. **Q 7 4**

K 9 3

West leads the 10 in a suit bid by East. Which cards does East hold? How should you play at trick 1?

Play the queen. You have one trick. The 10 lead denies the jack so that East can be expected to hold A-J-x-x-x. If East ducks your queen, your king will be a second trick later. If East takes the queen, you can confidently finesse your 9 when the suit is led next. If you play low in dummy, East can also play low, restricting you to one trick in the suit.

If West had led the jack, you have to judge whether West is likely to have J-10-x or J-x. The latter is more likely, giving East A-10-x-x-x. Accordingly, it is best to play the queen from dummy and finesse the 9 later.

66. **J 4 2**

A K 8

West leads the 9 in a suit bid by East. Who holds the queen? The 10? How should you plan the play?

The 9 lead marks East with Q-10-x-x-x at least. Play the jack. You have two tricks. If your assessment is correct, this play will give you three tricks. If East covers the jack with the queen, capture it with the ace. Your remaining K-8 tenace over East's 10 will provide two more tricks. You can safely finesse the 8 at your leisure. If you play low from dummy at trick 1, East will play low too, and you can score only two tricks.

67. **A 4 2**

K 10 3

West leads the jack in a suit bid by East. Who holds the queen? How should you plan the play?

Capture the jack with dummy's ace. The jack lead marks East with the queen. Your remaining K-10 tenace will produce two more tricks, since you can finesse your 10 whenever you feel like it.

68. **K 10 3**

Q 5 4

West leads the 9 in a suit bid by East. Who holds the ace? The jack? How should you plan the play?

The layout will be something like this :

```
          K 10 3
    9 6              A J 8 7 2
          Q 5 4
```

Play dummy's king. The 9 lead marks East with A-J-x-x-x at least. If you play low from dummy, East also plays low, retaining the A-J over the king. If you then duck, the suit is continued and East's long cards are set up. If you play low in dummy and capture the 9 with the queen, you are in trouble if West gains the lead and leads the suit again. East then scores four tricks.

If you play dummy's 10 on the 9, East should play the jack and you have the same problems.

Playing the king looks odd but it gives you a second stopper. If East plays low, your queen will be a second trick later. If East takes the king with the ace, East must switch (and you still have a stopper in the suit) or if East leads the suit back, you would play low from hand, allowing dummy's 10 to give you a second trick and still keeping your queen as a stopper. It is worth analysing each play with this combination particularly because it does not appear to be a natural play from dummy.

EXERCISE ON CARD PLAY AT TRICK 1

A. In each case, the contract is no-trumps, dummy is the top hand, declarer is the lower hand and West's lead is the 4. Which card should declarer play from dummy?

1.	K 6	2.	K 6	3.	K 6	4.	K 6	5.	K 6	6.	K 6
	8 3		10 8 3		J 8 3		Q 8 3		Q 10 3		A 10 3

7.	A 9 2	8.	A J 5	9.	A J 9	10.	A J 6	11.	J 6 3	12.	J 9 3
	K 10 3		Q 3		6 3		9 3		A 9		A 6

13.	Q 6	14.	Q 6	15.	Q 6	16.	Q 6	17.	Q 6 3	18.	Q 6 3
	10 5 3		J 5 3		A 5 3		A 10 3		A 10		A 9 5

19.	10 6	20.	J 6	21.	10 6	22.	J 6	23.	J 6	24.	10 6
	A K 3		A K 3		K Q 3		A 3 2		A 10 2		A Q 2

HANDS ON DECLARER'S PLAY AT TRICK 1

Hand 45 : Dealer North : Both vulnerable

NORTH
♠ K 7 4 2
♡ A 10 9 3
◇ 9 4
♣ 6 5 2

WEST
♠ Q J 9 5 3
♡ 7
◇ Q 8 7 5
♣ K J 4

EAST
♠ A 10 8
♡ 5 2
◇ K J 6 3
♣ 10 9 8 7

SOUTH
♠ 6
♡ K Q J 8 6 4
◇ A 10 2
♣ A Q 3

WEST	NORTH	EAST	SOUTH
	Pass	Pass	1♡
1♠	2♡	2♠	4♡
Pass	Pass	Pass	

Lead : ♠ Q. Normal top of a near sequence.

Play : If declarer wrongly plays the king of spades from dummy on the first or second lead of spades, the contract should fail, losing one spade, one diamond and two clubs when the club finesse is off. The correct play is to duck the queen of spades and duck the spade continuation, ruffing in hand. Draw trumps, ending in dummy, and lead a *low* spade, ruffing East's ace. The king of spades is now a winner. Just as well you did not squander it earlier. Play ace and another diamond and after ruffing a diamond in dummy, discard a club loser on the king of spades. This secures your game and if the club finesse were to succeed as well, this line would give you 11 tricks.

Notes : (1) West should overcall 1♠. The suit is respectable and the 1-level overcall promises no more than 8-15 HCP, a good suit and 8 losers or better.
(2) East should readily support partner's overcall with a top honor in the suit.
(3) With 19 points (3 for the singleton) South is worth a shot at game. A raise to the 2-level usually includes two cover cards. As South has 5 losers, this should reduce the losers to 3. Note that, to succeed, South has to make the ♠ K into a winner (a 'cover card', that is, a card which covers one of declarer's losers).
(4) Do not play an honor which cannot win the trick (unless playing the honor helps to build up a winner later).
(5) If West switches after trick 1, say to a diamond, declarer should win and lead a trump to dummy's 9, ruff a low spade, cross back to dummy with a trump to the 10 and again ruff a low spade. This sets up the ♠ K for a club discard later.

Hand 46 : Dealer East : Nil vulnerable

NORTH
♠ 8 6 3
♡ 10 4
◇ 8 7 5 3
♣ A 9 8 2

WEST
♠ A K Q 10 4 2
♡ K 8 3
◇ 4 2
♣ K Q

EAST
♠ 9 7 5
♡ Q 9 2
◇ K Q 6
♣ 7 6 5 4

SOUTH
♠ J
♡ A J 7 6 5
◇ A J 10 9
♣ J 10 3

WEST	NORTH	EAST	SOUTH
		Pass	1♡
Double	Pass	1NT	Pass
4♠	Pass	Pass	Pass

Lead: ♡ 10. It is normal to lead partner's suit and the 10 is correct, top from a doubleton. That turns out to be an unfortunate choice in this case, but in the long run leading partner's suit is best.

Play: Declarer should play dummy's *queen* of hearts on the 10 at trick 1. After South takes the ace, West is left with the K-8 tenace over South's J-7-6-5. Whenever hearts are led next, declarer finesses the 8 and this marked finesse will hold the heart losers to one. This is vital as the three aces are inescapable losers.

Notes : (1) South has an absolute minimum but just worth an opening with the J-10 combinations.
(2) Double-then-bid-your-suit shows this strength (16-18 points, 5-6 losers) when strong jump overcalls are not used.
(3) The 1NT response shows 6-9 points plus a stopper in their suit. It normally denies a 4-card unbid major.
(4) With length in hearts, 3NT by West is a reasonable alternative to 4♠.
(5) North's *ten* of hearts lead marks the jack with South and so dummy's 9 of hearts and West's 8 of hearts become highly significant. By playing the queen, West utilises the knowledge about the location of the jack of hearts. If West plays low from dummy, South plays the 7, *not the ace.* Later North will gain the lead with the ace of clubs and another heart gives the defense two heart tricks, plus the minor suit aces.

Hand 47 : Dealer South : N-S vulnerable

NORTH
- ♠ A 5
- ♡ A 8 7
- ◇ A Q 10 7 4
- ♣ K 6 2

WEST	EAST
♠ J 10 9 7	♠ 8 4 2
♡ Q J 9 3	♡ 10 6 5
◇ 6 5	◇ K 3
♣ 10 9 4	♣ A J 8 7 3

SOUTH
- ♠ K Q 6 3
- ♡ K 4 2
- ◇ J 9 8 2
- ♣ Q 5

WEST	NORTH	EAST	SOUTH
			Pass
Pass	1NT	Pass	2♣
Pass	2◇	Pass	3NT
Pass	Pass	Pass	

Lead : ♣7. Unless partner has bid a suit or the opponents have bid your suit, it is normal to lead your long suit.

Play : Declarer should play the *queen* of clubs from dummy. When this wins, the diamond finesse is taken (lead the jack, 9 or 8 and let it run, keeping the lead in dummy if the finesse is working). In with the king of diamonds, East cannot continue clubs without giving declarer a second club trick. By playing the queen of clubs at trick 1, North has K-x, a stopper in clubs against East, the 'safe hand'. If East switches after winning the king of diamonds, declarer has ten tricks. A club continuation would give North eleven tricks.

Notes : (1) Use Stayman with a 4-card major plus a short suit (doubleton or shorter) and prospects for game. South intends to bid 4♠ over a 2♠ reply and 3NT over any other reply.
(2) It would be fatal for declarer to play low from dummy at trick 1 : West plays the 9 (the cheaper of touching cards when playing third-hand-high) and East's club tricks will be set up and ready to cash when in with the king of diamonds.
(3) If the queen of clubs had been captured by West, declarer should duck the next club and win king of clubs on the third round as a hold-up play. Then cash the ace of diamonds rather than finessing as a safety play in case East has the king of diamonds singleton. North does not need five diamond tricks for the contract and if West has the king of diamonds, West is probably out of clubs, thanks to the hold-up.

Hand 48 : Dealer West : E-W vulnerable

NORTH
- ♠ J 10 5 3
- ♡ Q 8
- ◇ Q 8 7 3 2
- ♣ K 8

WEST	EAST
♠ A 4	♠ K 8 7
♡ 9 6 5	♡ K J 4
◇ K 10	◇ A 6 5 4
♣ A J 10 9 3 2	♣ Q 5 4

SOUTH
- ♠ Q 9 6 2
- ♡ A 10 7 3 2
- ◇ J 9
- ♣ 7 6

WEST	NORTH	EAST	SOUTH
1♣	Pass	2NT	Pass
3NT	Pass	Pass	Pass

Lead : ♡3. Normal lead. There is no reason to choose spades rather than hearts.

Play : North plays the queen of hearts but declarer plays low, a form of hold-up play. A low heart is continued but declarer is safe whether South wins this or ducks. When East takes the club finesse into the North hand, North is out of hearts and declarer comes home with two spades, one heart, two diamonds and five clubs, 10 tricks.

Notes : (1) A 2NT response is preferable to a minor suit reply if the hand is suitable for no-trumps. If East bid 1◇, West would rebid 2♣ and East would then jump to 3NT.
(2) With a semi-balanced hand and no major, West should rebid 3NT, not 3♣ which would suggest an unbalanced hand or slam prospects.
(3) If East takes North's queen of hearts with the king, an instinctive almost reflex move, 3NT will be defeated. When the club finesse loses, the heart return through declarer's J-x gives South four heart tricks.
(4) As the club finesse has to be taken into North, it is North who is the 'danger hand'. Therefore the hold-up manoeuvre of ducking the queen of hearts is adopted. Note that declarer makes one heart trick whether declarer wins the first heart or ducks it. The decision hinges on which opponent is likely to gain the lead early. If North, duck the first heart. If North has a third heart to return later, this would mean that South had started with only four hearts. Therefore, the defense could take only three hearts and one club anyway.
(5) If the club finesse had to be taken into the South hand, declarer would take the first heart. That would leave East with J-x in hearts, a stopper against South.

CHAPTER 13

RUFFING LOSERS — DELAYING TRUMPS

Recollecting our earliest days of bridge, we can hear someone's voice saying "Draw trumps. You must draw trumps." This is sound advice and on most hands it is good technique to draw trumps early. It is a shattering blow to have one of your winners ruffed when you could have saved this trick by drawing trumps first.

Nevertheless, there are occasions when drawing trumps must be delayed. If you have more losers than you can afford, you may be able to eliminate some losers by ruffing them in dummy or by discarding them on dummy's excess winners. When discarding losers is the correct approach, it is often a race between declarer and the defenders. Will declarer have the discard in time? Will the defenders cash their tricks first? In these cases, it is sound to draw trumps if you can do so without losing the lead, but if you have to give up the lead in trumps, it may be wiser to go after the discards first.

Take these hands for example :

NORTH
♠ 10 5
♡ 8 6 4
♢ A K 7 2
♣ 9 8 4 3

SOUTH
♠ K Q J 7 3 2
♡ A 5 2
♢ Q
♣ J 10 7

South is playing in 2♠ after 1♠ : 1NT, 2♠. West leads the queen of hearts. How should South plan the play?

If South wins the ace and leads trumps, the defense can win and cash two hearts and three clubs for one down. Correct is to win ♡ A, lead ♢ Q to the king and discard a loser on the ♢ A first.

NORTH
♠ 10 5 4 2
♡ A K Q
♢ 8 7 2
♣ 6 4 2

SOUTH
♠ K Q J 7 6 3
♡ 4 2
♢ K Q
♣ A 10 7

South is playing in 4♠ after 1♠ : 2♠, 3♠ : 4♠. West leads the king of clubs. How should South plan the play?

If South leads a trump at once, the defense can win and cash two clubs and the ♢ A. Correct is to win the ♣ A and play three rounds of hearts first to discard a club loser. Then start trumps.

Where the winners are sitting in dummy ready and waiting, things are easy. Sometimes the winners have to be established swiftly :

NORTH
♠ Q 10 7 4
♡ A 6 4 3
♢ 5 2
♣ K J 4

SOUTH
♠ K J 9 8 5
♡ K 8 2
♢ K Q J
♣ Q 7

South is in 4♠ (North passed and raised South's 1♠ to 3♠). West leads the queen of hearts. How should South plan the play?

If declarer wins and leads a trump, the defense can win and lead another heart. As declarer has to lose three aces, declarer cannot afford to lose a heart as well.

Dummy has no extra winners yet, but declarer can set up an extra winner in clubs. The correct order is win the ♡ K (keeping the ♡ A as an entry to dummy), lead the ♣ Q to knock out the ace (and a second club if they duck the queen), win the next heart and discard a heart from hand on the third round of clubs. Then and only then should trumps be started.

NORTH
♠ 3
♡ Q J 8 6 4 3
♢ A 6 4
♣ J 7 2

SOUTH
♠ Q J 5
♡ K 10 9 5 2
♢ K 5 2
♣ A Q

South is in 4♡ after North raised South's 1♡ opening to game. West leads the queen of diamonds. Plan South's play.

South has to lose one spade and one heart. The danger is that there will also be a club loser and a diamond loser. Winning the ♢ A and finessing clubs gives you a 50% chance. Anything better?

The club finesse is an illusion. If the club finesse works you have two club tricks. If the club finesse fails you have two club tricks. If you reject the club finesse and play ace of clubs and queen of clubs, you have two club tricks. Thus, the club finesse does not gain a trick and may cost the contract. Suppose you take the club finesse and it loses. Back comes a diamond, taken by the king. You can cash the ♣ A but there is no easy access to the ♣ J. They will win the race and reach their diamond trick before you come to your discard.

The solution is simple once you see it, but it is easy to have a blind spot. Win the ♢ K, cash the ♣ A and lead the ♣ Q. After they take the king, the ♣ J is available for a diamond discard and the ♢ A is still in dummy as an entry. (Of course, if they duck the ♣ Q, you have no club loser.)

When you have too many losers, you may be able to eliminate some by ruffing losers in the shorter trump hand, usually in dummy.

A 6 3   If this is your trump suit, you
K Q J 10 9   have five winners. If you can ruff
           one loser in dummy, this produces
a sixth trick. Note that if you ruff once in hand, you still have only five trump winners.

If you can manage to ruff two losers in dummy, you score seven trump tricks : the five winners in hand and the two ruffs in dummy. Note that if you ruff twice in hand, you still have only five trump tricks, the same number with which you started.

It rarely gains an extra trick to ruff in the long trump hand.

Where dummy has few trumps, you may have to start ruffing before drawing any rounds of trumps. Sometimes you can afford one round or two rounds. Check on how many ruffs you need in dummy and that is the number of trumps dummy must retain. Sometimes it is convenient to take a ruff in dummy, return to hand via the trump suit (thus drawing one round of trumps) and ruff another loser in dummy.

Short-suiting dummy

Dummy may not be void in a suit and you may have to play one or two rounds of a suit first to create the void. You may need to do this before starting on trumps.

'Don't send a boy on a man's errand.'

If you can afford to ruff high in dummy, do so. It is painful to be overruffed when it was perfectly safe to ruff high.

How many winners can you cash without risking an opposition ruff?

If you have fewer cards in a suit than the opposition, three rounds of the suit will usually survive. If you hold six cards, they have seven and the chance for a 4-3 split is a bit over 60%. With only five cards in a suit, three rounds are very likely to escape a ruff. When you have seven cards in a suit, you can probably cash two rounds without a ruff but the third round is risky. The chance of a 3-3 break is only 36%. With eight cards in a suit, you may be able to cash two rounds but someone is bound to be out of the suit on the third round. In addition, even the second round is risky. The chance of a 4-1 split is about 1-in-4, around 28%.

These figures may be helpful when you need to decide how many rounds of a suit you can play in order to take a quick discard or two.

The cross ruff

A cross ruff enables you make your trumps and dummy's trumps separately. You ruff in dummy, ruff in hand, ruff in dummy, ruff in hand, back and forth, hopefully without an overruff on the way. In most cases, it is best not to draw any trumps before starting the cross ruff. The signs that a cross ruff will work better than drawing trumps are when dummy is short in your long side suit and you are short in dummy's suit(s). If your side suit is a 'running suit' (no losers expected, such as AKQxxx or AKQJx) or solid bar one loser (such as KQJ10x), normal technique is to draw trumps and use your strong side suit later. However, if your long suit is broken and not easy to establish, prefer to cross ruff.

You may have to short suit dummy or your own hand before starting the cross ruff. In addition, it is usually best to cash all your side suit winners before commencing the cross ruff. Once the opponents start discarding, they may be able to ruff those winners later.

Defending agains declarer's ruffs in dummy

If dummy has no useful long suit but has ruffing values, the defense should lead trumps at every opportunity. If dummy has a long suit but your strength in that suit means that declarer will not be able to use it for discarding, again you should lead trumps in defense if dummy has some ruffing value.

The best defense against a cross ruff is repeated trump leads. The more trumps you draw, the fewer trumps declarer has for ruffing. Each time you lead a trump and take out one trump from declarer and one trump from dummy, you reduce the value of the cross ruff by one trick.

The bidding and the appearance of dummy may indicate the likelihood of a cross ruff. If the opponents are playing in their third suit (for example, after an auction like 1♠ : 2◇, 2♡ : 3♡, 4♡), a cross ruff is likely. Declarer figures to be shortish in diamonds, dummy will be shortish in spades and so all the ingredients of a cross ruff are apparent in the auction. A trump lead is sensible in such cases, particularly if you are strong in one of their other suits.

If declarer has drawn trumps and left you with the top trump, it is usually your best move to cash that top trump when you gain the lead. By drawing a trump from declarer and from dummy, you are reducing their potential for tricks by ruffing.

PLAY HANDS ON RUFFING LOSERS IN DUMMY

Hand 49 : Dealer North : Nil vulnerable

NORTH
♠ A J 9 8 4
♡ A J 7 4
◇ A K
♣ J 3

WEST
♠ 10
♡ Q 9 5
◇ Q 10 8 5 3 2
♣ A 8 5

EAST
♠ 7 3 2
♡ K 10 8 2
◇ 9 6
♣ K Q 10 9

SOUTH
♠ K Q 6 5
♡ 6 3
◇ J 7 4
♣ 7 6 4 2

WEST	NORTH	EAST	SOUTH
	1♠	Pass	2♠
Pass	4♠	All pass	

Lead: ♣ K. It is more attractive to lead from a suit with touching honors than from a broken suit (such as the hearts). A near sequence such as the K-Q-10 is also more attractive than a doubleton lead. If the clubs were not so strong, a trump lead from three rags would be quite reasonable.

Play: West signals with the 8 of clubs and East continues with the ♣ 10 (rather than the ♣ Q, just in case West started with ace-doubleton and did not unblock the ace on the first round). West wins the ♣ A and plays a third round, ruffed by North. Declarer should continue by drawing one round of trumps, followed by ace and another heart. No matter how the defense continues, declarer regains the lead and ruffs a heart, plays a trump to hand, ruffs the last heart, comes to hand with a diamond and draws the last trump.

Notes: (1) It would be an error to draw trumps first before voiding dummy in hearts. If North takes three rounds of trumps, dummy has only one trump left. However, North needs to ruff two hearts in dummy and so needs to keep two trumps in dummy.

(2) One round of trumps first is safe but it would be wrong to draw two rounds of trumps before playing the hearts. If so, the defense might play a third round when in with the second round of hearts. That is exactly what East should do when East sees declarer is playing for heart ruffs in dummy. If the defense leads a third round, dummy has only one trump left.

Hand 50 : Dealer East : N-S vulnerable

NORTH
♠ K 9
♡ Q J 4
◇ A 8 7 3 2
♣ K 5 4

WEST
♠ Q 10 8 7 5 4
♡ 6
◇ K 9
♣ Q J 10 6

EAST
♠ J 6
♡ 8 7 5
◇ Q J 10 6 4
♣ A 8 7

SOUTH
♠ A 3 2
♡ A K 10 9 3 2
◇ 5
♣ 9 3 2

WEST	NORTH	EAST	SOUTH
		Pass	1♡
1♠	2◇	Pass	2♡
Pass	4♡	All pass	

Lead : ♣ Q. Top of sequence is usually best.

Play: Declarer should play low in dummy in case East has the ♣ A singleton or doubleton. East signals encouragement with the 8. West plays a second club, low from dummy again and the third club is taken by East. East should switch to the queen of diamonds and dummy's ace wins. Declarer's best sequence of plays is to cash the queen of hearts, lead the 4 of hearts to the ace and continue with a spade to the king, a spade to the ace and a spade ruffed with the ♡ J. Ruff a diamond and draw the last trump.

Notes: (1) The trap to avoid is to win the ace of diamonds and continue with the king of spades, spade to the ace and a spade ruffed with the four of hearts. East overruffs. One down.

(2) Don't send a boy on a man's errand. Holding the A, K, Q, J, 10 and 9 of trumps between the two hands, declarer can afford to ruff high on the third round of spades.

(3) Declarer must also avoid drawing three rounds of trumps before going after the spade ruff. Dummy needs to have one trump left to ruff the spade loser.

(4) As the cards lie, it would be adequate to win the ◇ A, cash the ♠ K, lead a spade to the ace and ruff a spade with the queen or jack of hearts. There is very little risk in this line but it is possible that one opponent has a singleton spade and could therefore ruff the second round of spades. You can reduce the risk by drawing two rounds of trumps (dummy only needs one trump to ruff one loser), taking care to leave a high trump in dummy to ruff the third spade. Play as safely as possible.

Hand 51 : Dealer South : E-W vulnerable

NORTH
♠ K Q 5
♡ 8 6 5 2
◊ J 9 8 7
♣ J 10

WEST
♠ A 7 6 2
♡ 9
◊ A K Q 4
♣ A 5 4 3

EAST
♠ 9 8 4 3
♡ A K J 4
◊ 5 2
♣ 8 6 2

SOUTH
♠ J 10
♡ Q 10 7 3
◊ 10 6 3
♣ K Q 9 7

WEST	NORTH	EAST	SOUTH
			Pass
1◊	Pass	1♡	Pass
1♠	Pass	2♠	Pass
4♠	Pass	Pass	Pass

Lead : ♣J. The unbid suit is normal.

Play : Win ♣A and continue with ◊A, ◊K, ◊Q, discarding a club. Play the fourth diamond and discard the other club loser. Duck one round of trumps, then cash the ace of spades, ruff a club, cash the top hearts and discard a club, ruff a heart and ruff a club in dummy. Losing two spades and one diamond.

Notes : (1) East's 2♠ is 6-9 points, at most a poor 10.
(2) West is in danger of losing two spades and two clubs. One club can be discarded and two need to be ruffed. Do not start trumps.
(3) If West ruffs the fourth diamond, South overruffs and declarer goes down. Note this loser-on-loser technique to transfer the ruff.

Hand 52 : Dealer West : Both vulnerable

NORTH
♠ 7 6 2
♡ 7 2
◊ A 9 7 6 3
♣ A 10 9

WEST
♠ 8 4
♡ Q 4
◊ K 8 4 2
♣ K 8 7 5 2

EAST
♠ A K Q J 9
♡ A K 10 8 6
◊ 5
♣ 6 3

SOUTH
♠ 10 5 3
♡ J 9 5 3
◊ Q J 10
♣ Q J 4

WEST	NORTH	EAST	SOUTH
Pass	Pass	1♠	Pass
1NT	Pass	4♡	Pass
4♠	Pass	Pass	Pass

Lead : ◊Q. Top of sequence. A trump lead is also attractive, as dummy has shown preference for spades and South has a fair holding in declarer's second suit.

Play : Duck the first diamond and ruff the second diamond. Cash ♡Q, ♡A and ruff a heart with the 8 of spades. Draw trumps and try the club finesse. 10 tricks.

Notes : (1) With four losers and strong suits, East can rebid in game.
(2) With equal length in support, prefer partner's first bid suit.
(3) Declarer ruff a heart to cater for the common 4-2 split. The ruff costs nothing if hearts are 3-3. If the ♡J drops, draw trumps.
(4) On a trump lead, win ♠9, cash ♡Q, ♡A, ruff a heart and exit from dummy with ◊K, the best chance to avoid a heart ruff.

Hand 53 : Dealer North : N-S vulnerable

NORTH
♠ 10 3
♡ A K 9 4 3
◊ K Q 6 2
♣ Q 3

WEST
♠ A K 9 8 5 4 2
♡ - - -
◊ J 8
♣ A K 6 5

EAST
♠ J 7
♡ J 10 7 6
◊ 10 9 4 3
♣ 7 4 2

SOUTH
♠ Q 6
♡ Q 8 5 2
◊ A 7 5
♣ J 10 9 8

WEST	NORTH	EAST	SOUTH
	1♡	Pass	2♡
4♠	Pass	Pass	Pass

Lead : ♡K (or ace). A trump lead and a second trump when in with clubs would defeat the contract, but that is hard to tell in the auction. It is not recommended to lead a trump if dummy has not shown any support.

Play : West ruffs and continues with ♣A, ♣K and a third club. On regaining the lead, West leads the fourth club and ruffs it in dummy. A heart ruff back to hand is followed by the top spades. With trumps 2-2, West loses only two diamonds and one club.

Notes : (1) West's 4♠ is sound. It may make or be a good sacrifice.
(2) As clubs are unlikely to be 3-3, West must delay trumps and plan to ruff a club in dummy. Even one trump first could be fatal. South could play a second trump when in with the third club. If clubs are 3-3, West has lost nothing by playing clubs first.

Hand 54 : Dealer East : E-W vulnerable

NORTH
♠ K Q J 8 3
♡ J
♢ J 6 5 4 2
♣ 7 3

WEST
♠ 6 5 4
♡ K Q 7
♢ K 10 7
♣ Q J 9 8

EAST
♠ - - -
♡ 10 5 3 2
♢ A Q 9 8
♣ K 10 6 5 2

SOUTH
♠ A 10 9 7 2
♡ A 9 8 6 4
♢ 3
♣ A 4

WEST	NORTH	EAST	SOUTH
		Pass	1♠
Pass	4♠	All pass	

Lead : ♣ Q. Top of near sequence preferred to a K-Q-x suit. With strength in all outside suits, a trump lead is also sound.

Play : Win the lead and play a diamond to short suit yourself. On regaining the lead, embark on a cross ruff: ace of hearts, ruff a heart low, ruff a diamond low, ruff a heart, ruff a diamond, and so on. 11 tricks, losing one diamond and one club.

Notes : (1) North's 4♠ shows strong support (4-5 trumps), an unbalanced hand and no more than 10 HCP. The bid is normally based on 7 losers.
(2) The signs for a cross ruff are all there. Declarer short in dummy's long suit, dummy short in declarer's long suit.
(3) It would be an error to draw trumps. Three rounds of trumps cuts down your ruffing potential by two tricks.

Hand 55 : Dealer South : Both vulnerable

NORTH
♠ A Q 10 4
♡ 10 4
♢ Q 10 8 6
♣ 10 7 3

WEST
♠ 9 5
♡ A 7
♢ K J 9 7 4 3
♣ A 4 2

EAST
♠ K 7 6
♡ K Q J 9 6 3 2
♢ - - -
♣ 9 6 5

SOUTH
♠ J 8 3 2
♡ 8 5
♢ A 5 2
♣ K Q J 8

WEST	NORTH	EAST	SOUTH
			Pass
1♢	Pass	1♡	Pass
2♢	Pass	4♡	All pass

Lead : ♣ K. The top of sequence lead is normal. A trump lead would in fact defeat the contract but that is almost impossible to judge. It is usually not attractive to lead a trump if dummy has not indicated any support for declarer's suit.

Play : Win the ♣ A and lead a spade at once, playing the king when North plays low. After the king wins, exit with a low spade. The defense can cash two clubs, but declarer wins the next trick and ruffs a spade in dummy. 10 tricks, losing one spade and two clubs.

Notes : (1) With a 7-card suit and 3 honors, East can jump to 4♡.
(2) East must not draw trumps first. That could lead to two down. There are seven hearts tricks. The other three must come from the spade finesse, a spade ruff and the ♣ A.

Hand 56 : Dealer West : Nil vulnerable

NORTH
♠ Q 8 7 6 3
♡ 3
♢ A Q J 9 5 2
♣ A

WEST
♠ 9 5
♡ Q 9 7
♢ 10 8 7 6
♣ 9 8 6 2

EAST
♠ J 10 4 2
♡ J 10 6 5 2
♢ - - -
♣ K Q J 7

SOUTH
♠ A K
♡ A K 8 4
♢ K 4 3
♣ 10 5 4 3

WEST	NORTH	EAST	SOUTH
Pass	1♢	Pass	1♡
Pass	1♠	Pass	2♣
Pass	2♠	Pass	4♢
Pass	5♣	Pass	5NT
Pass	6♡	Pass	7♢
Pass	Pass	Pass	

Lead : ♣ K. A solid sequence is the safest lead against a slam.

Play : Win ♣ A, cash ♢ A, then ♠ A, ♠ K, ruff a club, ruff a low spade with the ♢ K, finesse ♢ 9, draw trumps and claim 13 tricks.

Notes : (1) 2♣ was fourth-suit forcing, 2♠ showed five spades and therefore six diamonds, 4♢ set trumps, 5♣ was a cue bid, 5NT asked for trump honors and 6♡ showed two top trumps.
(2) As spades figure not to be 3-3, you must plan to ruff a spade. Test trumps first in case they are 2-2. You must keep the ♢ K to ruff a spade high to prevent an overruff. The ♢ 9 finesse is marked.

CHAPTER 14

DUCKING AS DECLARER

There are many situations where declarer's best move is to give up a trick in order to set up extra winners. When developing a long suit in which a trick has to be lost anyway, it usually pays to lose the trick as early as possible.

```
                7 4 2
  J 10 9 5                   - - -
                A K Q 8 6 3
```

If this suit has to be developed at no-trumps and the lead comes from North, East shows out at once. As soon as a player shows out, calculate the holding in the other hand. Here declarer knows that West began with J-10-9-x and a trick has to be lost to establish the suit. With no sure entry to hand, lose the trick now. This is sound business: you give up one trick and receive two in return.

If South were on lead, the natural start would be to cash the ace. When East shows out, South should play a low card next. This concedes the trick that West must inevitably win and still leaves a card in the North hand. This eliminates any entry problems when cashing the winners in this suit.

When setting up winners, be prepared to lose one or more tricks. If bound to lose a trick in order to set up extra tricks, it is usually best to concede the inevitable loser as early as possible.

```
                K 6 2
  10 9 7                     Q J 8
                A 5 4 3
```

Hoping for an extra trick via a 3-3 break, declarer should duck one round in this suit. Either duck the first round or cash the king (the winner from the shorter hand) and duck the second round.

```
                A K 5 4 3
  Q 10 8                     J 9 7
                6 2
```

Suppose declarer needs to develop tricks in this suit at no-trumps. If there is no outside entry to the North hand, declarer should duck the first round. On regaining the lead, cash the ace and king. If the suit is indeed 3-3, you will be score four tricks. If the North hand had an outside entry, you could play ace, king and concede the third round. You still score two extra tricks.

However, even with an outside entry, it does not hurt to duck the first round and it may be wise to do so. By ducking the first round, you keep control of the suit and can check later whether the suit divides favourably or not. If not, you are on lead and can tackle another suit. However, if you start with ace, king and give up the third round, you may find you have set up two winners for the opponents if the suit divides 4–2 and three winners for them if the suit divides 5-1.

```
                A 7 6 4 3
  K Q                       J 10 9
                8 5 2
```

To develop extra tricks in this suit with no outside entry to North, duck two rounds of the suit. When you regain the lead, play to your ace. If the suit has divided 3-2, you score three tricks in the suit.

```
                A 7 6 3
  J 9 8                     K Q 10
                5 4 2
```

This position is similar. To develop one extra trick with no entry to dummy, duck the first two rounds.

```
                A Q 6 5 4
  K 10 8                    J 9 3
                7 2
```

To develop tricks in this suit with no outside entry to North, declarer should duck the first round of the suit. Later, finesse the queen. If the king is onside and the suit divides 3-3, you can score four tricks.

Note that if you finesse the queen on the first round, you score only two tricks if dummy has no side entry. Also, if West plays the king on the first round, you must still duck in dummy to score your four tricks.

```
                K 7 6 5 2
  A J 8                     Q 10 9
                4 3
```

To set up three tricks with only one unassailable entry in dummy, duck the first round. Later lead low towards the king. If the position is as shown, you will be able to make three tricks. You cannot achieve this if you play the king on the first round of the suit if dummy has only one outside entry.

PLAY HANDS ON DUCKING AS DECLARER

Hand 57 : Dealer North : E-W vulnerable

	WEST	NORTH	EAST	SOUTH
		3♣	Pass	3NT
	Pass	Pass	Pass	

NORTH
♠ J 7
♡ Q
♢ 7 5 3
♣ A 10 9 7 6 5 4

WEST
♠ Q 8 6
♡ J 10 7 5 3 2
♢ K 9
♣ K J

EAST
♠ K 9 4 2
♡ 9 8 6
♢ J 8 4 2
♣ Q 8

SOUTH
♠ A 10 5 3
♡ A K 4
♢ A Q 10 6
♣ 3 2

Lead : ♡5. Against a 3-Minor : 3NT auction, it is often best to lead from a short strong holding (such as A-K-x) — see Chapter 3, page 20. However, with no suitable strong short suit, the lead from the long suit is normal.

Play : The queen of hearts wins the first trick and dummy now has no entries outside clubs. Declarer can succeed by playing a low club from dummy at trick 2. Declarer wins any return and plays a club to the ace. As the clubs were 2-2 originally, dummy's remaining clubs are winners. Declarer scores 1 spade, 3 hearts, 1 diamond and 6 clubs for 11 tricks.

Notes: (1) At favourable vulnerability, North is definitely worth 3♣. (2) With a balanced hand and double stoppers in every outside suit, South is worth a shot at 3NT. This may fail if North's clubs cannot be established but the risk should be taken. The game must be bid even if it does not always succeed. (3) After the ♡Q scores, declarer's best chance for success is the 2-2 club break. However, declarer's best line is to finesse the 10 of diamonds at trick 2. With a double stopper still held in every suit, declarer can delay the club duck and add another chance for success. West wins the ◇K and leads another heart. Now South ducks a club and makes the contract as above. Imagine, however, that clubs were 3-1. Finessing the diamond at trick 2 would make the contract if East held K-J-x in diamonds. The ◇10 would win, a club would be ducked and when the clubs are not 2-2, another diamond finesse can be taken, This would bring in four diamond tricks, three hearts and two black aces. The diamond play may also work for other layouts.

Hand 58 : Dealer East : Both vulnerable

	WEST	NORTH	EAST	SOUTH
			1NT	Pass
	3NT	Pass	Pass	Pass

NORTH
♠ 10 9 7 5
♡ K 9 2
♢ J 10 9 8
♣ J 4

WEST
♠ J 6
♡ 7 3
♢ A K Q 7 6 4
♣ 10 8 3

EAST
♠ Q 8 3 2
♡ A Q 8
♢ 5 3 2
♣ A K Q

SOUTH
♠ A K 4
♡ J 10 6 5 4
♢ - - -
♣ 9 7 6 5 2

Lead : ♡5. With two equally long suits, prefer the stronger to the weaker and prefer the major to the minor. Responders tend not to bid 3NT when holding a major, but length in the minors is frequently concealed.

Play : North plays the king and declarer takes the ace. If the diamonds divide 2-2 or 3-1, there are eleven tricks. When declarer leads a diamond, South shows out. North's J-10-9-8 is a certain stopper in diamonds. Without extra diamond winners, declarer has only eight tricks. Declarer ducks the first diamond, conceding to North what has to be lost anyway. Declarer wins the heart return and cashes five diamonds and three clubs, scoring 10 tricks.

Notes: (1) There is little value in responding 3◇. With minor suit length, game values and no slam ambitions, stick with no-trumps. (2) There is no benefit in ducking the first round of hearts here. A switch to spades could be unwelcome. (3) A spade trick could be established but the defense would set up and cash their heart tricks first. (4) It would be futile to play ace, king, queen of diamonds and then concede the fourth round. There would be two diamond winners in dummy but no way to reach them. (5) If South had followed on the first round of diamonds, declarer would win in dummy. If North showed out, declarer would counter by ducking the second diamond. Declarer has another diamond to reach dummy. (6) If declarer had started with only two diamonds, declarer would duck the first round of diamonds if playing rubber bridge or teams bridge. This safeguards the contract if the diamonds turn out to be 4-1.

Hand 59 : Dealer South : Nil vulnerable

            NORTH
            ♠ A Q J
            ♡ A J 3 2
            ◇ A 10 6 3
            ♣ 5 4

WEST   EAST
♠ 9 8   ♠ K 10 5 4 3
♡ K 9 8 6   ♡ Q 7 5
◇ K 8 5 2   ◇ Q 9 4
♣ Q J 10   ♣ 9 3

            SOUTH
            ♠ 7 6 2
            ♡ 10 4
            ◇ J 7
            ♣ A K 8 7 6 2

WEST	NORTH	EAST	SOUTH
			Pass
Pass	1NT	Pass	3NT
Pass	Pass	Pass	

Lead : ♠4. No reason to avoid the normal.

Play : West plays the 8 (cheaper of high cards in third seat) and declarer wins with the queen (declarer should win with the higher of equals). With only four outside winners, declarer needs five club tricks. With five clubs missing, a club has to be lost anyway. As dummy has no outside entry, *duck the first round of clubs.* Win any return and cash the clubs, followed by the other winners.

Notes : (1) In replying to 1NT, count two extra points for a 6-card suit. With 10 points, South should bid game in no-trumps, not 5♣.
(2) If the clubs turn out to be 4-1, you will fail. However, you succeed on the normal 3-2 break which occurs 2/3 of the time.
(3) Do not play ♣A, ♣K and give up a club, as dummy has no entry.

Hand 60 : Dealer West : N-S vulnerable

            NORTH
            ♠ J 10 9 8 3
            ♡ 7 5
            ◇ Q 10 9
            ♣ K 5 3

WEST   EAST
♠ A K Q 5   ♠ 6 4
♡ A K 6 4   ♡ J 3 2
◇ K 8 5   ◇ A 7 6 4 3 2
♣ A 10   ♣ 9 2

            SOUTH
            ♠ 7 2
            ♡ Q 10 9 8
            ◇ J
            ♣ Q J 8 7 6 4

WEST	NORTH	EAST	SOUTH
2NT	Pass	3NT	All pass

Lead : ♠J. Top of sequence. A club lead would in fact defeat 3NT but there is no way for North to know.

Play : Win the first spade, cash the ◇ K and duck the next diamond. Win any return and cash the diamonds, then the other winners.

Notes : (1) If the ◇ K reveals a 4-0 diamond split, abandon the diamonds. Try for three winners in hearts instead.
(2) The 3-1 diamond split (50%) is more likely than a 2-2 split (40%) and ducking one round of diamonds guarantees the contract if the split is 3-1 at the cost of an overtrick if the break is 2-2. Even at pairs duplicate, cater for the most likely division.
(3) If the opening lead were a club, declarer could not afford to duck a diamond. Now declarer would have to pray that diamonds are 2-2 and cash the king and ace, taking the precaution of unblocking the 8 of diamonds on the second round.

Hand 61 : Dealer North : Both vulnerable

            NORTH
            ♠ A K Q
            ♡ A Q 10 7
            ◇ A K 5
            ♣ 8 5 3

WEST   EAST
♠ J 7 3   ♠ 10 8 6 4 2
♡ 9 5 3   ♡ K J 8
◇ Q 10 8 6   ◇ 9 7 4
♣ K Q 9   ♣ J 10

            SOUTH
            ♠ 9 5
            ♡ 6 4 2
            ◇ J 3 2
            ♣ A 7 6 4 2

WEST	NORTH	EAST	SOUTH
	2NT	Pass	3NT
Pass	Pass	Pass	

Lead : ♠4. Normal long suit lead.

Play : Declarer wins the lead and can count seven top winners. The best chance for two extra tricks is in clubs. Duck one round of clubs, win the return and duck a second round of clubs. If the suit has divided 3-2, there is only one club missing. On regaining the lead, cash the ace of clubs and the two club winners.

Notes : (1) Since dummy has no entry outside clubs, declarer must not play the ♣A on the first or second round of clubs. If the clubs split 3-2, the ace of clubs is the entry to the two extra club winners.
(2) If East were to show out on the second round of clubs, so that the club suit could not be established and cashed, declarer would take the ace of clubs and take a finesse in hearts. Declarer would have to hope that this finesse works and that the hearts are 3-3.

Hand 62 : Dealer East : Nil vulnerable

NORTH
♠ J 10 9 8 7 3
♡ 7 2
◇ 8
♣ 10 7 6 2

WEST
♠ K Q 6 4
♡ A Q 3
◇ Q 5 4
♣ A K Q

EAST
♠ A
♡ 9 6 5 4
◇ A K 10 7 2
♣ J 4 3

SOUTH
♠ 5 2
♡ K J 10 8
◇ J 9 6 3
♣ 9 8 5

WEST	NORTH	EAST	SOUTH
		1◇	Pass
1♠	Pass	2◇	Pass
4NT	Pass	5♡	Pass
5NT	Pass	6◇	Pass
6NT	Pass	Pass	Pass

Lead: ♠J. Solid sequence is best even though West bid the suit.

Play: Win ♠A and lead a diamond to the queen, followed by a diamond towards dummy. When North shows out, duck the second round of diamonds. You have 3 spades, 3 clubs, 4 diamonds and need the heart finesse for 12 tricks.

Notes: (1) West's 1♠ is better than an immediate jump. It allows West to gauge whether East has a minimum or a stronger opening. (2) Had North followed to the second diamond, it would be safe to play the ace. If South shows out, you can finesse the ◇ 10 later. (3) The trap to avoid is playing the ◇ A or ◇ K first.

Hand 63 : Dealer South : N-S vulnerable

NORTH
♠ A Q 7 4 2
♡ 7 3
◇ 8 6
♣ 7 4 3 2

WEST
♠ K 9 8
♡ Q J 9 8
◇ 10 7 5 2
♣ K 9

EAST
♠ J 10 5
♡ 10 6 4
◇ Q J 9
♣ Q 10 8 6

SOUTH
♠ 6 3
♡ A K 5 2
◇ A K 4 3
♣ A J 5

WEST	NORTH	EAST	SOUTH
			1◇
Pass	1♠	Pass	2NT
Pass	3♠	Pass	3NT
Pass	Pass	Pass	

Lead : ♡Q. Top of near sequence in an unbid major is best.

Play: East encourages with the 6 of hearts and South wins the ace. Declarer should duck the first round of spades, win any return and lead a spade towards dummy. Play the queen if West plays low and hope for the best. When the spade finesse works, cash the ♠A and two more spades when the suit breaks 3-3.

Notes: (1) 3♠ shows five spades but does not imply extra strength. (2) With only five tricks outside spades, you must play for four spade tricks. The ♠ K will have to be onside and the suit will have to be 3-3. Even then, a trick is bound to be lost, so follow the rule 'If a trick must be lost to set up extra winners, lose it early.'

Hand 64 : Dealer West : E-W vulnerable

NORTH
♠ 10 8 3
♡ J 10 6
◇ 10 9 4
♣ A K Q 2

WEST
♠ Q 5
♡ K 7 4 2
◇ Q 6 5 3 2
♣ J 3

EAST
♠ A K J 7 4 2
♡ A 5 3
◇ A
♣ 9 7 6

SOUTH
♠ 9 6
♡ Q 9 8
◇ K J 8 7
♣ 10 8 5 4

WEST	NORTH	EAST	SOUTH
Pass	Pass	1♠	Pass
1NT	Pass	3♠	Pass
4♠	Pass	Pass	Pass

Lead : ♣4. Safer than the heart lead from one top honor or the diamond from split honors. Reasonable second choice : a trump.

Play: From the ♣4 lead, North can read East for at least three clubs. North should win ♣ Q and switch to a trump to prevent declarer ruffing a club in dummy. Declarer wins and ducks a heart at once. After trumps are drawn, the 3-3 heart split provides the tenth trick.

Notes: (1) If North wins the club lead and plays a second club, declarer simply ruffs a club in dummy for the tenth trick. (2) After the trump switch, declarer cannot afford to play a club at trick 3 or to draw trumps before ducking the heart. Dummy's trumps prevent the defense cashing three clubs. Lack of entries to dummy preclude declarer's playing ace, king and a third heart.

CHAPTER 15

CARD READING & INFERENCES (1)

Card reading is a skill which enables you to deduce where the significant missing cards lie. It aims to solve problems such as these :

```
            K J
  ?                   ?
            7 3
```

Who has the ace? Do I finesse the king or the jack?

```
            A 10 2
  ?                   ?
            K J 3
```

Who has the queen? Which way do I finesse?

Solving these problems by logic, not guesswork, separates the competent player from the card puller. There are many inferences which can assist you in figuring out the answers. These inferences are available from the bidding (or lack of it), from the card led, from the play by third hand, from other cards played by the defenders and from the strategy adopted by the defense.

You should adopt a regular routine :

1. Do not play too quickly at trick 1. Count dummy's points as soon as dummy appears. Add your own and deduct from 40 to find out how many points they hold.

2. Before playing a card from dummy, decide which suit you propose to play next. Do you need to be in hand or in dummy to tackle this suit to best advantage? Do you have a choice of winning in dummy or in hand? Is there a best play from dummy with this combination (see Chapter 12)?

3. Analyse the opening lead. What does it show? What does it deny?

4. Count your clearcut winners. In a trump contract, count your losers as well, suit by suit.

5. Review the bidding. What does the bidding tell you about the location of the missing high cards?

A good player is constantly inquisitive. The thoughts that run through your mind might be along these lines "I wonder why West did not lead a heart. Obviously West cannot have both the ace and king. Therefore, East must have either the ace or the king, or both . . ." or "That's odd. East passed West's 1♠ opening but has led the ace of hearts. Obviously, East

cannot have more than a jack extra. Therefore, West must have all the other significant high cards . . ." or "Why did no one bid spades? They have 21 HCP and nine spades between them. I suppose the points are pretty evenly divided and neither of their hands can be very shapely . . ."

Thinking along such lines can produce very rewarding results. You may occasionally be able to tell the location of every ace, king and queen even before you have played from dummy at trick 1.

The most important habit and the one most frequently ignored by the average player is to count dummy's points. Do this regularly whether you are declarer or defending.

1. COUNT DUMMY'S HIGH CARD POINTS AT TRICK 1.

2. ADD YOUR OWN POINTS AND DEDUCT FROM 40.

3. TRY TO FIGURE OUT WHERE THE MISSING POINTS ARE LIKELY TO BE.

INFERENCES FROM THE BIDDING

1. An opening bidder usually has 12 HCP minimum. If you need to find a key queen, play an opponent to have opened with 13 HCP rather than 11 HCP. If missing a vital king, play an opening opponent to have started with 13 HCP, not 10, or 14 HCP, not 11. Though light openings are possible, they are not frequent. Play an opening for normal opening points.

2. An opponent who failed to open usually has less than 12 HCP. While players do pass with poor 12 point hands, this too is rare. Missing a key queen, play an opponent who could have opened for 10 HCP rather than 12 HCP. In placing a key king, assume a non-opening opponent holds 9 HCP, not 12. For example, if an opponent fails to open the bidding but turns up with 10 or 11 HCP, you would play for any king or queen still missing to be with the other opponent.

3. Note the high card strength for the opponents' 1NT opening. If an opponent opened with a suit bid, particularly 1♣ or 1◇, and turns up with a balanced pattern, you know their point count must be outside the range for their 1NT opening.

4. If a queen or a jack is missing, play the opponent with greater length in the suit to hold the missing honour. For example :

A 10 7 4   With no clues, play the ace and the king and hope the queen drops. If there

K J 5 3 2   has been a pre-empt by West, play the ace and finesse the jack on the second round. If East has pre-empted, cash the king and then finesse the 10. In other words, play the pre-emptor to be short in your suit — play the partner of the pre-emptor to hold a key honor in an outside suit.

5. Other clues :

(a) An overcaller will usually hold a 5-card suit which includes at least the queen, king or ace.

(b) A takeout doubler is likely to be short in the suit doubled.

(c) A pre-emptor usually has less than 10 HCP.

(d) An opponent who opened and has turned up with a balanced hand usually has a narrow range of points.

(e) Where both opponents have bid, consider not only what the stronger hand needs to hold, but also what the weaker hand must have had to justify its action.

(f) Where an opponent shows a freakish hand (such as the unusual 2NT — 5-5 in the minors — or other actions showing a two-suiter), expect bad breaks in the other suits. If a player has revealed length in two suits, it is easy to keep track of the holdings in the other two suits.

Inferences from the opening lead and the cards played by the opponents are covered in Chapter 29 — Card Reading & Inferences (2) — which also deals with 'playing on an assumption'.

EXERCISE ON CARD READING AND INFERENCES

1.

WEST	EAST
♠ 9 7 2	♠ 8 6 4
♡ Q J 10 6 4	♡ A 7 5 3 2
◇ A 6 3	◇ K Q
♣ A K	♣ 9 8 5

Dealer North : Nil vulnerable

WEST	NORTH	EAST	SOUTH
	Pass	Pass	Pass
1♡	Pass	3♡	Pass
4♡	Pass	Pass	Pass

North cashes the ace, king and queen of spades. At trick 4, a club is led to South's jack and your ace. How do you continue? How would you play if North had led the 3 of spades and South had cashed the ace-king-queen before switching to clubs?

2.

WEST	EAST
♠ A J 8 5 2	♠ K 10 4
♡ 6 4	♡ 10 7 3
◇ A K Q	◇ J 5 2
♣ K 6 4	♣ Q J 7 2

Dealer North : Both vulnerable

WEST	NORTH	EAST	SOUTH
	1♡	Pass	Pass
Double	Pass	2♣	Pass
2♠	Pass	3♠	Pass
4♠	Pass	Pass	Pass

North leads the king of hearts. South overtakes with the ace and returns the 8 of hearts to North's jack. North continues with the queen of hearts, South discards a club and you ruff. How do you continue?

3.

WEST	EAST
♠ A K 10 6 4 3	♠ 8 7 5
♡ 8 6 2	♡ Q 5 4
◇ J 5 3	◇ A 6 4
♣ 6	♣ A Q 7 3

Dealer South : Both vulnerable

WEST	NORTH	EAST	SOUTH
			Pass
2♠	Pass	Pass	Pass

North leads the jack of hearts, low, low, low. North continues with the 10 of hearts, low, king from South. South cashes the ace of hearts and switches to the 10 of diamonds, low, low, ace. You cash the ace and king of spades and South plays the Q-J and North the 2-9. You have six spade tricks and two aces. Do you risk the club finesse for an overtrick? What is the chance that the club finesse is on?

4.

WEST	EAST
♠ 8 7 6	♠ A K 5 2
♡ K 6 5	♡ A 10 4 3
◇ Q 10 6	◇ 5
♣ K 10 8 7	♣ A J 4 3

Dealer South : Nil vulnerable

WEST	NORTH	EAST	SOUTH
.			3◇
Pass	Pass	Double	Pass
3NT	Pass	Pass	Pass

North leads the 9 of diamonds. South plays the 8 and you win. How many top winners do you have? How do you continue at tricks 2 and 3?

PLAY HANDS ON CARD READING & INFERENCES (1)

Hand 65 : Dealer North : N-S vulnerable

NORTH
♠ 10
♡ 9 6 4
◇ 6 3
♣ A K Q 6 5 4 2

WEST
♠ K 9 6 5 3
♡ 3
◇ A J 10 5
♣ 8 7 3

EAST
♠ A J 8 4
♡ K Q J 5
◇ K Q 2
♣ J 9

SOUTH
♠ Q 7 2
♡ A 10 8 7 2
◇ 9 8 7 4
♣ 10

WEST	NORTH	EAST	SOUTH
	3♣	Double	Pass
4♠	Pass	Pass	Pass

Lead : ♣K (or ace). No second choice.

Play: North cashes two clubs and South discards on the second club. North continues with a third club. Declarer ruffs with dummy's *ace* of spades and continues with the jack of spades. If South plays low, declarer lets the jack run. When the 10 drops from North, declarer continues with a low spade and finesses the 9 if South plays low. Declarer makes 10 tricks, losing 1 heart and 2 clubs.

Notes : (1) At unfavourable vulnerability, a 3-level pre-empt should not hold fewer than 7 likely winners.
(2) 3♠ would be a very timid effort by West and East should pass a 3♠ response. As a takeout double at the 3-level should be worth around 16-17 points or 6 losers, or better, West is certainly worth 4♠.

(3) On the second club, South should signal, asking North to continue clubs. A discouraging diamond is best (North is more likely to be short in hearts and you would not mind a switch to a singleton heart).
(4) Declarer should realise after trick 2 that the ♠ Q is almost certainly with South. North who pre-empted has turned up with A-K-Q in clubs. Hardly likely that North has the ♠ Q as well. If you ruff low, South will overruff and you still have to lose a heart. The best genuine chance is to play North to hold the ♠ 10 singleton: ruff with the ♠ A and then lead the *jack* of spades (despite the general rule not to lead an honor for a finesse if not holding the touching honor). If this does not work, it is unlikely that anything would have worked.

Hand 66 : Dealer East : Nil vulnerable

NORTH
♠ K 8 5
♡ K 3
◇ Q J 6 4 3
♣ Q 4 3

WEST
♠ 9
♡ J 10 5
◇ 9 8 5 2
♣ 10 9 6 5 2

EAST
♠ Q 6 2
♡ A Q 9 8 4 2
◇ 10
♣ A 8 7

SOUTH
♠ A J 10 7 4 3
♡ 7 6
◇ A K 7
♣ K J

WEST	NORTH	EAST	SOUTH
		1♡	Double
Pass	3◇	Pass	3♠
Pass	4♠	All pass	

Lead : ♡J. Partner's suit and top from touching honors.

Play: After two heart tricks, East switches to the ace of clubs. West discourages, so East tries the 10 of diamonds. Declarer wins and leads a spade to the king. A low spade is returned and declarer finesses the jack when East plays low. The last trump is drawn and declarer has 10 tricks.

Notes: (1) With 16 useful HCP and a strong 6-card suit, South is too strong for a simple overcall. A jump overcall of 2♠ is acceptable if this is played as strong. If not using strong jump overcalls, double-then-bid-your-suit shows these values and at least a 5-suit.
(2) North might respond 2NT (and 3NT makes at least 11 tricks on the same play in spades), but 3◇ does not preclude a 3NT contract and on other layouts, that modest heart stopper may not be adequate.
(3) After leading ♡ J, West should drop the 10 on the second round (follow the sequence down). The benefit occurs in other situations where the jack is followed by a lower card. This promises a doubleton, as you did not continue with the 10.
(4) East tries the ace of clubs at trick 3 just in case West has the king.
(5) South counts 16 HCP in hand, 11 HCP in dummy. East opened and West led the jack of hearts. The remaining 12 points must be with East to justify the opening bid. The normal play with the spade suit is to cash the ace and king and hope the queen drops. That does not apply, of course, if you know who holds the queen. If East has a regular opening bid, the spade finesse is marked.

Hand 67 : Dealer South : E-W vulnerable

NORTH
- ♠ 8 3
- ♡ 9 6 3 2
- ◇ A Q 7 6
- ♣ K 9 8

WEST
- ♠ 10
- ♡ J 10 5
- ◇ K J 10 9
- ♣ A Q J 6 4

EAST
- ♠ A K Q J 9 6 2
- ♡ 8 4
- ◇ 2
- ♣ 10 3 2

SOUTH
- ♠ 7 5 4
- ♡ A K Q 7
- ◇ 8 5 4 3
- ♣ 7 5

WEST	NORTH	EAST	SOUTH
			Pass
1♣	Pass	1♠	Pass
2♣	Pass	4♠	All pass

Lead : ♡K (or ace). Natural to go for heart tricks.

Play : North gives a discouraging signal, but South continues hearts as they are so strong. East ruffs the third heart and should continue with a diamond to the jack and queen. If North tries to cash the ◇ A, East ruffs, draws trumps and there are two diamond winners for club discards. If North returns a trump, this is ducked to the 10 and the ◇ K led. If North covers, ruff and draw trumps. If North ducks, discard a club and lead another diamond. The object is discard two clubs on the diamonds and avoid the club finesse.

Notes : (1) East is too strong for an immediate 4♠ reply.
(2) With strength in the long suits, a 2♣ rebid is superior to 1NT. The hand is not good enough for a 2◇ reverse.
(3) 4♠ can be defeated if South switches to a trump or a club before trying the third heart. This is very tough and would not be found by one defender in ten. North can help South find the switch: play the 2 (discouraging) on the first heart and the 3 on the second heart. Where the card played on the second round of a suit is an idle card, it can sensibly be used as a suit preference signal (lowest card asks for low suit). See Chapter 20 : Suit Preference Signals & Secondary Signals for further information and examples in this area.
(4) After the A-K-Q of hearts, East knows the ◇ A and ♣K are with North (as South passed as dealer). Thus, the club finesse is futile and declarer finesses the ◇ J and takes the ruffing finesse in diamonds later for success.
(5) North might defeat the contract by winning the first diamond with the ace. If East places the ◇ Q with South, East might later win ◇ K and ruff a diamond hoping that the queen drops. North can find this play if South has shown an even number of diamonds (see Chapter 19 — Count Signals), as North knows that declarer can tell North has the ◇ A after the top hearts have been played. Even if unsure of the diamond count, winning ◇ A is unlikely to cost. With a second diamond, East will almost certainly repeat the diamond finesse.

Hand 68 : Dealer West : Both vulnerable

NORTH
- ♠ 9 6
- ♡ A 8 7 5 3
- ◇ A Q 2
- ♣ A Q 5

WEST
- ♠ A K 8 7 4
- ♡ 2
- ◇ 9 6 5
- ♣ K 9 8 3

EAST
- ♠ Q J 10 2
- ♡ Q 9 6
- ◇ 10 8 4
- ♣ J 10 7

SOUTH
- ♠ 5 3
- ♡ K J 10 4
- ◇ K J 7 3
- ♣ 6 4 2

WEST	NORTH	EAST	SOUTH
Pass	1♡	Pass	2♡
Dble	3♡	Pass	4♡
Pass	Pass	Pass	

Lead : ♠Q. Top of sequence is best.

Play : West plays the ♠8, encouraging, and overtakes the ♠J at trick 2 in order to switch to a club. North inserts the queen which holds, North continues with the ace of hearts and a heart to the jack when East follows low. The ♡K draws the last trump and declarer scores 11 tricks.

Notes : (1) West might bid 2♠ but double caters for all suits.
(2) North's 3♡ invites game if South has more than a minimum raise. The bid does not change its meaning after West's double. A new suit by North would be a trial bid, also inviting game but this is normally used only with a weakish suit, one with two or three losers. With only a doubleton spade and strength in the other outside suits, the general invitation via 3♡ is best.
(3) If the club finesse lost, North would have to try to avoid a trump loser. Even then, finessing the ♡ J is the better bet in view of West's double, less attractive with Q-x in hearts.
(4) When the club finesse works, North can place West with A-K in spades and the ♣K. That makes 10 HCP and since West passed as dealer, West will not hold the ♡Q as well. Therefore finesse East for the queen.

CHAPTER 16

DECEPTIVE STRATEGY BY DECLARER

There are many ways that declarer can make it more difficult for the defenders to know what to do. One of the most promising areas is the treatment of equal (or touching) honors.

	Dummy	
	7 5	
3 led		
	A K Q	

West leads the 3 and East plays the jack. To South, it is irrelevant whether the trick is won with the ace, king or queen. However, if South wins with the queen, West knows that East has no card higher than the jack. South should win with the ace. That leaves it open for East to hold Q-J-x or K-Q-J-x or jack only. As a result, West may later misguess the position and misdefend. It is normally correct for a defender to win with the cheapest card (in order not to mislead partner), but this is not the best strategy for declarer.

A. In general, declarer should win a trick with the highest of equal winning cards.

1. 7 6	**2.** 7 6	**3.** 7 6
K Q 9	A Q J	A K J 3

In each of the above positions, West leads the 4 and East plays the 10. Which card should declarer play?

1. Win with the king. The king and queen are equals.
2. Win with the queen. The queen and jack are equals.
3. Win the jack. The jack is not equal to the ace and king.

B. When attempting to win a trick, play the highest of equal cards from your hand.

Dummy	
7 5 2	
K Q J 6	

In setting up winners in this suit, declarer leads low from dummy to the honors in hand. If East plays low, South should play the king, not the jack. To South, it is immaterial which honor is played, but the king gives the defenders the hardest time.

Suppose that West has the ace. If you play the jack and West takes the ace, East knows you have the K-Q as well (West would have taken the jack with a cheaper card if possible). If you play the king and West takes the ace, East cannot tell who holds the queen and the jack. Similarly, if East has the ace, playing the king conceals the location of the queen and jack. When the king scores, East does not know who holds the lower honors. However, if you play the jack and it wins, East can tell you also hold the king and queen.

The same applies when declarer is taking a finesse :

Dummy	
7 4 3	
A Q J 10	

Lead low from dummy and finesse the queen, not the 10. To declarer, it is irrelevant which honor is finessed, but the queen hides the maximum information from the defenders. If you finesse the 10 and it wins, East knows you have the queen and jack. If you finesse the 10 and West takes with the *king*, again East knows you hold the queen and jack. If you finesse the queen, East cannot tell who has the jack and 10, whether the finesse wins or loses.

C. When winning a trick in dummy with equal but non-touching honors, play the higher honor from dummy.

Dummy	
A Q J 6	
K 5 2	

In a suit contract, if West leads this suit and you wish to win in dummy, win with the ace, not the queen or jack. If you play the queen, West knows East does not hold the king. If you take the ace, West cannot be certain. Perhaps you had a singleton and did not wish to risk a finesse. Perhaps you did not wish to risk the lead being a singleton and losing to East's king and having the return ruffed. Playing the queen or jack clarifies the position for West; playing the ace leaves the position ambiguous.

Dummy	
K J 6	
Q 5 4	

If leading low to dummy, play the king if West plays low. If you play the jack and it wins, West knows you have the queen. If the king is played, West cannot be sure who has the queen. If the king wins, return to hand if convenient and lead low towards the J-6. If West ducks again, your jack wins and perhaps you can discard your queen later. It may not be wrong for West to duck twice. For example :

```
                    K J 6
        A 10 9 8 2           Q 3
                    7 5 4
```

South leads low and puts up dummy's king when West plays low. The king wins. South returns to hand and leads low. If West plays the ace here, the jack is high! Study this position and the previous layout and note how you can give the defense a tough time.

D. When leading honor cards from hand, lead top from a sequence if you want a defender to cover your honor, but lead bottom or second bottom from a sequence if you want second player to play low.

K 4 3
A J 10 9 6 2

With nine cards missing the queen, the standard play is king and ace, hoping the queen drops. However, when you also hold the J-10-9, you can afford to lead the jack from hand. Every so often an unwary defender will play the queen from Q-x-x and you have avoided a loser. If West follows low smoothly, play the king and return to the ace. It was never your intention to finesse anyway. Even if only one defender in twenty covers your jack, your gain is pure profit. It costs nothing to lead the jack.

K 4 3 2
A J 10 9

With eight cards missing the queen, it is normal to finesse for the queen on the second round. With no idea who holds the queen, you could play the ace and then lead the jack or play the king first and finesse the jack on the way back. With no genuine clue as to the location of the queen, try leading the jack from hand. If West covers with Q-x or Q-x-x, you have saved a trick. If West plays low, you can still play the king from dummy and finesse the jack on the way back, playing East for the queen.

Against inexperienced defenders, the jack may locate the queen by their indecision. When you lead the jack, West may dither and hesitate, pull out a card, put it back. . . If West then plays low, you can reasonably place West with the queen and let the jack run.

NOTE : It is contrary to the laws of bridge to dither and hesitate with the deliberate intention of deceiving or misleading an opponent.

Suppose you fear that East may ruff a side suit and this is the trump position :

```
              7 5 4
  A 9                    8 2
          K Q J 10 6 3
```

If you lead the king and West has the ace, West will naturally take the ace and may give East the ruff. If you lead a lower honor, West may duck (second-hand-low) and your second round draws the rest of the trumps. By sneaking a trump trick past West, you have avoided the danger of the ruff by East. Which card should you lead to have the best chance of sneaking the trick past West? Generally, it is best to lead second bottom from sequences, so that the

jack from the above suit is the preferred choice. However, against inexperienced players, the 10 is probably more likely to succeed in inducing the error.

For defenders : If declarer leads an honor from hand and you hold the next lower card, declarer is trying to sneak a trick past you. Grab the trick and try to work out why declarer was anxious to avoid your taking the trick.

Corollary for declarers: If you lead second bottom from a sequence when trying to sneak past second player, they will not hold the next lower card. Thus, they will not be able to interpret your plan so easily.

Incidentally, if on the above layout, you feared a ruff by West, cross to dummy if convenient and lead towards your hand. East may duck with A-x in the belief that you crossed to dummy to take a finesse in this suit. If East ducks, the ruff is averted.

The Pretend Finesse

K 7 3
Q J 10 9 4

Fearing a ruff by East, you wish to draw as many trumps as possible. If you wish to sneak a round of trumps past West, your best move is to lead the jack. To West, this will look as though you are finessing for the queen and West may well play low from A-x or A-x-x. If so, you have achieved your aim and can draw a second round of trumps.

E. If you fear a ruff, drop the higher of equal winners to pretend you hold a singleton.

J 7 2
Q 10 5

Against your suit contract, West leads the king, confirming the ace. Drop your queen. It cannot hurt and if West believes your queen is singleton, West may discontinue the suit and may fail to give East a ruff.

For defenders : If you think declarer's card is a singleton, check carefully the card that partner played. Trust your partner's signal, not declarer's card. At any time if you think partner's card or declarer's card is a singleton, work out how many cards the other player would have. Is that holding consistent with the bidding? If not, the singleton holding is unlikely.

J 9 6 2
K Q 10

West leads the 7 and East plays the ace. Drop your king. If the 7 is a singleton, East may now read you to have the king singleton and West to have led the 7 from Q-10-7. If East discontinues the suit, you may have averted a ruff. In addition, you have started to unblock the suit. Later you can play the queen and overtake the 10 with the jack. Playing the king (or the queen) keeps the suit 'fluid'.

F. To cause the opening leader to misinterpret the signal by third hand, do not play your lowest card in a suit if you want it continued.

10 9 2

A K J 5   8 7 4

Q 6 3

West leads the king, East plays the 4 and South should drop the 6. If South plays the 3, West can read the 4 as East's lowest and therefore discouraging and West may well switch. If South drops the 6, West may read East's 4 as encouraging from Q-4-3 or from 4-3 doubleton wanting a ruff. If so, West may continue the suit and South scores an extra trick.

If the opponents are using standard signals :

Play your lowest as declarer if you are not keen to have the suit continued.

Play a high card if you want the suit continued.

This is the best strategy to try to interfere with their signalling as far as possible.

If they are using reverse signals (low to encourage, high to discourage), you reverse your strategy, too. Play lowest if you want the suit continued and high if you are not keen on the suit.

G. Win with a higher card than necessary if a greater risk lies elsewhere.

WEST	EAST
♠ Q 5 2	♠ 8 3
♡ A K J	♡ 7 2
◇ A K 8 3	◇ Q J 5 4
♣ J 8 4	♣ K Q 10 9 3

West is in 3NT and North leads the 4 of hearts, 10 from South... What should West do? Try to plan your play before playing a card from dummy. Do not play quickly and instinctively, winning the jack. With the spades so dangerous, West's best hope is to win with the ace of hearts, not the jack, and then tackle the clubs.

If North has the ace of clubs and you won trick 1 with the ♡ J, North may realise the futility of pursuing the hearts. A spade switch is likely to be fatal to you. However, if you won trick 1 with the ♡ A, North will imagine you cannot hold the jack and may well lead another 'safe' heart upon winning the ♣ A. Not only do you now make your contract, but you also score your three heart tricks after all.

A similar problem :

WEST	EAST
♠ A Q 5	♠ 7 2
♡ J 8	♡ 8 4 2
◇ A 9 3 2	◇ Q J 10 7 6
♣ A J 4 3	♣ K Q 9

West is in 3NT and North leads the 6 of spades, jack from South ... What should West do?

The natural move is to win the queen, cross to a club in dummy and take the diamond finesse. If this loses, North may switch to hearts as North knows you still hold the ace of spades. See the effect of winning trick 1 with the ♠ A. If the diamond finesse works, 3NT is secure, but if North wins the ◇ K, North will assume that South has the ♠ Q and played the jack from Q-J-x. North is then likely to continue with a low spade and you will score your ♠ Q after all (and have a story to tell for weeks to come).

An astute defender may wonder why you did not hold up if you had only the ace in spades. Fortunately, we do not play against thoughtful defenders very often. In any event, North is more likely to credit you with a silly mistake than with an imaginative deception.

H. Lead low from dummy towards your own hand to force second player to guess whether to play high or low.

1.	Q 7 6 4	2.	Q 7 6 4	3.	Q 7 6 4
	K		K J		K 3

With plenty of entries, best play is low from dummy to your king. If the king wins, East has the ace. Return to dummy and lead low from dummy again. If East rises with the ace, you have an extra trick in **1.** and **3.** If East plays low, you have lost nothing in **1.** and **3.** but in **2.** you have scored a second trick without loss.

Dummy   West leads the jack, East's bid suit.
A Q 5 4   The jack may be singleton or doubleton,
                   but as far as East knows, West may
10 6   have J-10. Win the ace and, sooner or
later, lead low from dummy. If East plays low, your 10 scores a second trick and you lose no tricks.

A Q 5 4

J 10 3   K 9 8 7 2

6

You should do the same in this situation. When West leads the jack, win the ace and lead low from dummy when it suits you. If East rises with the king, you ruff and dummy's queen has been set up. Thank you, East.

EXERCISE ON DECEPTIVE STRATEGY BY DECLARER

1.   A 9 5 4

   Q J 10 8 3

You do not know who has the king in this trump suit. You cannot afford to take the normal finesse because there is a danger of an immediate and fatal ruff if the finesse loses. You propose to play ace and another heart. However, you would naturally like to capture the king if West has it. What can you do to try to accomplish both objectives?

(a) Lead the queen?
(b) Lead the jack?
(c) Lead the 10?
(d) Lead the 8?
(e) Lead low from hand and finesse the 9?
(f) Makes no difference how you play?

2.   A Q 5 3 2
   K 7 6   9 8 4
        J 10

You need five tricks from this suit and dummy has no entry. How can you play to try to score the five tricks needed? What is the danger? How can try to enlist West's co-operation?

(a) Lead the jack?
(b) Lead the 10?
(c) Makes no difference which you lead first?

3.   **Dealer North : Nil vulnerable**

        NORTH
        ♠ 7 3
        ♡ J 10 8
        ◇ K Q J
        ♣ K Q J 8 5

        SOUTH
        ♠ K J
        ♡ A K Q 9 7 6 4 3
        ◇ - - -
        ♣ A 4 2

WEST	NORTH	EAST	SOUTH
	1♣	4♠	6♡
Pass	Pass	Pass	

West leads the queen of spades. How should South play? What do you make of the opening lead plus East's bid? What great danger threatens to defeat your excellent slam? How can you try to avert the impending disaster?

4. You have plenty of entries to dummy. How should you handle these combinations for maximum tricks in a suit contract?

(a)	**You**	**Dummy**
	K	J 6 4

(b)	**You**	**Dummy**
	K	Q J 6 4

(c)	**You**	**Dummy**
	10	Q J 6 4

(d)	**You**	**Dummy**
	10 9	Q J 6 4

(e)	**You**	**Dummy**
	Q 5	K 7 4 2

5.   **NORTH**
        ♠ A 5 3 2
        ♡ 8 2
        ◇ Q 3
        ♣ A Q 6 5 3

        SOUTH
        ♠ J 7 4
        ♡ A K 4 3
        ◇ A K 5
        ♣ 7 4 2

South is in 3NT and West leads the jack of diamonds. How should South plan the play? What is the best way to develop the club suit?

6.   **Dealer West : Both vulnerable**

        NORTH
        ♠ J 5 4
        ♡ J 6 2
        ◇ 8 4 3
        ♣ A J 10 4

        SOUTH
        ♠ K 2
        ♡ A K Q 9 8 7 4
        ◇ Q J
        ♣ K Q

WEST	NORTH	EAST	SOUTH
Pass	Pass	3♠	4♡
Pass	Pass	Pass	

West leads the 3 of spades to East's ace. How should South plan the play? What do you make of West's lead plus East's opening bid? How can you try to avert the likely calamity?

PLAY HANDS ON DECEPTIVE STRATEGY BY DECLARER

Hand 69 : Dealer North : N-S vulnerable

NORTH
- ♠ A 9 3
- ♡ A K 8 7 6 2
- ◇ J 3
- ♣ 4 2

WEST
- ♠ K Q J 10 5 4 2
- ♡ 10 5
- ◇ - - -
- ♣ K Q J 10

EAST
- ♠ - - -
- ♡ Q J 4
- ◇ A K 8 7 4 2
- ♣ A 9 7 6

SOUTH
- ♠ 8 7 6
- ♡ 9 3
- ◇ Q 10 9 6 5
- ♣ 8 5 3

WEST	NORTH	EAST	SOUTH
	1♡	2◇	Pass
4♠	Pass	Pass	Pass

Lead: ♡ K (or ace). Hard to beat an A-K suit for the opening lead.

Play: South encourages a heart continuation by signalling with the 9 of hearts. North cashes the ace of hearts and should continue with a third heart. This removes one of declarer's winners and if South can ruff high enough, it may create a second trump winner for North. South ruffs and West overruffs. When West leads a trump, North should take the ace and play a fourth heart. Again South ruffs and West is forced to overruff again. After West plays the next trump winner, North's 9 of spades becomes the top trump and the fourth trick for the defense. This play of ruffing with a highish trump and forcing declarer to overruff is called an 'uppercut' because it *knocks out* a top trump. This hand features a double uppercut.

Notes : (1) With a self-sufficient suit, West should waste no time and simply bid a direct 4♠.
(2) If South's spades were 8-7-2, South should still ruff high. This costs nothing and may create an uppercut.
(3) After overruffing the spade, West should continue with the jack or ten of spades, not the king. On the king, North will have no problem taking the ace. If West leads the jack or ten, North may make the mistake of playing low. When the next trump is led, South's third trump is drawn and the second uppercut disappears. When declarer wishes to draw a round of trumps without losing the lead, lead bottom or second bottom from a sequence, not the top card.

Hand 70 : Dealer East : E-W vulnerable

NORTH
- ♠ K 7 6 5
- ♡ A 10 9
- ◇ J 6 4
- ♣ K J 10

WEST
- ♠ A 8
- ♡ Q J 3
- ◇ K Q 10 9 7
- ♣ 8 7 3

EAST
- ♠ 3 2
- ♡ 8 7 6 5 2
- ◇ 8 2
- ♣ A 9 6 4

SOUTH
- ♠ Q J 10 9 4
- ♡ K 4
- ◇ A 5 3
- ♣ Q 5 2

WEST	NORTH	EAST	SOUTH
		Pass	1♠
2◇	3♠	Pass	4♠
Pass	Pass	Pass	

Lead : ◇ K. A heart lead would be reasonable (although not successful), but when choosing between two suits with touching honors, prefer the suit which has more cards in the sequence. The diamond suit has three cards in a near-sequence while the heart suit has only two.

Play : On the king of diamonds lead, East should signal for a continuation by playing the 8 of diamonds. South wins the ◇ A and should lead a trump. Best defense is for West to win the first round of trumps and continue with the queen of diamonds and a third diamond. East ruffs and cashes the ace of clubs for one down.

Notes: (1) After an overcall, a jump raise is best played as a limit raise, a strong invitation with about 10-12 points. That is what North is worth here. With sufficient high card values to force to game, responder can bid the enemy suit. After a limit raise, South should pass 3♠ but some partners are irrepressible.
(2) If declarer can draw two rounds of trumps, 4♠ will make, as East will be unable to ruff the third diamond. South's best chance to try to sneak a round of trumps past West is to lead the jack of spades, a pretend-finesse. It may appear to West that declarer is finessing for the queen. If West falls for it and plays low, declarer will be able to draw another round of trumps and escape the diamond ruff.
(3) West should rise with the ♠ A on the jack. Partner's ◇ 8 indicates a desire to ruff and partner is unlikely to hold more than two trumps. Even if East does have Q-x in spades, South is unlikely to misguess trumps in view of the bidding. Therefore it is vital to win the first trump to give partner the ruff.

Hand 71 : Dealer South : Both vulnerable

NORTH
- ♠ Q
- ♡ 9 6
- ◇ 10 7 6 3 2
- ♣ 9 8 6 5 2

WEST
- ♠ 10 9 5 4
- ♡ 7 5
- ◇ Q 8 5
- ♣ A Q 10 7

EAST
- ♠ 7 2
- ♡ K Q J 10 8 3 2
- ◇ A
- ♣ K J 3

SOUTH
- ♠ A K J 8 6 3
- ♡ A 4
- ◇ K J 9 4
- ♣ 4

WEST	NORTH	EAST	SOUTH
			1♠
Pass	Pass	4♡	All pass

Lead : ♠ K (or ace). It is tempting to lead the singleton club but an A-K suit is a superior start. After the first trick, you can still switch to your singleton if that seems best. However, if it appears best to continue the A-K suit, you are still on lead and can do so.

Play : When North follows with the queen of spades at trick 1, South realises this is a singleton (see Chapter 8), as South holds the jack. Now South leads the singleton club. Declarer wins and leads a trump. South wins, leads a low spade for North to ruff and receives a club ruff in return. One down.

Notes : (1) In the pass out seat, any decent hand containing a self-sufficient major should take a shot at 4♡/4♠. The suit is good enough if it passes the Suit Quality Test (length plus honors equals or exceeds tricks bid). Thus a 6-card suit with four honors or a 7-card suit with three honors justifies a bid at game-level without receiving trump support from partner.
(2) If South continues spades at trick 2, the contract cannot be defeated. North no longer has an entry to give South the club ruff.
(3) Declarer can see what is about to happen and should realise that South is angling for a club ruff. East's best chance is to lead a low heart honor, the jack or ten, and hope that South sleepily plays second-hand-low. If so, a second round of trumps can be drawn and the risk of the ruff has evaporated. Of course, South should take the ace if the jack or ten is led. South's plan was to receive a club ruff. If South does not take the ace on the first round of trumps, the club ruff may not eventuate.

Hand 72 : Dealer West : Nil vulnerable

NORTH
- ♠ A 10 6 4 2
- ♡ A K Q J 8
- ◇ A
- ♣ A 2

WEST
- ♠ 9
- ♡ 7 6 4 3
- ◇ 10 9 8 2
- ♣ K 9 4 3

EAST
- ♠ Q J 5
- ♡ 5 2
- ◇ K J 5 3
- ♣ Q J 10 8

SOUTH
- ♠ K 8 7 3
- ♡ 10 9
- ◇ Q 7 6 4
- ♣ 7 6 5

WEST	NORTH	EAST	SOUTH
Pass	2♣	Pass	2◇
Pass	2♠	Pass	3♠
Pass	6♠	All pass	

Lead : ♣ Q. Normal attractive sequence start.

Play : West encourages by playing the 9 of clubs. North wins the ace of clubs and tackles the trumps : a spade to the king (play first the honor opposite the tenace) and a spade to the ace. When trumps are 3-1, leave the last trump out. Lead the hearts and try to discard clubs on the third and fourth heart. East should ruff the third heart and cash a club for one down.

Notes : (1) North has enough to insist on game. Over South's negative, bid first the higher of two 5-card suits. South's raise to 3♠ promises at least one useful card (a king, an ace, a singleton or a void). That is enough for North to bid the slam and it is best to do so without revealing the heart values. The less the defense knows about the shape of your hand and where your strength lies, the better your chance of success.
(2) 6♠ is an excellent slam. It will succeed if there is no trump loser or if the opening lead is not a club or if the hand with the last trump holds three or more hearts (so that two clubs can be discarded before they ruff).
(3) As the cards lie, the slam cannot be made against best defense. However, declarer can try a little ruse to outfox East. After the king and ace of spades, cash the ace of hearts, king of hearts and lead the *eight* of hearts next. The 8 of hearts is a winner : you know that, but East does not know. East may believe you intend to ruff this 'loser' in dummy and may decide not to waste the trump winner on a loser. If East discards, a rude awakening is at hand. You discard a club on the ♡ 8 and lead another heart. East ruffs, but too late. Your remaining club loser is discarded and the slam is home. Note that the 8 of hearts is just as much a winner as the queen or jack but if the defender does not know it is a winner, you may be able to sneak the trick through.

REVISION TEST ON PART 2

The material in Chapters 9-16 will help you answer these questions. If you experience difficulty in producing the correct answers, it will pay you to read these chapters again.

A. On each of these hands, you have reached 6♡ after East opened 1♠ and you responded 2♡ :

1.

WEST	EAST
♠ 9	♠ Q 7 6 3 2
♡ A Q 9 8 5 3 2	♡ K J 7
◇ Q 4	◇ A K
♣ A K 3	♣ 5 4 2

North leads the jack of diamonds. What do you play at trick 2? How do you plan to win 12 tricks? What will you do if North started with 10-6-4 in trumps? What could defeat you?

2.

WEST	EAST
♠ 7	♠ A 8 6 5 4 2
♡ A Q 10 6 4 2	♡ K J 9 8
◇ A 6 3	◇ Q 4
♣ Q J 5	♣ K

North leads the jack of diamonds. You try the queen from dummy, but South plays the king. How do you plan your play in 6♡? What do you play at tricks 2 and 3?

B. What is the best way to play each of these combinations to lose no tricks?

1. K 9 3 2	2. Q 7 4 2	3. Q 10 4 2
A Q 5 4	A J 5 3	A J 5 3

4. K 7 2	5. K 7 2	6. J 6 4 2
A J 5 4 3	A J 6 5 4 3	A K 5 3

C. How should declarer, South, play these combinations in a trump contract to lose no tricks in hand?

1. A Q 10 6	2. A Q 10 6	3. A Q 10 6
5 4	7 5 4	7 5 4 3

4. A Q 10 6	5. A Q 10 6 2
8 7 5 4 3	8 7 5 4 3

D. You are playing 3NT and West leads a low card. Which card do you play from dummy (North)?

1. A J 9	2. A J 2	3. J 9 2
7 5 3	9 6 3	A 6 3

4. J 6 2	5. Q 7	6. Q 7
A 9 3	A 5 3	A 10 3

E. West is in 4♡. North leads ♠J. Plan the play.

WEST	EAST
♠ K 6 3	♠ A 7 4
♡ K Q J 8 7 6	♡ 5 4 3 2
◇ K Q	◇ J 4 2
♣ A Q	♣ J 4 2

F. On each of the next two hands, West is in 3NT. North leads the 5 of diamonds. Plan the play.

1.

WEST	EAST
♠ A Q J	♠ 6 3 2
♡ A 9 5 3	♡ J 2
◇ A K 4 2	◇ 7 6
♣ 7 3	♣ A K 6 5 4 2

2.

WEST	EAST
♠ A Q J	♠ 6 3 2
♡ A 9 5 3	♡ J 2
◇ A K 4 2	◇ 7 6
♣ 7 3	♣ A Q 6 5 4 2

G.

WEST	EAST
♠ K J 7 3 2	♠ A 10 6 4
♡ K Q	♡ J 7
◇ 6 5	◇ 8 4 3
♣ A 8 6 3	♣ K Q J 5

WEST	NORTH	EAST	SOUTH
	Pass	Pass	Pass
1♠	2◇	3♠	Pass
4♠	Pass	Pass	Pass

North leads ◇ K, ◇ Q, ◇ J. South follows with ◇ 9, ◇ 2 and ◇ A which West ruffs. How should West continue? How should West tackle the spades?

H. (a) In each of these layouts, West leads the 3, dummy follows low and East plays the 9. With which card should declarer win the trick?

1. 5 4	2. 5 4	3. 5 4
A Q J 7	A K J 10	A K 7

(b) With no entry problems, you want to draw two rounds of trumps without the ace taking the first round.

You	Dummy
K Q 10 7 5	J 6 2

1. How should you play if you want North to duck with the ace?

2. How should you play if you want South to duck with the ace?

PART 3

IMPROVE YOUR

DEFENSIVE PLAY

CHAPTER 17

PASSIVE & ACTIVE OPENING LEADS

Sequence leads are so attractive because they set up tricks with almost no risk of giving declarer an undeserved trick. Leading from suits with only one honor or two honors or non-touching honors is risky. It may give declarer an extra trick. Such leads are also known as 'active' or 'busy' or 'attacking' leads.

(1)
```
              8 7 3
     K J 6 2          10 9 5
              A Q 4
```

(2)
```
              8 7 3
     K J 6 2          Q 5 4
              A 10 9
```

(3)
```
              A Q 5
     K J 6 2          9 8 4
              10 7 3
```

(4)
```
              A Q 5
     K J 6 2          10 9 4
              8 7 3
```

In each case, West leads the 2, an active, attacking lead. In (1), this gives declarer an extra trick with the queen. If declarer has to tackle the suit, declarer makes only one trick. The same would apply if dummy held A-x-x and declarer Q-x-x.

In (2), the lead works out well, East's queen knocking out the ace and setting up West's honors. In (3), the lead gives declarer a third trick if declarer plays low from dummy. The 10 wins and South can later finesse dummy's queen. If West leaves the suit alone, declarer has only two tricks. In (4) the lead gives declarer nothing extra. Declarer always had two tricks by finessing the queen.

Even when partner holds the ace, the lead may cost a trick:

(5)
```
              Q 5 3
     K J 6 2          A 8 7
              10 9 4
```

If West leads the 2, declarer plays low from dummy and East plays the ace (else South scores the 10). Now dummy's queen becomes a trick, sooner or later. If the defense does not touch this suit, declarer cannot develop a trick in it. Whoever leads the suit first drops a trick.

Even when the honors are touching, there is risk attached :

(6)
```
              J 5 4
     K Q 6          10 9 7 2
              A 8 3
```

(7)
```
              8 5 4
     K Q 6          9 7 3 2
              A J 10
```

In each case, if West leads the suit, West gives declarer a second trick. Declarer wins the king with the ace and can lead to the jack later, in (6), or lead the 10 or jack in (7) to set up the second trick. If West does not lead the suit, declarer has only one trick. Of course, if East held the jack or the ace, the lead would have worked out well.

(8)
```
              K 10 4
     Q J 6          9 8 7 3
              A 5 2
```

(9)
```
              K 5 4
     Q J 6          8 7 3 2
              A 10 9
```

In each case, South has only two tricks and no legitimate way to make a third trick without help from the defense. However, if West leads the suit, this gives declarer a third trick. In (8), South wins the queen with the ace and can, sooner or later, finesse dummy's 10. In (9), South wins the ace and can, sooner or later, lead the 10, finessing if West plays low or setting up the 9 if West covers the 10. Of course, Q-J-x as an opening lead could work out well if partner held the ace, king or 10.

Active leads such as the above do entail risk but sometimes the risk has to be taken. Passive leads are from suits with no honors, commonly three or four rags, or a trump lead from two or three rags. Passive leads rarely give declarer anything that declarer does not already have or could have won anyway. Passive leads are usually not effective if your objective is setting up tricks (although you might be lucky and strike gold in partner's hand). Passive leads are selected because they are unlikely to give away a trick. They usually do not give declarer more than declarer already has.

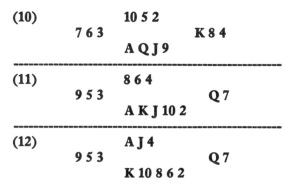

(10)

10 5 2

7 6 3   K 8 4

A Q J 9

----

(11)

8 6 4

9 5 3   Q 7

A K J 10 2

----

(12)

A J 4

9 5 3   Q 7

K 10 8 6 2

If West leads this suit, East's honor is captured. Still, in (10) and (11), the lead did not cost. East's honor was always doomed. The lead made it happen a little sooner. In (12), East might have scored the queen but for the lead. South might have led low to the jack or cashed the king and then led low to the jack. East should accept the loss philosophically. After all, declarer might have played to the ace and then led the jack (the best play when South has K-10-8-x-x). If so, the queen would not have won anyway. Perhaps some other lead by partner would have been more damaging. Even if the queen almost certainly would have taken a trick, be gracious (as always) and do not berate partner for the choice of lead.

Sometimes it is best to make an attacking lead and accept the risk. On other occasions, a passive lead is best. Here are some guidelines if you have no attractive lead such as a sequence or an A-K suit.

When To Make A Passive Lead

1. Against a grand slam

Lead a trump from two or more rags as long as partner cannot reasonably hold Q-x-x or J-x-x-x. Against 7NT, do not lead from any suit that contains an honor card (unless it is a sequence, of course).

2. Against 6NT

Choose a suit with no honor card, if possible. Your aims against 6NT are not the same as against 3NT or lower contracts. Remember that if you hold 6 or 7 points, partner probably has no high cards.

3. Against 1NT/2NT with no 5-card or longer suit

Tend to avoid a 4-card suit with no sequence. Prefer 3 or 4 rags to a 4-card suit with just one honor or two non-touching honors. Holdings such as J-10-x or 10-9-x are often more productive than a modest 4-card suit. Against a 1NT or 2NT opening, passed out, or a 1NT : 2NT auction, it is often best to stick with a passive lead. Leading into the strong hand from a 4-card suit with just one honor will often cost a trick.

4. Against a trump contract when there is no evidence that dummy has a long suit

After bidding like 1♠ : 2♠, 4♠ or 1♡ : 4♡, if you have no outstanding lead elsewhere, a trump lead from two or three rags may be best.

When To Make An Attacking Lead

1. Against a suit contract when dummy is known to hold a 5-card or longer side suit

How does the play normally develop when dummy has a long suit? Trumps are drawn and the long suit is used to discard losers. If you lead trumps or lead dummy's long suit, this simply gives declarer the initiative. When dummy has a useful long suit, you must collect your tricks in the other suits as quickly as possible. If you do not get them early, you will not get them at all. The rule then is: 'When dummy has a useful long suit, you should lead one of the unbid suits, even if this is a risky lead.'

This advice does not apply if you are so strong in dummy's suit that there is no prospect of discards for declarer. For example, if their bidding proceeded 1♠ : 2♡, 2♠ : 4♠, lead a club or a diamond, as dummy's five (or more) hearts may provide discards for declarer. However, if you held Q-J-10-x-x in hearts, it would not be necessary to make a risky minor suit lead. The hearts will be of little use to declarer.

2. Against a small slam in a suit

An ace lead against a suit slam is usually more attractive than against lower contracts, especially if you have a likely trump trick. Again, if dummy has shown a long suit, an attacking lead in an unbid suit may be best. However, if you hold so much strength that partner cannot hold a significant high card, do not lead from any honors other than a sequence lead.

3. Against a pre-emptive opening

Often dummy produces a useful suit which will furnish declarer with discards. An ace lead against a pre-empt is quite reasonable. Declarer will rarely hold the king in that suit, so that you have not set up an extra trick for declarer, and by leading the ace you see dummy and can judge which suit to tackle.

4. Against 3NT when dummy is expected to hold a long, running suit

After an auction like 3♣ : 3NT, it is often better to attack from a suit like A-K-x or K-Q-x than from a weakish 4-card or 5-card suit. Against that kind of dummy, you have little time to set up a long suit. Unless you collect your five tricks quickly, you will not be collecting them at all.

EXERCISE ON PASSIVE AND ACTIVE LEADS

In each question, you are given West's hand and the auction. What should West lead?

1.

WEST
- ♠ K J 8 3
- ♡ 8 3 2
- ◇ Q J 6
- ♣ J 8 2

WEST	NORTH	EAST	SOUTH
			1♠
Pass	1NT	Pass	2♡
Pass	Pass	Pass	

2.

WEST
- ♠ J 8 6 4
- ♡ 8 6 2
- ◇ K 7 4 2
- ♣ A 5

South opened 1NT and all passed.

3.

WEST
- ♠ 7 5 4
- ♡ J 9 6 2
- ◇ K 5 4
- ♣ Q J 2

South opened 1NT and North made a quantitative raise to 4NT. South bid 6NT, accepting the invitation.

4.

WEST
- ♠ 10 8 6 4 2
- ♡ 8 5 3
- ◇ A 6
- ♣ Q 5 4

WEST	NORTH	EAST	SOUTH
			1♡
Pass	3◇	Pass	4◇
Pass	4NT	Pass	5◇
Pass	6♡	All pass	

5.

WEST
- ♠ 8 6 5 2
- ♡ Q 3 2
- ◇ Q 7 6
- ♣ J 3 2

WEST	NORTH	EAST	SOUTH
			2NT
Pass	3♠	Pass	4♠
Pass	4NT	Pass	5♡
Pass	5NT	Pass	6♠
Pass	6NT	All pass	

6.

WEST
- ♠ 9 5 2
- ♡ A 7 3
- ◇ K 6 4
- ♣ 10 9 6 4

WEST	NORTH	EAST	SOUTH
	1♣	Pass	1♡
Pass	3♣	Pass	3♡
Pass	4♡	All pass	

7.

WEST
- ♠ 6 4 2
- ♡ K J 9
- ◇ A J 6
- ♣ Q 7 5 2

WEST	NORTH	EAST	SOUTH
			1♠
Pass	2♠	Pass	2NT
Pass	3♠	All pass	

8.

WEST
- ♠ J 8 7 2
- ♡ Q 5 4
- ◇ 9 6 2
- ♣ 7 4 3

WEST	NORTH	EAST	SOUTH
			1◇
Pass	1♡	Pass	1NT
Pass	2NT	Pass	3NT
Pass	Pass	Pass	

9.

WEST
- ♠ 9 7 4
- ♡ K 9 6 2
- ◇ K J 4
- ♣ J 7 3

WEST	NORTH	EAST	SOUTH
	1NT	Pass	3♠
Pass	4♠	All pass	

10.

WEST
- ♠ Q 9 6 5 2
- ♡ 2
- ◇ A K 7 3
- ♣ 9 8 2

North opened 3♣ and South bid 3NT.

HANDS ON PASSIVE AND ACTIVE LEADS

Hand 73 : Dealer North : E-W vulnerable

WEST	NORTH	EAST	SOUTH
	1NT	Pass	2NT
Pass	3NT	All pass	

NORTH
- ♠ 10 9 5 2
- ♡ A K J
- ◇ A Q 10
- ♣ K 6 2

WEST
- ♠ K 8 7 3
- ♡ 10 6 2
- ◇ 9 2
- ♣ A J 9 7

EAST
- ♠ A 6
- ♡ Q 9 4 3
- ◇ J 8 7 6
- ♣ 8 5 4

SOUTH
- ♠ Q J 4
- ♡ 8 7 5
- ◇ K 5 4 3
- ♣ Q 10 3

Lead : ♣5. East has no attractive lead (no long suit, no sequence). As it is very dangerous to lead from Q-x-x-x or J-x-x-x, East should prefer a passive lead, especially when the auction is invitational.

Play : On a club lead, the contract can be defeated. Declarer should play the 10 of clubs : jack, king. On a spade shift, East should take the ace at once and lead a second club. This gives the defense three club tricks plus the ace and king of spades.

Notes : (1) 17 points plus two tens is enough to accept the invitation.
(2) If declarer plays the ♣3 from dummy at trick 1, West plays the 9. If declarer were to play the queen of clubs from dummy, West should win the ace and switch (to a heart, dummy's weak suit). Again, if East wins the ace of spades at once, a second club lead will defeat 3NT.

(3) On a heart lead, declarer is given a present, winning the jack of hearts. Declarer can make game by leading spades and scoring two spades, three hearts, three diamonds and one club. Most players would make the inferior lead of a heart on the East cards. "4th-highest-of-your-longest-and-strongest" is sensible from a 5-card or 6-card suit, not so attractive from just a broken 4-card suit.
(4) On a diamond lead, North wins the ◇ 10 at trick 1, another present, cashes the ◇ A-Q, unblocking, and then leads spades. Declarer makes two spades, two hearts, four diamonds and one club. The heart or diamond lead not only costs a trick but also gives declarer the time to set up the spades. Declarer wins the race to nine tricks before the defense can come to five tricks.
(5) The club lead will not always work out as well as this, but the heart or diamond lead will often work out badly. When defending, accept the idea that partner may often make a passive lead. If so, do not be too anxious to return your partner's lead if something better is beckoning.

Hand 74 : Dealer East : Both vulnerable

WEST	NORTH	EAST	SOUTH
		1◇	Pass
1♡	Pass	3◇	Pass
3♠	Pass	4◇	Pass
5◇	Pass	Pass	Pass

NORTH
- ♠ Q 8 7 6 2
- ♡ J 10
- ◇ 10
- ♣ K 10 8 4 2

WEST
- ♠ K J 4 3
- ♡ K Q 7 5 3
- ◇ Q 7
- ♣ 9 7

EAST
- ♠ A 5
- ♡ A 4
- ◇ A K 8 6 5 3
- ♣ J 6 3

SOUTH
- ♠ 10 9
- ♡ 9 8 6 2
- ◇ J 9 4 2
- ♣ A Q 5

Lead : ♣A. A-Q-x is usually one of the least attractive leads of all but here the bidding calls for a club lead. If either opponent held the ♣K, the bidding would have ended in 3NT. Over 3◇, West with spades and hearts and the ♣K would have had an easy 3NT and likewise, East would have bid 3NT over 3♠ with a club stopper. Therefore, the club suit is unguarded and the ♣A is the correct card (just in case an opponent holds a singleton king).

Play : North signals with the ♣10 and a second club is cashed. Later South comes to a trump trick. One down.

Notes : (1) West's 3♠ is used to show a stopper in spades and worry about the clubs for 3NT.
(2) Without a club stopper, East can do no better than 4◇. 3NT can be defeated on a club lead. 4♡ is tough to reach but can be made as the cards lie.
(3) On a spade or a heart lead, 5◇ can be made. East wins and cashes the Q, K and A of diamonds. Leaving the ◇ J out, East switches to hearts : A, K, Q (discarding a club), heart ruff, back to dummy with the ♠ K and a second club is discarded on the last heart. South ruffs but the defense takes just one club and one trump trick.

Hand 75 : Dealer South : Nil vulnerable

NORTH
- ♠ 2
- ♡ 10 5 4
- ◇ A 9 8 3 2
- ♣ K 6 5 2

WEST
- ♠ A Q 10 8
- ♡ 7 3
- ◇ K 7 6 4
- ♣ J 10 7

EAST
- ♠ 5 4 3
- ♡ K Q 6 2
- ◇ Q J 10
- ♣ Q 8 4

SOUTH
- ♠ K J 9 7 6
- ♡ A J 9 8
- ◇ 5
- ♣ A 9 3

WEST	NORTH	EAST	SOUTH
			1♠
Pass	1NT	Pass	2♡
Pass	Pass	Pass	

Lead : ♡3. Of the unbid suits, clubs offers the better choice. Rather lead from two honors than from one. It is reasonably appealing to lead from a 3-card suit with two touching honours. However, a trump lead is best on the bidding (declarer bid two suits, dummy showed preference for hearts and West is very strong in declarer's other suit). The trump lead cuts down dummy's ruffing power and preserves West's potential for spade tricks.

Play : On a trump lead, East plays the queen and South wins the ace. South would normally cross to dummy to lead a spade. When East plays low, the jack is finessed (East would probably have played the ace when a singleton is led from dummy). However, the jack loses to the queen and another trump is led.

East takes the king and plays a third round of trumps. This removes all of dummy's trumps and prevents any spade ruffs. Declarer is one off and has to manage the rest of the play well to avoid going two down.

Notes : (1) Where declarer has bid two suits and dummy has shown a preference, a trump lead is attractive in general and particularly appealing when you are strong in declarer's second suit. Dummy is frequently short in that second suit and by leading trumps, you reduce dummy's capacity to ruff declarer's losers in the second suit.

(2) On a club lead, declarer should win with the ♣ K and lead a spade. The jack finesse loses to the queen. Declarer can win any return and proceeds to ruff spade losers in dummy. Say clubs are continued : South wins, ruffs a spade, cashes the ◇ A and ruffs a diamond, ruffs a spade, ruffs a diamond and ruffs a third spade with the ♡ 10. East may overruff but South still has the ♡ A-J over East's honor and can come to nine tricks.

Hand 76 : Dealer West : N-S vulnerable

NORTH
- ♠ Q 9 7 2
- ♡ A 9 3
- ◇ K 8 7
- ♣ 9 7 5

WEST
- ♠ A K 8
- ♡ K Q 6 2
- ◇ A 6
- ♣ J 8 4 3

EAST
- ♠ J 10 5
- ♡ J 10 5
- ◇ 10 5 4
- ♣ Q 10 6 2

SOUTH
- ♠ 6 4 3
- ♡ 8 7 4
- ◇ Q J 9 3 2
- ♣ A K

WEST	NORTH	EAST	SOUTH
1NT	Pass	Pass	Pass

Lead : ♣7. In the bridge cradle we learn to lead fourth highest of our long suit. To reach a higher plane, one must appreciate that such leads are not automatic. 5-card and 6-card suits are attractive leads. The risk of giving declarer an extra trick is balanced by the gain of two or three length tricks. When holding only a 4-card suit, the risk of leading from a single honor is great and the chance of setting up a length trick is poor. Thus, it is best to reserve leads from 4-card suits for strong suits. Here it is best to try a passive club lead. Of course, the spade lead could work out all right and the club lead might not be best, but in the long run you will find that it works better not to lead from Q-x-x-x or J-x-x-x.

Play : South should win with the king of clubs and switch to the queen of diamonds (top from a near sequence). North encourages with the 8. If West ducks, a low diamond is continued, the ace is played and North should unblock the king. South's queen lead promised the jack. West would lead a heart next, but the defense can come to seven tricks before declarer does. The defense takes 1 heart, 4 diamonds and 2 clubs.

Notes : (1) On a spade lead, dummy's jack wins the trick and declarer continues with the jack of hearts. Even if North finds the diamond switch after taking the ace of hearts, declarer wins the race to the seventh trick, taking 3 spades, 3 hearts and 1 diamond.

(2) As it happens, 1NT could also be defeated on a diamond lead or a heart lead. Only the spade lead is a fatal attraction for the defense.

CHAPTER 18

THE FORCING DEFENSE

Suppose the trump suit looks like this :

```
          875
A 4 3 2             6
          K Q J 10 9
```

How many trump tricks can West take in defense? It appears that West has only one winner, and much of the time one trick will be the limit for West. However, West may score extra trump tricks either by ruffing low *or by reducing declarer's trump length.* If West has the means to weaken South's trumps, West may take two or more tricks in trumps.

Suppose West is able to force South to ruff. If South's trumps are reduced to four, West has still only one trick, but if South can be forced to ruff twice, West will have one trump more than South. Except in unusual circumstances, the extra trump will score an extra trick. The key is to force declarer to ruff and ruff again. To achieve this, lead your long suit. That is where declarer figures to be shortest. That will usually be the best chance to force declarer to ruff. The principle is :

TRUMP LENGTH, LEAD LENGTH

Similar results can be achieved in these layouts :

```
          875
Q 4 3 2             6
          A K J 10 9
-------------------------------------
          875
K 4 3 2             6
          A Q J 10 9
```

West has only one trick on top but if South can be forced to ruff twice, West's long trump will usually produce an extra trick. This kind of defense is known as the 'forcing defense', because the strategy depends on forcing declarer to ruff again and again.

Actually, the strategy is force the long trump hand to ruff. Usually the long trump hand is declarer's but if dummy has the long trumps, then that is the hand that must be forced to ruff. If both declarer and dummy are void in a suit, it may be necessary to hold off with your winning trump. You will not gain by forcing the shorter trump hand to ruff. Otherwise, you may give declarer a ruff-and-discard without any tangible benefit to you.

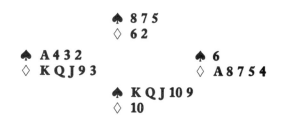

Suppose West has led diamonds and forced South to ruff once. Now both declarer and dummy are void in diamonds. Down to four trumps, South leads the king. West must hold off with the ace. If West takes the ace at this point and leads another diamond, dummy will ruff (dummy will 'take the force') and declarer can draw your trumps. There is no benefit in making the short trump hand ruff. This has no effect in reducing declarer's trump length.

After the king wins, South leads another trump. Again West must hold off with the ace (for the same reason). The ace should be taken when it draws the last trump in the short trump hand. South and West are now down to two trumps apiece :

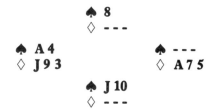

If South now leads a third spade, West can win and continue diamonds, forcing out South's last trump. West is left with the only trump plus two more diamonds.

Few Souths would make the mistake of leading a third trump. South's best play is to abandon trumps and play on the other suits. Normally West will be able to ruff in at some stage and thus the ♠4 scores that extra trick.

The forcing defense is most effective when you hold four trumps against declarer's five or six. It is also possible to force declarer off when you hold only three trumps if declarer is bound to lose the lead several times. In practice, however, it is almost impossible to force off a declarer who holds seven or more trumps.

You may also force off a declarer in a 4-4 fit :

```
          ♠ Q J 10 8
          ♢ 9 8 3
♠ A 6 4 3              ♠ 2
♢ K Q 7 6 5           ♢ A 10 2
          ♠ K 9 7 5
          ♢ J 4
```

West leads diamonds and South ruffs the third round. South leads a trump and West ducks. A second round of trumps is led and again West ducks. This time declarer is the shorter trump hand (after ruffing the diamond) and the ace should be taken only when it draws the last trump from the shorter hand.

Now if declarer plays a third trump (error), West takes the ace and forces dummy's last trump with another diamond. West later scores the last trump plus a diamond. If South abandons trumps after two rounds, West has to hope to ruff with the low trump.

When you hold a singleton trump and can diagnose that the opponents are playing a 5-3 or a 4-4 fit, you should adopt the same strategy. Partner holds four trumps and a forcing defense is usually best. Again, lead your long suit and help partner to start the force.

Declarer may overcome the threat of the forcing defense if there is a secondary long suit which can be played through the defender with the long trumps and no ruff is available to that defender. For example :

```
             NORTH
             ♠ 8 6 4
             ♡ 5 4 3
             ♢ Q J
             ♣ A 10 9 3 2
WEST                      EAST
♠ A 7 3 2                 ♠ 5
♡ K Q J 6 2               ♡ A 9 8
♢ 9 8                     ♢ 7 6 4 3 2
♣ 8 7                     ♣ Q J 6 4
             SOUTH
             ♠ K Q J 10 9
             ♡ 10 7
             ♢ A K 10 5
             ♣ K 5
```

WEST	NORTH	EAST	SOUTH
	Pass	Pass	1♠
2♡	2♠	3♡	4♠
Pass	Pass	Pass	

West leads the king of hearts and continues hearts. South ruffs the third round and leads spades. West ducks the first and second round of spades (otherwise

declarer has no problem). When the bad break in trumps is revealed, declarer must not lead a third round of spades (West would take the ace and force out declarer's last trump). Instead, the queen and jack of diamonds are cashed, followed by the ace of clubs and a club to the king. Provided that West has not been able to ruff any of these, the position will be :

```
          ♠ 8
          ♡ - - -
          ♢ - - -
          ♣ 10 9 3
♠ A 7                 ♠ - - -
♡ J 6                 ♡ - - -
♢ - - -               ♢ 7 6 4
♣ - - -               ♣ Q
          ♠ J 10
          ♡ - - -
          ♢ A K
          ♣ - - -
```

South leads the top diamonds and West cannot score the ♠ 7. If West ruffs low, dummy overruffs, and West makes only the ♠ A. If West ruffs with the ♠ A, South wins the return and draws West's trump. If West discards, a club is discarded from dummy and South leads the ♢ K for the same result.

Before leading a suit through the hand with the long trumps, it may be vital to cash a side trick to avoid it being ruffed later. For example :

```
             ♠ 10 9 7
             ♡ 7 6 5
             ♢ K 6
             ♣ Q J 9 7 2
♠ A 8 4 3                 ♠ 5
♡ K J 9 3 2               ♡ A Q 4
♢ 9 8 4                   ♢ 10 7 2
♣ 10                      ♣ K 8 6 5 4 3
             ♠ K Q J 6 2
             ♡ 10 8
             ♢ A Q J 5 3
             ♣ A
```

South has reached 4♠ and West attacks hearts. South ruffs the third heart and leads the ♠ K, low, low, low. A second low spade to dummy is also ducked by West. Declarer now plans to lead diamonds through West but must cash the ♣ A early. If South plays four rounds of diamonds without cashing the ♣ A first, West can discard the club and South will be unable to score the ♣ A at all. If the ♣ A is played early followed by diamonds, West will be unable to take a second trump trick.

PLAY HANDS ON THE FORCING DEFENSE

Hand 77 : Dealer North : Both vulnerable

NORTH
- ♠ 6 4 3
- ♡ Q J 5
- ◇ 7 6 3 2
- ♣ A K J

WEST	EAST
♠ 9 8 5 2	♠ 7
♡ 4	♡ A 8 6 3 2
◇ A K Q 8	◇ 10 9 5 4
♣ 7 4 3 2	♣ 10 9 6

SOUTH
- ♠ A K Q J 10
- ♡ K 10 9 7
- ◇ J
- ♣ Q 8 5

WEST	NORTH	EAST	SOUTH
	Pass	Pass	1♠
Pass	2NT	Pass	3♡
Pass	3♠	Pass	4♠
Pass	Pass	Pass	

Lead : ◇ K (or ace). Even without the length in trumps, it is obvious to start with diamonds. West's strategy, however, is not just to cash tricks. With four or more trumps, try to force declarer to ruff.

Play : Ignoring East's discouraging signal, West continues with the queen of diamonds and South ruffs. South starts on trumps. If they were 3-2, South would simply draw trumps and concede a trick to the ace of hearts. With the actual 4-1 break, declarer can be defeated. If declarer draws all of West's trumps, East wins when a heart is led and the defense can take two diamond tricks. Declarer's best chance is to draw just two rounds of trumps and then lead a heart. East wins and a diamond continuation ensures that declarer will fail. West can ruff the next heart and play a fourth diamond.

Notes : (1) North's 2NT is not pretty but best of the available choices.
(2) If West leads the singleton heart, there is good news and bad news. The good news is that East has the ace and can give West a heart ruff. The bad news is that you can no longer defeat the contract. Declarer would lose just 1 heart, 1 diamond and 1 ruff. Note : Trump length, lead length.
(3) If declarer draws two rounds of trumps and then leads hearts, East must not play a second heart after winning the ace. If West wanted the heart ruff, West would have led the singleton. When partner embarks on a forcing defense, do not thwart partner's plan.

Hand 78 : Dealer East : Nil vulnerable

NORTH
- ♠ 5
- ♡ 10 9 6
- ◇ A 10
- ♣ 9 7 6 5 4 3 2

WEST	EAST
♠ Q 7 6	♠ K J 10 9 8
♡ J 4 3	♡ A K Q 8 2
◇ 7 6 4 2	◇ 5 3
♣ K Q J	♣ A

SOUTH
- ♠ A 4 3 2
- ♡ 7 5
- ◇ K Q J 9 8
- ♣ 10 8

WEST	NORTH	EAST	SOUTH
		1♠	2◇
2♠	Pass	4♠	All pass

Lead : ◇ K. Top of sequence is the natural choice and leading the long suit is best anyway when holding four trumps.

Play : North should overtake with the ace and return the 10 of diamonds. South overtakes with the jack and continues diamonds. East ruffs the third diamond and leads trumps. South takes the ace and forces declarer again with a diamond. Declarer will be one down at least.

Notes : (1) 2♠ is not an attractive response but is best after the overcall. Had South passed, West would reply 1 NT, East would rebid 4♡ and West would give preference to 4♠.
(2) After the support, East ought not to reveal the second suit.
(3) If South led a club or a heart, declarer would make 4♠ easily, losing 1 spade and 2 diamonds at most. On a club lead declarer might make 11 tricks : win ♣ A, cross to ♡ J, play ♣ K and ♣ Q, discarding the diamond losers. Even though South ruffs the third club, declarer loses only two tricks.
(4) If North fails to overtake the first diamond with the ace, declarer makes 4♠. Declarer escapes the force and can keep control of trumps.
(5) If East ends in 4♡, the defense should go : ◇ K lead; North takes with the ace to switch to the ♠ 5; South wins the ace of spades and gives North a spade ruff. North returns the ◇ 10, overtaken by South to give North another spade ruff. Two down. Note the difference in strategy : when trumps are 4-1, play to force declarer; when trumps break 3-2, play for the ruff.

Hand 79 : Dealer South : N-S vulnerable

	NORTH		
	♠ K J 10 9 8		
	♡ 8 7		
	◇ A 9 3		
	♣ A J 10		

WEST		EAST	
♠ A 4 3 2		♠ 5	
♡ A J 10 6 3		♡ K 4 2	
◇ J 6		◇ 10 8 7 5 4 2	
♣ 7 3		♣ 9 5 4	

	SOUTH		
	♠ Q 7 6		
	♡ Q 9 5		
	◇ K Q		
	♣ K Q 8 6 2		

WEST	NORTH	EAST	SOUTH
			1♣
1♡	1♠	Pass	1NT
Pass	3♠	Pass	4♠
Pass	Pass	Pass	

Lead : ♡2. It is normal to lead partner's suit. In addition, with just one spade, East can expect that partner might have four trumps and wish to embark on a forcing defense. The standard lead from K-x-x is the bottom card, even in partner's suit.

Play : If dummy plays low, West should play the 10, not the ace (see Chapter 5, page 35). West continues with the ace of hearts and a third heart, North ruffing. Declarer starts on trumps and West should duck the first two rounds. If a third round of trumps is played, West takes the ace (as the last trump from the short trump hand is now drawn) and plays another heart. Declarer will fail by two tricks. Declarer should abandon trumps after two tricks and start on the clubs. However, West ruffs the third club and defeats 4♠ by one trick.

Notes : (1) West is too weak to double 1♣. A diamond response would be embarrassing and you are not strong enough to double and bid again. When doubling with a weak hand, you must be prepared to pass any weak reply.
(2) South might raise to 2♠ and should do so if North's 1♠ must be a 5-card suit (for example, if North-South are playing negative doubles where the double of 1♡ shows four spades while bidding 1♠ shows five spades). If 1♠ could be a 4-card suit, prefer not to give a 3-card raise with a hand which is suitable for no-trumps.
(3) The 2 of hearts lead, bottom card, signifies an honor in the suit or a singleton. As East is marked with a singleton or void spade, it is more likely that the 2 is from honor-third and the only honor missing is the king.
(4) If West wins the first or second round of trumps, declarer can make the contract. If West plays another heart, dummy still has a trump left and can 'take the force'. As West wants to shorten declarer's trumps, West holds off with the ace till the third round.

Hand 80 : Dealer West : E-W vulnerable

	NORTH		
	♠ 7 6 2		
	♡ A K Q 2		
	◇ Q 10 8 4 3		
	♣ 5		

WEST		EAST	
♠ 9 8		♠ A K	
♡ 10 9 6 5 4		♡ J 8 7	
◇ A K		◇ 7 6 5 2	
♣ A Q 8 3		♣ K J 10 9	

	SOUTH		
	♠ Q J 10 5 4 3		
	♡ 3		
	◇ J 9		
	♣ 7 6 4 2		

WEST	NORTH	EAST	SOUTH
1♡	Pass	2♣	Pass
3♣	Pass	3♡	Pass
4♡	Pass	Pass	Pass

Lead : ◇4. Trump length, lead length.

Play : West wins and leads a trump. North wins and leads a second diamond. West wins and leads another trump. North wins and leads a third diamond, ruffed by West. West and North now have two trumps each. If West leads a third trump, North wins and the next diamond forces West's last trump. If West abandons trumps (best), North ruffs the second round of clubs for one down.

Notes : (1) 2NT by East would not be foolish, intending to support the hearts next. 4♡ is a good contract, defeated only because of the foul break. 3NT could be defeated on a spade lead or a diamond lead. North might double 4♡ but this will be justified only if the correct defense is produced.
(2) If North leads the top trumps, West will succeed, drawing North's trumps as soon as West gains the lead.
(3) If North leads even one trump, West can make 10 tricks in comfort by leading trumps at every opportunity and drawing North's fourth trump.
(4) There is no rush to lead the singleton club. If this is the best defense, there is time enough to switch to clubs after winning a trump lead. On a club lead, West wins and by leading trumps every time, North's trumps can be drawn without North obtaining the club ruff. When holding a strong hand, a singleton lead is unlikely to work, as partner probably does not have the required entry to give you the ruff.

CHAPTER 19

COUNT SIGNALS

In standard methods, when partner leads a suit and third hand signals, the primary message is "Please continue this suit" or "This is not best. Find a switch, please." This information is considered usually more useful than knowing the number of cards partner holds in the suit led.

However, when declarer is the one leading a suit, it would rarely be of value to use this signal. The defense is almost never interested in continuing a suit which declarer is attacking. If the suit is good for declarer, it is probably bad for the defense. Now it is more useful to transmit and receive information as to the length of the suit. If you can find out how many cards partner has in the suit, simple arithmetic will tell you how many cards declarer has in the suit. Just add your cards to dummy's and the number shown by partner and deduct from 13.

Signalling how many cards you hold in a suit is called 'giving count'. The standard method of giving count is :

LOWEST CARD = Odd number

HIGH-THEN-LOW = Even number

When playing high-then-low with four or six cards, try not to choose the second lowest card as your first signal. Play the highest card you can afford.

From 10-7-4-3, signal with the 7 first, then the 3. Do not play the 4 first, then the 3. After you have played 4-then-3, partner will know you have an even number, but the 4 first can create an ambiguity for partner. The 4 could be the bottom card from 10-7-4 and thus an odd card signal. Whenever possible, make the first card of your signal as clear as possible. It is easier for partner to read the 7 as the beginning of a high-then-low signal.

However, it may not be feasible for you to play a particularly high card. You would not squander a trick for the sake of a signal. From Q-J-5-2, for example, play the 5, then the 2, if you are giving count. It is the best you can do with the cards you have been dealt.

The count signal is most useful when declarer is attempting to set up a long suit in dummy and a defender needs to know when to take the ace. The ace should be taken when declarer's last card in the

suit is played. Take the ace too soon and declarer has an entry to dummy's suit. Hold off with the ace too long and declarer may score an undeserved trick.

Suppose dummy has no outside entry and the position is this :

Dummy
K Q J 6 2

EAST
A 7 5

East needs to know whether to take the ace on the second or the third round of the suit. If South has only two cards, East should win the second round. If South has three cards, East should hold off until the third round. (If South has four cards, East cannot prevent declarer using this suit.) Many players hold up the ace until the third round each time because they have no method of discovering how many cards declarer has.

In an experienced partnership, West will give count. If South leads and West drops the 3, East can read this as West's lowest card, deduces West holds three cards and therefore declarer has a doubleton. East then takes the ace on the second round. If West plays the 9 or 10, however, East can read this as the start of a high-then-low signal, deduce that West has a doubleton and therefore declarer has three. East would now hold off until the third round.

Count signals are not obligatory each time declarer starts a suit but are very useful on most occasions. Beware of giving habitual count. The information you are giving to partner can be read also by declarer. A competent declarer may be able to make more use of the information than partner and will be able to read the hand too easily.

Quite a good idea against a good declarer is to give false count when you can tell that the information will not damage partner. If partner will never gain the lead or you know that declarer has a specific number of tricks but no way of making more, be prepared to play false count signals. If declarer notices, declarer will know that your signals cannot be relied upon and will not be too confident in future about adopting a line of play based on your signals. You want partner to trust your signals and all opponents to distrust them.

In particular, **beware of giving count in a suit where this gives away to declarer the location of a critical honor.** Neither you nor partner will be pleased if declarer successfully finesses for a jack or drops a queen offside because you assiduously signalled the number of cards you held.

PRESENT COUNT

If giving count after the first round of a suit, you can indicate the number of cards you have left : high-then-low = an even number of cards remaining, lowest from an odd number of cards remaining. This is commonly used when discarding from a suit after an earlier encouraging/discouraging signal.

NON-STANDARD COUNT SIGNALS

Some partnerships use 'reverse count', a sound method in which :

HIGH-THEN-LOW = Odd number

LOWEST CARD = Even number

This is just the opposite of standard count signals, but the same warning about excessive signalling applies. Reverse count has the advantage of being able to show a doubleton (play your bottom card) without wasting the top card of the doubleton.

When starting a high-then-low signal, play the highest of touching cards. For example, in standard count, play the 9 from 9-8-4-2, not the 8. Likewise, with reverse count, play the 8 from 8-7-3, not the 7.

THE TRUMP ECHO OR TRUMP PETER

Count signals are also available in the trump suit, but these are less common. Again, it would be foolish to give away the location of an honor by signalling your trump length. When you do wish to give count in the trump suit, the standard method is :

LOWEST = An even number of trumps

HIGH-THEN-LOW = An odd number

This happens to be the same as reverse count in non-trump suits (see above). An advantage of reverse count is that all count signals mean the same, in the trump suit and in non-trump suits.

The high-then-low signal in trumps to show an odd number of trumps is called the 'trump echo' or 'trump peter'. Giving count in trumps is useful in two situations :

1. When ruffing, it indicates how often you can ruff. If you ruff low, then ruff high, (low-then-high = even number), either you have no more trumps and cannot ruff again or you began with four trumps.

Partner is expected to work out whether you began with two trumps or with four. If you ruff high, then ruff low, you still have another trump with which to ruff. High-then-low whether ruffing or whether following suit shows an odd number of trumps.

2. It tells partner the number of trumps you hold. This enables partner to calculate declarer's length in trumps. This information may be useful for partner in calculating declarer's tricks or whether to try to give you a ruff or whether to pursue a forcing defense. Knowing declarer's length in one suit may assist you in working out declarer's length in the other suits. Giving partner information by count is valuable provided that declarer does not benefit from the information.

EXERCISE

1.   **Dummy**
                K Q J 3
                                EAST
                                7 4

(a) Declarer leads the 5 to dummy's king. Which card should East play?

(b) What should East play if East held 7-6-4-2?

2.   **Dummy**
                K Q J 2
                                EAST
                                9 4 3

(a) Declarer leads the 5 to the king. Which card should East play?

(b) What should East play if East held 9-8-6-4-3?

3. Which cards should East play in questions 1 and 2 if East-West are using 'reverse count'?

4.   **Dummy**
                        Q J 10 7 4
                WEST
                K 6 5

Dummy has no further entries. Declarer leads the ace and continues with the 9. Do you play the king on the second round or do you duck?

(a) East played the 8 on the ace.

(b) East played the 2 on the ace.

5. What would your answers be in question 4 if East-West are using 'reverse count'?

6. (a) Partner plays the 4 of trumps followed by the 3 of trumps. What can you deduce from that?

(b) What would your answer be if partner had first played the 6 of trumps followed by the 9?

PLAY HANDS ON COUNT SIGNALS

Hand 81 : Dealer North : Nil vulnerable

NORTH
- ♠ 2
- ♡ K Q J 10
- ◇ 7 6 5 2
- ♣ 7 5 4 2

WEST	EAST
♠ 5 4 3	♠ 9 7 6
♡ 9 8 7 2	♡ A 6 5
◇ Q 10 9	◇ J 8 4
♣ A K 10	♣ Q J 9 8

SOUTH
- ♠ A K Q J 10 8
- ♡ 4 3
- ◇ A K 3
- ♣ 6 3

WEST	NORTH	EAST	SOUTH
	Pass	Pass	1♠
Pass	1NT	Pass	4♠
Pass	Pass	Pass	

Lead : ♣ K (or ace). No reason to prefer another lead. Hard to go past an A-K suit to find a good start.

Play : East encourages the clubs (East should drop the queen to show the jack, although this is not safe if partner is the sort of player who fancies the occasional king lead from king-doubleton). West cashes the ace and leads a third club, ruffed by South. Trumps are drawn and South leads a heart. In order to defeat the contract, East must take the ace of hearts on the second round. If East wins the first heart, dummy's hearts will allow South to discard the diamond loser. If East ducks the first heart and ducks the second heart also, South has no loser in hearts. If East wins the second heart and plays a club or a diamond, South will be stuck with a diamond loser at the end. In order for East to know when to take the ace of hearts, East needs to know the number of hearts declarer has. It is this 'need to know' that is the basis for all signalling. If West can let East know the number of hearts West holds, East can calculate the number declarer has.

Notes: (1) South's 4♠ is a reasonable gamble. If North's 6 points happened to be ◇ Q plus the ♡ A or the ♣ A, 4♠ would be laydown. Likewise if North had A-Q-J in hearts. Even as it is, with North providing a minimum and not particularly suitable dummy, the defense has to be faultless to defeat 4♠.
(2) When the first heart is led, West should play the 9 of hearts (top card to show an even number). East knows that if West has two hearts and South has four, that there is no defense. Therefore, East plays West to hold four hearts and South to have two and wins the ♡ A on the second round.

Hand 82 : Dealer East : N-S vulnerable

NORTH
- ♠ 4 2
- ♡ A 10 9 8
- ◇ Q 9 8 6
- ♣ A 7 2

WEST	EAST
♠ 8 6 5	♠ A K Q
♡ Q 6 5	♡ K J 4 2
◇ 7 4 3	◇ A K 5 2
♣ Q J 10 6	♣ K 5

SOUTH
- ♠ J 10 9 7 3
- ♡ 7 3
- ◇ J 10
- ♣ 9 8 4 3

WEST	NORTH	EAST	SOUTH
		2NT	Pass
3NT	Pass	Pass	Pass

Lead : ♠ J. Top of sequence is best.

Play : East wins with the ace or king. Either makes it tough for the defense to gauge East's strength. North discourages, playing the ♠ 2. Do *not* play count on partner's lead — tell partner whether you wish the suit continued. East leads the ♣ K. If North wins this, declarer is home. If North ducks and a second club is played, North must win the second club. If North ducks the second club, declarer is home. North must win precisely the second round of clubs. Later when East leads ♡ K and ♡ J, North must not take the ace, lest ♡ Q becomes declarer's entry to dummy. Once dummy's clubs are high, North must ensure East has no entry to dummy to reach them.

Notes: (1) There are other ways to show a balanced 23-24 HCP : 2♣ demand, negative reply, 2NT rebid by East, 3NT by West.
(2) Against many defenders, East would succeed. Many Norths would duck twice in clubs and then East has nine tricks : 3 spades, 2 hearts, 2 diamonds, 2 clubs.
(3) When a club is led, South should signal with the 9, top card to show an even number. North can work out that East must therefore have two or four clubs. North will then win the second round of clubs, since there is no defense if East has four clubs.
(4) Double dummy, there are ways that East can succeed as the cards lie. However, in practice, East would start with the clubs and if North takes the second club, declarer would try to reach dummy via the ♡ Q.

Hand 83 : Dealer South : E-W vulnerable

WEST	**NORTH**	**EAST**	**SOUTH**
			Pass
1NT	Pass	3NT	All pass

NORTH
♠ J 10 9 8 4
♡ K 10 9 2
♢ J 7
♣ 9 2

WEST
♠ Q 6 2
♡ A Q J
♢ A K 5 3
♣ 5 4 3

EAST
♠ A 3
♡ 7 5 4
♢ 8 6 2
♣ K Q J 7 6

SOUTH
♠ K 7 5
♡ 8 6 3
♢ Q 10 9 4
♣ A 10 8

Lead : ♠ J. Longest suit and top of sequence is normal.

Play : Declarer plays low in dummy and South wins with the king. A spade is returned, removing dummy's only entry outside clubs. Declarer starts on the clubs. If South wins the first or the second round of clubs, declarer will succeed (2 spades, 1 heart, 2 diamonds, 4 clubs). South ducks the first two rounds of clubs and takes the third round. Dummy now has two club winners but there is no way to reach them. Declarer should now be held to eight tricks (2 spades, 2 hearts, 2 diamonds, 2 clubs).

Notes : (1) If South switches after winning the king of spades, declarer can succeed. On a heart or a diamond switch, declarer takes the ace and knocks out the ace of clubs. The ace of spades entry allows declarer to score four club tricks. As South can see the likelihood of being able to prevent declarer using the club length, South should return a spade even though West is known to hold the queen (it could be Q-doubleton).

(2) After South ducks the first round of clubs, declarer might take the heart finesse before playing a second round of clubs. If the heart finesse worked, declarer would lead a second club (the ace must duck again) and the heart finesse could be repeated. Declarer would make 2 spades, 3 hearts, 2 diamonds and 2 clubs. However, the heart finesse loses, a spade is returned and declarer should be held to eight tricks.

(3) On the first club, North signals with the *nine* of clubs, starting a high-then-low signal to show an even number. As West cannot hold a singleton, South knows that North's signal cannot show four clubs. Therefore, South plays North to show two clubs and therefore declarer has three. South knows to hold off with the ace of clubs until the third round.

Hand 84 : Dealer West : Both vulnerable

WEST	**NORTH**	**EAST**	**SOUTH**
Pass	1♢	Pass	1♠
Pass	1NT	Pass	3NT
Pass	Pass	Pass	

NORTH
♠ 8 6
♡ A Q 7
♢ A 9 8 5 4
♣ Q 8 5

WEST
♠ 10 9 7 5 4
♡ K 5
♢ 7 3 2
♣ K 9 7

EAST
♠ J 3
♡ J 10 6 4 2
♢ K 6
♣ A J 6 4

SOUTH
♠ A K Q 2
♡ 9 8 3
♢ Q J 10
♣ 10 3 2

Lead : ♡ 4. Normal long suit lead.

Play : West plays the king and North takes the ace. A spade is won in dummy and the queen of diamonds is led. The finesse loses to East's king. East switches to the 4 of clubs, won by West's king. West continues with the 9 of clubs (top of a remaining doubleton). East wins as cheaply as possible, cashes the top club and the thirteenth club is the fifth trick for the defense.

Notes : (1) East's hearts are too poor to justify an overcall.
(2) Many defenders would continue with the jack of hearts after taking the king of diamonds. That would allow declarer to succeed : 3 spades, 2 hearts and 4 diamonds. How can East tell that the switch to clubs is necessary?

(3) When the queen of diamonds is led, West should signal with the 2 of diamonds, bottom card, to show an odd number. East can count declarer's tricks : 3 spades in dummy, 2 hearts (North is marked with the ♡ Q after West plays the king at trick 1) and 4 diamonds. As West has an odd number, West will hold 3 diamonds and North 5 diamonds (including the ace, since declarer went to dummy to take the diamond finesse). That means North has nine tricks on a heart return. East does not know the club return will defeat the contract but does know that a heart continuation cannot defeat it.

(4) When West wins the ♣ K, West returns a club, not a heart. The *low-card-switch* by East asks partner to return the suit led. A *high-card-switch* shows no interest in the suit led.

CHAPTER 20

SUIT PREFERENCE SIGNALS & SECONDARY SIGNALS

Primary signals occur when you are following suit:

On partner's lead: In third seat, standard signals encourage or discourage the suit led. A discouraging signal asks for a switch but does not indicate which other suit is requested.

On declarer's lead: In second or fourth seat, standard signals give count in the suit led (for details, see Chapter 19).

Suit preference signals indicate which suit you wish partner to play. The key is:

HIGH CARD = HIGH SUIT

LOWEST CARD = LOW SUIT

The situations when a card will be a suit preference signal are normally clearly defined in partnership agreements.

STANDARD SITUATIONS

1. You are giving partner a ruff (or hoping to give partner a ruff).

Leading a high card for a ruff asks partner to return the higher outside suit. The trump suit is excluded. Leading your lowest card when giving partner a ruff asks partner to return the lower outside suit.

Dummy
♡ J 10 7 5 2

EAST
♡ A 9 8 6 4

Suppose you are East defending 4♠ and West leads the 3 of hearts, an obvious singleton. You win the ace of hearts and return a heart for partner to ruff. Which heart?

To you it is irrelevant which heart is returned. South's remaining honor will be trumped, so whether you play the 9, 8, 6 or 4 does not matter *to you*. Therefore, the actual card chosen can be used as a signal to partner to indicate your outside entry. As spades are trumps, the relevant suits are diamonds and clubs. If you want a diamond switch, play the 9: high card = high suit. If you want a club switch, return the 4: low card = low suit. (If you have no interest in either minor, play a middling card, neither your highest, nor your lowest).

2. You are defending against no-trumps and you are about to knock out declarer's stopper.

Dummy
♠ 7 4

WEST
♠ Q 10 6 5 3 2

Against no-trumps, you lead the 5 of spades. Partner wins the ace of spades and returns the 9. Declarer plays the jack and you win with the queen. Declarer clearly has only the king of spades left. Your next spade lead will knock out the king. Which spade do you lead?

To you it does not matter which spade forces out the king. Therefore, the card chosen can be used to signal to partner your outside entry. If dummy holds a powerful suit such as A-Q-J, A-K-J or A-K-Q, then only the other two suits will be relevant. Play the 10 if you want the higher suit, play the 2 if you want the lower suit.

Where dummy has a suit you cannot possibly want partner to lead, only two suits will be relevant. If dummy has no powerful suit, you might want any of the other three suits. In this case, the 10 would ask for a heart (high card = high suit), the 2 would ask for a club (low card = low suit) and the 6 would ask for a diamond (middle card = middle suit).

3. Partner has led A-then-K to show A-K doubleton.

Since partner is about to be void in this suit, partner needs to know your entry to obtain the ruff. You give partner a suit preference signal on the second round (your first round signal would have been an encourage/discourage signal). With trumps excluded, high card on the second round = high suit, low card = low suit.

4. Partner has led an obvious singleton.

Partner needs to know your entry to obtain the ruff. If the lead can be read as a singleton, third-hand-high does not apply if you cannot win the trick, and high-encourage/low-discourage is obviously futile. The card played by you should therefore be taken as a suit preference signal.

Dummy

◇ **K J 10 8 3**

EAST

◇ **9 7 6 5 4**

Against 4♠, West leads the 2 of diamonds, an obvious singleton (cannot be from Q-2, A-2 or A-Q-2). (If your partner does lead the 2 from such a holding, give partner this book as a present and highlight Chapter 1 and Chapter 4.) Whatever dummy plays, your card should be a suit preference signal to tell partner where to find your entry. Excluding trumps, the relevant suits are hearts and clubs. The ◇ 9 would ask for a heart (high card = high suit) and the ◇ 4 would ask for a club.

NORTH

♠ **A Q 4 3**

♡ **Q 6 4 2**

◇ **8 5**

♣ **Q 9 3**

EAST

♠ **6 2**

♡ **K 10 8 7 5 3**

◇ **A 7**

♣ **7 5 4**

WEST	NORTH	EAST	SOUTH
			1NT
Pass	2♣	Pass	2♠
Pass	4♠	All pass	

West leads the ace of hearts. Which card should East play?

Answer: Partner's lead must be a singleton. South, having opened 1NT, must hold the other two hearts. Partner needs to know your entry. Play the 10: high card for the high suit, diamonds (as trumps and hearts are excluded). Your 10 should not be read as an encouraging signal : why would you encourage another heart when you know partner does not have another heart? If your entry were in clubs, you would play the 3 of hearts at trick 1.

Suppose the West and South hands are :

WEST

♠ **J 10 8**

♡ **A**

◇ **J 9 6 4 3 2**

♣ **10 8 2**

SOUTH

♠ **K 9 7 5**

♡ **J 9**

◇ **K Q 10**

♣ **A K J 6**

After the ace of hearts and a diamond switch to the ace, East cashes the king of hearts. West discards to show no interest in clubs and East plays a third heart. This promotes a trump trick for the defense whether South ruffs high or low or discards. (Note, incidentally, that West should lead the 9 of diamonds, a high-card-switch to deny interest in the suit led.)

There is a common thread to all the above situations : When the problem is *knowing where the entry is,* the solution is the suit preference signal.

ADVANCED SITUATIONS FOR SUIT PREFERENCE SIGNALS

1. A switch is clearly necessary

When dummy turns up with a singleton in the suit led in a trump contract, should the signal by third hand be encouraging/discouraging or a suit preference signal? There can be merit in both approaches. It may be valuable to ask partner to continue the suit to force dummy to ruff. Suppose the trump position looks like this :

Q 6 2

7   **J 9 4 3**

A K 10 8 5

If declarer tackles the suit, South would play the ace and then lead low to the queen. When West shows out, declarer can finesse the 10 on the third round. However, if dummy can be forced to ruff, this manoeuvre will not be available to declarer and East may score a trump trick. Declarer may suspect what is going on but cannot be sure, and is not likely to finesse the 10 and risk losing to J-x or J-x-x.

It is also useful to use an encouraging signal even though dummy has a singleton to let partner know it is safe to continue the suit led. Many times you will prefer to have this suit continued rather than risk partner making one of those horrendous switches. If you want a switch, you can simply discourage. There are very few positions where partner needs to know which suit is needed. Most of the time, the appearance of dummy, the bidding and partner's own cards will indicate the switch desired.

A sensible working approach is :

1. If dummy holds three trumps or fewer, use standard encourage/discourage signals.

2. If dummy holds five or more trumps, give a suit preference signal if partner has led the ace or king and dummy turns up with a singleton.

3. When dummy has four trumps, use encourage/ discourage if their fit is 4-4, suit preference if their fit is 5-4 or better.

Consider this position :

        NORTH
        ♠ A 7 6 3
        ♡ 7
        ◇ K Q 5 2
        ♣ K J 3 2

WEST
♠ 9 2
♡ A K J 8 3
◇ 8 7 4
♣ 9 6 4

South opens 2♠, weak, showing six spades and 6-10 HCP. North raises to 4♠. West leads the king of hearts. How should West continue at trick 2?

This is clearly a suit preference position. If East plays a high heart, switch to diamonds. If East plays the lowest heart, switch to clubs.

The correct switch is not clear to West just by considering the cards visible. Help is needed from partner. Sometimes the switch may not matter, but sometimes it could be critical. East could have :

        ♠ 10
        ♡ Q 10 6 5 4
        ◇ A J 10
        ♣ A 8 7 5

The diamond switch is essential and East will play the 10 of hearts to ask for a diamond. If West were to switch to clubs, declarer would succeed. Holding Q-x in clubs, declarer would be able to set up a club winner to pitch a diamond before the defense could come to their second diamond trick. On the diamond shift, East can capture one of dummy's honors and return the jack, setting up the second diamond trick before the ace of clubs has been dislodged.

On the other hand, East could hold :

        ♠ 10
        ♡ Q 10 6 5 4
        ◇ A 10 6
        ♣ A Q 7 5

Now a club switch is necessary and East would play the 4 of hearts, lowest available card, to ask for a club. If West were to shift to a diamond here, declarer with ◇ J-9-x would succeed. Declarer would be able to set up the thirteenth diamond for a club discard without the defense being able to take their two club tricks. If West switches to the club, East can take the two club tricks and the ace of diamonds, defeating the contract before declarer gets started.

2. Suit preference signals by playing cards in abnormal order

        Dummy
        6 5 2
                EAST
                A K Q 7 4

If West leads this suit, East wins. It is normal to win with the queen, as defenders take tricks with the cheapest possible card. If East plays the ace, then the king, then the queen, East has played these winners in an abnormal order. The abnormal order carries a suit preference meaning and indicates interest in the high suit. At each opportunity, East played the highest card available : high card = high suit. If cards are played in the normal order, there is either no message or the preference is for the lower suit. The normal order certainly indicates there is no outstanding preference for the higher suit.

3. Suit preference leads

When the card led cannot possibly be the correct card to lead, it carries a suit preference message. A striking example would be the lead of the 2 by a pre-emptor. The 2 cannot be the legitimate fourth highest when the pre-emptor has a 7-card (or 6-card) suit. Therefore the 2 should be taken to mean "Please play back the lowest suit, trumps excluded." The pre-emptor is likely to be void in the low suit and this is the best way to transmit that information to partner.

The same logic would apply for a 2 lead (or bottom card lead) from a known 5-card or 6-card suit. As it cannot be a legitimate fourth highest, it is meant as a suit preference signal for the low suit.

Where the 9 cannot be a short suit lead (singleton or top of a doubleton), it is a suit preference for the high suit. The 9 cannot be a genuine fourth highest lead from a long suit because when the 9 is the fourth card from the top, there are three honor cards in the suit and some top-of-touching-honors sequence lead applies). Therefore, the 9 lead from a suit which the leader has bid, a known 4-card or longer suit, is a suit preference signal for the high suit. Again, there is a strong likelihood that the leader is void in the high suit.

Where you know or expect that partner can ruff your opening lead, you should also choose a suit preference lead. This can arise when the bidding has indicated that partner is void in a suit or partner has made a bid which indicates a likely void. Take this situation, for example :

WEST	NORTH	EAST	SOUTH
Pass	1◇	Pass	2♡
Pass	3♡	Pass	4NT
Pass	5♡	Pass	6♡
Pass	Pass	Double	All pass

What should West lead from :

♠ A 8 6
♡ 7
◇ 8 7 5 4 3 2
♣ J 5 2

Partner has made a Lightner double, asking for an unusual lead (see Chapter 4, page 29), normally the first suit bid by dummy. Lead a diamond, expecting partner to ruff. The correct card is the *eight* of diamonds, high card asking partner to return the high suit after ruffing. If West held the ace of clubs instead of the ace of spades, West would lead the *two* of diamonds.

WEST	NORTH	EAST	SOUTH
		Pass	1♡
Pass	2◇	Pass	3◇
Pass	4♡	All pass	

What should West lead from :

♠ Q 3 2
♡ 9 7 4
◇ 10 9 8 5 3
♣ A Q

Their bidding suggests that they hold eight diamonds and partner is void. Lead the *three* of diamonds. Expecting East to ruff, you are asking partner to return the lowest suit after ruffing. When giving a ruff, forget about top of sequence or fourth highest. Partner is not interested in the cards you hold in the suit, only in which suit to return. If your A-Q were in spades, you would lead the ◇ 10.

4. Secondary signals

Where your first signal (either encourage/discourage or count) has been made, you will often have spare cards for the second round of the suit. You may be able to use these spare cards for a suit preference signal on the next round. For example :

```
            Q J
A K 10 9 5         8 6 3 2
            7 4
```

In a suit contract, West leads the king and East discourages with the 2. West cashes the ace. What should East play? To East the actual card cannot matter, but as West is about to switch, it makes sense to signal the preferred switch. The 8 (high card) would show interest in the high suit. The 3 (lowest) would indicate preference for the low suit, or at least no great desire for the high suit.

There is a normal order in which cards are played. With 8-6-3-2, it would be 2, then 3, then 6, then 8 in a standard approach. The departure from standard by playing the 8 on the second round is the suit preference signal. The normal order indicates no significant preference for the high suit and perhaps strong preference for the low suit.

```
            K Q J 6 4
A 7                    9 3 2
            10 8 5
```

In no-trumps, South leads the 10, West plays low and East plays the 2 to show an odd number (primary count signal — see Chapter 19). South leads the suit again, West plays the ace and East plays . . .?

The normal order is 2, then 3, then 9. Sensibly, East would play the 9 on the second round to ask for the higher suit from West, while the 3 would say, "I prefer the lower suit, or at least I have no special interest in the higher suit."

Which suit to request will depend on both the bidding and your holding. It may be no more than a preference for Q-x-x over x-x-x. Partner is expected to work out how many points you could possibly hold by referring to the bidding (for declarer's strength), dummy's points and partner's own points.

```
            A K 8
4                    7 5 3 2
            Q J 10 9 6
```

Declarer is drawing trumps and plays the ace, king, over to the queen and then the jack. If East follows with the 7, 5, 3 and finally the 2, highest card at each opportunity, East is giving a strong suit preference signal for the high suit. However, 2, 3, 5 and 7, lowest card at every opportunity shows no interest at all in the high suit and suggests preference for the low suit.

```
            10 8 5 2
9 6 3                    A K Q J 4
            7
```

West leads the 6 (middle-up-down) and East wins with the jack. East continues the suit but South ruffs. Here West can use the 9 for the higher suit and the 3 for the lower suit. The normal card now would be the 3, since West's holding is known when South ruffs. (The normal order if South followed on the second round would be 6, then 9 and lastly, the 3.)

NON-STANDARD METHODS

1. SUIT PREFERENCE DISCARDS

These are also known as McKenney Discards or as Lavinthal Discards after the inventors of this concept whereby the principles of suit preference are extended to discards :

THE SUIT DISCARDED IS NOT WANTED.

HIGH DISCARD ASKS FOR HIGH SUIT.

LOW DISCARD ASKS FOR LOW SUIT.

The discard carries a double attitude message. The suit of the discard is discouraging, the number of the card encourages the suit indicated. Thus, if spades are trumps and partner discards the 9 of clubs when declarer draws trumps, partner is asking for a heart. The club discard discourages clubs, the 9 asks for the high suit of the remaining suits, hearts and diamonds.

Only two suits count as the player is out of one suit and the suit discarded is not wanted. It is also possible to ask partner to play the suit on which you are discarding. For example :

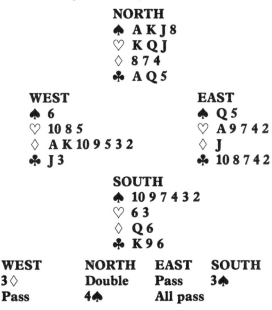

```
                NORTH
                ♠ A K J 8
                ♡ K Q J
                ♢ 8 7 4
                ♣ A Q 5
  WEST                        EAST
  ♠ 6                         ♠ Q 5
  ♡ 10 8 5                    ♡ A 9 7 4 2
  ♢ A K 10 9 5 3 2            ♢ J
  ♣ J 3                       ♣ 10 8 7 4 2
                SOUTH
                ♠ 10 9 7 4 3 2
                ♡ 6 3
                ♢ Q 6
                ♣ K 9 6
```

WEST	NORTH	EAST	SOUTH
3♢	Double	Pass	3♠
Pass	4♠	All pass	

West leads the king of diamonds followed by the ace of diamonds. What should East do?

East wants a third diamond in order to ruff with the queen of spades. Without a third diamond, declarer would succeed. Using standard discards, East can only signal with the 2 of clubs ("I do not want clubs.") or the 2 of hearts ("I do not want hearts."). In either case, West may switch to the other suit. East's best chance would be to discourage clubs and hope West can work it out.

With suit preference discards, East throws the 9 of hearts, saying "Do not play a heart. Play the higher of the other two suits." With trumps excluded, this leaves diamonds and clubs, with diamonds, of course, the higher suit requested. The 2 of clubs would lead to the same result : "Do not play clubs. Play the lower of the other two suits."

When using suit preference discards, a middling discard such as a 5 or 6 is normally unreadable, if it is not clearly your lowest or highest card. If unreadable, the 5 or 6 discard suggests you have no special preference.

2. REVOLVING DISCARDS

The idea here is the same as for suit preference discards, but the approach is slightly different.

THE SUIT DISCARDED IS NOT WANTED.

A HIGH DISCARD ASKS FOR THE SUIT "ABOVE" THE DISCARDED SUIT.

A LOW DISCARD ASKS FOR THE SUIT "BELOW" THE DISCARDED SUIT.

For example, if diamonds are trumps and you discard a heart when declarer is drawing trumps, the heart means, "Do not play hearts." A high heart asks for a spade (the suit above hearts), a low heart asks for a club (the suit below hearts, excluding trumps). As it happens, this is the same as a suit preference discard. However, if you throw a spade, rejecting spades, a high spade asks for the next suit up, clubs, and a low spade asks for the suit below spades, that is, hearts. Again, an unreadable discard of a 5 or 6 indicates no special preference.

There is no advantage in using revolving discards rather than straightforward suit preference discards, unless the opponents are unaware that you are using them and misread your signals. However, you are required to disclose your defensive methods (including signalling) on your system card and if the opponents ask about your methods. Revolving discards are different to suit preference discards but no better.

3. ODD-EVEN DISCARDS

Version A : $E = E, O = O$. Even Encouraging, Odd Offputting.

An even discard asks you to lead that suit.

An odd discard says "Do not lead this suit."

High odd discard = Lead the high suit.

Low odd discard = Lead the low suit.

Playing high-then-low with even cards (8-then-4, for example) cancels the encouraging message.

Version B : An odd discard encourages the suit discarded, an even discard is suit preference (and simultaneously discourages the suit discarded).

An odd discard asks you to lead that suit.
An even discard says "Do not lead this suit."
High even discard = Lead the high suit.
Low even discard = Lead the low suit.

Playing high-then-low with odd cards (9-then-3, for example) cancels the encouraging mesage.

Suit Preference Discards and Odd-Even Discards are recommended for regular partnerships. Make sure you and partner have discussed and agreed upon the method before you use it. These methods are not for casual or inexperienced partnerships.

EXERCISE ON SUIT PREFERENCE SIGNALS

1.

	NORTH		
	♠ 10 7 5		
	♡ 3 2		
	◇ 7 6 3		
	♣ A K Q J 4		

WEST			
♠ K 6 2			
♡ 9 8 6 5			
◇ Q 10 8 5 2			
♣ 2			

WEST	NORTH	EAST	SOUTH
Pass	Pass	1♡	1♠
2♡	3♠	Pass	4♠
Pass	Pass	Pass	

You, West, lead your singleton club. Dummy wins, partner plays the 3 and South the 5. The 10 of spades is led, 8 from partner, 2 from declarer and you win with the king. How do you put partner on lead to receive your club ruff?

2.

	NORTH	
	♠ K 4 3	
	♡ A 10 7 5	
	◇ K Q 7 4	
	♣ K Q	

WEST	
♠ J 10 9 8 5	
♡ 9 2	
◇ A 8	
♣ 10 4 3 2	

North opens 1 NT, South bids 3♡ and North raises to 4♡. You lead the jack of spades, low from dummy and partner's ♠ Q wins the trick. Partner now plays the ace of spades. What do you play on the second spade and why? What is partner's spade holding?

3. West holds :

	♠ 7 6
	♡ 9 4
	◇ 9 8 6 4 2
	♣ A 4 3 2

North opens 1 ◇, South jumps to 2♠. North raises to 3♠, South bids 6♠, passed to East whose double ends the auction. What should West lead and why?

4.

	NORTH		
	♠ 8 7		
	♡ 9 6		
	◇ K J 10 8		
	♣ K J 10 4 3		

WEST			
♠ J 9 6 4 3			
♡ A			
◇ 9 6 5 4			
♣ 9 7 2			

WEST	NORTH	EAST	SOUTH
Pass	Pass	1♠	4♡
4♠	Pass	Pass	5♡
Double	Pass	Pass	Pass

West leads ♠ 4, East plays ♠ A, South ruffs. A heart is led. West wins. How should West continue and why?

5.

	NORTH	
	♠ Q J 9 7 6	
	♡ Q 6 5	
	◇ 7	
	♣ Q 8 6 4	

	EAST
	♠ A K
	♡ 9 7
	◇ Q 6 5 4
	♣ 10 9 5 3 2

South opens 1♡, North replies 1♠ and South rebids 2NT, showing 16-18 points. North's 4♡ ends the auction. West leads ♣ A. What should East play?

6.

	NORTH
	♠ Q 9 6
	♡ 7 4
	◇ Q 9 3
	♣ K Q 10 5 3

WEST	
♠ 4	
♡ Q J 10 9 3	
◇ 8 7 5 4 2	
♣ A 4	

South: 1NT, North: 3NT. West leads the ♡ Q: 4 − 2 − A. South leads the jack of clubs: 4 − 3 − 2 from East. The next club is won by the ace: 5 from dummy − 9 from East. What should West play next?

PLAY HANDS ON SUIT PREFERENCE SIGNALS

Hand 85 : Dealer North : N-S vulnerable

NORTH
♠ K Q 10 4 3
♡ K 7 6 5
♢ Q 10
♣ A 8

WEST
♠ J
♡ A 8 4 3 2
♢ A 9 5 3
♣ 10 9 6

EAST
♠ 9 7
♡ 9
♢ J 7 6 4 2
♣ Q J 4 3 2

SOUTH
♠ A 8 6 5 2
♡ Q J 10
♢ K 8
♣ K 7 5

WEST	NORTH	EAST	SOUTH
	1♠	Pass	3♠
Pass	4♠	All pass	

Lead: ♡9. The weaker the hand, the more appealing it is to lead a singleton as partner is likely to have the entries needed to give you the ruffs.

Play: West wins the ace of hearts and returns the *eight* of hearts. East ruffs and returns a diamond to West's ace. A second heart ruff defeats the game.

Notes: (1) On any lead but a heart, declarer can make the game easily. Declarer will draw trumps at once and concede the two red aces.
(2) West cannot be sure that East has led a singleton but should defend hoping that East can ruff the next heart. West therefore gives East a suit preference signal with the 8 of hearts, asking East to return the high suit. With the trump suit, spades, excluded, this is a request for diamonds (clubs would be the low suit). If West's outside entry were in clubs, West would return the 2 of hearts.
(3) If East returns a club after ruffing the heart, declarer succeeds. East misses out on the second ruff. This may happen if East does not notice West's 8 of hearts or if West carelessly returns a low heart. After ruffing the heart return, look at East's quandary without the suit preference signal. East has no other clue whether to try clubs or diamonds to find West's entry. The suit preference signal replaces guesswork with partnership co-operation.

Hand 86 : Dealer East : E-W vulnerable

NORTH
♠ 10 6 3
♡ A J 5 4 2
♢ - - -
♣ A 8 4 3 2

WEST
♠ K 9
♡ Q 9 7
♢ A K J 8
♣ K J 10 7

EAST
♠ A Q J 8 5 4
♡ 10
♢ Q 10 4
♣ 9 6 5

SOUTH
♠ 7 2
♡ K 8 6 3
♢ 9 7 6 5 3 2
♣ Q

WEST	NORTH	EAST	SOUTH
		2♠	Pass
4♠	Pass	Pass	Pass

Lead : ♣Q. Honor doubleton is not an attractive start but a singleton queen or jack is reasonable if the hand is very weak and you hold worthless trumps for ruffing.

Play: The lead is covered by dummy's king and North wins the ace. Taking the lead as a singleton, North returns a suit preference 2 of clubs, lowest to ask for the low suit, diamonds. South ruffs and should recognise that North's request for a diamond must mean that North intends to ruff the diamond. South leads the 2 of diamonds, low card, low suit, to ask for another club ruff. North ruffs and returns the 3 of clubs, asking for another diamond ruff. When South ruffs this, South is out of trumps. South now plays the 9 of diamonds, high card for the high suit, hearts. When North ruffs this, North deduces that the request for hearts must mean that South has the king of hearts. Why else ask for a heart? North leads a low heart, not the ace, to South and receives another diamond ruff. The next heart is ruffed by East who can claim the rest, but the defense has taken the first seven tricks. Down four.

Notes: (1) If not using weak twos, East would pass, West would open 1NT and East might then bid 4♠.
(2) If North wins the ♣A and returns the 8 of clubs for South to ruff, South would return a heart to North's ace and receive a second club ruff. If South then tries to cash the king of hearts, East ruffs and draws trumps. The contract is defeated by one trick but North-South can do much, much better via the recommended defense.
(3) When South ruffs, South should ruff with the 2 first, 7 next. Low-high in trumps shows an even number. When North ruffs, North should ruff with the 6 first, 3 next. High-low in trumps shows an odd number.

Hand 87 : Dealer South : Both vulnerable

NORTH
- ♠ 2
- ♡ K Q 8 4
- ◇ 10 7 4 2
- ♣ A J 10 8

WEST
- ♠ K Q 10
- ♡ A 10 9 7 6 5
- ◇ J 9 5
- ♣ 5

EAST
- ♠ J 6 5 4
- ♡ 2
- ◇ K 8 6 3
- ♣ K 9 7 2

SOUTH
- ♠ A 9 8 7 3
- ♡ J 3
- ◇ A Q
- ♣ Q 6 4 3

WEST	NORTH	EAST	SOUTH
			1♠
2♡	Pass	Pass	Double
Pass	Pass	Pass	

Lead : ♠ 2. With four trumps, a singleton lead may not be best, but it is still normal to lead partner's suit. It may be necessary to set up winners in partner's suit.

Play : South wins the ace of spades and figures partner to have led a singleton. Playing for penalties at a low level is not attractive with 3-card or longer support for partner. South returns the *nine* of spades for North to ruff. North returns a diamond as South's high spade asked for the high suit (of clubs and diamonds). The correct card is the 2 of diamonds. Unless you know partner will ruff, lead the normal card (fourth highest, M.U.D., top from a doubleton, and so on). South wins the queen of diamonds and, reading North to hold four diamonds because of the lead of the 2, cashes the ace of diamonds. Then the *eight* of spades is returned (again, high card, asking for the high suit). North ruffs and plays the lowest diamond for South to ruff. South should now return a club (North should hold the ace to justify playing for penalties and North's *seven* of diamonds, the lower of the 10-7 remaining, asks for a club). North takes the ace of clubs and leads another diamond. South ruffs with the jack of hearts, uppercutting declarer. If West overruffs, North scores the K-Q of hearts. Either way the defense takes two more tricks and declarer is four down!

Notes : (1) If using penalty doubles, North would double 2♡. When using negative doubles, you pass for penalties and pass partner's expected takeout double. Playing for penalties at a low level is best with strong trumps, about 8 HCP or more and a shortage in partner's suit.
(2) If South plays a fourth spade before the ♣ A is cashed, West can save a trick by discarding the club loser.
(3) Note South's play of the ace of diamonds after winning the queen of diamonds. This creates the void and enables South to score ruffs as well as North.

Hand 88 : Dealer West : Nil vulnerable

NORTH
- ♠ 8 6 2
- ♡ K J 10
- ◇ Q J 9 6 5
- ♣ K 10

WEST
- ♠ Q J 10 9 3
- ♡ A 6 4
- ◇ 8 3
- ♣ 9 6 5

EAST
- ♠ A K
- ♡ 8 7 5 2
- ◇ 7 4 2
- ♣ 7 4 3 2

SOUTH
- ♠ 7 5 4
- ♡ Q 9 3
- ◇ A K 10
- ♣ A Q J 8

WEST	NORTH	EAST	SOUTH
Pass	Pass	Pass	1NT
Pass	3NT	All pass	

Lead : ♠ Q. Normal long suit lead.

Play : East wins the ace of spades, followed by the king of spades. West plays the jack of spades under the king. East switches to a heart. West wins the ace and cashes three more spades. Down two.

Notes : (1) Any lead other than a spade and any switch other than a heart at trick 3 allows South to make nine tricks.
(2) East should play ♠ A, then ♠ K, not the other way round. Ace first, king next shows the doubleton and begs partner to signal on the second round to indicate the suit with the entry. King first, ace next implies a third spade is held and West may not appreciate the need to signal the entry.
(3) When giving a high card suit preference signal, play the highest you can afford. That is why West plays the jack, not the 10 or 9.
(4) If West held the ace of clubs instead of the ace of hearts, West would play the *three* of spades at trick 2. The low card asks partner to play the low suit next.
(5) 3NT is a very poor contract but tough to avoid. With 26 HCP and no short suits, most pairs would land there. 3NT would succeed if West happened to lead a club or a diamond or even a heart away from the ace. If East were on lead, 3NT would be almost certain to succeed. Even as it is, declarer may make 3NT unless East-West are versed in showing entries via suit preference signals.

CHAPTER 21
UNBLOCKING, SURROUND LEADS & ENTRY-KILLING PLAYS

UNBLOCKING

When partner leads an honor and third player holds a higher honor-doubleton, it is usually correct for third hand to unblock that honor. Third hand should play low only if unblocking clearly gives declarer an extra trick.

$$
\begin{array}{ccc}
 & 10\ 7\ 4 & \\
K\ Q\ J\ 6\ 5 & & A\ 3 \\
 & 9\ 8\ 2 &
\end{array}
$$

West leads the king. East should play the ace and return the suit. If East plays low, only two tricks are available to the defense unless West has an outside entry. It may be vital to cash three quicks quickly.

$$
\begin{array}{ccc}
 & 10\ 7\ 4\ 2 & \\
K\ Q\ J\ 6\ 5 & & A\ 3 \\
 & 9\ 8 &
\end{array}
$$

West leads the king. At no-trumps East should play low if West could have an entry outside. To rise ace and return the suit allows declarer to set up a trick with dummy's 10. In a suit contract, East should take ace and return the suit. West can lead low on the third round and East's ruff puts paid to any trick for declarer in that suit. Also, the layout could be:

$$
\begin{array}{ccc}
 & 10\ 7\ 4\ 2 & \\
K\ Q\ J\ 6 & & A\ 3 \\
 & 9\ 8\ 5 &
\end{array}
$$

or :

$$
\begin{array}{ccc}
 & 10\ 7\ 4\ 2 & \\
K\ Q\ 6\ 5 & & A\ 3 \\
 & J\ 9\ 8 &
\end{array}
$$

In both cases, if East plays low, the defense scores two tricks. In a trump contract, if East plays ace and returns the suit, the defense can take three tricks.

$$
\begin{array}{ccc}
 & 8\ 4\ 3 & \\
Q\ J\ 10\ 6\ 5 & & K\ 7 \\
 & A\ 9\ 2 &
\end{array}
$$

West leads the queen. If East plays low, South could take the ace and the suit is blocked. If East plays the king (correct with honor-doubleton) and South wins the ace, the defense can take as many tricks as are available as soon as either defender gains the lead. At no-trumps, if East plays low, South could duck the first and second rounds. This leaves East on lead, unable to continue the suit, and South still has a stopper in the suit. If East plays the king and South ducks, East continues the suit. If South ducks again, West wins and can play a third round (including a suit preference signal) to knock out declarer's stopper.

LATER UNBLOCKS

If partner is cashing a long suit from the top, you are expected to unblock your cards from the top.

$$
\begin{array}{ccc}
 & Q\ 4 & \\
J\ 10\ 9\ 6\ 2 & & K\ 8\ 7\ 3 \\
 & A\ 5 &
\end{array}
$$

In no-trumps, West leads the jack: queen, king, ace. West regains the lead and cashes the 10 and 9. East should unblock the 8 and 7. Otherwise, the suit blocks, East wins on the fourth round and West's last card will not score if West has no entry.

$$
\begin{array}{ccc}
 & 3 & \\
K\ J\ 10\ 8\ 5 & & 9\ 6\ 4\ 2 \\
 & A\ Q\ 7 &
\end{array}
$$

West leads the jack, won by the queen, East playing the 6 (in no-trumps, it usually pays to encourage when holding four cards in partner's long suit). Later, West continues with the king, East playing the 2, and South wins the ace. If West gains the lead and plays the 10, East with 9-4 left should unblock the 9. If not, the suit blocks, East's 9 wins the fourth round and West's fifth card goes begging if West has no entry.

$$
\begin{array}{ccc}
 & 9\ 6 & \\
K\ Q\ J\ 7\ 5 & & 10\ 8\ 4\ 2 \\
 & A\ 3 &
\end{array}
$$

West leads the king, South ducks and East plays the 8. West continues with the queen : 9 − 2 − A. When West regains the lead, if West continues with the jack, the normal play, East with 10-4 should unblock the 10. If partner were not prepared for this unblock, partner would not lead the suit from the top. If in doubt, it is best to unblock partner's long suit.

SURROUND LEADS

```
                 10 6 5
      A 8 7                 K J 9 4
                 Q 3 2
```

This position deserves close study. If East is on lead, which card should be led to ensure that declarer scores no trick?

Solution : East should lead the jack. If South plays low, the jack wins. A low card to the ace and back to the king gives the defense all the tricks. If South covers the jack with the queen, West takes the ace and returns the suit: North has 10-6, East has K-9-4, Whatever dummy plays, East wins as cheaply as possible and again the defense takes the maximum number of tricks.

No other card by East can ensure this result. If East leads low, South can duck it to the 10. After West wins the ace, South's Q-3 will make a trick, sooner or later. If East leads the king and continues with a low card, South can again duck in hand and set the queen up as a winner, while if East leads king, then jack, South covers the jack and dummy's 10 wins the third round.

The situation :

Dummy is on your right and holds the jack, 10 or 9. You have dummy's card (jack, 10 or 9) surrounded, *plus* a higher non-touching honor as well.

The rule :

Envisage dummy's card (the jack, 10 or 9) in your own hand and then lead top of the imaginary interior sequence.

```
                 10 6 5
      8 7 2                 K J 9 4
                 A Q 3
```

East has dummy's 10 surrounded (the J-9) plus a higher, non-touching honor (the king). Imagine dummy's 10 in East's hand, giving East K-J-10-9-4. From K-J-10-9-4, the jack would be led, so that is the correct card also in the surround position. When the jack is led, declarer can score only the queen and ace, two tricks, but if East led low, South could duck in hand and dummy's 10 would win. With the A-Q finesse still available, declarer could come to three tricks. After the jack and queen, if West can gain the lead and return the suit, South's ace can be forced out and East's winners established.

```
                 J 7 2
      8 6 3                 A Q 10 5
                 K 9 4
```

East's Q-10 surround dummy's jack. The ace is the higher honor, non-touching. Imagine the jack in East's hand. From A-Q-J-10-5, you would lead

the queen in no-trumps, so you also lead the queen in the surround position. If East leads a low card, South ducks and dummy's jack wins. South's K-9 remaining gives declarer a second trick. After the queen lead, won by the king, if West later leads through the J-7 to East's A-10-5, the defense collects all the available tricks.

```
                 9 5 4
      K 6 3                 Q 10 8 2
                 A J 7
```

The 10-8 surround the 9, the Q is the high non-touching honor. Imagine the 9 in East's hand. From Q-10-9-8-2, the correct lead is the 10. Likewise, the 10 is correct when you have the surround position.

A low lead by East gives South two tricks if South ducks it to the 9. West wins the king and South has the A-J over the queen. If East leads the 10, South is held to one trick. The proper play by East would be the same if East's suit were headed by the K-10-8.

```
                 9 5 4
      A 6 3                 Q 10 8 2
                 K J 7
```

The above analysis indicates East should lead the 10. This restricts South to one trick. A low card by East would give South two tricks if South elected to play low from hand.

```
                 A 9 4
      K 6 3                 Q 10 8 2
                 J 7 5
```

The 10-8 surround the 9. The queen is the higher non-touching honor. From Q-10-9-8-2, the 10 would be led, so lead the 10 also from the surround position. If East leads low, South has two tricks by playing low from hand. The 10 lead holds declarer to just one trick.

You should recognise that partner has made a surround lead if dummy holds the J, 10 or 9 and partner has led the next higher card. Partner would not lead the next higher card from other holdings.

The surround card should also be led if dummy is on your left and declarer might have the surrounded card:

```
                 Q 7 6
      K J 9 2
```

West should lead the jack. If South holds the ace, dummy's queen will win whether West leads the jack or leads low. However, if East has the ace and South has the 10, it is vital to lead the jack to prevent declarer winning a trick. West should also lead the jack from K-J-9-2 above if dummy held A-Q-x. If the 10 is with East, it would not matter which card West leads, but if the 10 is with South, the jack lead is necessary to prevent declarer scoring three tricks.

ENTRY-KILLING PLAYS

Where dummy has a long suit and few entries, there are several manoeuvres you may adopt to minimise declarer's tricks in this suit.

1. If you have a double stopper and dummy has only one entry, duck the first round of the long suit.

You may prevent the long suit being established.

```
            J 9 8 6 4 2
   A K 3                  7 5
            Q 10
```

When South plays the queen or 10, West should duck. If dummy has only one outside entry, this long suit is dead.

```
            K J 10 9 5 2
   8 7                    A Q 3
            6 4
```

South leads to dummy's jack. If East takes this, one more lead will set the suit up and one entry in dummy will do in order to reach the winners. If East ducks the jack, the suit cannot be established unless dummy has two entries. With only one outside entry, the suit is dead if East ducks the first round.

```
            K Q 8 6 4 3
   9 2                    A J 10
            7 5
```

South leads to dummy's king. East should duck. With only one outside entry to dummy, the long suit is dead. South might have done better by ducking the first round of the suit and playing to the king next time. Then the long suit can be set up and used as long as dummy has that outside entry.

2. Dummy has a long running suit and no entries outside trumps.

If you (or partner) hold more trumps than dummy, you may be able to kill the long suit by leading it. If you can run declarer out of this suit before your trumps are drawn, the suit will not be of any use to declarer. For example, see top of next column :

West leads the king of diamonds and cashes the ace. With 13 HCP with West and 10 HCP in dummy, all the significant high cards missing must be with South to justify the 3♡ rebid. The ♡K will be a trick but there is a great risk that West will not make a spade trick. The spade switch cannot work. South is almost certainly marked with the A-Q.

The solution is a club switch at trick 3 and a second club after winning the king of hearts. If declarer tries to play two more clubs to discard both spades, West ruffs. If South tries the spade finesse, that is one off, too.

NORTH
♠ J 7 3
♡ 10 8
♢ Q 4
♣ A Q J 8 7 3

WEST
♠ K 8 4
♡ K 4 2
♢ A K 8 7
♣ 10 5 2

WEST	NORTH	EAST	SOUTH
			1♡
Pass	2♣	Pass	3♡
Pass	4♡	All pass	

What should West lead after cashing two diamonds?

East's play of the lowest card on the second round of diamonds would also deny any interest in spades (see Chapter 20 on secondary signals). With the ♠Q as the only significant honor, East ought to play the top diamond on the second round to suggest some values in spades in a hand which partner can deduce to be hopelessly weak. The club switch is vital with South holding ♠ AQ10 ♡ AQJ963 ♢ 53 ♣ K4.

3. Knocking out dummy's entry.

NORTH
♠ A 9 3
♡ 7 2
♢ 8 6 3
♣ K Q J 9 3

EAST
♠ K Q 10 8
♡ A 4 3
♢ J 10
♣ A 7 5 2

South opens 1 NT and North raises to 3 NT. West leads the 10 of hearts and East wins the ace, South dropping the jack. How should East continue?

Staring at 14 HCP in hand and 10 HCP in dummy, East knows West has no useful high card. Dummy has only one entry to the clubs where East has a stopper. East should switch to the king of spades to attack dummy's entry. If declarer ducks the king of spades, East should continue with the queen of spades and, if South ducks again, a third spade. This cuts out dummy's club suit even if declarer has three clubs.

Holding K-Q in spades, knocking out the ♠A is not too difficult. Even if East's king is unsupported, it may be necessary to sacrifice the king to remove dummy's ace.

NORTH
♠ J 7 3
♡ A 4
♢ J 9 8 7 5 2
♣ 8 3

WEST
♠ 10 9 8 6
♡ K 7 2
♢ A K 4
♣ J 7 4

WEST	NORTH	EAST	SOUTH
			1♣
Pass	1♢	Pass	2NT (1)
Pass	3NT	All pass	

(1) Showing 19-20 points.

West leads the ♠10 : jack — queen — ace. South leads the queen of diamonds. West's play?

Answer: With a double stopper, West should hold off as there is only one outside entry in dummy. On the next diamond, West wins and East discards a discouraging heart. How should West continue?

Answer: East-West have 15 HCP at most between them. West has 11 and East has already turned up with the ♠ Q. East can hold at most two more points. Even so, West should switch to the king of hearts. Although this gives South heart tricks, it eliminates the entry to dummy's diamonds. If South ducks the king of hearts, a second heart is led. East-South are:

EAST
♠ Q 5 4
♡ 10 9 6 5 3
♢ 3
♣ Q 10 6 5

SOUTH
♠ A K 2
♡ Q J 8
♢ Q 10 6
♣ A K 9 2

If West fails to switch to the king of hearts, South makes four diamond tricks. The king of hearts switch holds South to one diamond trick and, on best defense, eight tricks in all.

EXERCISE ON UNBLOCKING, SURROUND LEADS & ENTRY-KILLING PLAYS

1.   **NORTH**
             6 5

                       EAST
                       A K 7

Against no-trumps, West leads the Q. Which card should East play?

2.   **NORTH**
             6 5 2

                       EAST
                       J 7

Against no-trumps, West leads the 10. Which card should East play?

3.   **NORTH**
             A 9 5

                       EAST
                       K 10 8 4

East is on lead and feels that a switch to this suit is required. Which card should East lead?

4.   **NORTH**
             10 7 4

                       EAST
                       K J 9 3

East is on lead and feels that a switch to this suit is essential. Which card should East lead?

5.   **NORTH**
             Q 7 3

WEST
K J 9

To defeat South's contract, West needs three tricks from this suit. Which card should West lead when switching to this suit?

6.   **NORTH**
             ♠ A 6 2
             ♡ 7 5
             ♢ K J 10 9 5 2
             ♣ J 6

                       EAST
                       ♠ 9 8 4
                       ♡ 6 4 3 2
                       ♢ A Q 6
                       ♣ Q 5 3

WEST	NORTH	EAST	SOUTH
Pass	Pass	Pass	1♣
Pass	1♢	Pass	2NT
Pass	3NT	All pass	

West leads the 10 of clubs : jack from dummy, covered by the queen and South wins the ace. South leads the 4 of diamonds, 7 from West and the jack from dummy. How should East plan the defense?

HANDS ON UNBLOCKING, SURROUND LEADS & ENTRY-KILLING PLAYS

Hand 89 : Dealer North : E-W vulnerable

NORTH
♠ Q J 10 8 5 2
♡ K Q 6 5
◇ A 5
♣ 7

WEST
♠ A 6 4 3
♡ 10 7 2
◇ J 8 6
♣ A Q 9

EAST
♠ 7
♡ A J 9 8
◇ K Q 9 3
♣ K J 8 6

SOUTH
♠ K 9
♡ 4 3
◇ 10 7 4 2
♣ 10 5 4 3 2

WEST	NORTH	EAST	SOUTH
	1♠	Double	Pass
2NT	Pass	3NT	All pass

Lead : ♠ Q. Best to lead your long, strong suit.

Play : South should play the king of spades on the queen. Declarer's best chance is to duck. South continues with the 9 of spades. Again West should duck. North overtakes with the 10 of spades and continues the spades to knock out the ace. Declarer should tackle the diamonds. North wins the ace and cashes the spades to defeat 3NT by two tricks.

Notes: (1) The 2NT response to the double shows 10-12 points, a stopper in opener's suit and denies four cards in the other major. Although not successful, 3NT is the normal contract. East's raise to 3NT is practical. An alternative would be 3♠, expressing concern about the spade position and inviting something other than 3NT. That might lead to a 4♡, also a reasonable spot.

(2) If South fails to play the king of spades at trick 1, declarer can succeed. Declarer could win the ♠A and lead a diamond towards dummy. If North ducks, the king wins. Declarer comes to hand with a club and leads a second diamond towards dummy. When the ace appears, declarer has 1 spade, 1 heart, 3 diamonds and 4 clubs and the blocking king of spades means that the defense cannot cash their spade tricks. Note West's technique in leading diamonds twice from hand, saving a trick when North has ace-doubleton.

(3) Declarer could also succeed by ducking both the first spade and the second spade if South does not play the king of spades at trick 1. South is on lead with the king of spades at trick 2 and cannot continue the spades. Again declarer can collect nine tricks before the defense can come to the spades.

(4) When South returns the 9 of spades, it is vital for North to overtake it to continue spades. Otherwise, South is stuck on lead and unable to continue the spades.

Hand 90 : Dealer East : Both vulnerable

NORTH
♠ K
♡ A 9 3 2
◇ 10 6 4
♣ A K 10 9 8

WEST
♠ 8 7 6 5
♡ 10 5
◇ A 7 3 2
♣ J 4 2

EAST
♠ A Q J 4 3 2
♡ J 4
◇ K J 9
♣ 7 5

SOUTH
♠ 10 9
♡ K Q 8 7 6
◇ Q 8 5
♣ Q 6 3

WEST	NORTH	EAST	SOUTH
		1♠	Pass
2♠	Double	Pass	4♡
Pass	Pass	Pass	

Lead: ♠7 (or 8). With four rags, middle-up-down is recommended. However, where you have raised partner's suit and cannot hold a doubleton, leading top-of-nothing is acceptable.

Play: East wins the ♠A and switches to the jack of diamonds. If South plays the queen, West takes the ace and returns a diamond. East's K-9 over the 10 is worth two tricks. If South plays low, the defense continues diamonds and takes 1 spade and 3 diamonds.

Notes: (1) It is better for North to double and risk a diamond reply than not to double and perhaps miss the hearts.

(2) South is worth 4♡ in reply to the double. 3♡ would be timid. Some use a variation of the Lebensohl convention in these auctions: a 2NT reply forces a 3♣ rebid by the doubler. A change of suit over 3♣ is then meant as a sign-off. A 3♡ reply without the use of the 2NT puppet shows invitational values and the jump to game obviously has game values. Using Lebensohl, South bids 3♡ and North passes.

(3) After winning ♠A, East sees that the only prospect of three more tricks is in diamonds. Dummy has the 10, East has the J-9 surrounding the 10, plus a higher, non-touching honor. This indicates a surround position, so that East leads the jack, the surround card. If East switched to a low diamond, declarer could succeed by playing low from hand. After West plays the ace, South's queen later scores a trick.

Hand 91 : Dealer South : Nil vulnerable

NORTH
♠ K J 10
♡ A Q
◇ A Q 8 3 2
♣ K 6 3

WEST	EAST
♠ A Q 5 3 2	♠ 9 6
♡ 9 8	♡ 7 6 5 4 2
◇ 5 4	◇ K 7 6
♣ A Q 10 8	♣ 7 5 2

SOUTH
♠ 8 7 4
♡ K J 10 3
◇ J 10 9
♣ J 9 4

WEST	NORTH	EAST	SOUTH
			Pass
1♠	Double	Pass	2♡
Pass	2NT	Pass	3NT
Pass	Pass	Pass	

Lead : ♠9. With a weak hand, it is usually preferable to lead partner's suit, not your own. It is best to choose the suit where there are entries after the suit is established.

Play : West wins the ace of spades and switches to the queen of clubs. Declarer's king wins. Declarer plays ♡ A, ♡ Q overtaking with the king, and leads the jack of diamonds, finessing. East wins with the king and returns the 7 of clubs. West is able to take 3 club tricks to defeat the contract.

Notes : (1) Double followed by no-trumps shows a hand too strong for a 1 NT overcall. North's 2NT thus shows 19-21 points or so, and South has enough to raise that to game.

(2) If West ducks the first spade or wins ♠A and returns a spade, declarer can make 3NT with ease.

(3) West can deduce from the 9 lead that declarer holds K-J-10 in spades. A count of points indicates East has 3 HCP at most. Declarer has a double stopper in spades but at most one stopper in clubs. The switch, therefore, should be to clubs. Dummy has the jack, West has the jack surrounded and a higher honor as well. Time to lead the surround card, the queen. If North ducks, a low club is continued. The club switch will work if East's 3 point holding is the king of clubs or a quick entry in a red suit.

(4) East should take the king of diamonds at the first opportunity and return a club. There are occasions when it pays to duck when declarer is likely to repeat a finesse. This is not one of those cases. If East ducks the first diamond, declarer can succeed by cashing the hearts and finessing in spades. East can judge that West has the given holding in clubs because the *queen* of clubs was led. With the jack in dummy, the queen switch is consistent only with a surround holding.

Hand 92 : Dealer West : Both vulnerable

NORTH
♠ K 9
♡ 10 7 6 4
◇ 9 8 7 5
♣ A Q 5

WEST	EAST
♠ A 3 2	♠ Q 10 6
♡ 5 2	♡ A K J 8
◇ 6 4	◇ A K 3 2
♣ K J 10 8 4 3	♣ 7 2

SOUTH
♠ J 8 7 5 4
♡ Q 9 3
◇ Q J 10
♣ 9 6

WEST	NORTH	EAST	SOUTH
Pass	Pass	1NT	Pass
3NT	Pass	Pass	Pass

Lead : ♠5. Normal long suit lead.

Play : Declarer plays low from dummy and North wins the king. North continues with a spade. Declarer takes the queen and plays a club to the jack. North ducks (smoothly, without a tell-tale trance). Declarer returns to hand and plays a club to the 10. North wins the queen and switches to a diamond or a heart. Declarer can no longer establish the club suit and can be held to eight tricks.

Notes : (1) With a strong 6-card minor, 8 HCP and an outside entry, West should bid game. 2NT would be timid.

(2) North returns a spade partly because no switch is attractive. In addition, the spade return may enable the defense to dislodge dummy's entry if South has the queen of spades.

(3) When declarer leads a club, South should play the 9 of clubs, top to indicate a doubleton.

(4) If North wins the first round of clubs, declarer can succeed. Declarer wins any return, knocks out the ace of clubs and has the ♠ A as an entry to the clubs. This would give East 2 spades, 2 hearts, 2 diamonds and 4 clubs.

(5) If possible, North should duck the club smoothly in order not to give the position away to declarer. Once you see dummy's clubs and appreciate the position, prepare your play in advance. You know declarer will finesse the jack of clubs. Make up your mind early to duck and you will manage it without allowing your indecision to give anything away.

CHAPTER 22
CREATING EXTRA TRUMP TRICKS
SIMPLE PROMOTIONS, OVERRUFFS & UPPERCUTS

PART 1 : SIMPLE PROMOTIONS

The defense has taken three spade tricks against 4♡ and East is on lead. If South were on lead, the A-K-Q would draw West's trumps. With East on lead, another spade will create a trump trick for West. If South ruffs low, West overruffs. If South ruffs high, (the best chance, in fact, with nine trumps missing the jack), West discards and the ♡J scores a trick later.

Simple promotions can also create a trick for the defense in these positions :

```
        J 8 6 5
Q 2               4 3
        A K 10 9 7
```

If South has the lead, the A-K drops West's queen. If East leads a suit where West is void, the queen will score a trick. If the East-West cards are reversed, and West leads a suit where dummy and East are void (but South has to follow), East can overruff dummy.

```
        K J 8 5
4 2               Q 10
        A 9 7 6 3
```

If South has the lead, A-K drops East's queen. If West leads a suit in which dummy and East are void (but South has to follow), East's Q-10 will yield a trick. If dummy ruffs with the jack or lower, East overruffs. If the king ruffs, East discards and the Q-10 over the jack ensures a trick later.

```
            A 8 7
10 9 4 2             5
            K Q J 6 3
```

If South has the lead, trumps can be drawn in four rounds. If East leads a suit in which declarer and West are void (but dummy must follow), West will score a trick. If South ruffs low, West overruffs. If South ruffs high (the best chance), West's 10 will become high later.

PART 2 : REFUSING TO OVERRUFF

```
        10 9 6 2
A J               4
        K Q 8 7 5 3
```

If South leads the king, taken by the ace, the queen later draws the jack. If East leads a suit where South and West are void, if South ruffs low, West overruffs with the jack and scores two tricks. If South ruffs high, however, West should discard, not overruff. This leaves A-J over South's honor and ensures two tricks. If West overruffs with the ace, South's honor draws the remaining trumps and the defense takes only one trick. This position is worth studying to appreciate the benefit in not overruffing.

PRINCIPLE : If given the chance to overruff, do so with a trump that is not sure to win a trick or with ace-singleton, king-doubleton or queen-tripleton. With ace-doubleton, king-tripleton or four to the queen, decline to overruff if you are bound to win a trick with your honor anyway and may score an extra trick with one of your lower cards.

```
        6 4 3
K 7               J 10
        A Q 9 8 5 2
```

If East leads a suit where South and West are void, if South ruffs with the queen, West should overruff (king-doubleton). East later scores a second trick. If West fails to overruff, South can hold the defense to just one trick. The same would hold if East had 10-9-8 and South ruffed with the jack of queen from A-Q-J-5-2. If West overruffs, East makes a trick later. If West fails to overruff, the defense might still make two tricks, but declarer could pick the position to lose only one trick.

```
        7 5
K 9 4             10 3
        A Q J 8 6 2
```

If East leads a suit where South and West are void, if South ruffs with the 8, overruff with the 9 for two tricks in trumps. If South ruffs with the queen or jack, do not overruff. If West does overruff, South's two remaining honors draw the trumps. one trick for the defense. If West discards, the defense will come to two trump tricks.

```
            6 4
   Q 9 3 2            5
         A K J 10 8 7
```

If East leads a suit where South and West are void, if South ruffs with the jack or 10, West should discard. This gives West two trump tricks. If West overruffs, South's three remaining honors can draw West's trumps and the defense takes only one trick.

These situations are not clearcut if the defense is uncertain about declarer's length in trumps.

DUMMY
```
            4 3
```
WEST
```
   Q 9 5
```

East leads a suit where South and West are void. South ruffs with the jack. Should West overruff?

If South began with A-K-J-x-x and East with 10-x-x, West can overruff with the queen and East makes a trick after the A-K are played. If West fails to overruff, declarer plays A, K and another and the defense comes to no more than their original entitlement.

However if South started with A-J-10-x-x-x and East with K-x, if West declines the overruff, the defense will come to two tricks whatever South does. However, if West overruffs the jack, declarer can cross to dummy and finesse against East's king. The defense makes only the queen.

There is no easy solution to such problems other than being able to read declarer's holding from the bidding and the points revealed.

PART 3 : UPPERCUTS

An uppercut is a ruff by a defender forcing an overruff with a high trump. The uppercut is so named because a high trump is *knocked out.*

```
            9 6 3
   A J                10 2
         K Q 8 7 5 4
```

The defense comes to only one trick if South can force out the ace with the king and later cash the queen. However, if West can lead a suit where East and South are void, the defense will come to two tricks if East ruffs with the 10. If South overruffs, West's A-J over South's remaining honor is worth two tricks.

```
            9 7 2
   Q 5                J 6
         A K 10 8 4 3
```

The defense has no tricks if South can cash the A-K. If West leads a suit where East and South are void, East's ruff with the jack gives the defense one trick. If South overruffs, West's queen will score later.

```
            9 8 2
   Q 10               K 6
         A J 7 5 4 3
```

If South plays ace and another, the defense has one trick. If West leads a suit which East can ruff with the king, the defense has two tricks. If South overruffs, West's Q-10 over South's jack will come to two tricks.

```
            5
   Q J 10 8            9
         A K 7 6 4 3 2
```

If South plays A-K, West has two tricks. If East can ruff with the 9, the defense comes to three tricks.

```
            Q J 10 5
   6                 K 8 7 2
         A 9 4 3
```

The defense has no tricks if declarer makes the normal play of leading dummy's honors for a finesse. However, if East leads a suit which West can ruff, the defense will take a trick. If South ruffs with the 9, South is down to three trumps and East's king scores. If South follows or discards, West's 6 uppercuts North's holding. If North overruffs, East can cover either of dummy's remaining honors to score a trick.

```
            4
   A 7 2               9 8 3
         K Q J 10 6 5
```

West seems to hold only one trump winner, yet even this innocuous holding can provide two winners if an uppercut is available. If West leads a suit where East and South are void, East ruffs with the 8, knocking out the 10. South leads any honor, taken by the ace. West leads the suit which East can ruff with the 9. If South discards, the 9 is the second trick for the defense. If South overruffs, South will have only one honor left. West's 7 becomes the top trump after South cashes the remaining honor.

NOTE: Before playing for a promotion, an overruff or an uppercut, cash your outside winners. Declarer may discard a loser to save a trick rather than ruff.

```
         ♠ Q 6 5
         ◇ K Q J 8 4
   ♠ J 9 3              ♠ 10 2
   ◇ A 9 7 5            ◇ 10 6 2
         ♠ A K 8 7 4
         ◇ 3
```

If East and South are out of clubs and West leads a club, ruffed by East's 10, South will discard the diamond loser. West must cash the ◇ A first and then lead a club. The defense then takes the diamond *and* comes to a trump trick via the uppercut.

PLAY HANDS ON CREATING EXTRA TRUMP TRICKS

Hand 93 : Dealer North : Both vulnerable

NORTH
♠ 10 6 5
♡ 10 3
◇ 8 5 3 2
♣ 9 8 6 3

WEST
♠ K Q J 8 7 4
♡ J 8
◇ A 6
♣ K 7 4

EAST
♠ 9 3 2
♡ 6 4 2
◇ K Q J 10
♣ A Q J

SOUTH
♠ A
♡ A K Q 9 7 5
◇ 9 7 4
♣ 10 5 2

WEST	NORTH	EAST	SOUTH
	Pass	1◇	1♡
1♠	Pass	2♠	Pass
4♠	Pass	Pass	Pass

Lead : ♡10. No excuse for anything else.

Play : South wins the queen of hearts and cashes the king. South continues with a third heart. West ruffs with the king, crosses to dummy with a club and leads a spade. South wins with the ace and leads a fourth heart. This promotes the ♠10 for North. If West ruffs low, North overruffs. If West ruffs with the queen (the best chance, hoping for trumps 2-2), North's 10 will be high after West cashes the jack.

Notes : (1) South's hand is worth an overcall and a rebid at the 2-level. However, the 3-level is too high if partner was not worth action over West's 1♠. Using intermediate jump overcalls, South could bid 2♡, West bids 2♠, forcing, and East would raise to 3♠.
(2) East has an awkward rebid after 1♠. The raise to 2♠ is unappetising with such a flat hand. Without the intervention, East would rebid 1NT. However, the raise to the 2-level with only three trumps is preferable to rebidding 1NT without a stopper in their suit. Playing negative doubles, a double by West would show four spades and 1♠ shows five. This would make East's raise to 2♠ easier to endure.
(3) South can deduce from West's jump to 4♠ that West has the ace of diamonds. With no more than K-Q-J in spades, the jack of hearts and the king of clubs, West would only invite game with 3♠. West needs the ace of diamonds to justify the jump to 4♠. In any event, on the third heart, North should discard to discourage diamonds. This also places the ◇ A with West so that South should lead a fourth heart when in with the ♠ A.
(4) After ruffing the third heart high, West should not lead a trump honor. This could cost the contract if South had A-x in trumps. Crossing to dummy to lead a spade caters for South holding ♠A-x.

Hand 94 : Dealer East : Nil vulnerable

NORTH
♠ Q 8
♡ A Q J 7 6 5
◇ K 10 8 3
♣ J

WEST
♠ A K 9 7 5 4 3
♡ 4
◇ 9 7
♣ 10 8 4

EAST
♠ 6 2
♡ K 10 2
◇ 6 5
♣ K 9 7 5 3 2

SOUTH
♠ J 10
♡ 9 8 3
◇ A Q J 4 2
♣ A Q 6

WEST	NORTH	EAST	SOUTH
		Pass	1◇
3♠	4♡	All pass	

Lead : ♠6. No reason to avoid the normal lead of partner's suit.

Play : West wins the king and cashes the ace. As a switch to either minor is appalling, West should continue with a third spade. If North discards or ruffs low, East can ruff with the 10. Later East scores the king of hearts for one off. Declarer's better chance is to ruff with the queen of hearts. This may tempt a defender to overruff with the king. If East does overruff with the king, North makes the rest, as the ♡ A-J can draw all the trumps. East should discard on the queen of hearts. Now East has K-10-x over North's A-J-7-6-5 and North cannot avoid losing two trump tricks to the king and the 10. One down.

Notes : (1) Not vulnerable, West is worth 3♠. Vulnerable, a weak jump overcall of 2♠ would be enough.
(2) North's 4♡ is the best practical move. 4♡ is likely to be the best contract and you cannot reach that if you support diamonds. 4◇ is too weak an action and 5◇ is more likely to fail than 4♡.
(3) When the third spade is led, declarer's best bet is to ruff with the queen or jack. This will allow 4♡ to make if trumps are 2-2. Ruffing with the queen is superior psychologically : if you want an opponent to overruff, make the bait attractive. East should not overruff anyway, but an unwary defender is more likely to overruff the queen (out of habit, instinct or greed) than the jack.

Hand 95 : Dealer South : N-S vulnerable

NORTH
♠ K Q 8 3
♡ J 10 7 2
♢ K Q
♣ 9 8 6

WEST
♠ J 9 7 5
♡ 9 3
♢ 9 8 5 3 2
♣ 10 4

EAST
♠ 10 4
♡ Q 8 6
♢ J 10 6
♣ A K Q 7 2

SOUTH
♠ A 6 2
♡ A K 5 4
♢ A 7 4
♣ J 5 3

WEST	NORTH	EAST	SOUTH
			1NT
Pass	2♣	Double	2♡
Pass	4♡	All pass	

Lead: ♣10. East's double called for a club lead and there is no reason to overrule that request.

Play: East wins the queen, king and ace of clubs. At trick 4, East plays a fourth club. West ruffs with the 9 of hearts and North overruffs. East now covers as cheaply as possible any trump led from dummy and must therefore come to a trump trick for one off.

Notes: (1) 3NT would make if a club is not led, but using Stayman on the North cards will lead to the best contract most of the time. (2) It is standard to reply normally to Stayman after the double. A better scheme is to give the normal reply only with a club stopper. Without a stopper, pass. Partner redoubles to ask for the normal reply. This method discovers whether opener has a club stopper.

(3) On the third club West should discard a low diamond. This discourages diamonds if using standard signals, or asks for a club if using Suit Preference discards (thus indicating no interest in spades or diamonds). (4) East does not need any such signal. East can count that West has no useful high card (East has 12 HCP, dummy has 11 and the 1NT showed 16-18). With no chance for another high card trick, East tries for a trump trick via a fourth club. Luckily West has the ♡9 and can uppercut dummy. East's queen and spot cards are now strong enough to force a defensive trump trick. (5) If East switches at trick 4, declarer wins, cashes ♡A, crosses to dummy and leads ♡J for a finesse.

Hand 96 : Dealer West : E-W vulnerable

NORTH
♠ 10
♡ Q J 10 7 6 4 3
♢ 9
♣ J 7 5 4

WEST
♠ Q 5 3
♡ A 5
♢ Q J 10 7 4
♣ A 9 3

EAST
♠ A K 8 7 6 4
♡ K 8
♢ 6
♣ K Q 8 2

SOUTH
♠ J 9 2
♡ 9 2
♢ A K 8 5 3 2
♣ 10 6

WEST	NORTH	EAST	SOUTH
1♢	3♡	3♠	Pass
4♠	Pass	4NT	Pass
5♡	Pass	6♠	All pass

Lead : ♢ K (or ace). A heart lead must be futile, as East-West must have the ace of hearts. A better chance is to hope for two diamond tricks.

Play: At trick 2, South continues with a low diamond. North ruffs with the 10 of spades. East overruffs but North's uppercut has created a trump trick for South. If East leads a low spade, South inserts the 9 to force the queen, and the jack is the setting trick.

Notes: (1) At favourable vulnerabilty, North is worth 3♡. Some macho players would bid 4♡ but 3♡ is what the hand is worth and will not mislead partner as to your playing potential. (2) 3♠ is forcing and West has an easy raise to 4♠. East is worth a slam move and with second round control in all suits, 4NT is best.

(3) If East-West were using Roman Key Card Blackwood, West would reply 5♠ to 4NT to show two key cards and the queen of trumps. That would give East more confidence to bid the slam. Using ordinary Blackwood, West's 5♡ shows only the two aces and East could be afraid of being off an ace and the trump queen. 6♠ is an excellent slam, beaten only by the vile breaks in diamonds and trumps.
(4) On a non-diamond lead, declarer can succeed by deducing the position in clubs. Suppose South leads a heart. East wins, draws trumps and leads a diamond. South wins and leads a second heart, taken in dummy. When declarer leads a diamond and ruffs, North shows out and the whole hand is revealed. When an opponent shows out in a suit, make a habit of noting the number of cards in that suit held by the other opponent. Here, South is known to have started with three spades, six diamonds and two hearts. Therefore, South cannot hold more than two clubs. Declarer continues by cashing the king of clubs, unblocking the 9 from dummy and leading a club to dummy's ace. When South's 10 drops, declarer takes the marked finesse against North's jack.

CHAPTER 23

SETTING UP RUFFS

To score a ruff, you may have to locate partner's entry. When giving partner a ruff, you can indicate the desired return by a suit preference signal. You may wish to delay giving partner a ruff to create a void in your own hand. The following hands illustrate the principles involved.

Hand 97 : Dealer North : Nil vulnerable

NORTH
♠ A 2
♡ J 10 8 6
♢ A K J 10 5
♣ K 5

WEST
♠ 10 8 6 4 3
♡ A Q 3
♢ 6
♣ J 9 7 4

EAST
♠ K 7 5
♡ 5
♢ 9 7 4 3 2
♣ Q 10 8 3

SOUTH
♠ Q J 9
♡ K 9 7 4 2
♢ Q 8
♣ A 6 2

WEST	NORTH	EAST	SOUTH
	1♢	Pass	1♡
Pass	3♡	Pass	4♡
Pass	Pass	Pass	

Lead: ♢ 6. Usually avoid leading dummy's suit but with a singleton, a weak hand and control of the trump suit, this is the best shot.

Play: The ace of diamonds wins, East playing the *nine* as a suit preference signal for spades. The jack of hearts finesse loses to the queen. A spade return is won by the ace and second trump led. East discards the 3 of clubs to deny interest there. West wins and plays a spade. East takes the king and returns a diamond. West ruffs for one down.

Notes: (1) East should read the lead as a singleton. It is strange to lead dummy's suit but a singleton lead is feasible. The lead could not be from 8-6 or Q-6 and to lead dummy's suit with Q-8-6 is far-fetched.

(2) If West wins the queen of hearts and switches to a club, declarer succeeds. Win the king of clubs, drive out the ace of hearts, spade switch (too late) won by the ace, draw the last trump and discard the spade losers on the diamonds. West should find the spade switch even without East's suit preference signal. With the ace of hearts still controlling trumps, West can afford to try the spades first. If the ace of spades wins and East discourages, West can try the clubs later.

Hand 98 : Dealer East : N-S vulnerable

NORTH
♠ 3
♡ K Q 9 6 5
♢ 9 8 2
♣ Q 8 6 4

WEST
♠ J 10 6 5
♡ 7 3 2
♢ K Q J 10
♣ 7 3

EAST
♠ K 9 8 7 2
♡ A J
♢ A 7 6 5 4
♣ A

SOUTH
♠ A Q 4
♡ 10 8 4
♢ 3
♣ K J 10 9 5 2

WEST	NORTH	EAST	SOUTH
		1♠	2♣
2♠	3♣	4♠	All pass

Lead: ♢ 3. South plans to score two top trumps, plus partner's probable entry as the means to the fourth trick, a diamond ruff.

Play: Dummy wins and North plays the *nine* of diamonds, a suit preference signal for hearts. The jack of spades loses to South's queen. A heart is led to the queen and ace. South wins the next round of trumps, North discarding the ♣4 to discourage clubs. South leads a heart to North's king and the diamond ruff sinks the contract.

Notes: (1) North can read the lead as a singleton. South has led the lowest diamond, consistent only with an honor combination or a singleton. South would not lead away from the ace and the other honors are in dummy. Therefore the lead is a singleton. South needs to know North's entry and North uses the ♢ 9 as a suit preference signal to show interest in the high suit, hearts.

(2) In view of the club raise, it would be 'natural' to play for North's entry to be the ace of clubs. South should switch to hearts at trick 3 even without North's signal. With control of trumps, South can switch to clubs later if that is North's entry. On the next round of trumps, North signals dislike of clubs to clarify the defense.

Hand 99 : Dealer South : E-W vulnerable

NORTH
- ♠ K Q J 9 4 3
- ♡ A Q
- ♢ 10 8 6
- ♣ 9 3

WEST
- ♠ 8
- ♡ K J 10 6 4
- ♢ 9 7 5 3
- ♣ A K J

EAST
- ♠ A 6
- ♡ 9 8 7 5
- ♢ 2
- ♣ Q 8 7 6 4 2

SOUTH
- ♠ 10 7 5 2
- ♡ 3 2
- ♢ A K Q J 4
- ♣ 10 5

WEST	NORTH	EAST	SOUTH
			Pass
1♡	1♠	2♡	3♠
Pass	4♠	All pass	

Lead : ♢ 2. With trump control, a singleton appeals.

Play : North should play low in dummy and win in hand in order to lead a low spade. East rises with the ace, leads a club to West, receives a diamond ruff and the next club defeats the contract.

Notes : (1) A pre-emptive 4♡ is attractive but South would bid 4♠. (2) West should read the lead as a singleton. When a suit is bid and raised, leading an outside suit usually heralds a singleton. Whether dummy plays low or wins, West should play the 3, a suit preference signal for clubs.
(3) North's low spade lead is a good try. If East ducks, 4♠ makes.
(4) If East tries to reach West via a heart, declarer makes twelve tricks, drawing the trump and discarding clubs on the diamonds.

Hand 100 : Dealer West : Both vulnerable

NORTH
- ♠ 8 7 4
- ♡ K Q J 4 2
- ♢ 2
- ♣ A 9 6 2

WEST
- ♠ A J 10 5
- ♡ 8
- ♢ Q 9 7 6
- ♣ J 10 7 4

EAST
- ♠ K Q 9 3
- ♡ A 10 5
- ♢ 10 3
- ♣ K Q 8 3

SOUTH
- ♠ 6 2
- ♡ 9 7 6 3
- ♢ A K J 8 5 4
- ♣ 5

WEST	NORTH	EAST	SOUTH
Pass	Pass	1♣	1♢
1♠	2♡	2♠	3♡
3♠	Pass	Pass	Pass

Lead : ♢ 2. A singleton in partner's suit is a good start.

Play : South wins ♢ K and switches to ♣ 5. North takes ♣ A and returns the ♣ 2 (suit preference for diamonds). South ruffs and leads a low diamond. North ruffs and the next club defeats 3♠.

Notes : (1) On a heart lead, 3♠ makes easily.
(2) South sees a heart switch is futile as West will hold a singleton. With only two diamond tricks possible, South tries for club ruffs. The switch is clearly a singleton (why else lead dummy's strength?).
(3) South must not cash the second diamond before switching to clubs and should lead a low diamond after ruffing the club return (perhaps North began with Q-x-x). If South plays a top diamond after the club ruff, North should ruff to play another club.

Hand 101 : Dealer North : N-S vulnerable

NORTH
- ♠ 10 7
- ♡ Q 10 6 5
- ♢ K J 3
- ♣ K J 10 3

WEST
- ♠ K Q J
- ♡ 8 3
- ♢ 7 6 4
- ♣ 9 8 6 4 2

EAST
- ♠ A 9 3 2
- ♡ A 7 4
- ♢ 10 9 8 5 2
- ♣ 7

SOUTH
- ♠ 8 6 5 4
- ♡ K J 9 2
- ♢ A Q
- ♣ A Q 5

WEST	NORTH	EAST	SOUTH
	Pass	Pass	1NT
Pass	2♣	Pass	2♡
Pass	4♡	All pass	

Lead : ♠ K. Normal top of sequence.

Play : East overtakes the king with the ace in order to switch to the singleton club. Declarer wins and leads a trump. East takes the ace, returns a spade to West and the club is ruffed by East for one off.

Notes : (1) East overtakes the first spade to clarify the defense for partner. East knows the club ruff is needed, West does not.
(2) With 10 HCP in dummy East can tell that West cannot hold anything useful beyond the K-Q of spades. The second spade is needed as the entry for the club ruff. East can also see that the defense will come to no more than two tricks in spades. The ♡ A makes three and the club ruff is the only possibility for a fourth trick for the defense.

Hand 102 : Dealer East : E-W vulnerable

NORTH
♠ K J 8 5 2
♡ K 7 2
♢ 5 4 3 2
♣ J

WEST
♠ 3
♡ Q J 10 9 6 5
♢ 9 8 7 6
♣ A 5

EAST
♠ A Q 7 6 4
♡ 3
♢ Q J 10
♣ K Q 9 2

SOUTH
♠ 10 9
♡ A 8 4
♢ A K
♣ 10 8 7 6 4 3

WEST	NORTH	EAST	SOUTH
		1♠	Pass
1NT	Pass	2♣	Pass
2♡	Pass	Pass	Pass

Lead : ♣ J. Against low level contracts, singletons are particularly attractive as partner is so likely to have entries.

Play : Declarer wins and leads a trump. South wins and cashes the A-K of diamonds (in that order, to show a doubleton), then club ruff, diamond ruff and the contract is one off. On the next club, West does best to discard a diamond to avoid two off.

Notes : (1) West is too weak for a 2♡ response. 1NT followed by a new suit is weak (5-8 HCP) and is taken as a 6-card suit. Therefore, East should pass 2♡. A rebid of 2♠ or 2NT would be misguided.
(2) Before giving partner a ruff, it is attractive to cash a singleton ace or A-K doubleton in order to receive a ruff yourself. North discourages on the ♢ A and signals suit preference on the king.

Hand 103 : Dealer South : Both vulnerable

NORTH
♠ K 10 9 8 3
♡ 8 6
♢ Q 8
♣ A K 10 4

WEST
♠ A 6 4
♡ A 9 2
♢ J 9 7 5 4 3
♣ 5

EAST
♠ 7 5 2
♡ K Q J
♢ A
♣ J 9 8 7 6 2

SOUTH
♠ Q J
♡ 10 7 5 4 3
♢ K 10 6 2
♣ Q 3

WEST	NORTH	EAST	SOUTH
			Pass
Pass	1♠	Pass	1NT
Pass	2♣	Pass	2♠
Pass	Pass	Pass	

Lead : ♡ K. Second choice, ace of diamonds, but the sequence is more attractive with the ♢ A as an entry later.

Play : West overtakes the ♡ K with the ace and switches to the 5 of clubs. Declarer starts on trumps and West wins the ace and leads a heart. East cashes the ♢ A before giving West the club ruff. The diamond return is ruffed for one down.

Notes : (1) Preference to 2♠ is better than introducing the hearts with only a 5-card suit (and a rotten one, at that).
(2) With East leading a sequence and dummy having length in hearts, West can see little future in hearts. West overtakes to take control of the defense and steer East to the club ruffs.

Hand 104 : Dealer West : Nil vulnerable

NORTH
♠ A
♡ A 2
♢ Q 8 4 3 2
♣ A 7 6 3 2

WEST
♠ K Q 10 8 6
♡ 5 3
♢ A J 10 7
♣ K J

EAST
♠ 4 2
♡ K Q J 8 6 4
♢ 5
♣ Q 10 5 4

SOUTH
♠ J 9 7 5 3
♡ 10 9 7
♢ K 9 6
♣ 9 8

WEST	NORTH	EAST	SOUTH
1♠	Pass	1NT	Pass
2♢	Pass	2♡	All pass

Lead : ♣9. With no attractive lead, the unbid suit is the best choice.

Play : North wins the ♣ A, cashes the ♠ A to create a void and returns the 7 of clubs (high card for the high suit). Declarer wins and leads a trump. North takes the ace and leads the 6 of clubs. South ruffs, gives North the spade ruff and ruffs the club return for one down.

Notes : (1) East is just too weak for a 2♡ response. The 1NT reply followed by hearts shows this type of hand.
(2) North need not cash the ♠ A at trick 2. Here it is safe but in other cases it may tip your hand to declarer. North could return a club at trick 2, win the ♡ A on the first round of trumps, *then* cash the ♠ A before embarking on the defensive crossruff. The defense scores three aces and three ruffs.

CHAPTER 24

CARD READING & INFERENCES IN DEFENSE

Just as declarer can take inferences from the bidding, so can the defenders. The opening lead can be very revealing and partner's signals can also pinpoint the location of the missing cards. In addition, declarer's plan of attack may itself provide valuable clues as to the appropriate countermeasures. The best preliminary rule for the defenders is the same as for declarer :

COUNT DUMMY'S POINTS

Then add your own. Deduct from 40 to gauge what partner and declarer hold. Often you can assess declarer's point count within a narrow range. Deduct that, too, and you are left with partner's point range. For example :

```
            NORTH
            ♠ K Q 8
            ♡ K Q 5 4
            ◇ Q 10
            ♣ A Q 4 3
WEST
♠ J
♡ A 7 6 2
◇ A K 9 8 2
♣ J 5 2
```

WEST	NORTH	EAST	SOUTH
1◇	Double	Pass	2♡
Pass	4♡	All pass	

You, West, lead the king of diamonds and dummy comes into view. How many points do you think partner holds?

The 18 HCP in dummy plus your 13 leave 9 for partner and declarer. Given declarer jumped to 2♡ in reply to the double rather than responding just 1♡, almost every missing high card will be with South. It would be futile, for instance, to switch to your singleton spade and hope for a spade ruff. Partner cannot hold the ♠ A. Likewise, do not expect the ♣ K with partner. You must plan to defend without benefit of partner (quite an attractive thought, really) and your best shot is to adopt a forcing defense. With only three winners in top cards, you must try to establish an extra trick in trumps. Lead the king of diamonds, ace of diamonds and a third diamond. Suppose the missing hands are :

```
            EAST
            ♠ 10 7 6 5 4 2
            ♡ 8
            ◇ 7 6 5 3
            ♣ 9 7
SOUTH
♠ A 9 3
♡ J 10 9 3
◇ J 4
♣ K 10 8 6
```

The third round of diamonds forces declarer or dummy to ruff. You then hold off with the ace of hearts for two rounds and declarer will fail (see Chapter 18, page 109, for forcing defense strategy).

ESTIMATE THE LENGTH OF DECLARER'S SUITS FROM THE BIDDING

	SOUTH	NORTH	
1.	**1♠**	**1NT**	How many spades will South hold?
	2♠	**Pass**	
2.	**1♠**	**2♣**	How many spades does South have? Also, how many diamonds?
	2◇	**2♡**	
	3◇	**3♠**	
	4♠	**Pass**	
3.	**1NT**	**3♠**	How many spades will South have?
	3NT	**Pass**	
4.	**1♣**	**1♠**	On this auction, how many clubs will South have? How many spades?
	3♣	**3◇**	
	3NT	**Pass**	
5.	**1♠**	**2♣**	South: How many spades? How many hearts? How many clubs? Diamonds?
	2♡	**2NT**	
	3♣ . . .		

Answers :

1. Normally six spades.   **2.** Five spades and five diamonds at least.   **3.** Two spades.   **4.** Six clubs at least and fewer than three spades.   **5.** Five spades, four hearts, three clubs and therefore one diamond. (Conceivably, six spades, four hearts, three clubs and therefore no diamond, or even 5-4-0-4.)

NORTH
♠ Q 8 3
♡ K J 8 7 3
♢ 8 3
♣ A J 9

WEST
♠ K 9 6 2
♡ A 6 4
♢ 7
♣ Q 10 6 4 2

SOUTH	NORTH
1♢	1♡
1♠	2NT
3♠	4♠
Pass	

West leads the 4 of clubs, dummy's ace wins, 7 from East and South follows with the 8. A diamond is led, 6 from East and South's queen wins. South now leads the 2 of hearts. Do you fly in with the ace or do you play low, hoping declarer mispicks the K-J combination?

Solution: South's hand pattern is an open book. Five spades (they were bid and rebid), longer diamonds (the diamonds were bid ahead of the 5-card spade suit), therefore six diamonds, one club (seen at trick 1) and therefore *only one* heart (now led). South is bound to be 5-1-6-1. You must grab your ace. You certainly are not taking two heart tricks in defense and if you duck, South is sure to play the king, leaving you with no heart trick.

INFERENCES FROM THE LEAD

1. Partner leads an honor card : You can usually deduce where the missing honors are.

2. Partner leads fourth highest : You can estimate partner's length and hence declarer's length. Apply the Rule of 11 and see whether that provides any useful information.

3. Partner makes an unexpected lead : If partner does not make the lead you expect from the bidding, try to work out partner's motive. An unexpected lead is frequently a singleton.

4. In no-trumps, if partner leads a suit which is known to be a 4-card suit or turns out to be a 4-card suit, partner figures not to have a longer unbid suit. Partner would usually prefer to lead the longer suit.

On the problem at the top of the next column, South opened 1 NT (15-17) and North raised to 3 NT. After West leads the 2 of hearts, can you as East deduce how many spades are held by South?

NORTH
♠ 8 7
♡ A 8 3
♢ K Q 8 4 2
♣ J 7 3

EAST
♠ 9 5
♡ Q 7 6
♢ J 10 7 5
♣ K 8 4 2

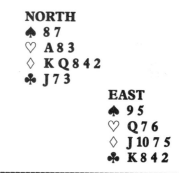

Solution: Partner's 2 of hearts, being fourth highest, indicates partner has precisely a 4-card heart suit. Therefore partner does not hold five spades (else partner would have preferred a spade lead). Since nine spades are missing and partner does not have five, declarer must have five spades. The lead marks South with five spades and three hearts. There are many opportunities for this kind of inference.

INFERENCES FROM LATER PLAY

1. If third hand plays high to try to win the trick, the card played denies the next lower card. A defender wins or tries to win as cheaply as possible.

The ace by third hand denies the king.
A king by third hand denies the queen.
A queen by third hand denies the jack.
A jack by third hand denies the 10.
A 10 by third hand denies the 9.
A 9 by third hand denies the 8, and so on.

2. A high card signal denies the next higher card.

A jack signal denies the queen. If you can afford to signal with the jack, you can afford the queen.

A 10 signal denies the jack.
A 9 signal denies the 10.
An 8 signal denies the 9.
A 7 signal denies the 8, and so on.

This applies whether the high card signal is the beginning of a come-on (encouraging) attitude signal or whether the high card signal is the beginning of a high-low count signal.

3. Partner's count signals when declarer is leading a suit enable you to calculate the number of cards held by declarer in that suit. See Chapter 19, page 113, which deals with count signals.

4. When returning partner's lead, play the top card from a remaining doubleton and the bottom card when three cards are remaining (unless you need to unblock this 3-card holding). From longer holdings, it is standard to return the card that was your original fourth highest.

MID-GAME SWITCHES

If you plan to switch to a new suit, the card you *lead* tells partner how much you would like to have this suit returned.

Low card switch = Please continue this suit.

High card switch = Not interested in this suit.

These guidelines are important. If partner comes on lead, partner needs to know which suit to tackle. The high card switch refers to high spot cards such as the 9, 8 or 7. An honor card switch follows the normal honor card rules for top of sequence leads.

INFERENCES FROM DECLARER'S PLAY

The correct play by a competent declarer is known for many card combinations, especially the play at trick 1 (see Chapter 12). A defender can often deduce declarer's and partner's holding in a suit from the card played by declarer. For example :

NORTH

A Q 5

WEST

K 10 6 3 2

West leads the 3 and dummy's queen is played, winning. Who holds the jack?

Answer: If declarer held the jack, the correct play would have been low from dummy (see page 78). As declarer did not do this, declarer does not hold the jack. Therefore partner has the jack and you can safely continue this suit later. Incidentally, when East signals here, East need not signal possession of the jack. West knows that already. East's signal has the usual meaning (high = please continue this suit; lowest = I prefer a switch).

NORTH

Q 5

EAST

K 10 8 4

Against 3NT, West leads the 3 and dummy plays the 5. Who has the ace? Which card should East play?

Answer: With Q-x opposite the ace or Q-x opposite A-J-x, declarer would have played the queen (see page 76). As declarer did not play the queen, declarer does not have the ace. Therefore, East should play the king, not the 10. It would be embarrassing to play the 10 and give declarer a trick for nothing, if declarer began with J-x and partner with A-x-x-x-x.

Take note of declarer's line of play. Is declarer going for ruffs in dummy? A switch to trumps may be best. Is declarer trying to set up a long suit in dummy? Perhaps you can knock out dummy's entry.

Does dummy have a long, running suit which will give declarer discards? Do not adopt a passive defense; go for your tricks in the outside suits quickly. Was the first suit led futile? Be prepared to switch. At no-trumps, note if dummy has a long semi-solid suit such as K-Q-J-x-x, A-Q-J-x-x or A-K-J-x-x and declarer is tackling some other suit. Declarer holds the missing honor in dummy's suit and can cash the tricks in that suit at will. Otherwise, declarer would be playing to establish dummy's suit.

COUNTING

A good defender will have noted declarer's likely point count and probable shape from the bidding. As the play develops, keep track of the honor cards played and relate it to declarer's expected holding. If declarer has a 6-9 point hand and has turned up with an ace, a king and a queen, the unseen points must be with partner. Also keep track of the cards in declarer's hand and note when declarer shows out. It requires only a little effort and concentration to deduce declarer's original hand pattern. If declarer is known to be 5-4 in spades-hearts from the bidding and follows to two diamonds and then ruffs, declarer cannot have more than two clubs. Gradually you will be able to build up a picture of declarer's shape (5-4-2-2, 6-3-3-1, 5-5-3-0, etc.) with ease.

The better your opponents, the more reliable their bidding and so the more accurate your assessment. Also, the more descriptive their auction, the easier it is for the defenders to build up an accurate picture of declarer's pattern.

It is vital for the defenders to keep in mind the number of tricks needed to defeat the contract. Particularly when it is clear that dummy can provide discards for declarer, you must attack the suits where the tricks needed are possible. It is all too common for defenders to follow some maxim blindly (such as 'return partner's lead') when a little thought will indicate that this line has to be futile and a switch is essential to defeat the contract.

However, if there is no prospect of a long suit in dummy providing discards for declarer, it is best to adopt a passive defense. You need not switch to a new suit just because a switch happens to be available. A switch can often assist declarer in building up tricks in a suit. The principle is : If dummy has a useful long suit, attack in the outside suits is essential. If dummy has no useful long suit, the defense usually does not need to break open new suits. Exit safely and let declarer struggle.

When dummy is on your right, a switch from a suit with one honor is particularly dangerous if dummy holds a lower honor. For example :

10 6 5

Q 9 8   K 7 4 2

A J 3

Declarer has one trick (the ace) and cannot develop another without help from the defense. If declarer leads the 10 from dummy, East covers and South is set to lose two tricks. However, if East is on lead and switches to this suit, declarer scores a second trick (low to West's queen and finesse the jack later). Likewise, if West were to switch to this suit, declarer has a second trick. As long as declarer has no discards, the defense will come to their tricks. Be patient.

Q 4 3

J 9 7 5   K 10 8 2

A 6

Declarer has one trick. If East switches to this suit, declarer ducks in hand and scores a second trick.

J 7 5

10 8 3   Q 9 6 2

A K 4

Declarer has two tricks. If East switches to this suit, declarer ducks and scores a third trick.

J 7 5

10 8 3   K 9 6 2

A Q 4

Declarer has two tricks. If East switches to this suit, declarer ducks in hand and can score three tricks.

10 7 5

K 9 8   J 6 4 2

A Q 3

Declarer has one trick and cannot score a second without the defense's co-operation. If either defender switches to this suit, declarer makes another trick. If East leads low, declarer ducks in hand and makes the A-Q when West plays the king.

The message is : **Hands off that switch!**

EXERCISE ON DEFENSIVE INFERENCES

1.   **NORTH**
                    Q 5

WEST   West leads the 3
J 9 8 3 2   against 3NT.

(a) Dummy's queen is played, king from East and South wins the ace. Who holds the 10?

(b) The 5 is played from dummy, 10 from East and South wins the ace. Who has the king?

2.   **NORTH**
             ♣ A Q 7 2
                     EAST
                     ♣ K 9 6 5

In 4♡, declarer cashes dummy's ♣ A and then leads low from dummy. Do you play low or do you play the king?

3.   **NORTH**
             ♠ Q J 10 6
    ♠ K 8 5 2

Declarer is in 4♡. Winning the opening lead, declarer leads a low spade. Dummy has entries. Who holds the ace? Do you play low or play the king?

4.   **NORTH**
             Q 10 5
       J 2

In desperation you lead the jack against a suit contract : low from dummy, low from partner and ace from declarer. Who holds the king?

5.   **NORTH**
             7 5
   J 8 6 4 2

Against no-trumps, you lead the 4, 10 from East and South wins the ace. What is South's holding in this suit? What do you play when you regain the lead?

6.   **NORTH**
             10 4 3
   K Q 8 5

Against a suit contract, you lead the king, partner plays the 2 and declarer the 6. Does declarer hold A-J?

7.   **NORTH**
             ♠ 4 2
    ♠ Q 10 7

With hearts trumps, declarer wins your minor suit lead in dummy and plays the ♠2, low from East and the 8 from declarer taken by your 10. Who has the king of spades? Who has the ace? What is declarer planning?

8.   **NORTH**
             ♠ A 10 4
    ♠ K 7 5 2

South opened the bidding and ended in 4♡. Your minor suit lead is won in dummy and the ♠4 is led : low from East, queen from declarer and won by your king. Who has the jack? Who has the 9?

9. In 3NT, your club holding is 7-6-2 and dummy has K-Q-J-10-4. Dummy has entries but declarer does not touch clubs. Who holds the ace of clubs?

PLAY HANDS ON CARD READING & INFERENCES IN DEFENSE

Hand 105 : Dealer North : E-W vulnerable

NORTH
- ♠ J 4
- ♡ A J 10 7 4
- ◊ A K J 9 2
- ♣ 5

WEST
- ♠ A Q 5
- ♡ Q 3
- ◊ 6 5 3
- ♣ Q J 9 4 3

EAST
- ♠ 10 8 6 3 2
- ♡ K 9 2
- ◊ 7 4
- ♣ 8 6 2

SOUTH
- ♠ K 9 7
- ♡ 8 6 5
- ◊ Q 10 8
- ♣ A K 10 7

WEST	NORTH	EAST	SOUTH
	1♡	Pass	2♣
Pass	2◊	Pass	2NT
Pass	3◊	Pass	4♡
Pass	Pass	Pass	

Lead : ♠3. With nothing obviously superior, the unbid suit is the normal start.

Play: Declarer plays low in dummy and West wins with the queen. West continues with the ace of spades and a third spade, taken in dummy. Declarer leads a heart to the jack, losing to the king. East plays a fourth spade, ruffed by West with the queen of hearts. This uppercuts declarer's ace. The upshot is that East's 9 of hearts will become a winner, the fourth trick for the defense. One down.

Notes : (1) A 2NT reply by South would be reasonable. In fact, 3NT is a superior spot, despite the heart fit and the unbalanced nature of the North hand. Most partnerships would find it too difficult to avoid 4♡ (a good contract that will usually make but can be beaten here).

(2) Declarer should drop the ♠J under West's queen. If West takes this to be a singleton and switches, declarer can later discard a spade on the second round of clubs.

(3) After winning the ♠Q, West can work out that it is vital to cash the ♠A. Declarer's bidding has shown five hearts and five diamonds. That leaves only three black cards. If West does not cash the ♠A, the clubs will allow a spade discard. East's ♠3 shows at most a 5-card suit so that North is marked with at least two spades.

(4) After the ♠A, a club switch is futile and a diamond switch is unnecessary as declarer is known to have five diamonds. Any diamond loser cannot be discarded and a spade continuation will not help declarer.

Hand 106 : Dealer East : Both vulnerable

NORTH
- ♠ A 10 5
- ♡ 10 7 4
- ◊ 9 6 5 3 2
- ♣ 8 3

WEST
- ♠ 7 6 4
- ♡ 5 3
- ◊ A K 10
- ♣ Q 10 7 5 4

EAST
- ♠ Q 9 2
- ♡ A K J
- ◊ Q J 8
- ♣ K J 9 2

SOUTH
- ♠ K J 8 3
- ♡ Q 9 8 6 2
- ◊ 7 4
- ♣ A 6

WEST	NORTH	EAST	SOUTH
		1NT	Pass
3NT	Pass	Pass	Pass

Lead : ♡6. With no bidding to guide you, it is usually best to start with your 5-card suit if the 4-card suit does not have a sequence.

Play: North plays the 10 and East wins with the jack. The king of clubs is led and South takes the ace. South switches to the 3 of spades and North wins. North returns the 10 of spades (top from the remaining doubleton) and South collects three more spade tricks to defeat the contract by one trick.

Notes : (1) If South wins the ace of clubs and continues with a heart, declarer makes three hearts, three diamonds and four clubs. From the play at trick 1, South should realise that East is very strong in hearts and that a heart continuation is futile.

(2) If North returns a heart after taking the ace of spades, again declarer comes to ten tricks. The spade return is essential. North can tell that a spade continuation is necessary and not a return to hearts from the spade chosen by South. South led the *three* of spades. The low lead asks for a return of the suit led. If South held something like ♠ 9 8 3 2 ♡ A Q 8 6 2 ◊ 7 4 ♣ A 6, South would win ♣A and switch to the *nine* of spades. The high card switch denies interest in the suit led. Then North would return to hearts after winning the ace of spades. Note this use of lead-signals for middle game switches.

(3) East might improve the chances of success by winning the first heart with the ace rather than the jack. Now South may place North with the jack of hearts and continue hearts when in with the ♣ A. If so, East still makes the jack of hearts and comes to ten tricks (see Chapter 16 — Deceptive Strategy By Declarer).

Hand 107 : Dealer South : Nil vulnerable

        NORTH
        ♠ K 9 8 7 3
        ♡ 10 7 2
        ◇ 2
        ♣ 10 7 6 5

WEST   **EAST**
♠ J 6 4   ♠ Q 2
♡ A K 8 6 3   ♡ Q J 9
◇ Q J   ◇ K 10 9 7 5
♣ A J 9   ♣ K Q 3

        SOUTH
        ♠ A 10 5
        ♡ 5 4
        ◇ A 8 6 4 3
        ♣ 8 4 2

WEST	NORTH	EAST	SOUTH
			Pass
1♡	Pass	2◇	Pass
2NT	Pass	3♡	Pass
4♡	Pass	Pass	Pass

Lead : ◇ 2. Leading dummy's suit is not attractive but acceptable when you have a weak hand and worthless trumps.

Play : South wins the ace of diamonds and returns the *eight* of diamonds, a suit preference signal for spades (high card, high suit). After North ruffs the diamond return, North switches to spades. North, however, is careful to play the king of spades first followed by a spade to the ace. This gives the defense four tricks. South plays another diamond but declarer ruffs high, draws trumps and claims the rest.

Notes : (1) On a club lead or a trump lead, declarer would win and draw trumps, losing at most two spades and a diamond.
(2) On a spade lead, the defense can still prevail, perhaps even more easily than on a diamond lead. South wins the ace of spades and switches to ace and another diamond. West's 2NT marks North with 0 or 1 diamond. Even if South returns a spade, North switches to the ◇ 2. South takes the ace and gives North the diamond ruff.
(3) Declarer should drop the queen of diamonds at trick 1. If South believes this is a singleton and switches, declarer may make. Of course, North's ◇ 2 lead could not be from J-2 and South should not be fooled.
(4) On ruffing the diamond, North notes the *eight*, asking for the high suit back. This must mean South has the ♠ A. Why else ask for spades? Therefore, leading the king next is safe and saves partner from making a mistake. On a low spade back, South might win and play a third diamond. Declarer ruffs high, draws trumps and discards two spades on the diamonds. A low spade does indeed ask for a spade back, but cashing the king first pays heed to the first Law of Defense : 'If you give partner the chance to do the wrong thing, partner will grab that chance.'
(5) If North began with ♠ 10 8 7 3 2 and ♡ Q 7 2, North would return the 8 of spades after ruffing the diamond. South would take the ace and, as the 8 showed no interest in spades, South would play another diamond, promoting North's ♡ Q.

Hand 108 : Dealer West : N-S vulnerable

        NORTH
        ♠ 8 7 3
        ♡ Q 5
        ◇ 8 4
        ♣ A Q 8 7 4 2

WEST   **EAST**
♠ A Q 5 2   ♠ K 9 4
♡ J 10 9 3 2   ♡ 8 7 6 4
◇ A 10   ◇ 9 7 3 2
♣ 6 3   ♣ 10 9

        SOUTH
        ♠ J 10 6
        ♡ A K
        ◇ K Q J 6 5
        ♣ K J 5

WEST	NORTH	EAST	SOUTH
Pass	Pass	Pass	1◇
Double	2♣	Pass	3NT
Pass	Pass	Pass	

Lead : ♡ J. It is hard to do better in no-trumps than a long suit headed by a sequence.

Play : Declarer plays low from dummy, East plays the 4 and South wins with the king (a good deceptive move here). Declarer's best shot is to lead the queen or jack of diamonds. If this holds the trick, declarer can then cash the clubs and the ♡ A for nine tricks. West should take the jack of diamonds with the ace and switch to the 2 of spades. East wins the king and returns the 9 of spades. West cashes the spades for one down.

Notes : (1) Declarer should try to steal the diamond trick before running the clubs. If the clubs are run first, it is easy for the defense to know which suit to attack and to signal strong and weak suits.
(2) At trick 1, West should realise that South has the ♡ A. East would have played a more encouraging signal than the 4 if holding the ace of hearts. Therefore, South will have the ace of hearts. Declarer's diamond at trick 2 rather than a club marks declarer with the king of clubs. Otherwise, declarer would be setting up the clubs. With six clubs and two hearts for declarer, West cannot afford to duck the diamond. The only chance is in spades and West switches to the the 2, the low spade, to ask for a spade back.

REVISION TEST ON PART 3

The material in Chapters 17-24 will help you answer these questions. If you experience diffuculty in producing the correct answers, it will pay you to read these chapters again.

1.

NORTH
♠ J 9 3
♡ 10 9 6 5
◇ A 7 5
♣ Q 8 6

EAST
♠ Q 6 5
♡ K Q 8 4 3
◇ 6
♣ J 9 7 4

Dealer South : Nil vulnerable

WEST	NORTH	EAST	SOUTH
			1♠
Pass	1NT	Pass	2♣
2◇	2♠	All pass	

West leads the 2 of hearts.

(a) What heart holding can West have consistent with the lead of the 2 of hearts?
(b) Who has the ace of hearts?
(c) What is South's length in each black suit?
(d) What is the heart position?
(e) What are the precise shapes for South and West?

2.

NORTH
♠ Q J 8 6 4
♡ K 3
◇ 9 8 7
♣ A 6 3

EAST
♠ K 9 2
♡ 8 6
◇ J 6 4 3 2
♣ Q 9 2

Dealer North : Both vulnerable

WEST	NORTH	EAST	SOUTH
	Pass	Pass	1NT
Pass	3♠	Pass	3NT
Pass	Pass	Pass	

South's 1NT is 15-17. West leads the 4 of clubs.

(a) How many clubs did West hold originally?
(b) How many clubs has South?
(c) How many hearts does West have?
(d) How many hearts does South have?
(e) What is South's spade length?
(f) What is South's exact pattern?

3.

NORTH
♠ K J 7 4
♡ 3 2
◇ 6 4
♣ A J 10 5 2

WEST
♠ - - -
♡ K Q 10 8 4
◇ A 8 3
♣ Q 9 8 7 3

Dealer East : Nil vulnerable

WEST	NORTH	EAST	SOUTH
		2♠	3♡
Double	Pass	Pass	Pass

East's 2♠ is a weak two which, according to your system, will not be a 6-5 pattern and will not have a void in first or second seat. West's double is for penalties.

(a) Thank heavens South bid! What would you have done if South had passed 2♠?
(b) You lead the 7 of clubs : 2 from dummy, 4 from East and South wins with the king. How many hearts will South have? And how many does East have?
(c) What is the club position?
(d) What is the spade position?
(e) What is the diamond layout?

4.

NORTH
♠ J 8 3
♡ A 9 3
◇ 8 3
♣ 10 9 8 7 3

EAST
♠ 9 6 5 2
♡ Q 10 8 4
◇ A 6
♣ A 5 2

Dealer East : East-West vulnerable

WEST	NORTH	EAST	SOUTH
		Pass	1NT
Pass	Pass	Pass	

South's 1NT is 16-18. West leads the 2 of diamonds.

(a) How many diamonds will West hold?
(b) How many diamonds do you place with South?
(c) How many spades will South have? Hearts?
(d) After winning ◇ A, will you return a diamond?
(e) If not, which card will you play at trick 2?

PART 4

IMPROVE YOUR

DECLARER PLAY

CHAPTER 25

SETTING UP A LONG SUIT (2)

One of the major problems in setting up a long suit is shortage of entries in the hand which contains the long suit. There are certain techniques which can improve your chances.

DUMMY	DUMMY
A 7 6 4 3	A 7 6 4 3 2
8 5	8 5

With such holdings, it is often best to duck the first round. This leaves the ace as an entry. Later you can lead a second round to the ace and ruff the third round. If you start by playing the ace and another round, you need an outside entry to dummy before you can ruff the third round of the suit. If dummy has plenty of entries, playing the ace on the first round may not hurt your chances. If entries are precious, ducking the first round may be necessary.

Similar considerations may indicate the best way to handle these suits :

DUMMY	DUMMY
A K 6 4 3	A K 6 4 3 2
8 5	8 5

If you need two extra tricks from the first combination or three extra tricks from the second, the normal play is to cash the ace and king and ruff the third round. If the break is friendly, you will succeed. If you are after the maximum number of tricks possible and dummy has two or more entries, again it is best to cash the ace and king, ruff a third round, return to dummy to ruff a fourth round if necessary and return to dummy to cash your winners.

However, if dummy is short of entries *and* you need only one extra trick from the first combination or two from the second *and* you can afford to give up the lead, a sound move is to duck one round. This caters for one opponent holding four cards in the suit. When you regain the lead, you then cash the ace and king and ruff the fourth round. Use dummy's only outside entry to reach the established winners.

When you can afford to give up a trick, it can often be worthwhile to concede a trick to the opponents in order to set up the rest of the suit as winners. This is attractive when the long suit has good pips provided you can afford to lose the lead.

A J 10 6 2	Play the king and ace. If all have
K 4	followed, lead the jack. If East plays the queen, ruff, but if East follows low

or shows out, you can discard a loser. This will set up two tricks in dummy no matter where the queen lies.

A J 9 6 2	You play the king and ace. If the 10
K 4	has fallen, the position is the same as above. Lead the jack. If East plays the

queen, ruff, but if East follows low or shows out, you can discard a loser on a loser. West may win with the queen, but dummy's 9-6 are then good for two tricks.

A 10 9 6 2	Play the king and ace. If either the
K 4	queen or jack has dropped, you can lead the 10, ruffing if East plays the

other honor, or discarding if East follows low or shows out. West may win the third round but dummy has two winners.

The above are variations of the ruffing finesse which is often used to set up a long suit. These cases have a common thread :

A Q J 10 6 2	A J 10 9 6 2	A J 10 9 6 2
4	Q	K

In each case, you can lead your singleton and take it with dummy's ace. Then lead dummy's top card. If East covers with the missing honor, ruff it. If East follows low, you discard. West may win but the rest of this suit in dummy is now high.

A K J 10 6 2	A K 10 9 6 2	A K 10 9 6 2
5	J	Q

In each case you can overtake your singleton and cash dummy's ace and king. Then lead dummy's top honor. If East covers with the missing honor, ruff it and dummy's remaining cards are high. If East plays low on the third round, discard. Dummy's remaining cards will be winners if West takes this trick. When you need to cash two rounds before taking the ruffing finesse, it is usually best to have drawn all the opposition trumps. Where your singleton was the queen and dummy has plenty of entries, you could play the queen, cross to dummy in another suit and then cash the ace and king. You will know what is going on in the suit by then. To overtake the queen and use the ruffing finesse may be vital if dummy has only one outside entry.

When you are setting up a long suit in dummy and the only entries are in the trump suit, you may have to delay drawing trumps until the suit has been set up. If dummy has entries in the trump suit and in outside suits, use the trump entries first when setting up the long suit. This enables you to start drawing trumps. Trumps need to be drawn before you cash the established winners later. If an opponent holds more trumps than dummy, the entries in dummy in the trump suit will not be suitable to cash your winners later as there will still be one or more trumps at large.

PLAY HANDS ON SETTING UP A LONG SUIT (2)

Hand 109 : Dealer North : Both vulnerable

NORTH
- ♠ K 3 2
- ♡ 10 4
- ◇ 7 4
- ♣ K 9 7 6 4 2

WEST
- ♠ 10
- ♡ A Q J 9 3
- ◇ A Q 10 5
- ♣ J 8 5

EAST
- ♠ 7 6 4
- ♡ 8 7 6
- ◇ J 9 8 6 2
- ♣ Q 10

SOUTH
- ♠ A Q J 9 8 5
- ♡ K 5 2
- ◇ K 3
- ♣ A 3

WEST	NORTH	EAST	SOUTH
	Pass	Pass	1♠
2♡	2♠	Pass	4♠
Pass	Pass	Pass	

Lead: ♣5. West has no attractive lead. The club lead is the least of evils. Leading from an A-Q suit is the worst and a singleton trump is also riskier than the club. As the cards lie, a red suit lead costs a trick but either black suit lead is cost free.

Play : Declarer should win the club in hand and cash the the A-Q of spades. Next comes a club to the king and a third club, ruffed. Dummy's clubs are now high. A trump to the king draws the last trump and the clubs provide three discards. 11 tricks.

Notes : (1) South, with only five losers, is worth a shot at game. A raise to the 2-level, usually two tricks, reduces the losers to three. (2) In view of West's bid, it is likely that both red finesses will lose. Setting up the clubs is the best line even with no enemy bidding.

(3) Declarer cannot afford to draw all the trumps before starting the clubs. The king of spades is needed as an entry to the clubs and is the only entry to dummy outside clubs. Likewise, the king of spades must not be played on the first or second round of trumps, else there is no later entry to the clubs.

Hand 110 : Dealer East : Nil vulnerable

NORTH
- ♠ 10 5
- ♡ 9 8 6
- ◇ 10 9 5
- ♣ K Q 10 4 3

WEST
- ♠ A 7 6 4 3
- ♡ A K 5
- ◇ 7 6 4
- ♣ J 6

EAST
- ♠ J 2
- ♡ Q J 10 4 3 2
- ◇ A 8 3
- ♣ A 7

SOUTH
- ♠ K Q 9 8
- ♡ 7
- ◇ K Q J 2
- ♣ 9 8 5 2

WEST	NORTH	EAST	SOUTH
		1♡	Pass
1♠	Pass	2♡	Pass
4♡	Pass	Pass	Pass

Lead : ◇ K. Nothing else is as attractive.

Play : Declarer wins and leads a spade at trick 2, playing low in dummy. The defense can cash two diamonds and should then switch to a club or a trump. Declarer wins in hand and continues with a spade to the ace and a spade, ruffing. A heart to the king allows another spade ruff. Dummy's fifth spade is now a winner. Declarer cashes the queen of hearts and leads a heart to dummy. The club loser is discarded on the established spade. 10 tricks via 2 spades, 6 hearts and the minor suit aces.

Notes : (1) With nine top winners 3NT would be easy. With the same nine winners, 4♡ requires an extra trick. The extra trick can come only by setting up an extra spade.

(2) Declarer cannot afford to draw trumps first. Dummy's trumps are the only entries to dummy to ruff the spades and reach the established spade winner. Even one round of trumps could be fatal for declarer.
(3) If South leads a trump, declarer should win in hand and lead the jack of spades, ducking when South plays the queen. As South is out of hearts, South cannot remove one of dummy's trump entries.
(4) It would be an error to play a spade to the ace at trick 2 and lose the second round of spades. If trumps are 3-1, dummy no longer has enough entries to ruff spades twice and return to reach the spade winner. Ace and another spade would see declarer home if spades were 3-3 or hearts 2-2. Ducking the first spade to keep the ♠ A as an extra entry caters also for spades 4-2 and trumps 3-1 (both are the most likely divisions).

Hand 111 : Dealer South : N-S vulnerable

NORTH
♠ A K J 9 4
♡ 9 5
♢ 7 4 3
♣ A K Q

WEST
♠ 8 5
♡ A Q 7 6 4
♢ 10 9 8 5
♣ 6 3

EAST
♠ 7 6 3
♡ K 10 8 3
♢ K Q J
♣ 8 7 4

SOUTH
♠ Q 10 2
♡ J 2
♢ A 6 2
♣ J 10 9 5 2

WEST	NORTH	EAST	SOUTH
			Pass
Pass	1♠	Pass	2♠
Pass	3♢	Pass	4♠
Pass	Pass	Pass	

Lead : ♢ K. Cannot go past top of sequence.

Play : Declarer wins the ace of diamonds, cashes the ace and king of spades and does not draw the missing trump. Next, declarer plays off the ace, king and queen of clubs. Having survived thus far, declarer leads a spade to dummy, drawing the last trump in the process, and cashes two club winners, discarding two red losers.

Notes : (1) 3♢ is a trial bid, inviting game and seeking help in diamonds. It is suitable where the trial suit has two or three losers.
(2) Declarer cannot afford to draw three rounds of trumps, else there is no entry to the clubs. Cashing the ♣ A-K-Q while a trump is out is risky, but any other line has zero chance of success.

Hand 112 : Dealer West : E-W vulnerable

NORTH
♠ 8 7
♡ A J 5
♢ Q J 10 2
♣ Q 8 7 3

WEST
♠ A Q J 4 3 2
♡ K 9 8
♢ 8 4
♣ A K

EAST
♠ K 10 6
♡ 4 3 2
♢ A 6
♣ J 10 9 5 2

SOUTH
♠ 9 5
♡ Q 10 7 6
♢ K 9 7 5 3
♣ 6 4

WEST	NORTH	EAST	SOUTH
1♠	Pass	2♠	Pass
4♠	Pass	Pass	Pass

Lead : ♢ Q. Easy choice.

Play : Declarer wins ♢ A, cashes the A-K of clubs, leads a spade to dummy's 10 and plays the jack of clubs. If South discards, West discards the diamond loser. Later declarer can cash the ♠ A, lead a trump to dummy and cash the remaining club winner(s). If South ruffs the club, West overruffs, leads a trump to the king (drawing the last trump) and ruffs a club high. A low trump overtaken by dummy's 6 provides access to the club winner for a heart discard.

Notes : (1) West must not duck the diamond lead. South could overtake with the king and switch to hearts. Curtains.
(2) After ♢ A, ♣ A-K, it is not safe to cash ♠ A and lead a spade to the 10 before leading ♣ J. If trumps were 3-1, the last trump might ruff this club and the clubs could not be set up and cashed.

Hand 113 : Dealer North : Nil vulnerable

NORTH
♠ 7
♡ A K 10 9 6 4
♢ K Q J
♣ K 6 2

WEST
♠ A K 10 9
♡ 7 5 3
♢ 8 7 5
♣ 9 7 5

EAST
♠ 8 6 5
♡ 8 2
♢ 10 9 6 2
♣ Q J 10 4

SOUTH
♠ Q J 4 3 2
♡ Q J
♢ A 4 3
♣ A 8 3

WEST	NORTH	EAST	SOUTH
	1♡	Pass	1♠
Pass	3♡	Pass	4NT
Pass	5♢	Pass	6♡
Pass	Pass	Pass	

Lead : ♣ Q. Sequence leads occur frequently in textbooks.

Play : Win with the ♣ K and lead a spade. East plays the 5 (lowest from an odd number to give count), jack, king. West returns a club. (If West tries to cash the ♠ A, North's task is simplified.) Win ♣ A, ruff a spade, heart to the jack, ruff a spade, heart to the queen, ruff a spade. Draw the last trump. Cross to ♢ A and cash the spade.

Notes : (1) If Roman Key Card Blackwood is used, North bids 5♡ to show two key cards (♡ A and ♡ K).
(2) Win ♣ K at trick 1 and keep the ♣ A as an entry to dummy.
(3) Use dummy's trumps as entries before using the ♢ A as an entry.
(4) A trump lead would have defeated 6♡.

Hand 114 : Dealer East : N-S vulnerable

NORTH
♠ J 10 7 5
♡ 7 5
◇ J 10 9 7
♣ J 9 5

WEST
♠ 9 2
♡ A K Q 8 6 4 3
◇ A 5 4
♣ 7

EAST
♠ A K 4
♡ - - -
◇ Q 6 3
♣ A K 8 6 4 3 2

SOUTH
♠ Q 8 6 3
♡ J 10 9 2
◇ K 8 2
♣ Q 10

WEST	NORTH	EAST	SOUTH
		1♣	Pass
1♡	Pass	3♣	Pass
4NT	Pass	5♡	Pass
6♡	Pass	Pass	Pass

Lead : ◇ J. Speaks for itself.

Play : Try dummy's queen: South covers with the king and West wins the ace. Cash ♡ A-K-Q. Leave South with the top trump and continue with a club to the ace and the ♣ K, discarding a diamond. Play a third club: if South ruffs, discard your other diamond loser; if South discards, ruff the club, play a spade to the ace and lead club winners. South can ruff but your last diamond loser is discarded.

Notes: (1) Do not start clubs before trumps. Hearts could be 3-3.
(2) After ◇ A, ♡ A-K-Q and a club to the ace (correct), do not ruff a low club. Cash ♣ K first. Otherwise when you cross to dummy and lead ♣ K later, South ruffs before both diamonds are discarded.

Hand 115 : Dealer South : E-W vulnerable

NORTH
♠ 3 2
♡ 6 5 4
◇ K J 3
♣ A 10 9 3 2

WEST
♠ 8 5 4
♡ K J 3
◇ 10 9 8
♣ J 8 7 5

EAST
♠ 9 7
♡ 10 9 8 7
◇ Q 7 6 5 4
♣ Q 6

SOUTH
♠ A K Q J 10 6
♡ A Q 2
◇ A 2
♣ K 4

WEST	NORTH	EAST	SOUTH
			2♣
Pass	3♣	Pass	3♠
Pass	3NT	Pass	4NT
Pass	5◇	Pass	5NT
Pass	6◇	Pass	6♠
Pass	Pass	Pass	

Lead : ◇ 10. A poor sequence is better than no sequence at all.

Play : Try the ◇ J, a free finesse, and capture the queen with the ace. Draw trumps in three rounds, discarding a heart from dummy. Then ♣ K, a club to the ace and when the queen drops, lead ♣ 10 and discard a heart (loser on loser) when East shows out. The ♣ 9 is now high for another heart discard and the ◇ K is the entry.

Notes: (1) With a self-sufficient suit, insist on your suit as trumps.
(2) Trumps must be drawn before starting on the clubs.
(3) Resort to the heart finesse only if all else fails.

Hand 116 : Dealer West : Both vulnerable

NORTH
♠ 7 2
♡ K Q 10 5
◇ 7 5
♣ 10 9 8 5 2

WEST
♠ A 9
♡ A J 9 4 3 2
◇ A 10 2
♣ 6 4

EAST
♠ K Q J 10 8 3
♡ 6
◇ K Q J 3
♣ A Q

SOUTH
♠ 6 5 4
♡ 8 7
◇ 9 8 6 4
♣ K J 7 3

WEST	NORTH	EAST	SOUTH
1♡	Pass	2♠	Pass
3♡	Pass	4NT	Pass
5♠	Pass	5NT	Pass
6♣	Pass	7♠	All pass

Lead : ♠ 5. Against a grand slam, choose a safe lead. With no sequence (surprise!), a trump lead from three or four rags is usually safest against a grand slam.

Play : Win the ♠ 9, cash the ♡ A, ruff a heart, spade to the ace, ruff a heart, draw the last trump (discarding a club), diamond to the 10, ruff a heart. Dummy's two remaining hearts are now high. Cross to the ◇ A and discard ♣ Q on a heart winner.

Notes: (1) If West shows 3 aces and a king, East would bid 7NT.
(2) Knowing West has long hearts makes the grand slam a good bet.
(3) Do not draw trumps first. Dummy's trumps are vital entries.
(4) Do not resort to the club finesse unless all else fails.

CHAPTER 26

CARD COMBINATIONS FOR DECLARER (2)

1. Precautionary plays — Guarding against a bad break

These are plays which do not cost you a trick but improve your chances of avoiding a loser or reducing the number of losers you might have.

K 10 6 5

J 8 7 4   **- - -**

A Q 9 3 2

You risk losing a trick only if the suit breaks 4-0. When missing only J-x-x-x and holding the 10 and 9 as well as the A, K and Q, retain a top honor in each hand. In other words, cash an honor from the suit which contains two honors. In the above case, play the ace or queen first. If both follow, no problem. If either opponent shows out, you can finesse and capture the jack held by the other opponent. If you play the king first, you lose a trick when West holds J-x-x-x.

K Q 7 3 2

A 10 9 5

Play the king or queen first. If East shows out, lead low to the ace and then lead the 10, finessing if West plays low. If West is the one to show out, you can lead low and finesse against East's remaining J-x-x. If you play the ace first, you lose a trick if East began with J-x-x-x.

A Q 9 2

J 10 8 7   **- - -**

K 6 5 4 3

When holding the A, K, Q and the 9, too (i.e. missing J-10-x-x, *the 10 as well as the jack*), you need to keep two honors in the same hand to capture the two missing honors if you do run into a 4-0 break. In the example above, play the king first, retaining the A-Q-9. When the bad break is revealed, lead low towards dummy. West will play an honor (else you finesse the 9). You capture this, come back to your hand via some other suit and again lead low towards dummy, finessing the 9 if West follows low.

This is your only chance to cope with a 4-0 split. If East began with J-10-8-7, you cannot capture both honors, no matter how you play. Note that you lose a trick to either 4-0 split if you play ace or queen first. West is bound to win a trick with the remaining J-10-8.

The above principles apply also when you hold the K, Q and J and need to drive out the ace. If you are missing A-10-x-x (you hold the 9 and 8), keep one honor card in each hand.

K J 8 3 2

- - -   **A 10 7 6**

Q 9 5 4

Play the king or the jack on the first round. If you strike a 4-0 split, you can finesse against the 10 in either opponent's hand. If you play the queen first, you lose a trick when East has the four missing cards.

However, if you are missing A-10-**9**-x, play the honor first that is on its own and retain the other two honors to capture the 10 and 9 later.

K Q 8 4

A 10 9 6   **- - -**

J 7 5 3 2

Play the jack first. If West ducks, no problem : lead low twice towards the K-Q-8 later. If West takes the ace, you see the position when East shows out. You lead from your hand twice later, capturing West's card each time as cheaply as possible.

If you lead low, West should play the 6 and if you play the king or queen, West's remaining A-10-9 will score two tricks. Note that you can do nothing if East began with A-10-9-6. Lady Luck has saddled you with two losers.

The above principles take precedence over the high-card-from-shortage rule (see page 60).

K 2	K 5 2	K 7 4 3
A 10 9 6 5 3	A 10 7 4 3	A 10 5 2

In each of the above cases, play the king from dummy first. When you next lead low towards your hand, play the 10 if East plays low. This saves a trick if East started with Q-J-x-x. If you play the king and ace (or ace and king) you lose two tricks whenever East started with Q-J-x-x.

A 9 5 2   To guard against two losers, you can cash the ace first and then lead low to **K 10 4 3**   the 10 (in case East began with Q-J-x-x) or cash the king first and then lead low to the 9 (if West has the 4-card holding). You need to judge (or guess) which opponent is more likely to hold the singleton.

2. Sacrifice plays

These are also included in the category known as 'safety plays' or 'sure trick plays'. They sacrifice a possible overtrick but guarantee a specific number of tricks against any bad break. Because they reduce the number of tricks possible, sacrifice plays are not attractive at duplicate pairs (except in a doubled contract). They are useful at rubber bridge or at teams play to guarantee your contract.

7 6 5

A K 9 8 4 2

If you need six tricks, cash the ace and king and pray for a 2-2 break. If you need only five tricks, cross to dummy and lead the 5 : if East follows with the 3, play low from hand. This guards against East holding Q-J-10-3 (if you cash the ace or king first, East would score two tricks).

If West wins the trick, the two remaining cards in the suit can be captured by your ace and king later. You have lost an overtrick when the suit breaks 2-2 (40% of the time) but guaranteed five tricks when East started with Q-J-10-3 (5% of the time).

Q 6 4 3

A 10 8 7 5 2

If you need six tricks, the best chance is to play the ace and hope the king is singleton. You do the same if your aim is to win the maximum number of tricks. However, playing the ace costs two tricks if East began with K-J-9. If you need only five tricks, leading low towards the queen will cost one trick for sure but you guarantee not to lose two tricks. If the suit divides 2-1, the ace captures the remaining card on the next round. If West follows low, play the queen from dummy. You have only one loser if West began with K-J-9. If West shows out, play the queen. East wins but you later can cross to dummy and finesse against East's remaining J-9.

K 9 5 2

A J 4 3

To make all four tricks, the best play is lead low from dummy (North) and take a first round finesse of the jack if East follows low. You succeed if East started with Q-singleton, Q-x or Q-x-x. If you need only three tricks, play the ace first and then lead low towards dummy's K-9-x. If West follows low, play the 9 from dummy. This is certain to yield three winners. If the suit breaks 3-2, the king will capture the remaining card, if the 9 loses to the 10 or queen. If West began with

Q-10-x-x, dummy's 9 will win on the second round (it does not help West to insert the 10 on the second round).

If West shows out on the second round, take the king and lead towards your J-x. East who began with Q-10-x-x makes only one trick. The sacrifice play is less likely to score four tricks (you do make four tricks if West began with Q-x or East with Q-singleton), but low to the jack will lose two tricks if West started with Q-singleton. Playing the king first loses two tricks if West began with Q-10-x-x or Q-10-x-x-x.

NOTE : Precautionary plays and sacrifice plays which involve losing an early trick in the trump suit should be avoided if there is a danger of a ruff.

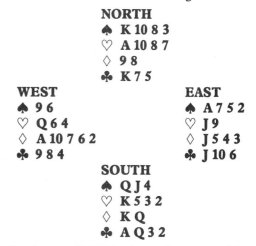

```
              NORTH
              ♠ K 10 8 3
              ♡ A 10 8 7
              ◇ 9 8
              ♣ K 7 5
WEST                        EAST
♠ 9 6                       ♠ A 7 5 2
♡ Q 6 4                     ♡ J 9
◇ A 10 7 6 2                ◇ J 5 4 3
♣ 9 8 4                     ♣ J 10 6
              SOUTH
              ♠ Q J 4
              ♡ K 5 3 2
              ◇ K Q
              ♣ A Q 3 2
```

South opens 1 NT, North uses Stayman and South ends in 4♡. If West leads ace and another diamond, South should guard against a 4-1 trump break by playing ♡ K followed by a heart to the 10. This loses to the jack, but the ace later captures West's queen.

However, if West leads the ♠9, East wins and returns a spade. As West's play clearly indicates a doubleton, declarer should play ♡ K and a heart to the ace. Declarer cannot afford the luxury of guarding against the 4-1 break. If South cashes ♡ K and leads a heart to the 10, East wins the jack and plays a third spade, ruffed by West. The defense scores two trump tricks and defeats the game. Beware of losing a trick to guard against a bad break when a ruff is threatened.

3. Taking the best chance

Partners being what they are, you will often find less than ideal support after you have pre-empted. There is a technique in scoring the most tricks possible when partner puts down the usual void.

How do you manage each of these combinations?

- - -   - - -   - - -

A J 10 6 5 4 3   A Q 10 9 5 4 2   K Q 10 9 4 3 2

A J 10 6 5 4 3
- - -

The best chance to lose only two tricks is to lead the ace followed by a low card, not the jack or 10. This succeeds whenever the suit is 3-3 or when an opponent holds Q-doubleton or K-doubleton. To play ace followed by an honor will lose three tricks if either opponent has Q-x or K-x.

A Q 10 9 5 4 2
- - -

To lose just one trick, cash the ace and continue with the queen. If either opponent has J-x, you succeed. If the suit is 3-3, you always have two losers. To play ace followed by a low card loses two tricks if either opponent has J-x or K-x. Even though you drop K-doubleton, the other opponent started with J-x-x-x and still has the guarded jack left.

K Q 10 9 4 3 2
- - -

Start with the king. If this is taken by the ace, continue with the queen next time. If the king is allowed to hold, continue with the queen anyway. You lose just one trick when an opponent has J-x. To play the king (allowed to win) and a low card next will lose two tricks when an opponent has J-x or A-x. It does not help to drop ace-doubleton since the other opponent began with J-x-x-x and still has the guarded jack.

4. Leading an honor card for a finesse when you do not hold touching honors

Although in many cases it is unsound to lead an honor for a finesse unless you hold touching honors in the same hand (see page 63), there are exceptions.

J 6 4 3
- - -   **K 10 8**
A Q 9 7 5 2

With ten cards missing the king, the best chance is to finesse. With A-Q-9 or A-J-9 in one hand, it is best to lead the honor opposite. In the above case, lead the jack. If East plays low, let the jack run. If the finesse works, you can repeat the finesse if East began with three trumps. If East covers the jack, capture the king. When West shows out, return to dummy via another suit and finesse against East's remaining 10-8. Note that if you lead low from dummy, East should play the 8 and you finesse the queen. The queen wins but East's K-10 is now bound to score a trick.

Q 10 9 8

A 6 4 2

You could lead the ace followed by low towards dummy. If West plays low, you have to guess whether to play the queen or finesse the 10. (The 10 is superior:

it gains when West started with K-J-x-x.) However, the better play, if you have enough entries, is to lead the queen from dummy, planning to finesse twice. If the queen is covered, capture the king and force out the jack. If East plays low, let the queen run. If it loses to the king, later cross to dummy and lead the 10, letting it run if East plays low. You hold the losers to one trick whenever East started with the king, the jack or the king and jack. You lose two tricks only when West began with king and jack.

A K 10 8

J 5 4 2

The best play to lose no trick is to finesse for the queen on the second round. Cash the ace first, in case the queen is singleton. If the queen does not drop, come to hand, intending to finesse for the queen next. The presence of the 8 in dummy means it is best to lead the jack on the second round. Without the 8, low to the 10 next would be fine.

A K 10 8
Q 9 6 3   7
J 5 4 2

You cash the ace, come to hand and lead the jack. If West plays low, the jack wins. If West covers, you capture the queen and the bad break is revealed. Return to hand and you can trap West's 9-6 by finessing dummy's 10-8. Had you led low to the 10 on the second round of the suit (instead of leading the jack), West would still have the Q-9 and dummy the K-8. West would be bound to win a trick.

5. When only one finesse is available

A Q 10 9 5 3
(A) K 7 4 2   (A) J 8
(B) J 7 4 2   (B) K 8
6

Although it is often best to finesse the 10 first when tackling an A-Q-10 combination (see pages 68-69), it is superior to finesse the queen if you can finesse only once. In the above case, if the missing cards split 3-3, it is a 50-50 guess whether to finesse the 10 or the queen. Finessing the queen may gain when the suit breaks 4-2. In (A) or (B) above, finessing the 10 loses two tricks. However, if you finesse the queen, you lose only one trick in (A). When you continue with the ace and the jack drops, you lose just one trick to the king.

K Q 10 7 4 3

6

Should you lead low to the king first or low to the 10 first? For five tricks, you should finesse the 10 on the first round of the suit.

```
            K Q 10 7 4 3
A 8 2                       J 9 5
            6
```

With this layout, you lose two tricks whatever you do. Finesse the 10 and you lose to the jack. Playing low to the king wins this trick, but you lose to the ace and the jack later anyway.

```
            K Q 10 7 4 3
J 9 5                       A 8 2
            6
```

If you lead low to the king, East can win this and you lose a trick to the jack later on. However, if you lead low to the 10, you lose just one trick. If East takes the ace, the king and queen eliminate the missing cards later. If East ducks, continue with the king and again you lose only to the ace.

6. Two-way finesses for the queen

```
            A 10 5 3

            K J 4 2
```

With no clue as to the location of the queen, you can cash the king and finesse the 10 next or cash the ace and finesse the jack next. Often there will be some clue as to the likely location of the queen. Play the opponent with greater strength to have the queen. Play the opponent with greater length in this suit to hold the queen. If left-hand opponent made a takeout double of this suit, play the other hand to hold the length in this suit. If left-hand opponent made a takeout double of some other suit, play the doubler to hold length in this suit.

```
            A J 10 2

            K 5 4 3
```

If you have a strong indication where the queen is, finesse accordingly. With no clue as to the queen's whereabouts, the better play is to cash the king and lead low to dummy's jack. Because the jack and 10 are in the one hand, this play captures the queen with West even if West started with Q-x-x-x. Playing the ace and then leading the jack works if East has Q-x or Q-x-x but a trick is lost if East has Q-x-x-x. Playing West for the queen is superior since it works when West has Q-x, Q-x-x, Q-x-x-x and even Q-x-x-x-x.

```
            A 10 8 2

            K J 4 3
```

The presence of the 8 can affect your approach. With tenaces in both hands plus the 8, cash the honor opposite the 8 first unless you are confident where the queen lies. Here, cash the king first, then *lead the jack*. This wins not only when West has Q-x or Q-x-x but also when West started with Q-9-x-x.

```
            A 10 8 2
Q 9 7 6                      5
            K J 4 3
```

If you cash the king and then lead low to the 10, West will later score a trick with the Q-9 poised over the jack. When you cash the king and then lead the jack, West makes no trick. If West plays low, the jack wins and you continue by finessing the 10. If West covers the jack, you capture the queen. When East shows out, you return to hand via another suit and continue by finessing against West's 9-7.

7. First round finesses for the queen

When the best chance to avoid losing a trick is to finesse against the queen, it is usually best to take this finesse on the second round of the suit. Cashing the ace or king first can save a trick when the queen is singleton (see page 65). However, there are certain combinations where it is superior to finesse for the queen on the first round of the suit.

```
            A K J 8 7 4 3

            2
```

To gives yourself the best chance for most tricks, you should finesse for the queen. As you have only one card in this suit you must finesse for the queen on the first round of the suit. Cashing the A-K gains when East has Q-singleton or Q-x. Finessing gains when West has Q-x-x or Q-x-x-x or longer. These holdings with West are more frequent than Q-x or the singleton Q with East.

```
            A K J 10 5 3
Q 9 8 7                      4
Q 9 8 4                      7
Q 9 7 4                      8
Q 8 7 4                      9
9 8 7 4                      Q
            6 2
```

You should finesse on the first round of the suit when your suit is divided 6-2 and the 6-card suit is headed by A-K-J-10. Finessing on the first round gains in the first four cases above since you can repeat the finesse later. Cashing the king first gains in only one case when East has the singleton Q. It loses in the other four positions since you have only one finesse left later.

```
            A K J 7 5 3

            6 2
```

This time you should cash the ace first and finesse the jack on the second round. As the suit is headed by A-K-J without the 10, two finesses are not available.

A K J 10 3

6 5 2

This time you do have the jack and the 10, but you should again cash the ace first and finesse on the second round. As you have *three* cards in hand you can afford to cash the ace first to cater for the possibility of the singleton queen. You still have two finesses available and can pick up Q-x-x-x with West.

A J 10

K 5 4 3 2

With A-J-10 opposite K-x-x-x or K-x-x-x-x, you should lead low to the jack on the first round. This gains when West has Q-x, Q-x-x and Q-x-x-x. If the finesse works, you can repeat the finesse. Playing the ace first and then leading the jack for a finesse gains when East has Q-singleton, Q-x or Q-x-x. Again, Q-x-x-x is four times more frequent than the singleton-Q. (With A-J-10 opposite K-x-x, you can finesse either way but cash the ace or king first.)

A J

K 6 5 3 2

Lead low to the jack. This saves a trick when West has Q-x or Q-x-x. Cashing the ace first saves a trick only when East has Q-singleton.

A J

K 10 5 3 2

Holding the 10 does not change the best chance. Again, lead low to the jack on the first round of the suit. You lose no trick if West started with Q-x or Q-x-x. Playing the ace first and leading the jack for a finesse loses no trick only when East has Q-x-x and saves a trick if East has Q-singleton (much less frequent than Q-x with West).

A J 4

K 9 5 3 2

The best chance to make all five tricks is to lead low from hand and finesse the jack on the first round. You lose no trick if West started with Q-x, Q-x-x or Q-singleton. If the queen appears, the ace wins and when you cash the jack, you can next finesse the 9 if West has shown out. Cashing the king first will lose no trick if West has Q-x or Q-x-x. It saves a trick if East has the singleton-Q but in this case you will lose a trick ultimately as West began with 10-x-x-x. In addition, cashing the king first costs you a trick when West has the singleton-Q. You can no longer pick up East's 10-x-x-x.

8. Restricted choice

The theory of restricted choice may be useful when you are faced with the choice of finessing or playing for the drop on the second or third round of a suit. The theory states that if an opponent follows with an honor card when you cash a winner, it is more likely that this honor is a singleton than from two touching honors doubleton.

Firstly, an obvious example :

Q 10 4 2

A 7 6 5 3

You cash the ace and East drops the king. Obviously you will continue by finessing the 10. There is no doubt that East began with K-singleton. With K-J doubleton, East would not have played the king. East's choice was restricted in either case.

K 10 4 2

A 7 6 5 3

When you cash the ace, East drops the queen (or the jack). Here the honor could be singleton or from Q-J-doubleton. The theory of restricted choice indicates that the singleton holding is the more likely. With Q-J, East might have played either honor. With a singleton, the choice was restricted. The restricted choice is the better chance. Thus, in this case, even though it is usual to play for the 2-2 break with 9 trumps, your plan changes if an honor appears on the first round. Take a second round finesse if available. In the above case, you finesse the 10 on the second round.

Q 9 4 2

A 6 5 3

The best chance to lose only one trick with this layout is to cash the ace and then lead low to the queen. You survive if West began K-x or K-x-x (or if East has K-singleton, you can pick up J-10-x-x with West by leading twice towards the Q-9-x tenace).

However, suppose when you cash the ace East drops the jack (or the 10). This could be from K-J (or K-10) or from J-10 or the honor could be singleton. With K-J or J-singleton, East's choice was restricted. With J-10, East could play either honor. Play for the restricted choice holding. Therefore, on the next round you should lead low to the 9, not low to the queen. You gain a trick when East began with K-J (or K-10) or when East's honor is singleton. You drop a trick when East has J-10-doubleton, the less frequent possibility.

PLAY HANDS ON CARD COMBINATIONS FOR DECLARER (2)

Hand 117 : Dealer North : N-S vulnerable

	WEST	**NORTH**	**EAST**	**SOUTH**
		1◇	Pass	1♡
	Pass	1NT	Pass	4♡
	Pass	Pass	Pass	

```
              NORTH
              ♠ A Q 6
              ♡ 6 2
              ◇ K Q J 8 4
              ♣ J 8 3
WEST                        EAST
♠ 10 7 5 3 2                ♠ 9 4
♡ 7                         ♡ Q 9 8 4
◇ A 9 5 2                   ◇ 10 6
♣ K Q 7                     ♣ A 10 9 5 4
              SOUTH
              ♠ K J 8
              ♡ A K J 10 5 3
              ◇ 7 3
              ♣ 6 2
```

Lead : ♣K. Top from K-Q-x appeals more than 10-x-x-x-x.

Play : East signals with the 10 of clubs and West continues with the ♣Q. East follows with the ♣4. The third club is ruffed. Declarer should cross to dummy with a spade to the queen, lead a low heart to the jack, finessing against the queen on the first round. When this wins, another spade to dummy is followed by another heart finesse which wins. Trumps are drawn and declarer concedes just the ◇ A. 10 tricks.

Notes : (1) Opposite a 1NT rebid, South has a comfortable 4♡ rebid. Even if North rebid 2◇, South should rebid 4♡. A 6-card suit with four honors is strong enough to bid to game-level without support opposite. Likewise, a 7-card suit with three honors.

(2) When signalling partner to continue, play the highest card you can afford. East therefore signals with the 10 of clubs : if you can afford the 9, you can afford the 10. If intending to make a high card signal with one of touching cards, signal with the top of the touching cards.

(3) As a diamond is sure to be lost in addition to the two clubs, declarer needs to avoid a heart loser. The best chance is to finesse for the queen. Normally with 8 trumps missing the queen, one cashes the ace or king first and finesses on the second round. With the suit divided 6-2 and the 6-card suit headed by A-K-J-10, the odds favour a first round finesse (see page 153 for details of this combination).

(4) When crossing to dummy to take the heart finesse, it is safer to use the spade suit. As North-South have fewer spades between them than diamonds, an opponent is less likely to hold a singleton spade than a singleton diamond.

Hand 118 : Dealer East : E-W vulnerable

	WEST	**NORTH**	**EAST**	**SOUTH**
			1♣	Pass
	1♠	Pass	1NT	Pass
	6NT	Pass	Pass	Pass

```
              NORTH
              ♠ J 10 8 7 4
              ♡ 10 7 5
              ◇ 10 9 5 3 2
              ♣ - - -
WEST                        EAST
♠ A K 3 2                   ♠ Q 6
♡ A J 3                     ♡ K Q 4
◇ A 8                       ◇ K Q 6
♣ K Q 8 6                   ♣ J 5 4 3 2
              SOUTH
              ♠ 9 5
              ♡ 9 8 6 2
              ◇ J 7 4
              ♣ A 10 9 7
```

Lead : ♡8. Against 6NT, avoid leading a suit bid by the opposition unless you hold a solid sequence. Also, against 6NT, it is usually best not to lead a suit which contains an honor. That leaves only hearts and middle-up-down is recommended from three or four rags. With four rags, middle = second highest. The higher the lead, the less likely it is the leader has an honor card in that suit.

Play : East plays ♣J at trick 2. If South ducks, continue with a second club, return to hand and lead another club until South takes the ace. It is better for South to capture the ♣J. With the bad break revealed, East wins any return in hand and leads a club : if South plays the 7, finesse the 8; if South plays the 9 or 10, capture it, return to hand and lead another club, finessing the 8 if South plays low.

Notes : (1) With a powerful hand but no strong 5-card suit, it is better for West to change suit and not jump. West can bid 6NT later, but the question is whether to bid six or seven. On hearing East's rebid, West can judge whether the grand slam is worth a shot. Any minimum rebid will limit the ambition to a small slam.

(2) If the clubs are 2-2 or 3-1, it would not matter which honor is played first. However, it is vital to play the *jack* first to guard against A-10-9-7 with South. If North has the four clubs, you cannot escape two losers. Ignore that possibility. When you lead the jack you will find out whether there is a bad break and you have retained dummy's two honors to take care of the 10 and 9. If you play the ♣K or ♣Q first, you can be beaten.

Hand 119 : Dealer South : Both vulnerable

NORTH
- ♠ K Q 5 3
- ♡ A 10 5 3
- ◇ A 6 5 4
- ♣ 4

WEST
- ♠ 10 8 7 6
- ♡ K 6
- ◇ 9 8 7 3
- ♣ A 9 5

EAST
- ♠ J 9 4
- ♡ Q 9 8 7 2
- ◇ K 10
- ♣ J 8 3

SOUTH
- ♠ A 2
- ♡ J 4
- ◇ Q J 2
- ♣ K Q 10 7 6 2

WEST	NORTH	EAST	SOUTH
			1♣
Pass	1◇	Pass	2♣
Pass	3NT	All pass	

Lead : ♡7. Fourth highest from the unbid long suit is normal. Not the 9 : for top of sequence, the sequence must have an honor.

Play : Declarer plays low from dummy, West plays the king of hearts and North wins with the ace. There are six top tricks and the club suit is the best source for extra tricks. Declarer leads a club at trick 2 and finesses dummy's 10. West should take the ace and return a heart. East wins and continues hearts, but declarer makes the rest. If West ducks the ace of clubs, declarer continues with the king of clubs. When the ♣Q is played, the rest of the clubs are winners. 11 tricks.

Notes : (1) With 4-card suits, it is normal to respond 'up-the-line' (cheapest suit first). North should not respond 2NT.
(2) When South rebids 2♣, there is no point in North's bidding a major. The 2♣ rebid has denied a major. With no major fit and no unguarded suit, bid 3NT without further ado.
(3) With only one finesse available opposite a K-Q-10 suit, it is best to finesse the 10 if you need more than one trick. If declarer leads a club to the king, West takes the ace and the hearts are cleared. When declarer cashes the ♣Q, the ♣J is still out. Finessing the ♣10 gains when East has J-x-x and also when East has A-J-x. Leading low to the king loses two tricks in both these cases.
(4) Finessing the ♣10 would be the best chance to lose just one trick even if South's clubs were K-Q-10-9-8-7. However, with a singleton opposite A-Q-10-9-x-x, finessing the queen on the first round is superior.

Hand 120 : Dealer West : Nil vulnerable

NORTH
- ♠ K 7 6 4
- ♡ 10 8 4 2
- ◇ 10 7
- ♣ A K Q

WEST
- ♠ A Q 10 9 8 3 2
- ♡ 7
- ◇ 6 4
- ♣ J 8 2

EAST
- ♠ - - -
- ♡ A K 6 5 3
- ◇ A 9 8 5 2
- ♣ 7 6 5

SOUTH
- ♠ J 5
- ♡ Q J 9
- ◇ K Q J 3
- ♣ 10 9 4 3

WEST	NORTH	EAST	SOUTH
3♠	Pass	Pass	Pass

Lead : ♣K (or ace). It is natural to cash the clubs.

Play : South would discourage the clubs but North continues despite partner's signal. As North's clubs are so strong, North expects a discouraging signal anyway. North plays the king, then queen, then ace of clubs. South follows with the 3, the 4 and then the 9. It is normal for North to switch to diamonds anyway, but South's carding has confirmed that diamonds are wanted. At every opportunity, South has followed with the lowest club possible. Lowest, lowest, lowest asks for the low suit. This is a secondary suit preference signal for diamonds. Declarer takes the ace of diamonds, cashes the top hearts to discard the diamond loser and ruffs a diamond. Next comes the ace of spades, followed by the queen of spades. When the ♠J is 'pinned' by the queen, declarer holds the trump losers to one and makes 9 tricks.

Notes : (1) Neither North nor South is strong enough to act over 3♠. East would be itching to inflict a penalty double if North-South did enter the auction.
(2) East should not change suit or push higher. With a void opposite the pre-empt, deduct one trick from your playing strength.
(3) After taking the diamond discard on the top hearts, it is slightly safer to come to hand by ruffing the second round of diamonds than via the third round of hearts.
(4) If the missing spades are 3-3, there are always two trump losers. When the spades are 4-2, playing ace, then queen holds the losers to one when the jack is doubleton. Playing ace, then 10 does not save a trick when the king is doubleton. In that case, the other defender began with J-x-x-x and still has the guarded jack. You can deal with J-x and K-x-x-x, but if their spades are K-x and J-x-x-x, you are saddled with two losers.

CHAPTER 27

AVOIDANCE PLAYS & DUMMY REVERSALS

AVOIDANCE PLAYS

There are many situations where you can afford to have one opponent on lead but not the other. The 'safe hand' is the one whom you do not mind having the lead. The 'danger hand' is the opponent you cannot afford to have on lead.

The reasons vary. At no-trumps, the danger hand may have winners to cash. In trumps, the danger hand may hold the master trump and be able to draw two of your trumps. In any contract, you may have a precarious holding which only one opponent can successfully attack. Avoidance plays are concerned with playing suits in a particular way to keep the danger hand off lead.

These are precarious holdings :

```
        K 7 2
Q J 4           A 10 9 6
        8 5 3
```

West is the danger hand. With East on lead, the king is a stopper. East is the safe hand. With West on lead, the defense can run through this suit. West is the danger hand. Play the other suits to keep West off lead.

```
        7 4 2
K 9 8 6         J 10 5 3
        A Q
```

West is the safe hand. With West on lead, South has a double stopper. East is the danger hand. If East leads the suit, South has only one stopper and wins only one trick. Play the other suits to keep East off lead.

Some holdings become precarious after the opening lead :

```
        7 4
A 10 6 5 3      Q 8 2
        K J 9
```

At no-trumps, West leads the 5 to the queen and king. South's J-9 is now at risk if East gains the lead, but is a stopper if West is on lead. East is the danger hand. Play to keep East off lead.

```
        9 8
A J 7 4 2       10 6 3
        K Q 5
```

At no-trumps, West leads the 4 to the 10 and king. South's Q-5 is now in jeopardy if East gains the lead, but is a stopper if West is on lead. East is the danger hand. Play to keep East off lead.

```
        9 6
Q 10 7 4 2      K 8 5
        A J 3
```

At no-trumps, West leads the 4 to East's king. How should South play?

If South can keep East off lead, take the ace. The J-3 is a further stopper against West. If South can keep only West off lead, duck the king and duck the next round, too. East is out of the suit and is safe.

Keeping the danger hand off lead

1. The two-way finesse

```
K J 9 2     If East is the danger hand, play the king,
A 10 7 3    then run the jack. If the danger hand is
            West, cash the ace, then run the 10. If
```
the finesse loses, the trick is won by the safe hand.

2. Taking a finesse instead of playing for the drop

```
K 10 4 3    The normal technique is to play ace
A J 6 5 2   and king and hope the queen drops. If
            you can afford to lose a trick, you can cater
```
for any 3-1 break. If East is the danger hand, cash the king and then finesse your jack if East plays low. If West is the danger hand, cash the ace and then finesse the 10 if West plays low. If a trick is lost, it is lost only to the safe hand.

3. Playing for the drop instead of taking a finesse

```
A Q J 7     A Q 7 3     A Q 7 4 3
8 6 5 3     8 6 5 4 2   9 8 6 5 2
```

The normal play in each case is to finesse the queen, losing to East when the king is offside. However, if East is the danger hand and you can afford to lose a trick, play the ace from dummy first. If the king has not dropped, come to hand and lead up to the queen. If West has the king, West is the safe hand. If East did start with king singleton, you have prevented the danger hand from coming on lead. If East started with K-x or longer, you cannot stop East getting in.

```
A K J 4     The normal play is to cash the ace,
8 7 5 3     come to hand and finesse the jack. If East
            is the danger hand and you can afford to
```
lose a trick, play the ace and king. If West wins the queen, West is the safe hand. If East started with Q-singleton or Q-x, East's queen is captured and East cannot gain the lead. With Q-x-x or longer, East cannot be prevented from gaining the lead in this suit.

4. The double finesse

A Q 10 5

7 6 3 2

The standard play is to finesse the 10 first and the queen later in order to win the maximum number of tricks. However, if East is the danger hand, it is better to finesse the queen first if you can afford to lose a trick. If the queen wins, come to hand and lead low, ducking if West plays the king. Better still is to lead towards the ace, ducking if West plays the king, cashing the ace otherwise. Then, cross back to hand and lead low to your queen. This prevents East gaining the lead with K-singleton, J-singleton, J-x or J-x-x. With K-x or longer, East cannot be prevented from coming in. If West is the danger hand, make the normal play of finessing the 10 first and the queen later.

K J 6

7 4 3

If you need one trick only, lead low to the king if East is the danger hand, but low to the jack if West is the danger hand.

5. The deep finesse

As long as you are prepared to give up a trick, many suits can be developed by conceding a trick to the safe hand.

A Q 9 4 3 2

K 10

For six tricks, play the king, ace and queen. If only five tricks are needed and East is the danger hand, lead low from dummy and finesse the 10. If West is the danger hand, lead the king and then run the 10 if West plays low. You may lose a trick to J-x or J-x-x but only to the safe hand. You prevent the danger hand coming in with J-x-x-x.

K Q 9 4 2

A 8

If you need only four tricks and can afford to lose one: If East is the danger, play low from dummy and insert the 8 if East plays low. If West is the danger, cash the ace and then run the 8 if West plays low. You concede a trick when the suit is 3-3 but the trick is lost to the safe hand. When the suit is 4-2, you can always keep the danger hand off lead unless it holds J-10-x-x.

A K Q 8 2

6 5 3

If you need only four tricks and can afford to lose a trick but not to West, the danger hand, lead low and insert dummy's 8 if West plays low. If West plays the 9 or higher, capture it, come back to hand and lead low, again playing the 8 if West plays low. You can prevent West coming in with J-10-9-x, J-10-x-x, J-9-x-x, or 10-9-x-x. You lose a trick to East when the suit is 3-2, but you can afford a loser and East is the safe hand.

6. Ducking a trick into the safe hand

With the deep finesse, you are prepared to lose a trick which perhaps need not have been lost at all.

In ducking a trick, you are conceding a trick that has to be lost anyway. However, you intend to lose it to the safe hand if possible. Various manoeuvres exist.

A 10 4 3

K 9 5 2

If East is the danger hand, cash the ace and lead low, playing the 9 if East plays low. East is kept off lead unless East holds both the queen and the jack. If East started with Q-J-x, there was nothing you could do. If West is the danger, cash the king and then lead low, playing the 10 if West plays low. West is kept off lead, if it is possible to do so.

K 8 2

A 9 6 4 3

Lead low through the danger hand and play the 8 or 9 if the danger hand plays low. You prevent the danger hand taking the lead with Q-x-x, J-x-x or 10-x-x.

```
             A K 5 3 2
   Q 8                      J 10 9
             7 6 4
```

Lead low from your hand. If West is the danger, duck in dummy if West plays the 8. If East is the danger, lead low to dummy and duck if West plays the queen: West is the safe hand. If West plays low, take the ace. Return to hand in another suit and lead low again. When West plays the queen, duck in dummy. If West plays low on the second round, from J-10-8, say, win the king and concede the next round. East is kept off lead whenever West has Q-x or any three cards. Note that it would be an error to lead the ace or king *from dummy* first: West could unblock the queen. You must lead lead low from hand towards the ace-king.

7. The ruffing finesse

A Q J 10 6

4

You wish to develop this side suit in a trump contract. If West is the danger hand, finesse the queen, cash the ace and ruff the next round if the king has not dropped. If East is the danger hand, play the ace first, then lead the queen. Ruff if East plays the king. If East plays low, let the queen run. If it loses, it is to West, the safe hand.

A K J 10

5 2

If you need four tricks from this suit, take two finesses. If only three tricks are needed and you can afford a loser, you can take avoidance measures. If West is the danger, take the normal finesse. If East is the danger, cash the ace and king and continue with the jack. If the queen is with West, you are losing to the safe hand. At no-trumps, you gain when East, the danger hand, started with Q-doubleton. In trumps, you let the jack run if East plays low, taking the ruffing finesse.

PLAY HANDS ON AVOIDANCE TECHNIQUE

Hand 121 : Dealer North : E-W vulnerable

NORTH
♠ A 9 5
♡ A 6 3
◇ K 10 5 2
♣ K Q 4

WEST
♠ 8 7 3
♡ Q 10 8 7 4
◇ J 7
♣ J 6 3

EAST
♠ K Q J 10 2
♡ J
◇ Q 8 3
♣ 10 9 8 2

SOUTH
♠ 6 4
♡ K 9 5 2
◇ A 9 6 4
♣ A 7 5

WEST	NORTH	EAST	SOUTH
	1NT	Pass	2♣
Pass	2◇	Pass	3NT
Pass	Pass	Pass	

Lead : ♠K. Obvious top of sequence.

Play : Declarer ducks the first two rounds of spades and takes the ace on the third round. At trick 4 declarer leads a low diamond and plays dummy's 9 when East plays low. West wins but is out of spades. Declarer wins any return and plays a diamond to the ace. When they break, declarer has nine tricks.

Notes : (1) Having led spades, East is likely to have the rest of the spades and is the danger hand. East is unlikely to be long in diamonds.
(2) Declarer would fail by cashing ◇A, ◇K and playing a third diamond. East wins and cashes the rest of the spades.
(3) The avoidance play in diamonds is designed to keep East off lead. It gains when East has J-x-x or Q-x-x (or any singleton).

Hand 122 : Dealer East : Both vulnerable

NORTH
♠ 7 5 2
♡ A K J
◇ Q 10 6 5
♣ 6 4 2

WEST
♠ 9 3
♡ 10 9 6 5 4
◇ 8 7 4 2
♣ J 8

EAST
♠ A Q J 8 6
♡ 8 3
◇ K J 9
♣ Q 10 7

SOUTH
♠ K 10 4
♡ Q 7 2
◇ A 3
♣ A K 9 5 3

WEST	NORTH	EAST	SOUTH
		1♠	1NT
Pass	3NT	All pass	

Lead : ♠9. Lead your own suit only if you have entries.

Play : East inserts the ♠J and South ducks, a hold-up play. East continues with ♠A and a third spade. South plays a heart to dummy to lead a club. If East plays low, South plays the 9 (avoidance play). If East plays an honor, South takes it, returns to dummy with a heart and leads another club, inserting the 9 if East plays low. South scores four club tricks without letting East in.

Notes : (1) If South wins the first spade, West has a spade left and declarer fails when either defender obtains the lead.
(2) If South plays ♣A, ♣K and a third club, East wins and cashes the spades. With the spades set up, East is the danger hand.
(3) The avoidance technique of ducking the club into the safe hand works whenever East has Q-J-x or worse in clubs.

Hand 123 : Dealer South : Nil vulnerable

NORTH
♠ Q 10 4
♡ K 9 8
◇ J 8 7 5 4 2
♣ 9

WEST
♠ A 9 5 2
♡ 7 6 2
◇ 3
♣ A K J 7 2

EAST
♠ K J 7 6 3
♡ A J 4
◇ Q 10
♣ Q 5 3

SOUTH
♠ 8
♡ Q 10 5 3
◇ A K 9 6
♣ 10 8 6 4

WEST	NORTH	EAST	SOUTH
			Pass
1♣	Pass	1♠	Pass
2♠	Pass	4♠	All pass

Lead : ◇K (or ace). Clearcut choice.

Play : With no more tricks in diamonds and dummy's clubs likely to provide declarer with plenty of discards, South switches to dummy's weakness and leads the 3 of hearts. North plays the king and East wins the ace. North is the danger hand since a heart lead from North could give the defense two heart tricks. East draws trumps to keep North off lead : a spade to the ace and a spade back to the jack. The last trump is drawn and the hearts discarded on the clubs.

Notes : (1) If declarer plays ♠A and ♠K, North can ruff the second round of clubs and return a heart : one down.
(2) Even if the ♠J lost to South's queen, South could cash only one heart. The spade finesse guarantees the contract.

Hand 124 : Dealer West : N-S vulnerable

NORTH
- ♠ A J 9 5 3
- ♡ 10 8 6
- ◇ K 8
- ♣ 10 8 3

WEST
- ♠ K Q 4
- ♡ K Q 3
- ◇ 5 4 3
- ♣ A K 6 5

EAST
- ♠ 8 2
- ♡ A 9 5
- ◇ A Q 9 6 2
- ♣ 7 4 2

SOUTH
- ♠ 10 7 6
- ♡ J 7 4 2
- ◇ J 10 7
- ♣ Q J 9

WEST	NORTH	EAST	SOUTH
1NT	Pass	3NT	All pass

Lead : ♠5. Normal fourth highest.

Play : South plays the ♠10 and West wins the king. Best is to lead a diamond to the ace, a heart back to hand and another diamond. North wins ◇ K but cannot run the spades as West's ♠ Q-4 is still a stopper. On a non-spade return, West has 10 tricks.

Notes : (1) It does not help West to duck the first spade. A second spade is played, *ducked by North,* and West will fail. (2) It would be an error to finesse ◇ Q, cash the ace and play a third diamond. South wins and a spade back will defeat 3NT. (3) Declarer could lead a diamond to the queen, play a heart to hand and lead another diamond. When North plays the king, declarer ducks and allows North, the safe hand, to hold the trick. The recommended line has a slight edge over this play as it gains when South has the ◇ K singleton.

DUMMY REVERSALS

Normally, the long trump hand draws trumps and the short trump hand ruffs losers. You cannot usually score more tricks by ruffing with the long trump hand.

A 8 7

K Q J 10 9

If this suit is trumps, there are five winners if you draw trumps. If you can ruff with the 7, you make six tricks. You still have the five in the long trump hand. If you can ruff with the 8 and 7, you have seven tricks. Ruff with the A, 8 and 7 and you have eight tricks.

Ruffing with the 9 produces no extra trick. This was one of the original five tricks. Likewise, ruffing twice in the long hand produces no extra tricks.

However, in the above layout, ruffing with the long trump hand three times or more gains extra tricks. Three ruffs in hand and three trump winners in dummy is six tricks. Four ruffs in hand and you have seven tricks.

If dummy's trumps are powerful enough to draw the opponents' trumps, or most of them, then you can produce extra tricks by ruffing in the long trump hand. You need to ruff often enough to reduce the length in the long trump hand to below the length in the short trump hand.

This play is known as 'dummy reversal' since it reverses the normal roles : dummy's hand draws the trumps and declarer's hand does the ruffing.

PLAY HANDS ON DUMMY REVERSALS

Hand 125 : Dealer North : Both vulnerable

NORTH
- ♠ A J 5 2
- ♡ 10 9 6
- ◇ J 8 3
- ♣ K Q 6

WEST
- ♠ 10 9 8 7
- ♡ 4 2
- ◇ A K Q
- ♣ J 10 5 2

EAST
- ♠ K Q 6 3
- ♡ 8 5 3
- ◇ 9 7 6 5
- ♣ 9 8

SOUTH
- ♠ 4
- ♡ A K Q J 7
- ◇ 10 4 2
- ♣ A 7 4 3

WEST	NORTH	EAST	SOUTH
	Pass	Pass	1♡
Pass	1♠	Pass	2♣
Pass	3♡	Pass	4♡
Pass	Pass	Pass	

Lead : ◇ K (or ace). Natural to cash tricks.

Play : West cashes three diamonds and switches to the 10 of spades. Declarer wins the ace and ruffs a spade high. ♡ A and a low trump to dummy is followed by another spade ruff. A club to dummy allows the last spade to be ruffed. Declarer crosses to dummy with a club and uses dummy's remaining trump to draw the last trump. On this, South's club loser is discarded.

Notes : (1) The likely club split is 4–2. If declarer draws trumps, there figures to be a club loser. The same reason argues against trying to ruff the fourth round of clubs in dummy. (2) As dummy can draw trumps, a dummy reversal is possible.

(3) If West switches to a trump at trick 4, win ♡ A, play a spade to the ace, ruff a spade *high*, low heart to dummy, ruff a spade, club to dummy, ruff a spade, club to dummy and draw the last trump.

Hand 126 : Dealer East : Nil vulnerable

           NORTH
           ♠ 8
           ♡ 7 6
           ◊ J 10 7 6 3
           ♣ 10 8 7 5 2

WEST   **EAST**
♠ A K 5 2   ♠ 7 6 4
♡ A Q J 8 3   ♡ K 10 9
◊ 9 5 4   ◊ A 8 2
♣ 9   ♣ A 6 4 3

           SOUTH
           ♠ Q J 10 9 3
           ♡ 5 4 2
           ◊ K Q
           ♣ K Q J

WEST	NORTH	EAST	SOUTH
		Pass	1♠
2♡	Pass	3♡	Pass
4♡	Pass	Pass	Pass

Lead : ♠8. Partner's suit, what else?

Play: West wins the spade lead and continues with a club to the ace, a club ruffed high, a low trump to dummy, a club ruffed high, a trump to dummy and the last club ruffed. A diamond to the ace allows the last trump to be drawn. Declarer makes 2 spade tricks, 3 trumps in dummy, 3 ruffs in hand, 1 diamond and 1 club.

Notes: (1) 3NT is easier but very difficult to reach. East could try 2♠ over 2♡. West should then rebid 3NT.
(2) If declarer draws trumps, there are only 9 winners. Declarer cannot afford to try to ruff a spade in dummy. The second spade will be ruffed, leaving declarer a trick short. With dummy strong enough to draw trumps, a dummy reversal is indicated.

Hand 127 : Dealer South : N-S vulnerable

           NORTH
           ♠ A 9 7 5 2
           ♡ 9
           ◊ Q 7 5
           ♣ A Q 6 2

WEST   **EAST**
♠ 10 6   ♠ K Q J
♡ K 7 5 4 3   ♡ Q 10 8
◊ 10 6 4 2   ◊ K J 9 3
♣ 8 7   ♣ 9 5 3

           SOUTH
           ♠ 8 4 3
           ♡ A J 6 2
           ◊ A 8
           ♣ K J 10 4

WEST	NORTH	EAST	SOUTH
			1♣
Pass	1♠	Pass	1NT
Pass	3♣	Pass	3♠
Pass	4♠	All pass	

Lead : ♠K. A solid sequence in trumps is an attractive start.

Play : Declarer ducks the first spade and wins the next spade. Leaving the last trump out, North aims to score three ruffs in hand. A heart to the ace and a heart ruff is followed by a club to dummy, another heart ruff, a club to dummy and a final heart ruff. Declarer continues clubs and later cashes the ace of diamonds.

Notes : (1) South should give delayed 3-card spade support.
(2) An inferior plan that fails is to win ♠A, play a diamond to the ace and a diamond to the queen. East wins ◊K and draws dummy's last trump. This would work if the ◊K were onside or without a trump lead, but the recommended line works on any layout.

Hand 128 : Dealer West : E-W vulnerable

           NORTH
           ♠ 8 7 4
           ♡ 9 6 5 2
           ◊ Q 10 8 2
           ♣ 10 6

WEST   **EAST**
♠ Q J 10   ♠ A K 6 5 2
♡ 8 7 3   ♡ A 10 4
◊ A J 9 4   ◊ 5
♣ A J 3   ♣ K Q 7 4

           SOUTH
           ♠ 9 3
           ♡ K Q J
           ◊ K 7 6 3
           ♣ 9 8 5 2

WEST	NORTH	EAST	SOUTH
1◊	Pass	1♠	Pass
1NT	Pass	3♣	Pass
3♠	Pass	4NT	Pass
5♡	Pass	6♠	All pass

Lead : ♡K. No problem.

Play: Win ♡A, play a diamond to the ace and ruff a diamond. A club to dummy is followed by another diamond, ruffed high. Play a low trump to dummy and ruff another diamond high. A trump to dummy enables trumps to be drawn. The clubs are cashed for 12 tricks.

Notes: (1) Dummy's strong trumps indicate a dummy reversal.
(2) If declarer draws trumps, there are only 11 tricks.
(3) An inferior plan which fails is to duck the first heart, win ♡A, draw two rounds of trumps, then four rounds of clubs to discard a heart. This would work if the hand with 3 spades had 4 clubs.

CHAPTER 28

THE COMPULSORY DUCK & TRUMP REDUCTION PLAYS

THE COMPULSORY DUCK

There are certain card combinations where it is vital not to lose an honor card to an opponent's ace. How do you handle this combination to lose only one trick?

Q 7 3 2 Barring opposition error, the only hope
K 6 5 4 to hold your losers to one is that the ace is doubleton. If either opponent has A-9-8 or better, you are bound to lose two tricks. When the ace is doubleton, you can succeed if you lead low through the ace on the first round and duck the second round.

```
              Q 7 3 2
     A 9                 J 10 8
              K 6 5 4
```

If you lead an honor on the first round, the ace takes it and you are sure to lose a second trick. If you lead from the North hand you will lose two tricks when West has the ace. On the above layout, you must lead low from the South hand. If West plays the ace, no problems. If West ducks (best), play the queen which wins. Then lead low and duck in the South hand. West's ace drops and your king can capture East's jack later. Note that you lose a second trick if you put up the king on the second round. You must duck the second round, hence the name 'compulsory duck'. The tricky part is knowing that West holds the ace.

If the ace were with East, you would have to lead low from the North hand first. After your king wins, again you duck the second round. The technique is to make the player with the ace play second on the first round of the suit. You place the ace from the bidding if possible (an opponent who opened the bidding is likely to have the ace; an opponent who pre-empted is unlikely to have the ace, etc.). Otherwise you will have to guess well.

The same play applies if the suit is divided 5-3 but if the layout is 6-2, something like this :

Q 3 you must lead low towards your
K 7 6 5 4 2 doubleton honor first and pray the ace is under the doubleton.

This ducking play also applies whenever playing an honor card is certain to lose.

```
              8 6 4 2
     K 9                 J 10 7
              A Q 5 3
```

If you know from the bidding or early play that the king sits over your ace, it is futile to finesse the queen. That will lose to the king and you will have a second loser. *Don't squander the honor.* Play the ace and duck the second round, or duck the first round and later play the ace. If the king does fall doubleton, you lose only one trick.

PLAY HANDS ON THE COMPULSORY DUCK

Hand 129 : Dealer North : Nil vulnerable

NORTH
♠ 8
♡ K 7 5 2
♢ Q 9 7
♣ A 9 6 4 3

WEST
♠ 6 5 3 2
♡ J 9 8
♢ 10 5 4 3
♣ 10 8

EAST
♠ Q J 10 9 4
♡ A 10
♢ 8 6 2
♣ K Q J

SOUTH
♠ A K 7
♡ Q 6 4 3
♢ A K J
♣ 7 5 2

WEST	NORTH	EAST	SOUTH
	Pass	1♠	1NT
Pass	2♣	Pass	2♡
Pass	4♡	All pass	

Lead: ♠5. Partner's suit. M.U.D. from rags. However, the ♣10 is not a bad shot. With so many cards in partner's suit, a short suit lead from a very weak hand is reasonable.

Play: South wins ♠A, ruffs a low spade in dummy and leads a low heart from the North hand. East plays low and the queen wins. South continues with a low heart, ducking in dummy. East's ace falls and South can later draw West's last trump with the king.

Notes: (1) South is bound to lose two club tricks and must hold the trump suit to one loser.
(2) 4♡ fails on a low heart from the South hand.
(3) The ♡A is marked with East because of the opening bid. To lead through the ace, the first heart must come from North.

Hand 130 : Dealer East : Nil vulnerable

NORTH
♠ Q J 10
♡ K 8 5 4 2
♢ A 3
♣ Q 8 3

WEST
♠ 9 8 5 4 3 2
♡ A
♢ 10 9 7 6
♣ 10 9

EAST
♠ A 7 6
♡ J 10 9
♢ K Q J 8
♣ 7 6 2

SOUTH
♠ K
♡ Q 7 6 3
♢ 5 4 2
♣ A K J 5 4

WEST	NORTH	EAST	SOUTH
		Pass	1♣
Pass	1♡	Pass	2♡
Pass	4♡	All pass	

Lead : ♢ K. Clearcut choice.

Play : North wins the ace of diamonds and plays a spade at trick 2. East wins and continues with ♢ Q and ♢ J. North ruffs and, because of the early spade play, is able to place 10 HCP with East. As East passed as dealer, East cannot hold the ace of hearts as well. North ruffs a spade (a club to the ace is riskier) and leads a low trump from dummy. When the ace pops up, declarer has no further loser.

Notes : (1) Leading from either hand works if trumps are 2-2. If either opponent has A-10-9 or better, there are two trump losers, regardless how you play. You can deal with a 3-1 split if the ace is singleton by leading through the player who holds the ace.
(2) If West had ♠ A, you have to guess where the ♡ A might be.

Hand 131 : Dealer South : E-W vulnerable

NORTH
♠ 9 7
♡ 8 7 6 5
♢ 9 8 6 3
♣ J 10 9

WEST
♠ A Q 5
♡ A K
♢ Q J 10
♣ 8 7 5 4 2

EAST
♠ K J 4 3 2
♡ 4 2
♢ 7 5 2
♣ A Q 3

SOUTH
♠ 10 8 6
♡ Q J 10 9 3
♢ A K 4
♣ K 6

WEST	NORTH	EAST	SOUTH
			1♡
1NT	Pass	3♠	Pass
4♠	Pass	Pass	Pass

Lead : ♢ K (or ace) or ♡ Q. Little to choose between the two.

Play : If South starts with the diamonds, South should not switch to clubs at any stage. When declarer wins the lead, declarer draws trumps and continues with the ace of clubs and a low club (or duck a club and cash the ace next time). When the king falls on the second round, declarer loses just two diamonds and one club.

Notes : (1) Better to overcall 1NT than to double.
(2) Declarer fails by finessing the ♣ Q. This loses to the king and there is a second club loser. The club finesse is futile.
(3) There are 26 HCP between declarer and dummy. As South opened the bidding, almost all the missing HCP will be with South. Without ♣ K, South's opening = 11 HCP, possible but unlikely.

Hand 132 : Dealer West : Nil vulnerable

NORTH
♠ 5 3
♡ Q 10 9
♢ 10 7 6
♣ Q J 10 9 7

WEST
♠ A K 9 8 7 6
♡ K J 2
♢ A Q J
♣ 4

EAST
♠ Q J 10
♡ A 8 7
♢ K 9 8
♣ K 6 5 3

SOUTH
♠ 4 2
♡ 6 5 4 3
♢ 5 4 3 2
♣ A 8 2

WEST	NORTH	EAST	SOUTH
1♠	Pass	2NT	Pass
3♠	Pass	4♠	Pass
4NT	Pass	5♢	Pass
6♠	Pass	Pass	Pass

Lead : ♣ Q. Easy decision.

Play : Declarer ducks the first club and also the second if North continues clubs. After ruffing the club, declarer plays ♠ A and a spade to the queen, drawing trumps. A third club is ruffed and when the ace drops, the ♣ K is high for a heart discard.

Notes : (1) The heart finesse is a 50% play, but there is no rush to take it. Correct play makes the heart finesse unnecessary.
(2) If North switches after the first club, declarer can ruff low clubs twice, setting up the king if the ♣ A falls in two or three rounds.
(3) The ♣ A is marked with South on the lead. Playing the king of clubs must lose and cannot gain. *Don't squander the honor.*

TRUMP REDUCTION PLAYS

Often, too often it seems, you strike a bad trump break. Do not despair when things turn nasty. Those inevitable losers may not be inevitable after all. With trump reduction technique, if you know your counter-measures, you may yet survive even the worst of breaks.

There are certain basic positions in the trump suit:

J 4

3   K 7 6 2

A Q 10 9 8 5

The jack is led and the finesse repeated. When West shows out, East has K-x left and with no more trumps in dummy, the finesse cannot be repeated. East's king seems secure. However, if South can reduce the trump length to create this position, South can succeed:

\- \- \-

\- \- \-   K 7

A Q

If the lead is in dummy at trick 12, no matter which card is led from dummy, East's king is trapped. The key elements are to reduce your trump length to the same length held by the opponent *and* to place the lead in dummy with two tricks to go.

This position is equivalent:

A 4

5   J 8 7 3

K Q 10 9 6 2

Not knowing the position, declarer naturally starts with the ace and king, and the bad break is revealed.

Now declarer must ruff twice to reduce trump length to the same as East's and be in dummy at trick 12:

\- \- \-

\- \- \-   J 8

Q 10

On any lead from dummy, East's jack is caught.

8 4 3

Q J 5 2   \- \- \-

A K 10 9 7 6

With this trump layout, West seems to have two winners. After the ace reveals the break, South must reduce trump length to the same as West's.

8 4

Q J 5   \- \- \-

K 10 9

If there are only three tricks to go, South leads the 9 or 10. West wins but is said to be 'endplayed'. Forced to lead into South's tenace, West makes only one trick.

8 4 3

K Q J 5   \- \- \-

A 10 9 7 6 2

West seems to have three sure trump tricks. A trump is led from dummy. When East shows out, South inserts the 10 (or 9 or 7 or 6). South must reduce the trump length to create this end-position:

8 4

K Q 5   \- \- \-

A 9 7

If there are only three tricks to go, South plays the 9 or 7 and West makes only one more trick.

PLAY HANDS ON TRUMP REDUCTIONS

Hand 133 : Dealer North : N-S vulnerable

NORTH
♠ A 8 6 5 2
♡ A 3
◇ A K J
♣ 7 5 3

WEST
♠ Q 7 4 3
♡ 6
◇ 9 4 3 2
♣ A K 10 4

EAST
♠ J 10 9
♡ Q 9 8 5
◇ 10 8 7
♣ Q 8 2

SOUTH
♠ K
♡ K J 10 7 4 2
◇ Q 6 5
♣ J 9 6

WEST	NORTH	EAST	SOUTH
	1♠	Pass	2♡
Pass	2NT	Pass	4♡
Pass	Pass	Pass	

Lead : ♣K. Nothing else is even remotely appealing.

Play : East signals encouragement and the defense cashes the first three tricks. East switches to the jack of spades. South wins and makes the normal play in trumps: cash the ace and finesse the jack. There is good news and bad news. The finesse works but West shows out. Time to reduce trumps: diamond to dummy's jack, ruff a spade, diamond to dummy, ruff a spade. Next, a diamond to dummy leaves the lead in the North hand at trick 12. On the next spade, East ruffs and South overruffs and draws the last trump.

Notes : (1) If East switches to a diamond at trick 4, South later overtakes the ♠K with the ace to regain the entry lost.
(2) South fails if the lead is in the South hand at trick 12.

Hand 134 : Dealer East : E-W vulnerable

NORTH
♠ J 9 5 3
♡ Q 7 5
♢ J 10 2
♣ K 9 7

WEST
♠ 8
♡ A K 8 4
♢ A K 7 6
♣ A 8 5 2

EAST
♠ A K Q 10 7 6 4
♡ 10
♢ 9 4
♣ 6 4 3

SOUTH
♠ 2
♡ J 9 6 3 2
♢ Q 8 5 3
♣ Q J 10

WEST	NORTH	EAST	SOUTH
		3♠	Pass
5♠	Pass	6♠	All pass

Lead : ♣Q. Best available choice.

Play : Win ♣A. Cash ♠A, ♠K. Bad news. Time to reduce trumps. ♡A, ♡K discarding a club, heart ruff, ♢A, heart ruff, ♢K, diamond ruff. Down to ♠Q-10 and ♣6, East exits with the club and scores the last two tricks.

Notes : (1) At the vulnerability, East should have seven sound playing tricks. 5♠ asks partner to bid 6♠ with strong trumps.
(2) Hearts are ruffed ahead of diamonds to preserve entries. East must ruff three times and needs three entries to dummy. Playing ♢A, ♢K before hearts removes one entry.
(3) After ruffing three times to come down to ♠Q-10, declarer can simply exit to ensure the last two tricks. As long as the lead is not with East at trick 12, the ending will succeed.

Hand 135 : Dealer South : Both vulnerable

NORTH
♠ A 10 9 8 4 3
♡ 6
♢ J 7 5
♣ A K 8

WEST
♠ J 6 5 2
♡ K 10
♢ Q 10 2
♣ 10 9 5 2

EAST
♠ 7
♡ Q 9 8 7 5
♢ A K 9 6
♣ 7 4 3

SOUTH
♠ K Q
♡ A J 4 3 2
♢ 8 4 3
♣ Q J 6

WEST	NORTH	EAST	SOUTH
			1♡
Pass	1♠	Pass	1NT
Pass	4♠	All pass	

Lead : ♢K (or ace). The most attractive start.

Play : West encourages and the defense takes the first three tricks. West's natural switch is to a club, ♣2. Declarer wins the ace, *next plays a heart to the ace and ruffs a heart,* and then cashes the king and queen of spades. When the bad break appears, another heart is ruffed, bringing North down to ♠A-10. After ♣K and a club to the queen, West is caught in a 'trump coup'.

Notes : (1) Win ♣A at trick 4 to keep the ♣Q entry in dummy.
(2) Note the precautionary heart ruff before touching trumps. If North plays ♠K-Q first, dummy is an entry short for the trump reduction. After ♠K-Q, ♡A, heart ruff, club to dummy, heart ruff, North is down to ♠A-10 but is in hand instead of dummy at trick 12.

Hand 136 : Dealer West : Nil vulnerable

NORTH
♠ Q J 8 3
♡ K J 5
♢ 10 9 8 2
♣ J 9

WEST
♠ A K 10 6 4 2
♡ 6
♢ A 6 3
♣ A 7 3

EAST
♠ 9 7 5
♡ A 8 3
♢ K Q J 5
♣ K Q J

SOUTH
♠ - - -
♡ Q 10 9 7 4 2
♢ 7 4
♣ 10 8 6 5 2

WEST	NORTH	EAST	SOUTH
1♠	Pass	3NT	Pass
6♠	Pass	Pass	Pass

Lead : ♢10. As partner will have little, lead safely.

Play : Win ♢K and lead a trump to the ace. The bad break is a blow, but never give up. Time to reduce trumps. Heart to ace, ruff a heart, club to the king, ruff a heart. Continue with ♢A and a diamond to dummy. When South shows out, cash ♢J and pitch a club. West is down to ♠K-10-6 and ♣A. Cash the ♣A and exit with the ♠6 towards dummy's 9. North wins but is endplayed.

Notes : (1) The 3NT response shows 16-18 balanced, enough for West to take off for slam. West does not gain by asking for aces.
(2) Note the technique in tackling diamonds before clubs. After two heart ruffs, North is known to have at most six minor cards. When North turns up with four diamonds, North cannot have more than two clubs. Therefore discard a club on the diamonds.

CHAPTER 29

CARD READING & INFERENCES (2)

Declarer can make useful inferences not only from the bidding, or lack of it, but also from the opening lead and the approach adopted by the defense. If you are not sure about the opponents' methods, do not hesitate to ask. Do they lead top of sequence or second honor from sequences? Do they lead 4th-highest or 3rds and 5ths? Do they signal high encouraging or do they use reverse signals or do they signal count only? Do you know which system of discards they use? To be able to make intelligent decisions, you need the answers to these questions. You do not appear foolish by asking about their methods and even if you did, it is better to appear foolish by asking than to be really foolish by failing in a contract which you should have made if you knew the methods they were using.

The importance of knowing their methods can be gauged from this example :

Q 7 4

A 6 2

Playing no-trumps you receive the lead of the 10. Which card do you play from dummy? What if the lead were the jack? Or the 3?

In standard methods, the lead of the 10 may be from a 10-9-sequence or from a K-10-9-interior-sequence. Playing the queen may or may not succeed. However, some pairs use the lead of the 10 to *guarantee* an interior sequence. Against such a pair, you can play the queen with confidence. The lead will be from a K-J-10 or K-10-9 holding.

The standard lead of the jack may be from a J-10-sequence or a K-J-10-interior-sequence. You cannot be sure to play the queen. Against a pair that always leads the 10 from an interior sequence, the jack lead denies that holding. Therefore the king will be with East and it cannot gain to play the queen. If the opponents are reliable, play low in dummy. On the next round of the suit, play low in dummy again. You must hope East began with K-singleton or K-doubleton.

On the standard lead of the 3, it may work to play the queen or to play low. Some pairs use 'attitude leads' where the lower the card led, the greater the interest in the suit. The 3 is the lowest card missing, so that West is very keen on the suit. That makes it very likely that West has the king.

Inferences from the opening lead at no-trumps

1. An honor card lead indicates a 3-card sequence or near-sequence. Note from their methods which honor is denied or promised by the honor led.

2. What can you tell from a low card lead? If it is fourth highest, how many cards can the opening leader hold in the suit? How many will be held by third hand? Apply the Rule of 11 and note any relevant information from that source.

3. Was the lead from a 4-card suit precisely? If so, it is unlikely that the opening leader has a 5-card or longer holding in an unbid suit.

4. Is the opening lead an unexpected short suit lead? A doubleton lead at no-trumps is rare and a 3-card holding not common. If you or dummy has bid a suit, a short suit lead often implies that the leader has length in your suit(s). If no suit was bid, a short suit lead suggests that the leader is very weak and is hoping to strike partner's suit. When the lead is from three or four rags, the leader might have unattractive tenace holdings in the other suits.

5. If the lead is in a suit bid by third player, which cards can you place with third hand from the card led?

Inferences from third hand's play at no-trumps

1. Did third player play an honor on the leader's honor? If the leader is long in that suit, third player is short in the suit and is unblocking.

2. Did third hand play high? Which cards can you place from the card played?

3. Did third hand signal on the lead? What did the signal mean? Encouraging? Discouraging? Count?

Inferences from the lead in a suit contract

1. Note the card led. Just as in no-trumps, you can take valuable inferences if the card led is an honor or if it is a low card.

2. Is the opening lead a trump? This implies trumps are breaking favourably. A trump lead is not likely from a singleton or from four or more.

3. A low card lead denies a strong lead such as a sequence or an A-K-suit. A low card lead implies the leader does not have the ace, A-K or K-Q in the suit led.

4. If you and dummy have an unbid suit no better than jack high between you, the leader does not have the A-K or K-Q in that suit if the lead is some other suit.

5. Was the lead in a suit bid by you or dummy? If so, it is almost certainly a singleton. Did the leader bid the unusual no-trump or pre-empt and then lead some other suit? Such a lead is usually a singleton. Did the defenders bid and raise a suit? If so, a lead in some other suit is usually a singleton, perhaps a doubleton.

6. Is the lead a singleton? If so, trumps are likely to break favourably. Defenders tend not to lead singletons when trumps are 4-1 or worse. The lead of a singleton tends to suggest the leader has some worthless trumps, perhaps A-x, A-x-x or K-x-x, but not likely Q-x-x or other holdings which need a low trump to guard an honor.

7. If the bidding suggested a trump lead, a (good) defender who does not lead a trump wishes to protect an honor in trumps.

8. If the opponent on lead has bid a suit and fails to lead it, the suit is headed by a tenace and not a sequence.

9. If the lead is clearly unorthodox, the leader has no normal lead and has a hand strewn with tenaces.

10. If a sound defender underleads an ace-high suit at trick 1, there will be no sound lead available. Such a risky manoeuvre smacks of desperation and implies tenaces in all suits.

The stronger the opposition, the more reliable the inferences.

Inferences from the play by third hand

Similar inferences apply as for no-trumps. Third hand may be unblocking a top honor, third hand high reveals something about the cards held, signals by third hand are a valuable source of information.

You can also judge third hand's holding when third hand returns the leader's suit. Top card return is standard from a remaining doubleton, lowest from three remaining.

In any contract, declarer may deduce something not only from the card led but also from the speed with which it was led. While such inferences are at your own risk, they are usually valid. After 1NT : 3NT, what is your opening lead on these hands?

	1.		2.	
♠	Q J 10 9 2		8 7 6 2	
♡	A 5 2		K J 4	
◇	J 6		J 6	
♣	5 3 2		10 6 3 2	

No problem with hand 1, was there? A defender with that hand will lead the queen of spades at the speed of light. What about hand 2? Not so easy, right?

Here a defender is likely to dither for some time before choosing a lead. A trance before leading tends to suggest that the leader has no clearcut lead and has some holdings which are undesirable leads. A very swift lead indicates an obvious choice.

Mid-game switches

When a defender is faced with a switch, there are valuable inferences available. If there is an obvious switch and a defender fails to make that switch, you can expect the defender to have a critical honor in that suit. With a switch available through an A-Q-x suit in dummy, failure to switch implies the defender has the king.

If you have K-J-x in dummy opposite rags, failure to lead through the K-J suggests the defender has the queen (or no honor). Leading the suit suggests the defender has the ace. It is riskier to lead from the queen than the ace as declarer may have A-10-x and have a two-way guess. Leading from the ace in mid-game is safer: if declarer has the queen, the lead is unlikely to cost.

A defender who leads round to an unsupported queen in dummy is most unlikely to have the king. A defender who leads round to an unsupported jack is not likely to have the queen. Defenders are not in the habit of giving declarer a gift. When you have no entry to dummy but a defender (kindly) gives you an entry so that a finesse now becomes possible, that finesse will lose. Play for the drop.

Playing on an assumption

You will often be in a position that a finesse will have to work in order for you to succeed. If so, assume that the finesse works and credit the relevant opponent with that card. That may assist in placing other missing cards. The train of thought may be "I can afford to lose only one club, so West will have to have the ace. West has already produced 7 points and the ♣A makes 11. As West did not open the bidding, all the other points must be with East."

1. *If you cannot make your contract unless the cards lie in a certain way, assume that they do lie as you wish, and see what consequences follow.*

2. *If your contract seems safe and is in jeopardy only if the cards lie in a certain way, assume that they do lie as you fear and see what precautions you can take.*

3. *Do not make more assumptions than necessary. It is easier to have one prayer answered than two.*

4. *If an assumption produces consequences that are absurd, discard the assumption.*

PLAY HANDS ON CARD READING AND INFERENCES (2)

Hand 137 : Dealer North : E-W vulnerable

NORTH
♠ 6
♡ A Q 7 4
♢ 8 7 6 5
♣ K Q 6 3

WEST
♠ A 7 5 4 3
♡ 8 5 3
♢ K Q J
♣ J 10

EAST
♠ K J 10 2
♡ K J 6 2
♢ A 9 3
♣ 7 2

SOUTH
♠ Q 9 8
♡ 10 9
♢ 10 4 2
♣ A 9 8 5 4

WEST	NORTH	EAST	SOUTH
	Pass	1♢	Pass
1♠	Double	2♠	3♣
4♠	Pass	Pass	Pass

Lead : ♣K. Even if South did not bid, this is best.

Play : South encourages the lead and North continues with the queen. At trick 3, the diamond switch is best. Declarer wins ♢ A and plays the king of spades, followed by the jack of spades. When South plays low, West ducks and the jack wins. The last trump is drawn and a heart is led to the jack. When this holds, a diamond back to hand is followed by another heart. Declarer loses just one heart and two clubs.

Notes : (1) South's 3♣ is marginal and West might be content with just 3♠ which would end the auction.
(2) The defense should avoid playing a third club which gives declarer a ruff and discard.
(3) The standard play in spades is ace, then king but there are overwhelming indications that South has the queen. North's takeout double is a clue. North figures to be short in spades. More compelling is the heart position. To make 10 tricks, declarer needs to find North with A-Q in hearts. North has already shown up with ♣ K-Q. Assuming North has ♡ A-Q as well gives North 11 HCP. North cannot have the ♠ Q as well. That would make 13 HCP and North passed as dealer. The same logic applies even if North-South did not bid at all.
(4) If North rises with the ace when a heart is led towards dummy, that is a sure tip-off that North has ace and queen. With ace only, North would duck smoothly and let you finesse the jack.

Hand 138 : Dealer East : Both vulnerable

NORTH
♠ Q 5 2
♡ 7 4 3
♢ J 10 6
♣ K Q 10 2

WEST
♠ J 8 7 3
♡ K 10 6 2
♢ 2
♣ J 8 6 4

EAST
♠ K 10 9
♡ Q J 5
♢ A 8 7 5 4
♣ 9 7

SOUTH
♠ A 6 4
♡ A 9 8
♢ K Q 9 3
♣ A 5 3

WEST	NORTH	EAST	SOUTH
		Pass	1NT
Pass	2NT	Pass	3NT
Pass	Pass	Pass	

Lead : ♡2. No suit appeals greatly but it is more attractive to lead from a king than from a jack. It is better to lead from a suit with two honors than a suit with only one honor.

Play : East plays the ♡ J and declarer takes the ace. A diamond to the jack is taken by the ace and East continues with the ♡ Q and a heart to West who cashes the thirteenth heart. East discards a diamond and declarer discards a spade from dummy and from hand. West switches to a spade, and the queen is covered by the king and ace. Declarer cashes the diamonds, West discarding all the spades ('keep length with dummy'). A spade is discarded from dummy. South continues with a club to the king, a club to the ace and finesses the 10 of clubs on the third round. The ♣ Q is the ninth trick.

Notes : (1) South should not hold up at trick 1. West's lead of the 2 indicates no more than a 4-card suit. A duck could lead to a spade shift and on other layouts declarer might lose a spade, a diamond and three hearts.
(2) South should cash the diamonds before starting clubs. A defender may err by discarding a club.
(3) The best chance normally with this club suit is to play ace, king and queen, hoping the jack falls in three rounds. However, South should read West to have started with four clubs and therefore the finesse on the third round of clubs is marked. The clues? A defender who leads a 4-card suit against no-trumps is unlikely to have a 5-card holding in an unbid suit. West led an unspectacular 4-card heart suit and turned up with a singleton in diamonds. How are West's eight black cards divided? As West would lead a 5-card or longer suit if possible, West's shape with a singleton diamond and four hearts should be 4-4 in spades and clubs.

Hand 139 : Dealer South : Nil vulnerable

NORTH
♠ 9 7 5
♡ K 2
♢ J 7 5
♣ 8 7 6 4 3

WEST
♠ 10 6 4
♡ 9 5 4
♢ K Q 9
♣ A Q 9 2

EAST
♠ A Q J 8 3 2
♡ J 10 6
♢ A 8 3
♣ 10

SOUTH
♠ K
♡ A Q 8 7 3
♢ 10 6 4 2
♣ K J 5

WEST	NORTH	EAST	SOUTH
			1♡
Pass	Pass	2♠	Pass
3♠	Pass	4♠	All pass

Lead: ♢ 2. Not an attractive choice but everything else is worse. As partner passed your opening bid, partner can have very little and you should be reluctant to lead from any tenace.

Play: East plays the 9 from dummy and captures North's jack. East continues with the ace of spades. The singleton king is a lucky break (at least virtue is rewarded here, if not always at the table). Trumps are drawn and declarer continues with a club to the queen. A heart loser is discarded on the ace of clubs and declarer has made 11 tricks.

Notes: (1) North is too weak to respond to 1♡ with only 4 points. (2) East's 2♠ shows opening values, 12-15 points, and a strong suit. West is just worth a raise.

(3) East picks the location of the black kings from the opening lead. It is not the diamond lead that is telling but the failure to lead hearts. With A-K in hearts, South would have led a heart, not a nondescript diamond. Therefore, South does not have A-K in hearts. So North must have a top heart. Yet North passed the opening bid, indicating 0-5 points, so North cannot have ♡ K and another king as well. Therefore both black kings are with South. The normal play in spades is the finesse, but when the finesse is sure to fail, play for the drop. The ♠ K being singleton was pure luck. East did not know the king was singleton, only that the spade finesse was futile. The club finesse was not necessary for the contract but the overtrick is worth taking, especially at duplicate, when you know that the club finesse will work. Had the king of spades not dropped under the ace, declarer would have taken the club finesse and discarded a heart loser before continuing spades.

Hand 140 : Dealer West : N-S vulnerable

NORTH
♠ Q J 10 9 6 3
♡ 6 3
♢ A 10 3 2
♣ A

WEST
♠ K 7 2
♡ A Q 9 7 5
♢ J
♣ K J 7 3

EAST
♠ 5
♡ K J 8 2
♢ 9 8 5 4
♣ 10 5 4 2

SOUTH
♠ A 8 4
♡ 10 4
♢ K Q 7 6
♣ Q 9 8 6

WEST	NORTH	EAST	SOUTH
1♡	1♠	2♡	2♠
Pass	3♠	Pass	4♠
Pass	Pass	Pass	

Lead: ♡2. No reason to choose anything other than partner's suit.

Play: West wins the ace and switches to the jack of diamonds. Declarer wins and continues with the ace of clubs, ♠ Q to the ace and the *queen of clubs*. When West produces the king, declarer does not ruff but discards the heart loser, a loser-on-loser play. Declarer wins any return by West and leads trumps. Later the last trump is drawn and declarer loses just one spade, one heart and one club.

Notes: (1) The ♠ Q is led to tempt a defender to cover with the king. (2) If West wins the heart and returns a heart, the defense cannot defeat the contract. West should plan to ruff a diamond and hopes East has either the ace of diamonds or the king of hearts entry.

(3) If North wins the diamond switch and takes the spade finesse, West wins, leads a low heart to East and receives the diamond ruff. One off. The same result ensues if declarer, fearing the ruff, foregoes the spade finesse and plays ace and another spade. Trying to clear as many trumps as possible is sound and would succeed if spades were 2-2. However, when West has three spades, this play also fails.

(4) North should note that West won the *ace* of hearts, thus denying the king. The switch to a diamond is startling. Clearly West has a singleton diamond and plans to lead a heart to East to receive a diamond ruff. North thwarts this plan by cutting communications between East and West. By cashing ♣ A, crossing to ♠ A and leading ♣ Q, North can discard the heart loser. Although this trick is lost, West no longer has access to East and the threat of the diamond ruff has evaporated. North's communication cutting is called the 'scissors coup'.

CHAPTER 30

ENDPLAYS : STRIP-AND-THROW-IN TECHNIQUE

These are known as 'strip-and-throw-in' plays because the technique is to exhaust the opponents of safe exit cards ('strip' or 'eliminate') and then give the lead to an opponent ('throw-in') who is obliged to make a lead favourable to you. They occur mostly when you have trumps left in hand and trumps left in dummy with voids in each hand in the suits that are irrelevant. Thus, if one of these suits is led, you benefit from the ruff and discard.

A strip and throw-in may avoid a losing finesse, solve a guess or create a trick where you did not have one.

```
                    Q 4 2
        K 10 8                   A 9 6 5
                    J 7 3
```

South has no trick but if either opponent is forced to lead the suit, declarer scores a trick by playing second hand low. The following hands illustrate the principles.

PLAY HANDS ON STRIP-AND-THROW-INS

Hand 141 : Dealer North : Both vulnerable

```
        NORTH
        ♠ A Q 10
        ♡ A Q J 3 2
        ◇ K Q J
        ♣ 7 2

WEST                    EAST
♠ 9 8 7 5               ♠ K J 4
♡ 4                     ♡ 10 7
◇ 10 9 3                ◇ 8 7 6 2
♣ 9 6 5 4 3             ♣ Q J 10 8

        SOUTH
        ♠ 6 3 2
        ♡ K 9 8 6 5
        ◇ A 5 4
        ♣ A K
```

WEST	NORTH	EAST	SOUTH
	1♡	Pass	3♡
Pass	3♠	Pass	4♣
Pass	4NT	Pass	5♡
Pass	5NT	Pass	6♡
Pass	Pass	Pass	

Lead : ♣Q. Not a hard selection.

Play : Declarer wins, draws trumps, plays off the diamonds and clubs (stripping the side suits) ending in dummy and leads a spade to the 10 (throw-in). East wins but must return a spade or concede a ruff-and-discard. 12 tricks.

Notes : (1) 3♠ and 4♣ were cue bids, showing control of the suits bid. Once North finds clubs guarded, a switch to Blackwood is sensible. (2) At duplicate pairs, top pairs would try 6NT for a better score. (3) The double spade finesse is a good bet (75%) but the strip and throw-in is even better (100%). The latter would not work in 6NT.

Hand 142 : Dealer East : Nil vulnerable

```
        NORTH
        ♠ - - -
        ♡ Q 7 6 5
        ◇ 8 7 4 3
        ♣ J 9 6 3 2

WEST                    EAST
♠ 9 8 7 5 4             ♠ A K 6 3 2
♡ A 4 2                 ♡ K 3
◇ A 6 2                 ◇ K J 5
♣ K 5                   ♣ A 8 4

        SOUTH
        ♠ Q J 10
        ♡ J 10 9 8
        ◇ Q 10 9
        ♣ Q 10 7
```

WEST	NORTH	EAST	SOUTH
		1♠	Pass
3♠	Pass	4NT	Pass
5♡	Pass	6♠	All pass

Lead : ♡J (or ♠Q). Not a minor. North will have very little.

Play : East wins, cashes ♠A, ♠K, plays ♡A and ruffs a heart (strip), then ♣K, ♣A, and ruffs a club (strip). Now a third spade puts South on lead (throw-in). South has to lead a diamond (East thus avoids a losing finesse) or give a ruff-and-discard. 12 tricks.

Notes : (1) West is too strong for a pre-emptive 4♠ raise. (2) With ace or king in every suit, Blackwood is more suitable than cue bids. Missing the queens in all four suits East should forego the grand slam. 4 aces + 4 kings = only 8 tricks. (3) East should not take the diamond finesse (only 50%). The strip and throw-in is far superior and succeeds even though trumps do not break and the diamond finesse loses.

Hand 143 : Dealer South : N-S vulnerable

```
            NORTH
            ♠ 6 4 3
            ♡ Q J 9 8
            ◇ Q 6
            ♣ A Q 5 2
WEST                    EAST
♠ K 7 5                 ♠ J 10 9 8
♡ 6 2                   ♡ 10 3
◇ 9 5 4 3               ◇ J 10 8 7 2
♣ J 10 7 6             ♣ 9 8
            SOUTH
            ♠ A Q 2
            ♡ A K 7 5 4
            ◇ A K
            ♣ K 4 3
```

WEST	NORTH	EAST	SOUTH
			2♣
Pass	2NT	Pass	3♡
Pass	4♣	Pass	4◇
Pass	4♡	Pass	6♡
Pass	Pass	Pass	

Lead : ♣6. Leading through dummy's control is attractive.

Play : Declarer wins, draws trumps, eliminates diamonds and cashes the clubs. When the clubs are not 3-3, South does not ruff the last club. It is used as the throw-in card, South discarding the ♠2 on it. West is on lead and has to lead a spade into South's A-Q or concede a ruff-and-discard (ruff in dummy and discard ♠Q).

Notes : (1) 4♣ is a cue with heart support and denies the ♠A. 4♡ denies any king, so South knows ♠K is missing.
(2) The spade finesse is 50%. The throw-in avoids the finesse.
(3) Note the use of the fourth club as the throw-in card.

Hand 144 : Dealer West : E-W vulnerable

```
            NORTH
            ♠ 8
            ♡ J 9 8 4
            ◇ 8 7 6
            ♣ Q J 10 3 2
WEST                    EAST
♠ J 10 9 7 2            ♠ A K 4 3
♡ A K 5                 ♡ 7 6 3 2
◇ A K Q                 ◇ J 10 2
♣ A K                   ♣ 7 6
            SOUTH
            ♠ Q 6 5
            ♡ Q 10
            ◇ 9 5 4 3
            ♣ 9 8 5 4
```

WEST	NORTH	EAST	SOUTH
2♣	Pass	2NT	Pass
3♠	Pass	4♠	Pass
4NT	Pass	5◇	Pass
6♠	Pass	Pass	Pass

Lead : ♣Q. No problem.

Play : Win ♣A, lead ♠J (in case a foolish opponent covers) but rise with ♠A when North follows low. Cash ♠K, strip clubs and diamonds, cash ♡A and ♡K, then throw South in with the third spade. Out of hearts, South has to concede a ruff-and-discard.

Notes : (1) Even if West found East with A-K-Q in trumps, third round control in hearts is needed to try the grand slam.
(2) Faced with a sure trump loser and a probable heart loser, West must pray that the hand with the last trump is short in hearts. The forced ruff-and-discard is the only hope of eliminating the heart loser. If South has a third heart, the slam could not be made.

Hand 145 : Dealer North : Nil vulnerable

```
            NORTH
            ♠ 8 7 6
            ♡ Q 10 9 8
            ◇ 7 6 5 4
            ♣ 8 5
WEST                    EAST
♠ A 10 5               ♠ K J 3
♡ A K 4                ♡ 7 3 2
◇ 8 3                  ◇ A K 2
♣ A K J 10 3           ♣ Q 7 6 4
            SOUTH
            ♠ Q 9 4 2
            ♡ J 6 5
            ◇ Q J 10 9
            ♣ 9 2
```

WEST	NORTH	EAST	SOUTH
	Pass	1♣	Pass
3♣	Pass	3NT	Pass
4♣	Pass	4◇	Pass
6♣	Pass	Pass	Pass

Lead : ◇Q. No other choice.

Play : East wins, draws trumps, cashes the second diamond, ruffs a diamond in dummy (strip), cashes the ace and king of hearts and exits with the third heart (strip and throw-in simultaneously). Whoever wins the third heart can lead a spade, solving declarer's two-way guess, or concede a ruff-and-discard for the same result.

Notes : (1) 3NT showed a minimum, balanced opening. 4♣ was slam-bound, asking East to cue. West was anxious about diamonds. After hearing 4◇, West could bid the slam confidently.
(2) Note the use of the third heart as the throw-in. 6NT needs the spade finesse. In 6♣, the opposition find the ♠Q for you.

Hand 146 : Dealer East : N-S vulnerable

      NORTH
      ♠ J 10
      ♡ A K 3
      ◇ Q 10 9 5 4 2
      ♣ Q 3

WEST   **EAST**
♠ K 7 6   ♠ 9 8 5
♡ 9 7 5 2   ♡ 10 8 6 4
◇ A   ◇ 3
♣ K 10 6 4 2   ♣ J 9 8 7 5

      SOUTH
      ♠ A Q 4 3 2
      ♡ Q J
      ◇ K J 8 7 6
      ♣ A

WEST	NORTH	EAST	SOUTH
		Pass	1♠
Pass	2◇	Pass	4◇
Pass	4♡	Pass	4♠
Pass	5◇	Pass	6◇
Pass	Pass	Pass	

Lead : ♣7. The suit that was not cue bid is often best.

Play : North plans to use the trump suit as a throw-in to avoid the spade finesse. Win ♣ A, cash ♡ Q, ♡ K, ♡ A, ruff the ♣ Q, then lead a low trump. With diamonds 1-1 and West holding the ace, West must lead a spade into the A-Q or concede a ruff-and-discard.

Notes : (1) North's 4♡ cue, then sign off, shows slam interest without club control. With club control, South bids the slam.
(2) A diamond or a spade lead defeats 6◇. Had West doubled for an unusual lead, East would have led a spade (dummy's first bid suit).
(3) Had diamonds been 2-0, North would need the spade finesse.

Hand 147 : Dealer South : E-W vulnerable

      NORTH
      ♠ K J 9
      ♡ 10 5
      ◇ Q 10 8 3
      ♣ 8 7 6 2

WEST   **EAST**
♠ A Q 8   ♠ 6 3 2
♡ A Q 6 3 2   ♡ K J 9 8 7
◇ 7 2   ◇ A K
♣ K Q J   ♣ A 5 4

      SOUTH
      ♠ 10 7 5 4
      ♡ 4
      ◇ J 9 6 5 4
      ♣ 10 9 3

WEST	NORTH	EAST	SOUTH
			Pass
1♡	Pass	3♡	Pass
3♠	Pass	4♣	Pass
5♣	Pass	6♡	All pass

Lead : ◇ 3. The suit not cue bid. Second choice : A club, the suit cue bid by dummy. The suit cue bid by declarer is not attractive.

Play : West wins, draws trumps, eliminates clubs and diamonds, ending in dummy and leads a spade. If South plays low, West inserts the 8, endplaying North.

Notes : (1) West's 3♠ cue (♠ A) followed by 5♣ is searching for diamond control. With it, East bids the slam.
(2) With A-Q-9 or A-Q-10 in spades, the endplay is unbeatable.
(3) South can defeat the slam by playing ♠ 10 on the spade lead from dummy. West's play is clearly a strip-and-throw-in. To prevent partner being thrown in, you must play high on the throw-in round.

Hand 148 : Dealer West : Nil vulnerable

      NORTH
      ♠ A K 4
      ♡ A J 8 7
      ◇ A 2
      ♣ A Q 4 3

WEST   **EAST**
♠ J 10 6 3   ♠ Q 9 8
♡ 5   ♡ 10 9
◇ J 10 9 8 7   ◇ 6 5 4 3
♣ 9 7 5   ♣ K J 10 2

      SOUTH
      ♠ 7 5 2
      ♡ K Q 6 4 3 2
      ◇ K Q
      ♣ 8 6

WEST	NORTH	EAST	SOUTH
Pass	2NT	Pass	3♡
Pass	3♠	Pass	4NT
Pass	5♣	Pass	6♡
Pass	Pass	Pass	

Lead : ◇ J. A club lead defeats 6♡ but the diamond lead is normal. East could have doubled 5♣ for the lead. A transfer sequence making North declarer avoids the damaging club lead at trick 1.

Play : South wins, draws trumps, cashes the other diamond and plays ace, king and another spade. If East wins ♠ Q, East has to lead a club into the A-Q or concede a ruff-and-discard.

Notes : (1) 3♠ was a cue bid promising heart support. With no cue bid available, South launched into Blackwood.
(2) East defeats the slam by discarding the ♠ Q under the ace or king. East can foresee the endplay if the ♠ Q is retained. To escape an endplay, unblock your high cards and hope partner gets in.

CHAPTER 31

TRUMP CONTROL TECHNIQUES

When you have an 8-card trump fit, you will strike a 4-1 trump break about 25% of the time. With just a 7-card trump fit, the awkward 4-2 break occurs around 50% of the time. These setbacks are frequent enough to justify insurance strategy. Some techniques to protect yourself against the possibility of a bad break are illustrated in the hands that follow.

These are some of the measures that may be possible to keep control of the trump suit :

1. Do not shorten the long trump hand by ruffing. Discard from other suits until dummy can ruff or otherwise control the danger suit.

2. Delay trumps until your second suit is set up.

3. Duck a round of trumps. Instead of cashing your trumps from the top, let one round go in order to keep at least one trump in dummy to ruff their suit.

4. With weak trumps, manoeuvre to draw two rounds of trumps without letting them draw a third round.

PLAY HANDS ON TRUMP CONTROL TECHNIQUES

Hand 149 : Dealer North : N-S vulnerable

> **NORTH**
> ♠ A K 10 7 6 2
> ♡ 4
> ♢ Q 9 4
> ♣ A 8 5

> **WEST**
> ♠ Q 3
> ♡ Q 9 7
> ♢ A 6 5 3
> ♣ K Q J 10

> **EAST**
> ♠ J
> ♡ A K J 8 5
> ♢ K 7 2
> ♣ 9 6 4 3

> **SOUTH**
> ♠ 9 8 5 4
> ♡ 10 6 3 2
> ♢ J 10 8
> ♣ 7 2

WEST	NORTH	EAST	SOUTH
	1♠	2♡	Pass
4♡	Pass	Pass	Pass

Lead : ♠8. Second highest from four rags, like M.U.D.

Play : North plays ♠K and ♠A. East discards a diamond on the second spade. Declarer will draw trumps and knock out the ace of clubs, losing just two spades and the ♣A.

Notes : (1) An opening hand plus support is enough to raise a 2♡ overcall to game.
(2) It would be an error to ruff the second spade and draw trumps. East then has no trumps left and is at the mercy of the spades after knocking out the ♣A. Even if trumps were 3-2, you make just as many tricks by discarding the inevitable diamond loser at trick 2.
(3) A third spade from North is ruffed in dummy.
(4) If East ruffs the second spade and leads a club, North can duck and give South a club ruff if clubs are continued.

Hand 150 : Dealer East : E-W vulnerable

> **NORTH**
> ♠ 7 5 3
> ♡ A 4 2
> ♢ 8 6 3
> ♣ K 7 5 2

> **WEST**
> ♠ J 9 8
> ♡ 10 9 7 5
> ♢ A K J 2
> ♣ 10 8

> **EAST**
> ♠ Q 10 6
> ♡ 8 6
> ♢ Q 10 9 5 4
> ♣ 9 6 3

> **SOUTH**
> ♠ A K 4 2
> ♡ K Q J 3
> ♢ 7
> ♣ A Q J 4

WEST	NORTH	EAST	SOUTH
		Pass	1♣
Pass	1NT	Pass	2♡
Pass	3♣	Pass	3♠
Pass	4♡	All pass	

Lead : ♢ K (or ace). The unbid suit is usually best.

Play : East encourages and another diamond is led. South discards a spade and discards another spade on the third diamond. South wins the next trick, draws trumps and claims.

Notes : (1) 4-4-4-1s are often unwieldy if no strong fit is found. 5♣ is a sensible spot, but 3NT is ludicrous. 4♡ is more attractive at duplicate. North's 4♡ offers South the choice between 4♡ and 5♣.
(2) With only seven trumps, the 4-2 split is the most common. If South ruffs the second diamond, shortening the long trump hand could lose control of the trump suit. Discarding the spade losers keeps control until dummy can take the ruff.

Hand 151 : Dealer South : Both vulnerable

NORTH
- ♠ A 6 4 3
- ♡ 5
- ◇ Q J 6
- ♣ A 8 5 4 2

WEST
- ♠ J 8 7 5
- ♡ K 10 9 7
- ◇ 9 8 5 4
- ♣ 6

EAST
- ♠ K Q 10 9
- ♡ Q 8 3
- ◇ 7 2
- ♣ J 10 9 3

SOUTH
- ♠ 2
- ♡ A J 6 4 2
- ◇ A K 10 3
- ♣ K Q 7

WEST	NORTH	EAST	SOUTH
			1♡
Pass	2♣	Pass	2◇
Pass	2♠	Pass	4♣
Pass	5♣	All pass	

Lead : ♠K. The K-Q-10 holding is the most attractive.

Play: North ducks the first spade. A spade continuation is ruffed in dummy, followed by ♣K, ♣Q, a diamond to hand and ♣A. The other spade loser is discarded on the diamonds. The play is similar, including the spade ruff, on a diamond or a club switch. A heart switch is taken by the ace, then ♣K, ♣Q, diamond to hand, spade ruff, diamond to hand, ace *and another club*.

Notes: (1) 6♣ is a good contract, succeeding if clubs are 3-2 (ruff a spade and draw trumps). North might have done more over 4♣.
(2) If North wins ♠A and draws trumps or ruffs a spade first, East will be able to take three tricks in the black suits. East can ruff and continue spades before North can obtain a discard on the diamonds.

Hand 152 : Dealer West : Nil vulnerable

NORTH
- ♠ J 7 6 4
- ♡ A K Q 7
- ◇ 8 4
- ♣ K 8 4

WEST
- ♠ A K Q 5 3
- ♡ 8 3
- ◇ K 5
- ♣ A J 6 3

EAST
- ♠ 10 9
- ♡ J 4 2
- ◇ A Q J 6 2
- ♣ Q 7 2

SOUTH
- ♠ 8 2
- ♡ 10 9 6 5
- ◇ 10 9 7 3
- ♣ 10 9 5

WEST	NORTH	EAST	SOUTH
1♠	Pass	2◇	Pass
3♣	Pass	3♡	Pass
3♠	Pass	4♠	All pass

Lead : ♡K (or ace). What else?

Play: North plays three rounds of hearts. West ruffs. West continues with a low spade. North wins but another heart can be ruffed in dummy. On any other switch, West wins, draws all the trumps and discards the club losers on the diamonds.

Notes: (1) East's 3♡, fourth suit, asks for a stopper for no-trumps. 3NT is not a good spot but succeeds on the lucky 4-4 heart break.
(2) West must ruff the third heart or lose three hearts and a spade.
(3) By ducking the first round of trumps, declarer retains trump control as dummy still has a trump to deal with a fourth heart. You never know, North might even duck the trump!
(4) West loses trump control by ruffing and cashing ♠A-K-Q.

Hand 153 : Dealer North : E-W vulnerable

NORTH
- ♠ A 7 6 3
- ♡ A 6 5 3
- ◇ 6 2
- ♣ 8 6 4

WEST
- ♠ K Q 9
- ♡ Q 10 4
- ◇ J 9 8 7 4
- ♣ J 10

EAST
- ♠ J 10
- ♡ J 9 8 7
- ◇ Q 10
- ♣ Q 9 7 5 2

SOUTH
- ♠ 8 5 4 2
- ♡ K 2
- ◇ A K 5 3
- ♣ A K 3

WEST	NORTH	EAST	SOUTH
	Pass	Pass	1NT
Pass	2♣	Pass	2♠
Pass	3♠	Pass	4♠
Pass	Pass	Pass	

Lead : ♣J. Two touching honors doubleton is a sound start. It is not appealing to lead a major after they have used Stayman.

Play: South wins and ducks a trump. Any return is won and the ♠A is cashed. The last trump is left out and declarer cashes all the winners and cross ruffs the red suits. Ten tricks.

Notes: (1) At best there are eight tricks in no-trumps. The 4-4 fit generates two extra tricks in spades.
(2) South must not lead ace and another spade. West could draw a third round of trumps leaving declarer a trick short.
(3) It would be an error to cross ruff before drawing two rounds of trumps. The defender with the two spades might overruff.

Hand 154 : Dealer East : Both vulnerable

NORTH
- ♠ 8 3
- ♡ Q J 9 7
- ◇ 9 8 6 4 3 2
- ♣ A

WEST
- ♠ A 5 4
- ♡ A K 4 3
- ◇ 7
- ♣ J 7 5 4 2

EAST
- ♠ 7 6
- ♡ 8 6 5 2
- ◇ A K Q
- ♣ K Q 10 6

SOUTH
- ♠ K Q J 10 9 2
- ♡ 10
- ◇ J 10 5
- ♣ 9 8 3

WEST	NORTH	EAST	SOUTH
		1♣	1♠
Double	Pass	2♡	Pass
4♡	Pass	Pass	Pass

Lead : ♠K. Anything else is fanciful.

Play : Declarer wins, plays one top trump only and then cashes the diamonds discarding two spade losers from dummy. Still leaving the trumps alone, declarer leads clubs to knock out the ♣A. Declarer wins any return, cashes the other top trump and then runs the clubs. North can ruff with the master trumps but declarer loses just two trumps and the ace of clubs.

Notes : (1) West's negative double promises four hearts.
(2) A key strategy in trump control is to set up the second suit before playing off the top trumps. If East plays ♡ A-K before clubs, North will draw declarer's trumps when in with the ♣A. If trumps are 3-2, the contract still succeeds by playing clubs first.

Hand 155 : Dealer South : Nil vulnerable

NORTH
- ♠ A K J 7 6
- ♡ 8 3
- ◇ A 4
- ♣ 9 8 7 2

WEST
- ♠ 8 5 4 2
- ♡ A K Q 10 4
- ◇ 8
- ♣ Q 6 4

EAST
- ♠ 10 3
- ♡ 7 5 2
- ◇ Q J 7 6 5 3
- ♣ J 10

SOUTH
- ♠ Q 9
- ♡ J 9 6
- ◇ K 10 9 2
- ♣ A K 5 3

WEST	NORTH	EAST	SOUTH
			1◇
1♡	1♠	Pass	2♣
Pass	2♡	Pass	2♠
Pass	4♠	All pass	

Lead : ♡5. Partner's suit. Middle from three rags.

Play : West plays ♡ Q, ♡ K and ♡ A. North ruffs and continues with ace, king and a third club, won by West. North wins a diamond or trump switch and draws trumps. On a heart return, the ruff is taken in dummy, overruffing East if necessary. Dummy's trump is cashed and a diamond to hand allows trumps to be drawn.

Notes : (1) With 4-4 in the minors, the 1◇ opening is preferred, as it allows a 2♣ rebid if interference makes 1NT unattractive.
(2) Over North's 2♡, South has a tough rebid. 2♠ is the least evil.
(3) If North plays two or more trumps after ruffing the heart, 4♠ can be beaten. Set up the club winner and let dummy take the ruff.

Hand 156 : Dealer West : N-S vulnerable

NORTH
- ♠ J 10 8 7 5
- ♡ 3
- ◇ K J 10
- ♣ Q 10 9 2

WEST
- ♠ 2
- ♡ A K J 10 8 2
- ◇ A 7 5 2
- ♣ K 7

EAST
- ♠ K 9 3
- ♡ Q 5
- ◇ 8 6 4 3
- ♣ A 8 5 4

SOUTH
- ♠ A Q 6 4
- ♡ 9 7 6 4
- ◇ Q 9
- ♣ J 6 3

WEST	NORTH	EAST	SOUTH
1♡	Pass	1NT	Pass
3♡	Pass	4♡	All pass

Lead : ♠J. Top of near sequence is superior to tenace leads.

Play : Declarer ducks in dummy, South encourages with the 6 and North plays a second spade. West ruffs and continues with ace and another diamond. A third spade is ruffed by West and another diamond is led, setting up the fourth round. On a club or trump switch, West wins and draws trumps, making 6 hearts, 2 diamonds and 2 clubs. If a fourth spade is led, dummy ruffs and declarer makes the rest after drawing trumps.

Notes : (1) West has 9 top winners and needs to establish an extra trick in diamonds. Even if trumps were 3-2, it would not hurt to establish the diamond trick before tackling trumps.
(2) If West plays trumps before diamonds, 4♡ can be defeated. Set up the side winner first and let dummy take the ruff.

CHAPTER 32

COUNTING & DISCOVERY PLAYS

Declarer has a lot of counting to do. You have to count tricks, count points and count cards. You start by counting your winners and in a trump contract, count the losers as well. You count the tricks you are bound to lose and the tricks which you might lose (if a finesse fails or if a bad break occurs). In addition, you count the high card points of each opponent and relate that to their bidding (or lack of bidding). Finding the location of the missing high cards is covered in the chapters on inferences and card reading.

However, the main aspect of counting is keeping track of the cards they play and gradually building up a picture of the unseen hands. It is this ability to reconstruct the opponents' hands that is the hallmark of the talented declarer.

There is no single area of card play that brings with it so many rewards as hand construction, the counting out of the enemy hands. It is second nature to the expert and it is the dividing line between mere competence and expert technique.

Counting is not beyond any player but regrettably the vast majority of players do not bother. Failing to count, they put contracts on the floor which they could have made easily. It is true that counting is a chore but no one said that bridge was meant to be easy. The fruits of labour are there to be enjoyed, but only by the labourer, not by the idler.

If you are not already counting regularly, make a resolution now that you will make a start and attempt to count out their hands. Start with just a few hands each session, then extend that number each time you play until you are counting out every hand. Once you make that start, the effort will become less and less and when you start doing it regularly, almost without effort, you will be amazed at the store of knowledge that is now at your fingertips. You will wonder how you ever managed before.

Counting begins in the auction. If you do not wake up until the opening lead, you have already missed a valuable source of information. Did they open the bidding? A suit opening will include some minimum length in that suit. Did they open 1NT? The possible hand patterns for 1NT are very limited. A no-trump opener who turns up with a 5-card suit will almost always have a 5-3-3-2 pattern.

The opening lead is the next important clue. You can almost always derive some information about suit length from the lead. Is the lead fourth-highest? Can you tell how many cards the leader had? If so, you can work out how many cards third hand will hold. Is the lead a doubleton or a singleton? Again, you can calculate the number of cards held by each opponent.

The clearest indication occurs during the play when an opponent shows out in a suit. The moment this occurs, STOP AND COUNT. Work out the number of cards with which that player started and hence the number of cards originally in the other hand. The good news is that the sums are simple. Everything adds up to 13. It will help if you make a mental note at the start of the hand of the number of cards held by you and dummy together in each suit. Then, as soon as someone shows out, make another mental note of the number of cards thus revealed in each hand.

Once you have been able to count out three suits, the fourth suit holding is obvious. Just deduct from 13 again. The thinking runs along lines like "West must have had five spades for the opening bid. He has turned up with four diamonds and three clubs, so he cannot hold more than one heart."

Sometimes you will be able obtain an absolute count, knowing the exact number of cards originally held in each suit. On other occasions, you will obtain only an approximate count but even that may be enough on which to base your play. Sometimes, knowing the number of cards held by an opponent may make the play of a suit an absolute certainty:

K 10 5 2

  ?   **?????**

A J 4

You need three tricks from this suit and cannot afford to lose a trick. You have been able to count that West began with a singleton and East began with five cards in the suit. There are no other clues and you now have to tackle this suit. How do you play?

Obvious, isn't it? You cash the king which draws West's only card and finesse the jack on the next round. If your count is right, West cannot hold a second card and the finesse *must* succeed.

Similarly :

K 5 3

??   ????

A Q 10 2

You need four tricks from this suit. You have been able to count West for a doubleton and East for four cards in the suit. How do you play it?

Easy, right? You cash the ace and lead to the king which draws West's two cards. If your count is right, West cannot hold any more cards in this suit and the finesse of the 10 on the next round *must* succeed.

On many occasions, knowing the count will only improve your chance of success without guaranteeing it. For example :

K 10 5 2

??   ????

A J 4

You need three tricks from this suit and cannot afford to lose a trick. You have counted West for a doubleton and East for four cards. There are no other clues. How do you tackle this suit?

The principle is clear : *When missing one vital card in a suit, play the opponent who is known to hold more cards in the suit to hold the critical missing card.* As East has four cards and West two, play East for the queen. Cash the king, then finesse the jack. If West were the one known to have started with four cards, you would cash the ace, then finesse the 10. The odds of success are exactly the same as the number of cards held by each opponent, 4-2 or 2-1 in your favour. You may lose to a doubleton queen, but that occurs only ⅓ of the time. The finesse will succeed ⅔ of the time if your count is correct.

K 10 3

????   ??

A Q 9 2

You need four tricks from this suit and know that West began with four cards and East with a doubleton. With no other clues, how do you play this suit?

As long as your count is correct, the best chance is to cash the ace and then lead to the 10. The odds are 4-2 (2-1) that this finesse will work. Playing ace and king will succeed only ⅓ of the time.

Knowing the number of cards held by each opponent can allow you to plan the play perfectly.

K 10 3

?   ?

A 9 4 2

Needing three tricks, how do you handle this suit?

If you know the suit is split 3-3, duck one round and cash the rest later. If you know West has two and East has four, lead low to the 10 first. Later cash the king, drawing West's last card and play to the 9 next. If your count is right, the 9 *must* win. If West has four and East has two, there is no sure way to guarantee three tricks. King and ace will cater for honor-doubleton with East. Ace and low to the 10 plays West to have started with Q-J-x-x.

Against some opponents you can use their signals to deduce the number of cards held. Opponents who signal count relentlessly (whether standard count or reverse count) give away valuable information. Of course, most opponents are not constantly helpful. You can gradually build up a dossier of those whose signals are reliable and those who cannot be trusted. The better your opponents, the less inclined they will be to help you through their signalling.

Other clues arise during the play. A player's first discard is often from a 5-card suit. Where dummy has a 4-card suit, a player discarding from that suit is likely to hold five cards or more, or three, but not four, because of the 'keep-length-with-dummy' rule.

Even with all the information from the bidding and early play, you will usually not have enough knowledge about the division of the critical suits. Most of the time you will have to ferret out the extra details, you will play to discover how the cards lie. Sometimes you will need to play off irrelevant suits to see how they have divided. Sometimes you may play off only one or two rounds of an irrelevant suit to check the number of cards held in that suit by one opponent. On other occasions, you will run your trumps or other long suit and watch their discards diligently. The basis of many squeezes and endplays is no more than keeping a close watch of their discards.

Once you have started to count out a hand and you know the division of one or two suits, the best approach is to work out the precise original pattern of just one opponent. Once you have one opponent's pattern worked out, it is straightforward to deduce the original pattern of the other hand (as long as you remember the number of cards held by you and dummy in each suit).

Obviously you could work on either opponent but it is easiest is to concentrate on the player who turns up with greater length in the early suits. If one opponent has shown up with a 6-card suit and the other with a doubleton, focus on the pattern of the player with the 6-card suit, as that hand has fewer gaps.

PLAY HANDS ON COUNTING AND DISCOVERY

Hand 157 : Dealer North : Both vulnerable

NORTH
♠ 7 3
♡ 10 9 8 6 5
♢ 4
♣ 10 8 5 3 2

WEST
♠ J 5 4
♡ K J 2
♢ A 9 5 2
♣ A K J

EAST
♠ A K Q
♡ A Q 4
♢ K Q 10 3
♣ Q 7 6

SOUTH
♠ 10 9 8 6 2
♡ 7 3
♢ J 8 7 6
♣ 9 4

WEST	NORTH	EAST	SOUTH
	Pass	2NT	Pass
7NT	Pass	Pass	Pass

Lead : ♠ 10. The sequence is the obvious lead. Against a grand slam, the opening lead should be as safe as possible and one would not lead away from any honor combination.

Play : The hands are the dreaded 'mirror shape', exactly the same number of cards in each suit in both hands. If the fourth diamond in either hand were in any other suit, there would be 13 top tricks. As it is, there are 12 tricks on top. If the diamonds divide 3-2, there is no problem. However if either player has J-x-x-x in diamonds, it is vital to discover which player has the four, so that the jack can be trapped. Declarer wins the lead and cashes two more spades, then cashes the hearts and the clubs. Next the ♢ K-Q are played, followed by the finesse of the 9 of diamonds, making 13 tricks.

Notes : (1) Declarer fails if the ♢ A is cashed first.
(2) It would be an error to try the diamonds early in the play. It would then be a matter of luck whether you played ♢ K-Q first or the ♢ A early on. One works, the other fails. Luck is not needed, counting is.
(3) By playing off the other suits, declarer discovers the count in each suit. North shows out on the third spade, so South began with five spades. South follows to two hearts, then shows out. South follows to two clubs, then shows out. With 5 spades, 2 hearts, 2 clubs, South must have four diamonds. Therefore ♢ K-Q first. If you counted the North hand, the same result would follow : 5 hearts, 5 clubs, 2 spades, so only one diamond.
(4) Even if the count is not exact, it may not matter. Suppose South turns up with five spades and both opponents follow to three rounds of hearts and clubs. As South is known to have started with 5-3-3 in the played suits, South cannot hold four diamonds. Therefore, ♢ K and a diamond to the ace will cater for J-x-x-x with North.

Hand 158 : Dealer East : Nil vulnerable

NORTH
♠ Q J 5
♡ 10 5 4
♢ 9
♣ A K J 9 3 2

WEST
♠ A K
♡ K Q J 3 2
♢ A 10 5
♣ Q 8 5

EAST
♠ 7 6 2
♡ A 9 8 6
♢ K J 3
♣ 7 6 4

SOUTH
♠ 10 9 8 4 3
♡ 7
♢ Q 8 7 6 4 2
♣ 10

WEST	NORTH	EAST	SOUTH
		Pass	Pass
1♡	2♣	2♡	Pass
4♡	Pass	Pass	Pass

Lead : ♣ K (or ace). Easily the best choice.

Play : North continues with the second top club and gives South a club ruff at trick 3. South switches to the 10 of spades at trick 4. Having lost three tricks, declarer needs to pick up the queen of diamonds. Declarer draws trumps in three rounds, then cashes the second spade. A trump to dummy is followed by a third spade, ruffed by declarer. Declarer can now claim the contract, playing a diamond to the king and finessing against South for the queen.

Notes : (1) West makes easily on a diamond lead or a diamond switch at trick 2. Even a major suit lead makes it easy : win the lead, cash ♡ K-Q, ♠ A-K, ♡ A, ruff a spade and exit with a club, forcing the opponents to locate the ♢ Q or give a ruff-and-discard.
(2) The diamond position may seem to be a 50-50 guess. Playing the bidder to hold the ♢ Q is logical but that analysis is superficial. If nothing further comes to light, you can still play North for the ♢ Q later. However, after the club ruff, North is known to have started with 6 clubs. When trumps are drawn, North follows three times, so North has 6 clubs-3 hearts. Cashing the spades and ruffing the third spade is a discovery play. North turns up with 3 spades as well, therefore at most one diamond. The diamond play is now not a 50-50 guess but an absolute certainty. Even if North turned up with only 2 spades and diamonds were known to be 2 with North and 5 with South, the odds strongly favor playing for the queen with South, the long hand.

Hand 159 : Dealer South : N-S vulnerable

NORTH
♠ K Q J 9
♡ 9 6
♢ A 6 4
♣ K 9 5 2

WEST
♠ 6 2
♡ J 10
♢ Q J 10 9 3
♣ Q J 8 7

EAST
♠ 10 8 4
♡ A K 7 5 3 2
♢ 8 5
♣ 6 3

SOUTH
♠ A 7 5 3
♡ Q 8 4
♢ K 7 2
♣ A 10 4

WEST	NORTH	EAST	SOUTH
			1♣
Pass	1♠	Pass	2♠
Pass	4♠	All pass	

Lead : ♡K (or ace). Nothing else appeals.

Play : West follows with the jack of hearts. East continues with the other top heart and a third heart. West ruffs the queen and North overruffs. North continues with the K-Q-J of spades, drawing trumps, followed by a club to dummy's 10. West wins and exits with the queen of diamonds. Declarer cashes the top diamonds, followed by the ♣A and a club to the 9. When this (marked) finesse works, declarer cashes the ♣K and discards the diamond loser.

Notes : (1) The 1♠ response is far superior to 2NT or 3♣. Even at this vulnerability, East is not worth a 2♡ overcall. If East did bid 2♡, South would still bid 2♠ and if West made a competitive double (takeout), North would still bid 4♠ to end the auction.

(2) Declarer needs three club tricks to dispose of a diamond loser. You could duck a club and hope for a 3-3 break, cash ♣A, ♣K and hope clubs are 3-3 or an honor drops, but after the early play, the recommended line is almost a certainty. At trick 3, East has shown up with 6 hearts. When trumps are drawn, East is known to have started with 3 spades-6 hearts. It is unlikely that East's remaining four cards are 4 clubs and 0 diamonds. If not, you can guarantee success. A club to the 10 fetches an honor and when the diamond comes back, you cash both diamonds to discover the diamonds held by East. When East follows to both diamonds, East is 3 spades-6 hearts-2 diamonds and cannot hold three clubs. Therefore, ♣A and finesse the ♣9 is bound to work. Had East turned up with only one diamond, East would be marked with a 3-6-1-3 pattern and clubs would be known to be 3-3. Note that playing ♣A-K first fails on the actual hand.
(3) If ♣10 and ♣7 were interchanged, ducking a club first is still best. If East follows to two diamonds, so that clubs are not 3-3, the ♠A is cashed and this would squeeze West in clubs and diamonds if East is 2-2 in the minors.

Hand 160 : Dealer West : E-W vulnerable

NORTH
♠ A 3 2
♡ J 5 3
♢ A 6 4 2
♣ K J 9

WEST
♠ 10
♡ A 10 9 8 7
♢ Q 10 7 5 3
♣ 10 2

EAST
♠ 7 6
♡ Q 6 4
♢ 9 8
♣ A Q 8 6 5 4

SOUTH
♠ K Q J 9 8 5 4
♡ K 2
♢ K J
♣ 7 3

WEST	NORTH	EAST	SOUTH
Pass	1♢	Pass	1♠
Pass	1NT	Pass	4♠
Pass	Pass	Pass	

Lead : ♣10. Not a great choice, but everything else seems worse. Diamonds were bid by dummy, a singleton trump is usually a poor choice and to lead from the ♡A is worse than the others.

Play : East wins and cashes another club, followed by a third club. South ruffs high and draws trumps with the king and ace. Declarer continues by playing all the trumps, keeping track of West's discards. With four cards to go, South has ♡K-2 and ♢K-J. No matter which cards West retains, South loses only one more trick.

Notes : (1) West's ♣10 is clearly a singleton or top of a doubleton, so that East began with at least A-Q-x-x-x-x in clubs. East's failure to overcall marks the ♡A almost certainly with West and the heart finesse will therefore fail.

(2) As East shows up with eight black cards and West with three black cards, West is bound to have length in the red suits. With the ♡A and five or more diamonds West can be squeezed, the only hope with the ♡A wrong.
(3) Keep ♢A-6-4-2 in dummy and watch West's discards closely. At the end, you have to decide which four cards West has left. If West comes down to ♡A-x and two diamonds, king of diamonds and a diamond to the ace brings in all the diamonds. However, if West keeps three diamonds and bares the ♡A, play a low heart from hand, dropping the ace and setting up the king. There is no certainty here — you have to pick the ending. However, what joy and satisfaction when you do pick the position! Counting makes for happy bridging.

REVISION TEST ON PART 4

The material in Chapters 25-32 will help you answer these questions. If you experience difficulty in producing the correct answers, it will pay you to read these chapters again.

A. What is the best way to play each of these combinations to make the maximum number of tricks? You have no problems with entries.

1.	K Q 9 3	2.	K Q 9 2	3.	K Q 8 2
	A 8 6 5 2		J 8 7 4 3		J 7 6 4 3

4.	Void	5.	Void	6.	6
	A J 10 7 5 4 3		A Q 10 9 4 3 2		K Q 10 7 4 3

7.	A K J 8 7 4	8.	A K J 8 7 4 3	9.	A K J 10 7 4
	6 3		6		6 3

B. In each of these layouts, declarer South leads the ace and East drops the jack. On the next round, South leads the 3 and West plays the 8. Which card should declarer play from dummy?

1.	K 10 5 2	2.	Q 9 4 3
	A 7 6 4 3		A 6 5 2

C.

WEST	EAST
♠ K J 4	♠ 7 3
♡ K 7 3 2	♡ A Q 6
◊ K 10	◊ A Q 9 5 3 2
♣ A 9 8 4	♣ 7 6

WEST	EAST
	1◊
1♡	2◊
3NT	Pass

North leads the ♠5 and South plays the queen. Do you win this or duck? If you win it, how do you continue? Which cards will you play at tricks 2 and 3?

D.

WEST	EAST
♠ 6 3	♠ A Q 4
♡ A 10 9 4 2	♡ K Q J
◊ A K J 5 3	◊ Q 10 8
♣ 9	♣ Q 4 3 2

WEST	EAST
	1NT
3♡	4♡
4NT	5◊
6♡	Pass

North leads the ♣J : 2 − 8 − 9. North continues with the ♣10 : 3 − 5 − ruff. How should West plan the play?

E.

WEST	EAST
♠ Q 10 8	♠ A K J 5 3
♡ Q 6 5 3	♡ A 7
◊ K 4 2	◊ A 8 7
♣ A K Q	♣ 6 5 2

After a transfer sequence, West is in 6♠. North leads ◊ Q. You win the ace and draw trumps in three rounds. When you play ♡ A and another heart, South plays the 10 on the second round. How do you play?

F.

WEST	EAST
♠ A Q 7 6 4	♠ K 9 8 5 2
♡ A 5	♡ K 8
◊ A K 3	◊ 8 5 2
♣ Q 7 4	♣ J 9 2

After 1♠ : 2♠, 4♠, North leads the queen of diamonds. How should West plan the play?

G.

WEST	EAST
♠ K Q J 7	♠ A 10 4
♡ 7	♡ J 5 2
◊ A 8 3	◊ 9 7 6 2
♣ K 10 9 6 2	♣ A Q J

You are West in 4♠. You have bid well to avoid a foolish 3NT and a doomed 5♣ where there are three losers. After 1♣ : 1◊, 1♠, East tried 2♡, fourth suit, and opted for the 4–3 spade fit when West rebid 3◊. However, your bidding will be worth naught if your play is not just as delicate. North starts with the king and queen of hearts. How should West plan the play?

H.

WEST	EAST
♠ K Q J 2	♠ A 10 3
♡ K 8 2	♡ A Q
◊ A J 2	◊ K 10 5 3
♣ Q 9 6	♣ A K 10 3

You, West, opened 1NT and because you played the previous hand so well, partner bid a dashing 7NT. North leads ♡J. You win and cash a second heart, North playing the 10. All follow to three rounds of spades. On the fourth spade North discards a diamond and South a heart. When you cash ♡K, North discards another diamond. You play A-K of diamonds and South discards a heart on the second round. Do you know enough yet? You continue with ♣A and a club to the queen, all following. The jack has not appeared and when you lead a third club, North plays the 8. Do you finesse the 10 or play the K (for a 3-3 break)?

ANSWERS TO EXERCISES AND QUIZZES

Page 4. A. 1.6 2.9 3.8 4.3 5.8 6.5 7.10
8.10 9.10 10.2 11. J 12. J 13. J 14.8 15.4
16.5 17.2 18. J 19. J 20. J 21. Q 22. Q 23. Q
24. Q 25. Q 26.4 27.8 28.2 29.10 30.3 31. K
32. K 33. K 34.2 35. J 36.8 37.10 38. K 39.8
40. 4 41. A if leading K from A-K-x; K if leading A
from A-K-x 42. A 43. A 44.3 45.7 46.2 47.10
48. K or A, according to partnership agreement
49. K or A; see 41. & 48 50. J.

B. All the answers are the same for a trump contract
except for numbers 44, 45, 46, 47 and 50 where the
ace would be led. In a trump contract, do not lead a
low card at trick 1 from a suit where you have the ace.

C. 1. The Q lead is a singleton or a doubleton (not top
of sequence as the jack is in dummy). 2. The 8 lead
is a singleton or a doubleton. West **has** led top card.
East can see every higher card except the 10. There
is no combination headed by 10-8 where the 8 is led.
3. The 7 lead is a singleton or a doubleton. East can
account for every higher card except the queen.
There is no combination headed by Q-7 where the 7
is the right lead. 4. The 10 lead is a singleton or a
doubleton. As East has the 9, the 10 cannot be part
of a sequence lead. The only higher cards missing are
the Q and J. There is no combination of J-10 where
the 10 is led and no Q-10 combination where the 10
is led unless holding the 9 also. 5. The 2 lead is a
singleton (any lead could be a singleton) or from Q-x-x
or Q-x-x-x. The 2 is bottom card and if not a singleton,
bottom card is led only when holding an honor card
in the suit. East can see every honor other than the
queen. Importantly, East can win the lead and give
West the lead by playing a low card on the next round
of this suit. 6. The 4 lead is a singleton. With the 3
and 2 visible, East can tell that the 4 is bottom card lead.
If not a singleton, bottom card lead promises an honor,
but East can see all the honors. Therefore the lead
must be a singleton. The missing cards are the 9
and 6. The 4 is not the correct card from 9-4, 6-4 or
9-6-4. If declarer finesses the queen in a trump
contract, East can win and give West a ruff.

Page 9 : **A.** 1.6 2.3 3.8 4.6 — top of sequence
applies only if the sequence includes an honor card.
5. 5 6. 2 — the 10 is an honor; no M.U.D. when
holding an honor. 7. 10 8. 10 9. 5 10. 4 11. 4
12.7 13.2 14. J 15. J 16.3 17.4 18.10 19.2
20. Q 21.5 22. Q 23. Q 24.6 25.7 26.2 27.7
28.3 29.10 30.5 31.4 32. J 33.5 34. K 35. K
36.4 37.5 38.10 39.6 40. J 41.10 42. Q 43.4
44.3 45.8 46. A (recommended) or K 47. A (or K)
48. 7 49. 8 50. 10

B. All the leads are the same in a trump contract
except for 33 (lead the K) and 36, 37, 38, 39, 40, 41,
42, 43, 44, 45, 46, 47, 48, 49 and 50, where the ace is
led. In a trump contract, do not lead low at trick 1
from a suit headed by the ace. Prefer not to lead
such a suit at all, but if you must lead the suit, start
with the ace at trick 1.

Page 15 : **A.** 1.7 2. J 3.10 4.2 5.10 6. Q
B. 1. (i) ♢ J (ii) a. ♠5 b. ♡8 2. (i) ♠Q (ii) a. ♢2
b. ♢2 (North's 2♣ Stayman implies four spades)
3. (i) ♡5 (ii) a. ♠3 b. ♠3 — do not lead from an
honor card against 6NT or against a grand slam.
4. (i) ♠10 (ii) a. ♡3 b. ♣4 — if the defenders have
not bid, the double of 3NT asks for dummy's first suit.
5. (i) ♠ J (ii) a. ♠ J — lead your own good suit if
you have the entries b. ♢ A — after a pre-empt and
3NT, prefer a strong short suit to a weak long suit.

Page 24 : 1. (i) ♡7 (ii) a. ♡ J — a dangerous lead
but the others are worse still b. ♡ J — partner's suit
2. (i) ♢ 3 — not attractive but the others are riskier.
(ii) a. ♣A — partner is very likely to be short in clubs.
b. ♢3 — unbid suit 3. (i) ♡9 (ii) a. ♢5 b. ♣4
4. (i) ♢2 (ii) a. ♡3 b. ♡3 5. (i) ♣K (ii) a. ♢2
b. ♣K 6. (i) ♠8 or ♣7 (ii) a. ♢ 3 — when dummy
has a long suit, lead an unbid suit b. ♠8 — when
you are strong in declarer's other suit, lead a trump.
7. (i) ♡7 (ii) a. ♢ 2 — try to build up a second trick.
b. ♢ 2 — planning to give partner a diamond ruff.
8. (i) ♢ Q (ii) a. ♡8 — partner's double of 5♡ asks
for a heart lead b. ♣4 — partner's slam double
asks for an unusual lead, preferably dummy's first suit.

Page 27 : **(a)** 1. Declarer 2. Declarer 3. Declarer
(b) 1. Declarer 2. Declarer **(c)** Declarer **(d)** Declarer
Page 29 : 1. 10 2. J 3. Normally the 10. The
ace could be correct in a trump contract. 4. 10,
usually 5. 9, usually 6. 10, usually 7. 8
8. 9, usually 9. 9 10. 6, cheapest of equals.
Page 29 : **1.a.** 1. Declarer 2. Declarer 3. Partner
1.b. 1. Declarer 2. Declarer **1.c.** 1,2,3, Declarer
2.a. No, South began with A-Q-J-8. **2.b.** Yes, it is
safe. The ace is with declarer but partner has the jack.
2.c. Yes. Partner has the jack.
Page 33 : 1. No. 2. No. If South started with
10-9-7-6-4-3-2, to cover the 10 costs a trick. 3. No
4. No 5. No In each case, partner is short in spades.
Page 37 : **A.** 1.8 2.4 — East prefers a club switch.
3. 7 — East does not want a switch. Happy enough
to have hearts continued, East should encourage.
4. 2 — East would rather a switch (to clubs) than to
have diamonds continued 5. 6 — East wants spades
continued to ruff the third round 6. 3 — East has

no interest in clubs being continued. There is no prospect of a club ruff as declarer is bound to lead trumps next.   7. ◇7 — East's ♣5, the lowest, shows the entry is in the lowest suit.   8. ◇5 — East's ♡2 asks for a switch. As West is looking at the ♣K, East cannot want a switch to clubs.   9.♣2 — East's ♡7 was the lowest heart possible. East therefore wants a switch. When switching, usually avoid dummy's long suit. East has   ♠ 54   ♡ KQJ987   ◇ K5   ♣ KQ7. East can see there is no point having hearts continued if West has a second heart.

B. 1. 4   2. 8   3. 2   4. 7   5. 3   6. 8   7. ◇7   8.♡A 9. ♡5

Page 41 :   A. 1. ♡2   2. ♣9   3. ♠7 — ruff and cash the ♣ A. Do not rely on partner to understand and obey a signal if you can defeat the contract on your own.   4. ♣3 and ◇2 — discourage clubs and diamonds so that East will play a fourth heart. 5. ♣9 — West is desperate for a club switch. A third diamond from East will be disastrous if South holds ♠ A K Q J x x   ♡ K x   ◇ x x x   ♣ K x or similar.   6.♣4 — West wants a third diamond this time in order to score the ♠J. A club switch at trick 3 would give South the contract this time if South had ♠ A K Q x x x   ♡ x x   ◇ x x x   ♣ K Q.

B.   1. ♡10   2. ♣9   3. ♠7 — do not signal if you can defeat the contract yourself without cost. 4.♣10 and ◇8   5.♣9   6.♡10, asking for a diamond.

Page 45 :   1. Lead a diamond. East's *two* of clubs was a suit preference signal for the low suit, diamonds. East has   ♠ 9   ♡ KJ1086   ◇ AKJ   ♣ 9852. On a heart return, declarer succeeds.   2. East should overtake with the ♣Q and switch to diamonds. Win the ♠ A and lead a low club. East plans to take ♣Q, ♠ A, West's hoped-for ♣10 and a diamond ruff. 3. ◇ Q. East expects West to lead a low diamond next to East's 10. East switches to clubs, hoping West has A-Q.

Page 48 Revision Test :   A. 1. 3   2. 10   3. 8 4.6   5.4   6.2   7.10   8.3   9.6   10. Q 11. 4   12. J   13. 7   14. 3   15. 3.

B. Changes: 3. A   6. K   11. K or A   14. A

C. a. ♡Q   b. ◇3. North has five hearts. c. ♡Q. North has only four hearts.

D. a. ♡6. Do not lead from an honor against a grand slam.   b. ♡6. Everything else is risky and North's rejection of no-trumps implies ruffing values. c. ♡6. Do not lead from an honor against 6NT.

E.   1. Declarer   2. Partner   3. Declarer.

F. 1.Q   2.J   3.Q   4.J   5.A   6.A   7.K 8.6   9.9   10.K   11.A   12.K   13.A   14.K 15.Q   16.10   17.J   18.10   19.9   20.J. **G.**   1.10   2. K   3.10   4.9   5.6   6. A 7. J   8.9   9. K   10. J   11. 10   12. 9   13. 8 14. 10   15. 8   16. 6

H.   1. A   2. K   3. 8   4. K   5. 9. **I.**   1. 10, usually   2. Q   3. 9   4. 9, usually. **J.**   Any card except the jack. South must have the ace. If East plays the jack, declarer has five tricks. If East plays low, declarer has at most four tricks from this suit. As it would not make sense for East to encourage this suit (how can East want it continued?), East uses the 2 or the 6 as a suit preference signal.

Page 54 :   A. 1. K first, then A and Q.   2. A first, then Q, then over to the K   3. 10 first   4. Q first 5. K first, then J   6. J first.

B. 1. J, then 10   2. K, then Q   3. Q, then J   4. J first 5. K, then 10   6. 10 first   7. Q first   8. Q, then 10 9. K, then J

C.   1. A, then Q, then overtake the jack with the K 2. A, then K, then overtake the J   3. A, then overtake the Q with the K   4. K, then overtake the Q 5. Q, then J, then overtake the 10   6. K, then Q, then overtake the J   7. K first   8. A, then Q   9. A first

Page 55 :   D. 1. Lead low to the king, return to hand in another suit and lead low to the queen. You have 3 tricks if the suit is 3-3 or if West has ace singleton or ace doubleton   2. Same as 1   3. Low to the king, return to dummy and lead low to the jack   4. Low to the queen, return to hand and lead low to the jack 5. Low to the jack   6. Low to the jack. If the jack wins, cash the ace and then lead a low card next.

Page 74 :   1. K   2. K   3. 6   4. K   5. 6   6. 6 7. 2   8. 5   9. 9   10. 6   11. 3   12. 9   13. Q 14. 6   15. Q   16. 6   17. 3   18. 3   19. 10 20. J   21. 10   22. J   23. 6   24. 10.

Page 87 :   1. Play a heart to the ace. Do not take the normal heart finesse. North passed as dealer and has shown up with A-K-Q in spades, 9 points. North will not have K-x in hearts as well. If South turns up with ♠ A-K-Q, then do take the heart finesse. Having passed, too, South will not hold the ♡ K. 2. Lead a low spade to dummy's 10. The normal play in spades is low to the king, then lead the 10, ducking if South plays low (or shows out). Here, however, North has the ♠ Q, so finesse the 10. Why? Because South was unable to reply to North's 1♡ opening but has turned up with the ♡ A. With the ♠ Q as well, South would have answered.

3. The club finesse is almost 100% certain and you should finesse for the overtrick (certainly at pairs duplicate). South passed originally but has already turned up with ♡ A-K and ♠ Q-J, 10 points.

4. You have seven top tricks after you win the ◇ Q. The club suit offers the best chance for the extra tricks needed. North is more likely to hold the ♣ Q because of South's pre-empt. Cash ♣ K and lead ♣10, playing low (and praying low) if North plays low.

Page 93 : 1. (a) The best chance to have the king played is to lead the queen. You have to make the bait attractive. If West plays low, continue with your plan to play the ace and another trump.

2. (b) Lead the 10 first, not the jack. You want West to hold the king and to play low so that your 10 will score. Next you finesse the queen, cash the ace and rack up five tricks. The danger is that West will cover your honor card. This prevents the suit running. West is more likely to cover the jack than the 10. Therefore, lead the 10 and hope West plays a sleepy second-hand-low.

3. South should drop the king under East's ace. East's 4♠ without the king, queen or jack is almost certainly an 8-card suit. If you play the jack under East's ace, East will know West has led a singleton and will play a second spade for West to ruff. When you drop the ♠ K, East may believe you have the singleton and that West has led the ♠ Q from Q-J doubleton. If East tries to cash the ◇ A next, you will have a great hand to remember.

4. (a) Lead the jack from dummy. If South has the ace and, thinking you are finessing, plays low, your king scores. If you are certain North has the ace, lead low from dummy to the king. Return to dummy later and lead low. If South plays the Q, you can ruff and your jack is high.

(b) Lead low to the king. If this wins, return to dummy and lead low again (or lead the queen for a ruffing finesse if you want only one more trick).

(c) Lead low from dummy to the 10. Return to dummy later and lead low again (or lead the queen from dummy second time if you want only one trick).

(d) Lead low from dummy to your 10. Return to dummy later and lead low again. If your 9 wins, return to dummy and take a ruffing finesse. This may enable you to take two tricks but lose only one. If you can afford to lose two tricks and you have entry problems to dummy, simply lead the 10 and 9.

(e) Lead low from dummy to the queen. South may rise with the ace, fearing that you have Q singleton. You then score two tricks. If the queen wins, return to dummy in another suit and lead low from dummy again. If South has the ace but no jack, South may rise with the ace lest you have Q-J doubleton. If so, your king has been set up as a second trick. If you have entry problems to dummy, lead low to the queen, then lead low, ducking in dummy, hoping to drop the ace in two or three rounds. Leading low from dummy twice is psychologically superior.

5. Even if the club finesse works, there are only eight top tricks. You need to bring in the club suit. Best is to give up a club first and finesse the ♣ Q next round.

The best way to do this is to win the ◇ Q and lead a low club *from dummy*. Many players in the East seat with K-doubleton in clubs will rise with the king. Dummy's suit is now good and you have avoided taking a losing finesse. If East plays low, you will finesse the ♣ Q on the next round.

6. South should drop the ♠ K under East's ace. The 3♠ opening should be a 7-card suit and West's ♠ 3 is a singleton. When you drop the king, East is likely to place you with K-singleton and West with 3-2 doubleton. If East switches to diamonds and cannot regain the lead, you will be able to discard your spade loser later on the clubs. If you follow to trick 1 with the ♠ 2, East will know you have the king left. East will return a spade for West to ruff and two diamond losers later, you are one down. If you drop the king of spades without a trance and East still plays the queen next, either East is a duffer or you are not holding your cards back far enough.

Page 96 : Revision Test Part 2 : A. 1. You have 11 tricks and need to set up a spade for your 12th trick. Win the lead and give up a spade at once. Later, cross to dummy, ruff a spade, back to dummy, ruff a spade and so on, until dummy's fifth spade is high (you will need a 4–3 spade break). If North turns up with 10-6-4 in trumps, you will finesse dummy's ♡7 on one of your returns to dummy. You could be defeated if a second diamond is led after they win the spade trick and South has 10-6-4 in trumps. Dummy is now one entry short. You can set the spade up but cannot return to dummy to cash the fifth spade.

2. You need to set up two spade tricks to discard your diamond losers. At tricks 2 and 3, cash the ♠ A and ruff a spade. Trump to dummy, ruff a spade and, if necessary, trump to dummy and ruff another spade. As long as spades are 3-3 or 4-2, 6♡ makes.

B. 1. A first, then Q, preserving the K-9 tenace.

2. Low from dummy to your jack. If this wins, cash the ace next. You lose no tricks only if East started with K-doubleton. 3. With no entry problems, lead low from dummy to your jack. If this wins, return to dummy in another suit and lead the Q or 10 next for a finesse. This manoeuvre gains when East started with K-singleton. If entries to dummy are a precious commodity, lead the Q or 10 from dummy on the first round of the suit, finessing.

4. Play the king first and finesse the jack next round.

5. Play the king first and if both follow, cash the ace on the next round, hoping for a 2-2 split.

6. Cash the ace and king, hoping the queen falls on the second round. That is your only genuine chance to avoid a loser. The trap to avoid is to lead the jack. That cannot legitimately gain no matter who has the Q.

Page 96 continued: C. 1. Low to the queen. If the finesse works, you lose no tricks.   2. Low to the 10 first. You need West to have the king and the jack. 3. Same as 2.   4. Low to the queen. With 9 cards, the position changes. Low to the queen scores if West has K-doubleton or East has J-singleton. If the jack drops, under the queen, you return to hand, of course, to finesse the 10.   5. Low to the queen.
D. 1. 9   2. 2   3. 9   4. 2   5. Q   6. 7.
E. Win the ♠ K, cash the ♣ A and lead the ♣ Q next. You have set up the ♣ J for a spade discard. Playing diamonds instead of clubs may fail: they win the ◇ A on the first round and lead a second spade. The diamonds are blocked and the ◇ J is not accessible for a spade pitch.
F. 1. Win the ◇ A and duck a club. On regaining the lead, play the ♣ A-K. If clubs are 3-2, all is well. 2. Similar to 1. Win the ◇ A and duck a club. On regaining the lead, play a club to the queen. If clubs are 3-2 and North has K-x or K-x-x in clubs, you will be smiling. If not, there was nothing you could have done. The trap to avoid is finessing the ♣ Q on the first round of clubs. Even if this works, you are unable to use dummy's club length as dummy has no outside entries.
G. West should lead the ♡ K at trick 4 to discover who holds the ♡ A. If North, as expected, this gives North 10 HCP (with the ◇ K-Q-J). As North passed initially, the ♠ Q will be with South. If South turns up with the ♡ A, North will need to have the ♠ Q and even then, the overcall is very skimpy. West will play the spades by finessing against the player with the queen.
H. (a) 1. Q   2. J   3. A
(b) 1. Lead low from your hand towards the jack. 2. Lead low from dummy or lead the jack from dummy, as though planning to take a finesse.
Page 100 : 1. ♡3. You are strong in declarer's second suit. Lead a trump to reduce dummy's ruffing potential. With three trumps, play middle-down-up. 2. ♡6. 4-card suits with only one honor are most unattractive leads.
3. ♠5. Against 6NT (or 7NT), do not lead a suit with only one honor, or a suit with two honors unless they are part of a 3-card or longer sequence. 4. ♣4. The best chance is to find partner with the ♣K, so that your ♣Q can be set up as a winner before your ◇ A has been knocked out.
5. ♠6. Against 6NT do not lead a suit with only one honor. As East is short in spades, a spade lead will not cost a trick. Any other suit might.
6. ◇ 4. When dummy has a long suit, it is vital to lead an unbid suit. Lead from a king rather than an ace.

7. ♠4. When declarer suggests no-trumps and dummy reverts to the agreed suit, dummy has ruffing values. These can be minimised by trump leads.
8. ♣4. Neither diamonds, nor hearts, of course. Of the unbid suits, a major is usually more attractive. Here, however, East is marked with about 12 points and yet did not bid 1♠ or double. Therefore, East is more likely to hold clubs than spades.
9. ♠7. As dummy is balanced, a passive lead is fine. No suit is attractive and a spade is not likely to cost.
10. ◇ K (or ace). After a pre-empt, you need to cash tricks quickly or not at all. Dummy's long suit will generate plenty of tricks once declarer is in.
Page 108 : 1. (a) 7   (b) 7   **2.** (a) 3   (b) 3
3. 1. (a) The 4.   (b) The 2.   2. (a) and (b) The 9.
4. (a) Duck. East's 8 showed an even number and if East has two, South has a third card in the suit. (b) Play the king. East's 2 showed an odd number. If East began with three, South started with only two.
5 (a) Take the king.   (b) Duck.
6. (a) Partner has an odd number of trumps (probably three, but you are expected to work out from the bidding whether it is three or five.
(b) Partner has an even number of trumps, usually two but you are expected to deduce from the bidding whether it is two or four.
Page 116 : 1. Lead a diamond. Partner's *three* of clubs was a suit preference signal. Low card = low suit. Partner deduced from your club lead instead of a heart that you were leading a singleton and is indicating the entry. A heart back would disastrous if East holds ♠ 8   ♡ KQ1074   ◇ AK4   ♣ 9753.
2. Partner has A-Q-doubleton and needs to know your entry. You should drop the 10 of spades, high card for the higher suit, diamonds. As hearts are trumps the relevant suits are diamonds and clubs. With ♣ A as your entry, you would follow with the ♠ 5.
3. ◇ 2. Partner's double asks for a diamond lead, presumably because East is void in diamonds. You lead lowest diamond to ask for the low suit back after East ruffs. You could cash ♣ A and then lead a diamond but the recommended line produces two off.
4. West should switch to a diamond, not a club. The clue lies in East's *ace* of spades at trick 1. East began with A-K-Q-10-5-2 in spades and normally would play the queen at trick 1. The ace, an abnormal card, is suit preference: high card for the high suit.
5. ♣ 10. The ♣ A is very likely to be a singleton, as South rebid 2NT. West therefore needs to know your entry. High card, high suit, spade entry.
6. ♠ 4. East's ♡ 2 discouraged hearts and the ♣ 9, high card on the second round of clubs, was a suit preference signal. High card, high suit, spade switch.

Page 122 : 1. The king   2. The jack   3. The 10. The 10-8 surround the 9 and East has a higher honor as well. Lead the 10, the 'surround card'.   4. The jack, the 'surround card'.   5. The jack. To score three tricks, East will have to hold the ace. The 10 is now relevant and if South has it, you must lead the jack as the 'surround' smother of the 10.   6. Duck the first diamond. If South has only two diamonds, the diamond suit cannot be set up any more, as dummy has only one entry.

Page 135 : 1. (a) Almost certainly East. With A-10-x, South would have played low from dummy. South might have A-10 doubleton.   (b) Declarer. With Q-x opposite A-x or A-x-x, declarer would have played dummy's queen. Therefore South has the K.
2. Play low. South started with a singleton, else South would lead low from hand and finesse the Q.
3. Play low. East has the ace, else declarer would have crossed to dummy and led the queen to finesse.
4. Declarer has the king. With Q-10-x opposite A-x-x, declarer would have covered the J with the Q.
5. South has A-K-Q-9. When you regain the lead, play any suit other than this one or it costs a trick.
6. Declarer does not have the A-J. With A-J-x, declarer would have captured the king.
7. East has the K, declarer has the A. If East had A-K, East would have taken the trick. If South had A-K, South would have played high. With the king, South would have finessed the king. Therefore, South has the ace and East the king. South is ducking a round and planning to ruff a spade in dummy. A trump switch could be the best move.
8. East has the jack. With Q-J, South would have come to hand and finessed. East has the 9. With Q-9, declarer would probably have come to hand and taken two finesses (or inserted the 9 when East did not produce the king).
9. Declarer has the ace. Otherwise, declarer's first task would be dislodge the ace to set up the rest of the suit as winners. Do not expect partner to have the ace.

Page 138 Revision Test 3 : 1. (a) Singleton or J-7-2.   (b) Declarer. West would not lead away from the ace.   (c) Five spades - four clubs at least. (d) West has J-x-x in hearts and South has the ace singleton. South cannot have 3 hearts - 1 diamond, for that gives West 8 diamonds with which West would no doubt have bid somewhat more exuberantly. (e) South is 5-1-3-4 and West is 2-3-6-2. That is quite a deal of information after just the opening lead.
2. (a) Four, presumably.   (b) Three, if West started with four.   (c) and (d) West has four hearts. Nine hearts are missing. How can they be divided?

With four clubs and five hearts, West would have led a heart. South is wildly unlikely to have opened 1 NT with six hearts, but five hearts is feasible. Therefore, the position is almost certainly South five, West four. (e) Doubleton. With three spades, South would have raised spades.   (f) 2-5-3-3, virtually certain.
3. (a) Pass. Best not to bid higher with a weak misfit. (b) South five, East one. East should not hold a void. (c) East has two, South has one. East has a singleton heart but should not hold two singletons.
(d) East has six and South has three.
(e) East has 4, South 4. East 6-1-4-2, South 3-5-4-1.
4. (a) Four (from the lead of the 2)   (b) South has five if West has four.   (c) With five diamonds, South should have at most 3 spades and 3 hearts. (d) No, a diamond return will help declarer set up the long suit.   (e) The heart switch is the most attractive and the ♡10, the surround card, is the correct heart to lead.

Page 174 :   **A.** 1. Cash the ace first in case West has J-10-x-x.   2. Play the king first, guarding against A-10-x-x in either hand.   3. Play the jack first. You can guard against A-10-9-5 only with West. 4. Ace then low (not J or 10)   5. Ace, then Q   6. 6 from dummy to your 10   7. Cash ace, return to hand and finesse the jack   8. Finesse the jack on the first round.   9. Take a first round finesse of the 10.
B. 1. Finesse the 10 next   2. Finesse the 9 next.
C. You should win with the king, play a heart to dummy and lead a diamond to the 10 if South plays low. If North wins, a second spade cannot hurt you. You must keep South, the danger hand, off lead. This diamond play is essential if South started with ♠ Q-x-x   ♡ J-x-x-x   ◇ J-x-x-x   ♣ K-Q.   At duplicate pairs, play ◇ K, ◇ A. If diamonds are 3-2 (likely), this gives you an extra overtrick.
D. Play a heart to the king and cash ♡ Q. If all follow, ruff a club, play a diamond to dummy and ruff the last club, spade to the ace and draw the last trump. If hearts are 4-1, draw trumps and finesse ♠ Q.
E. Almost every South would play ♡ K if they had it. Therefore, ♡ K is likely to be with North. So, duck this heart, ruff a low heart and hope North started with K-x or K-x-x in hearts.
F. Win ◇ A, draw trumps, cash ♡ A-K and ◇ K, and exit with a diamond. The contract is guaranteed.
G. Discard diamonds on the second and third heart. Dummy can ruff high on the next heart. If you ruff a heart in hand, you will probably fail if spades are 4-2.
H. South has started with 6 hearts (North showed out on the third heart), 3 spades and only 1 diamond. Therefore, South has 3 clubs and you should play for the 3-3 break. Such counting makes *Happy Bridging.*

PLAY HANDS FOR NORTH

(After each hand number, the dealer is given, followed by the vulnerability, e.g. S/Nil means Dealer South, neither side vulnerable)

1 N/Nil	2 E/N-S	3 S/E-W	4 W/Both	5 N/N-S	6 E/E-W	7 S/Both	8 W/Nil
♠ Q109	♠ 43	♠ 6	♠ AKQ96	♠ 92	♠ K53	♠ J874	♠ 98732
♡ 10752	♡ Q72	♡ AKQ75	♡ J32	♡ QJ1076	♡ KQJ1072	♡ AK	♡ 752
◊ K	◊ 87652	◊ QJ5	◊ 76	◊ AQ1043	◊ K2	◊ 93	◊ AK
♣ AKQJ3	♣ 1098	♣ Q942	♣ 1082	♣ K	♣ Q7	♣ KQ1094	♣ 1097

9 N/E-W	10 E/Both	11 S/Nil	12 W/N-S	13 N/Both	14 E/Nil	15 S/N-S	16 W/E-W
♠ 83	♠ AQ62	♠ AKJ2	♠ 10	♠ 1083	♠ 92	♠ K9	♠ J74
♡ 76	♡ 1043	♡ J8	♡ 10542	♡ AQ87	♡ A765	♡ QJ98642	♡ 632
◊ AQJ7652	◊ K83	◊ KQ84	◊ AJ95	◊ 83	◊ K1052	◊ 95	◊ A107432
♣ J3	♣ 763	♣ Q107	♣ K742	♣ Q932	♣ 764	♣ K10	♣ 8

17 N/Nil	18 E/N-S	19 S/E-W	20 W/Both	21 N/N-S	22 E/Nil	23 S/Both	24 W/Nil
♠ AJ5	♠ KQ1095	♠ KJ1092	♠ J94	♠ 87	♠ 987	♠ 32	♠ Q5
♡ K62	♡ K	♡ A73	♡ 1095	♡ 9743	♡ K5	♡ 64	♡ AQJ76
◊ K743	◊ Q8762	◊ AJ	◊ Q873	◊ AQ	◊ K1098	◊ Q962	◊ 43
♣ 862	♣ 105	♣ 642	♣ 432	♣ J7643	♣ AK43	♣ Q10943	♣ KQJ10

25 N/E-W	26 E/Both	27 S/Nil	28 W/N-S	29 N/Both	30 E/Nil	31 S/N-S	32 W/E-W
♠ AJ	♠ 87432	♠ 9543	♠ K42	♠ KJ76	♠ 9	♠ AKQJ10	♠ 73
♡ 973	♡ KQ87	♡ 42	♡ 10	♡ AKJ65	♡ AQ1075	♡ J63	♡ 75
◊ AK84	◊ 86	◊ KQJ	◊ 1072	◊ 103	◊ 98542	◊ QJ10	◊ 975
♣ KQ76	♣ 105	♣ AQ86	♣ K107543	♣ 72	♣ 63	♣ 106	♣ KQ10953

33 N/Nil	34 E/N-S	35 S/E-W	36 W/Both	37 N/N-S	38 E/E-W	39 S/Both	40 W/E-W
♠ Q75	♠ AKQ932	♠ 7	♠ J102	♠ J9842	♠ J1076	♠ KQJ9875	♠ 985
♡ 4	♡ 62	♡ AQ6	♡ 865	♡ A942	♡ 42	♡ A	♡ AJ106
◊ AKQ952	◊ J109	◊ K98	◊ AK863	◊ Q10	◊ Q7	◊ 5	◊ Q10
♣ QJ10	♣ AQ	♣ A76543	♣ 72	♣ 106	♣ KQ643	♣ K753	♣ J532

41 N/E-W	42 E/Both	43 S/Nil	44 W/N-S	45 N/Both	46 E/Nil	47 S/N-S	48 W/E-W
♠ 8743	♠ J6	♠ AJ64	♠ AQ104	♠ K742	♠ 863	♠ A5	♠ J1053
♡ A9	♡ J852	♡ 864	♡ AK52	♡ A1093	♡ 104	♡ A87	♡ Q8
◊ AQ3	◊ Q965	◊ K95	◊ QJ	◊ 94	◊ 8753	◊ AQ1074	◊ Q8732
♣ AK52	♣ K92	♣ 763	♣ 432	♣ 652	♣ A982	♣ K62	♣ K8

49 N/Nil	50 E/N-S	51 S/E-W	52 W/Both	53 N/N-S	54 E/E-W	55 S/Both	56 W/Nil
♠ AJ984	♠ K9	♠ KQ5	♠ 762	♠ 103	♠ KQJ83	♠ AQ104	♠ Q8763
♡ AJ74	♡ QJ4	♡ 8652	♡ 72	♡ AK943	♡ J	♡ 104	♡ 3
◊ AK	◊ A8732	◊ J987	◊ A9763	◊ KQ62	◊ J6542	◊ Q1086	◊ AQJ952
♣ J3	♣ K54	♣ J10	♣ A109	♣ Q3	♣ 73	♣ 1073	♣ A

57 N/E-W	58 E/Both	59 S/Nil	60 W/N-S	61 N/Both	62 E/Nil	63 S/N-S	64 W/E-W
♠ J7	♠ 10975	♠ AQJ	♠ J10983	♠ AKQ	♠ J109873	♠ AQ742	♠ 1083
♡ Q	♡ K92	♡ AJ32	♡ 75	♡ AQ107	♡ 72	♡ 73	♡ J106
◊ 753	◊ J1098	◊ A1063	◊ Q109	◊ AK5	◊ 8	◊ 86	◊ 1094
♣ A1097654	♣ J4	♣ 54	♣ K53	♣ 853	♣ 10762	♣ 7432	♣ AKQ2

65 N/N-S	66 E/Nil	67 S/E-W	68 W/Both	69 N/N-S	70 E/E-W	71 S/Both	72 W/Nil
♠ 10	♠ K85	♠ 83	♠ 96	♠ A93	♠ K765	♠ Q	♠ A10642
♡ 964	♡ K3	♡ 9632	♡ A8753	♡ AK8762	♡ A109	♡ 96	♡ AKQJ8
◊ 63	◊ QJ643	◊ AQ76	◊ AQ2	◊ J3	◊ J64	◊ 107632	◊ A
♣ AKQ6542	♣ Q43	♣ K98	♣ AQ5	♣ 42	♣ KJ10	♣ 98652	♣ A2

73 N/E-W	74 E/Both	75 S/Nil	76 W/N-S	77 N/Both	78 E/Nil	79 S/N-S	80 W/E-W
♠ 10952	♠ Q8762	♠ 2	♠ Q972	♠ 643	♠ 5	♠ KJ1098	♠ 762
♡ AKJ	♡ J10	♡ 1054	♡ A93	♡ QJ5	♡ 1096	♡ 87	♡ AKQ2
◊ AQ10	◊ 10	◊ A9832	◊ K87	◊ 7632	◊ A10	◊ A93	◊ Q10843
♣ K62	♣ K10842	♣ K652	♣ 975	♣ AKJ	♣ 9765432	♣ AJ10	♣ 5

(After each hand number, the dealer is given, followed by the vulnerability, e.g. N/Nil means Dealer North, neither side vulnerable)

81 N/Nil	82 E/N-S	83 S/E-W	84 W/Both	85 N/N-S	86 E/E-W	87 S/Both	88 W/Nil
♠ 2	♠ 42	♠ J10984	♠ 86	♠ KQ1043	♠ 1063	♠ 2	♠ 862
♡ KQJ10	♡ A1098	♡ K1092	♡ AQ7	♡ K765	♡ AJ542	♡ KQ84	♡ KJ10
◇ 7652	◇ Q986	◇ J7	◇ A9854	◇ Q10	◇ ---	◇ 10742	◇ QJ965
♣ 7542	♣ A72	♣ 92	♣ Q85	♣ A8	♣ A8432	♣ AJ108	♣ K10

89 N/E-W	90 E/Both	91 S/Nil	92 W/Both	93 N/Both	94 E/Nil	95 S/N-S	96 W/E-W
♠ QJ10852	♠ K	♠ KJ10	♠ K9	♠ 1065	♠ Q8	♠ KQ83	♠ 10
♡ KQ65	♡ A932	♡ AQ	♡ 10764	♡ 103	♡ AQJ765	♡ J1072	♡ QJ107643
◇ A5	◇ 1064	◇ AQ832	◇ 9875	◇ 8532	◇ K1083	◇ KQ	◇ 9
♣ 7	♣ AK1098	♣ K63	♣ AQ5	♣ 9863	♣ J	♣ 986	♣ J754

97 N/Nil	98 E/N-S	99 S/E-W	100 W/Both	101 N/N-S	102 E/E-W	103 S/Both	104 W/Nil
♠ A2	♠ 3	♠ KQJ943	♠ 874	♠ 107	♠ KJ852	♠ K10983	♠ A
♡ J1086	♡ KQ965	♡ AQ	♡ KQJ42	♡ Q1065	♡ K72	♡ 86	♡ A2
◇ AKJ105	◇ 982	◇ 1086	◇ 2	◇ KJ3	◇ 5432	◇ Q8	◇ Q8432
♣ K5	♣ Q864	♣ 93	♣ A962	♣ KJ103	♣ J	♣ AK104	♣ A7632

105 N/E-W	106 E/Both	107 S/Nil	108 W/N-S	109 N/Both	110 E/Nil	111 S/N-S	112 W/E-W
♠ J4	♠ A105	♠ K9873	♠ 873	♠ K32	♠ 105	♠ AKJ94	♠ 87
♡ AJ1074	♡ 1074	♡ 1072	♡ Q5	♡ 104	♡ 986	♡ 95	♡ AJ5
◇ AKJ92	◇ 96532	◇ 2	◇ 84	◇ 74	◇ 1095	◇ 743	◇ QJ102
♣ 5	♣ 83	♣ 10765	♣ AQ8742	♣ K97642	♣ KQ1043	♣ AKQ	♣ Q873

113 N/Nil	114 E/N-S	115 S/E-W	116 W/Both	117 N/N-S	118 E/E-W	119 S/Both	120 W/Nil
♠ 7	♠ J1075	♠ 32	♠ 72	♠ AQ6	♠ J10874	♠ KQ53	♠ K764
♡ AK10964	♡ 75	♡ 654	♡ KQ105	♡ 62	♡ 1075	♡ A1053	♡ 10842
◇ KQJ	◇ J1097	◇ KJ3	◇ 75	◇ KQJ84	◇ 109532	◇ A654	◇ 107
♣ K62	♣ J95	♣ A10932	♣ 109852	♣ J83	♣ ---	♣ 4	♣ AKQ

121 N/E-W	122 E/Both	123 S/Nil	124 W/N-S	125 N/Both	126 E/Nil	127 S/N-S	128 W/E-W
♠ A95	♠ 752	♠ Q104	♠ AJ953	♠ AJ52	♠ 8	♠ A9752	♠ 874
♡ A63	♡ AKJ	♡ K98	♡ 1086	♡ 1096	♡ 76	♡ 9	♡ 9652
◇ K1052	◇ Q1065	◇ J87542	◇ K8	◇ J83	◇ J10763	◇ Q75	◇ Q1082
♣ KQ4	♣ 642	♣ 9	♣ 1083	♣ KQ6	♣ 108752	♣ AQ62	♣ 106

129 N/Nil	130 E/Nil	131 S/E-W	132 W/Nil	133 N/N-S	134 E/E-W	135 S/Both	136 W/Nil
♠ 8	♠ QJ10	♠ 97	♠ 53	♠ A8652	♠ J953	♠ A109843	♠ QJ83
♡ K752	♡ K8542	♡ 8765	♡ Q109	♡ A3	♡ Q75	♡ 6	♡ KJ5
◇ Q97	◇ A3	◇ 9863	◇ 1076	◇ AKJ	◇ J102	◇ J75	◇ 10982
♣ A9643	♣ Q83	♣ J109	♣ QJ1097	♣ 753	♣ K97	♣ AK8	♣ J9

137 N/E-W	138 E/Both	139 S/Nil	140 W/N-S	141 N/Both	142 E/Nil	143 S/N-S	144 W/E-W
♠ 6	♠ Q52	♠ 975	♠ QJ10963	♠ AQ10	♠ ---	♠ 643	♠ 8
♡ AQ74	♡ 743	♡ K2	♡ 63	♡ AQJ32	♡ Q765	♡ QJ98	♡ J984
◇ 8765	◇ J106	◇ J75	◇ A1032	◇ KQJ	◇ 8743	◇ Q6	◇ 876
♣ KQ63	♣ KQ102	♣ 87643	♣ A	♣ 72	♣ J9632	♣ AQ52	♣ QJ1032

145 N/Nil	146 E/N-S	147 S/E-W	148 W/Nil	149 N/N-S	150 E/E-W	151 S/Both	152 W/Nil
♠ 876	♠ J10	♠ KJ9	♠ AK4	♠ AK10762	♠ 753	♠ A643	♠ J764
♡ Q1098	♡ AK3	♡ 105	♡ AJ87	♡ 4	♡ A42	♡ 5	♡ AKQ7
◇ 7654	◇ Q109542	◇ Q1083	◇ A2	◇ Q94	◇ 863	◇ QJ6	◇ 84
♣ 85	♣ Q3	♣ 8762	♣ AQ43	♣ A85	♣ K752	♣ A8542	♣ K84

153 N/E-W	154 E/Both	155 S/Nil	156 W/N-S	157 N/Both	158 E/Nil	159 S/N-S	160 W/E-W
♠ A763	♠ 83	♠ AKJ76	♠ J10875	♠ 73	♠ QJ5	♠ KQJ9	♠ A32
♡ A653	♡ QJ97	♡ 83	♡ 3	♡ 109865	♡ 1054	♡ 96	♡ J53
◇ 62	◇ 986432	◇ A4	◇ KJ10	◇ 4	◇ 9	◇ A64	◇ A642
♣ 864	♣ A	♣ 9872	♣ Q1092	♣ 108532	♣ AKJ932	♣ K952	♣ KJ9

PLAY HANDS FOR EAST

(After each hand number, the dealer is given, followed by the vulnerability, e.g. W/N-S means Dealer West, North-South vulnerable)

1 N/Nil	2 E/N-S	3 S/E-W	4 W/Both	5 N/N-S	6 E/E-W	7 S/Both	8 W/Nil
♠ AKJ72	♠ A862	♠ AKQ109754	♠ 43	♠ Q	♠ AQ86	♠ 932	♠ 1065
♥ 3	♥ 105	♥ 42	♥ 104	♥ 854	♥ 84	♥ 965432	♥ KQJ1043
♦ Q654	♦ KQ1093	♦ 4	♦ 1098	♦ 9862	♦ QJ983	♦ AK7	♦ 962
♣ 972	♣ AK	♣ K10	♣ J96543	♣ AQ1098	♣ 103	♣ A	♣ A

9 N/E-W	10 E/Both	11 S/Nil	12 W/N-S	13 N/Both	14 E/Nil	15 S/N-S	16 W/E-W
♠ Q97	♠ 9854	♠ 865	♠ 865	♠ 75	♠ KQ6	♠ J72	♠ 6
♥ 108432	♥ Q6	♥ K10643	♥ AKQ6	♥ K2	♥ 84	♥ 53	♥ AKJ98
♦ K4	♦ 10742	♦ - - -	♦ Q10 ·	♦ 1096542	♦ A7	♦ 7642	♦ K8
♣ 1098	♣ 1084	♣ K8632	♣ AJ108	♣ 1076	♣ AQJ982	♣ AQ92	♣ KJ1065

17 N/Nil	18 E/N-S	19 S/E-W	20 W/Both	21 N/N-S	22 E/Nil	23 S/Both	24 W/Nil
♠ K103	♠ 874	♠ Q85	♠ AK10	♠ 104	♠ A65	♠ AK1098	♠ AK98
♥ 98	♥ J2	♥ KQJ8	♥ AJ72	♥ 1085	♥ J10874	♥ 97	♥ 54
♦ J862	♦ AK3	♦ Q74	♦ 109	♦ 109863	♦ 7	♦ J104	♦ J1052
♣ J1075	♣ KJ842	♣ 1095	♣ AJ87	♣ 852	♣ QJ85	♣ K65	♣ A94

25 N/E-W	26 E/Both	27 S/Nil	28 W/N-S	29 N/Both	30 E/Nil	31 S/N-S	32 W/E-W
♠ 764	♠ AK10	♠ 8	♠ 9853	♠ 43	♠ QJ875	♠ 87	♠ Q865
♥ 842	♥ J109	♥ J1093	♥ 98	♥ 432	♥ J9	♥ 102	♥ Q643
♦ 65	♦ KQ7	♦ 9862	♦ AQJ43	♦ QJ97	♦ A106	♦ K9643	♦ Q63
♣ A9854	♣ AKQ9	♣ 10754	♣ J8	♣ 10954	♣ KJ4	♣ 9832	♣ 87

33 N/Nil	34 E/N-S	35 S/E-W	36 W/Both	37 N/N-S	38 E/E-W	39 S/Both	40 W/E-W
♠ 9	♠ 76	♠ AQ8532	♠ 954	♠ Q7	♠ 8542	♠ A3	♠ J732
♥ AQJ9752	♥ Q10	♥ K10753	♥ K93	♥ 73	♥ K10865	♥ 9432	♥ Q4
♦ J6	♦ AK843	♦ - - -	♦ J2	♦ K76542	♦ J98	♦ J1094	♦ AK54
♣ 972	♣ KJ92	♣ 102	♣ AK654	♣ 832	♣ J	♣ AQ9	♣ AK8

41 N/E-W	42 E/Both	43 S/Nil	44 W/N-S	45 N/Both	46 E/Nil	47 S/N-S	48 W/E-W
♠ K62	♠ K93	♠ 753	♠ 8	♠ A108	♠ 975	♠ 842	♠ K87
♥ QJ1065	♥ AQ64	♥ 109	♥ 9876	♥ 52	♥ Q92	♥ 1065	♥ KJ4
♦ 762	♦ AK32	♦ AQ1074	♦ 75432	♦ KJ63	♦ KQ6	♦ K3	♦ A654
♣ J8	♣ 85	♣ J54	♣ Q98	♣ 10987	♣ 7654	♣ AJ873	♣ Q54

49 N/Nil	50 E/N-S	51 S/E-W	52 W/Both	53 N/N-S	54 E/E-W	55 S/Both	56 W/Nil
♠ 732	♠ J6	♠ 9843	♠ AKQJ9	♠ J7	♠ - - -	♠ K76	♠ J1042
♥ K1082	♥ 875	♥ AKJ4	♥ AK1086	♥ J1076	♥ 10532	♥ KQJ9632	♥ J10652
♦ 96	♦ QJ1064	♦ 52	♦ 5	♦ 10943	♦ AQ98	♦ - - -	♦ - - -
♣ KQ109	♣ A87	♣ 862	♣ 63	♣ 742	♣ K10652	♣ 965	♣ KQJ7

57 N/E-W	58 E/Both	59 S/Nil	60 W/N-S	61 N/Both	62 E/Nil	63 S/N-S	64 W/E-W
♠ K942	♠ Q832	♠ K10543	♠ 64	♠ 108642	♠ A	♠ J105	♠ AKJ742
♥ 986	♥ AQ8	♥ Q75	♥ J32	♥ KJ8	♥ 9654	♥ 1064	♥ A53
♦ J842	♦ 532	♦ Q94	♦ A76432	♦ 974	♦ AK1072	♦ QJ9	♦ A
♣ Q8	♣ AKQ	♣ 93	♣ 92	♣ J10	♣ J43	♣ Q1086	♣ 976

65 N/N-S	66 E/Nil	67 S/E-W	68 W/Both	69 N/N-S	70 E/E-W	71 S/Both	72 W/Nil
♠ AJ84	♠ Q62	♠ AKQJ962	♠ QJ102	♠ - - -	♠ 32	♠ 72	♠ QJ5
♥ KQJ5	♥ AQ9842	♥ 84	♥ Q96	♥ QJ4	♥ 87652	♥ KQJ10832	♥ 52
♦ KQ2	♦ 10	♦ 2	♦ 1084	♦ AK8742	♦ 82	♦ A	♦ KJ53
♣ J9	♣ A87	♣ 1032	♣ J107	♣ A976	♣ A964	♣ KJ3	♣ QJ108

73 N/E-W	74 E/Both	75 S/Nil	76 W/N-S	77 N/Both	78 E/Nil	79 S/N-S	80 W/E-W
♠ A6	♠ A5	♠ 543	♠ J105	♠ 7	♠ KJ1098	♠ 5	♠ AK
♥ Q943	♥ A4	♥ KQ62	♥ J105	♥ A8632	♥ AKQ82	♥ K42	♥ J87
♦ J876	♦ AK8653	♦ QJ10	♦ 1054	♦ 10954	♦ 53	♦ 1087542	♦ 7652
♣ 854	♣ J63	♣ Q84	♣ Q1062	♣ 1096	♣ A	♣ 954	♣ KJ109

(After each hand number, the dealer is given, followed by the vulnerability, e.g. E/N-S means Dealer East, North-South vulnerable)

81 N/Nil	82 E/N-S	83 S/E-W	84 W/Both	85 N/N-S	86 E/E-W	87 S/Both	88 W/Nil
♠ 976	♠ AKQ	♠ A3	♠ J3	♠ 97	♠ AQJ854	♠ J654	♠ AK
♡ A65	♡ KJ42	♡ 754	♡ J10642	♡ 9	♡ 10	♡ 2	♡ 8752
◇ J84	◇ AK52	◇ 862	◇ K6	◇ J7642	◇ Q104	◇ K863	◇ 742
♣ QJ98	♣ K5	♣ KQJ76	♣ AJ64	♣ QJ432	♣ 965	♣ K972	♣ 7432

89 N/E-W	90 E/Both	91 S/Nil	92 W/Both	93 N/Both	94 E/Nil	95 S/N-S	96 W/E-W
♠ 7	♠ AQJ432	♠ 96	♠ Q106	♠ 932	♠ 62	♠ 104	♠ AK8764
♡ AJ98	♡ J4	♡ 76542	♡ AKJ8	♡ 642	♡ K102	♡ Q86	♡ K8
◇ KQ93	◇ KJ9	◇ K76	◇ AK32	◇ KQJ10	◇ 65	◇ J106	◇ 6
♣ KJ86	♣ 75	♣ 752	♣ 72	♣ AQJ	♣ K97532	♣ AKQ72	♣ KQ82

97 N/Nil	98 E/N-S	99 S/E-W	100 W/Both	101 N/N-S	102 E/E-W	103 S/Both	104 W/Nil
♠ K75	♠ K9872	♠ A6	♠ KQ93	♠ A932	♠ AQ764	♠ 752	♠ 42
♡ 5	♡ AJ	♡ 9875	♡ A105	♡ A74	♡ 3	♡ KQJ	♡ KQJ864
◇ 97432	◇ A7654	◇ 2	◇ 103	◇ 109852	◇ QJ10	◇ A	◇ 5
♣ Q1083	♣ A	♣ Q87642	♣ KQ83	♣ 7	♣ KQ92	♣ J98762	♣ Q1054

105 N/E-W	106 E/Both	107 S/Nil	108 W/N-S	109 N/Both	110 E/Nil	111 S/N-S	112 W/E-W
♠ 108632	♠ Q92	♠ Q2	♠ K94	♠ 764	♠ J2	♠ 763	♠ K106
♡ K92	♡ AKJ	♡ QJ9	♡ 8764	♡ 876	♡ QJ10432	♡ K1083	♡ 432
◇ 74	◇ QJ8	◇ K10975	◇ 9732	◇ J9862	◇ A83	◇ KQJ	◇ A6
♣ 862	♣ KJ92	♣ KQ3	♣ 109	♣ Q10	♣ A7	♣ 874	♣ J10952

113 N/Nil	114 E/N-S	115 S/E-W	116 W/Both	117 N/N-S	118 E/E-W	119 S/Both	120 W/Nil
♠ 865	♠ AK4	♠ 97	♠ KQJ1083	♠ 94	♠ Q6	♠ J94	♠ - - -
♡ 82	♡ - - -	♡ 10987	♡ 6	♡ Q984	♡ KQ4	♡ Q9872	♡ AK653
◇ 10962	◇ Q63	◇ Q7654	◇ KQJ3	◇ 106	◇ KQ6	◇ K10	◇ A9852
♣ QJ104	♣ AK86432	♣ Q6	♣ AQ	♣ A10954	♣ J5432	♣ J83	♣ 765

121 N/E-W	122 E/Both	123 S/Nil	124 W/N-S	125 N/Both	126 E/Nil	127 S/N-S	128 W/E-W
♠ KQJ102	♠ AQJ86	♠ KJ763	♠ 82	♠ KQ63	♠ 764	♠ KQJ	♠ AK652
♡ J	♡ 83	♡ AJ4	♡ A95	♡ 853	♡ K109	♡ Q108	♡ A104
◇ Q83	◇ KJ9	◇ Q10	◇ AQ962	◇ 9765	◇ A82	◇ KJ93	◇ 5
♣ 10982	♣ Q107	♣ Q53	♣ 742	♣ 98	♣ A643	♣ 953	♣ KQ74

129 N/Nil	130 E/Nil	131 S/E-W	132 W/Nil	133 N/N-S	134 E/E-W	135 S/Both	136 W/Nil
♠ QJ1094	♠ A76	♠ KJ432	♠ QJ10	♠ J109	♠ AKQ10764	♠ 7	♠ 975
♡ A10	♡ J109	♡ 42	♡ A87	♡ Q985	♡ 10	♡ Q9875	♡ A83
◇ 862	◇ KQJ8	◇ 752	◇ K98	◇ 1087	◇ 94	◇ AK96	◇ KQJ5
♣ KQJ	♣ 762	♣ AQ3	♣ K653	♣ Q82	♣ 643	♣ 743	♣ KQJ

137 N/E-W	138 E/Both	139 S/Nil	140 W/N-S	141 N/Both	142 E/Nil	143 S/N-S	144 W/E-W
♠ KJ102	♠ K109	♠ AQJ832	♠ 5	♠ KJ4	♠ AK632	♠ J1098	♠ AK43
♡ KJ62	♡ QJ5	♡ J106	♡ KJ82	♡ 107	♡ K3	♡ 103	♡ 7632
◇ A93	◇ A8754	◇ A83	◇ 9854	◇ 8762	◇ KJ5	◇ J10872	◇ J102
♣ 72	♣ 97	♣ 10	♣ 10542	♣ QJ108	♣ A84	♣ 98	♣ 76

145 N/Nil	146 E/N-S	147 S/E-W	148 W/Nil	149 N/N-S	150 E/E-W	151 S/Both	152 W/Nil
♠ KJ3	♠ 985	♠ 632	♠ Q98	♠ J	♠ Q106	♠ KQ109	♠ 109
♡ 732	♡ 10864	♡ KJ987	♡ 109	♡ AKJ85	♡ 86	♡ Q83	♡ J42
◇ AK2	◇ 3	◇ AK	◇ 6543	◇ K72	◇ Q10954	◇ 72	◇ AQJ62
♣ Q764	♣ J9875	♣ A54	♣ KJ102	♣ 9643	♣ 963	♣ J1093	♣ Q72

153 N/E-W	154 E/Both	155 S/Nil	156 W/N-S	157 N/Both	158 E/Nil	159 S/N-S	160 W/E-W
♠ J10	♠ 76	♠ 103	♠ K93	♠ AKQ	♠ 762	♠ 1084	♠ 76
♡ J987	♡ 8652	♡ 752	♡ Q5	♡ AQ4	♡ A986	♡ AK7532	♡ Q64
◇ Q10	◇ AKQ	◇ QJ7653	◇ 8643	◇ KQ103	◇ KJ3	◇ 85	◇ 98
♣ Q9752	♣ KQ106	♣ J10	♣ A854	♣ Q76	♣ 764	♣ 63	♣ AQ8654

PLAY HANDS FOR SOUTH

(After each hand number, the dealer is given, followed by the vulnerability, e.g. N/E-W means Dealer North, East-West vulnerable)

1 N/Nil
♠ 653
♡ AKQ94
♢ A83
♣ 105

2 E/N-S
♠ 95
♡ AKJ86
♢ A
♣ 65432

3 S/E-W
♠ 83
♡ 863
♢ 8762
♣ AJ65

4 W/Both
♠ J1087
♡ 986
♢ AKQJ
♣ K7

5 N/N-S
♠ 653
♡ A932
♢ J
♣ 76543

6 E/E-W
♠ 942
♡ A6
♢ 106
♣ AKJ942

7 S/Both
♠ AKQ105
♡ QJ7
♢ 854
♣ J3

8 W/Nil
♠ A4
♡ 8
♢ J10843
♣ J6532

9 N/E-W
♠ AK10
♡ QJ9
♢ 1093
♣ AK62

10 E/Both
♠ J3
♡ KJ752
♢ 96
♣ AK92

11 S/Nil
♠ Q43
♡ AQ52
♢ J1093
♣ J5

12 W/N-S
♠ QJ732
♡ 83
♢ K6432
♣ 5

13 N/Both
♠ KJ4
♡ J10953
♢ AK
♣ AK5

14 E/Nil
♠ 54
♡ QJ93
♢ Q8643
♣ K5

15 S/N-S
♠ A1085
♡ AK
♢ KJ10
♣ J876

16 W/E-W
♠ AQ985
♡ Q
♢ QJ5
♣ A932

17 N/Nil
♠ 94
♡ QJ104
♢ A95
♣ AKQ3

18 E/N-S
♠ AJ62
♡ Q106
♢ J95
♣ Q97

19 S/E-W
♠ A643
♡ 942
♢ K3
♣ KQJ8

20 W/Both
♠ Q8763
♡ 843
♢ AK6
♣ K5

21 N/N-S
♠ Q652
♡ AKJ62
♢ KJ
♣ KQ

22 E/Nil
♠ KJ103
♡ AQ63
♢ 3
♣ 10962

23 S/Both
♠ Q4
♡ 10852
♢ AK7
♣ J872

24 W/Nil
♠ J64
♡ K1098
♢ AQ
♣ 8653

25 N/E-W
♠ KQ10
♡ Q65
♢ QJ3
♣ J1032

26 E/Both
♠ 65
♡ A2
♢ A32
♣ J86432

27 S/Nil
♠ A2
♡ KQ75
♢ A1075
♣ K93

28 W/N-S
♠ 76
♡ AKQJ76
♢ 96
♣ 962

29 N/Both
♠ AQ10952
♡ Q8
♢ 65
♣ KJ6

30 E/Nil
♠ AK
♡ 8642
♢ QJ3
♣ 10987

31 S/N-S
♠ 96543
♡ 94
♢ 85
♣ AKQJ

32 W/E-W
♠ J4
♡ 10982
♢ AKJ10
♣ AJ2

33 N/Nil
♠ K1083
♡ 63
♢ 1073
♣ K864

34 E/N-S
♠ J108
♡ AK843
♢ Q62
♣ 43

35 S/E-W
♠ 10
♡ 94
♢ AQJ1065432
♣ 8

36 W/Both
♠ KQ87
♡ 4
♢ 10954
♣ QJ98

37 N/N-S
♠ K1065
♡ 1085
♢ J9
♣ QJ97

38 E/E-W
♠ KQ
♡ AJ73
♢ K63
♣ A952

39 S/Both
♠ 42
♡ KQJ6
♢ AK6
♣ 8642

40 W/E-W
♠ K10
♡ K9532
♢ 987
♣ 1097

41 N/E-W
♠ AQ105
♡ 74
♢ KJ4
♣ 7643

42 E/Both
♠ Q10852
♡ K109
♢ J10
♣ Q74

43 S/Nil
♠ K82
♡ J7532
♢ J
♣ Q1082

44 W/N-S
♠ 97532
♡ Q4
♢ AK9
♣ J75

45 N/Both
♠ 6
♡ KQJ864
♢ A102
♣ AQ3

46 E/Nil
♠ J
♡ AJ765
♢ AJ109
♣ J103

47 S/N-S
♠ KQ63
♡ K42
♢ J982
♣ Q5

48 W/E-W
♠ Q962
♡ A10732
♢ J9
♣ 76

49 N/Nil
♠ KQ65
♡ 63
♢ J74
♣ 7642

50 E/N-S
♠ A32
♡ AK10932
♢ 5
♣ 932

51 S/E-W
♠ J10
♡ Q1073
♢ 1063
♣ KQ97

52 W/Both
♠ 1053
♡ J953
♢ QJ10
♣ QJ4

53 N/N-S
♠ Q6
♡ Q852
♢ A75
♣ J1098

54 E/E-W
♠ A10972
♡ A9864
♢ 3
♣ A4

55 S/Both
♠ J832
♡ 85
♢ A52
♣ KQJ8

56 W/Nil
♠ AK
♡ AK84
♢ K43
♣ 10543

57 N/E-W
♠ A1053
♡ AK4
♢ AQ106
♣ 32

58 E/Both
♠ AK4
♡ J10654
♢ - - -
♣ 97652

59 S/Nil
♠ 762
♡ 104
♢ J7
♣ AK8762

60 W/N-S
♠ 72
♡ Q1098
♢ J
♣ QJ8764

61 N/Both
♠ 95
♡ 642
♢ J32
♣ A7642

62 E/Nil
♠ 52
♡ KJ108
♢ J963
♣ 985

63 S/N-S
♠ 63
♡ AK52
♢ AK43
♣ AJ5

64 W/E-W
♠ 96
♡ Q98
♢ KJ87
♣ 10854

65 N/N-S
♠ Q72
♡ A10872
♢ 9874
♣ 10

66 E/Nil
♠ AJ10743
♡ 76
♢ AK7
♣ KJ

67 S/E-W
♠ 754
♡ AKQ7
♢ 8543
♣ 75

68 W/Both
♠ 53
♡ KJ104
♢ KJ73
♣ 642

69 N/N-S
♠ 876
♡ 93
♢ Q10965
♣ 853

70 E/E-W
♠ QJ1094
♡ K4
♢ A53
♣ Q52

71 S/Both
♠ AKJ863
♡ A4
♢ KJ94
♣ 4

72 W/Nil
♠ K873
♡ 109
♢ Q764
♣ 765

73 N/E-W
♠ QJ4
♡ 875
♢ K543
♣ Q103

74 E/Both
♠ 109
♡ 9862
♢ J942
♣ AQ5

75 S/Nil
♠ KJ976
♡ AJ98
♢ 5
♣ A93

76 W/N-S
♠ 643
♡ 874
♢ QJ932
♣ AK

77 N/Both
♠ AKQJ10
♡ K1097
♢ J
♣ Q85

78 E/Nil
♠ A432
♡ 75
♢ KQJ98
♣ 108

79 S/N-S
♠ Q76
♡ Q95
♢ KQ
♣ KQ862

80 W/E-W
♠ QJ10543
♡ 3
♢ J9
♣ 7642

(After each hand number, the dealer is given, followed by the vulnerability, e.g. S/E-W means Dealer South, East-West vulnerable)

81 N/Nil	82 E/N-S	83 S/E-W	84 W/Both	85 N/N-S	86 E/E-W	87 S/Both	88 W/Nil
♠ AKQJ108	♠ J10973	♠ K75	♠ AKQ2	♠ A8652	♠ 72	♠ A9873	♠ 754
♥ 43	♥ 73	♥ 863	♥ 983	♥ QJ10	♥ K863	♥ J3	♥ Q93
♦ AK3	♦ J10	♦ Q1094	♦ QJ10	♦ K8	♦ 976532	♦ AQ	♦ AK10
♣ 63	♣ 9843	♣ A108	♣ 1032	♣ K75	♣ Q	♣ Q643	♣ AQJ8

89 N/E-W	90 E/Both	91 S/Nil	92 W/Both	93 N/Both	94 E/Nil	95 S/N-S	96 W/E-W
♠ K9	♠ 109	♠ 874	♠ J8754	♠ A	♠ J10	♠ A62	♠ J92
♥ 43	♥ KQ876	♥ KJ103	♥ Q93	♥ AKQ975	♥ 983	♥ AK54	♥ 92
♦ 10742	♦ Q85	♦ J109	♦ QJ10	♦ 974	♦ AQJ42	♦ A74	♦ AK8532
♣ 105432	♣ Q63	♣ J94	♣ 96	♣ 1052	♣ AQ6	♣ J53	♣ 106

97 N/Nil	98 E/N-S	99 S/E-W	100 W/Both	101 N/N-S	102 E/E-W	103 S/Both	104 W/Nil
♠ QJ9	♠ AQ4	♠ 10752	♠ 62	♠ 8654	♠ 109	♠ QJ	♠ J9753
♥ K9742	♥ 1084	♥ 32	♥ 9763	♥ KJ92	♥ A84	♥ 107543	♥ 1097
♦ Q8	♦ 3	♦ AKQJ4	♦ AKJ854	♦ AQ	♦ AK	♦ K1062	♦ K96
♣ A62	♣ KJ10952	♣ 105	♣ 5	♣ AQ5	♣ 1087643	♣ Q3	♣ 98

105 N/E-W	106 E/Both	107 S/Nil	108 W/N-S	109 N/Both	110 E/Nil	111 S/N-S	112 W/E-W
♠ K97	♠ KJ83	♠ A105	♠ J106	♠ AQJ985	♠ KQ98	♠ Q102	♠ 95
♥ 865	♥ Q9862	♥ 54	♥ AK	♥ K52	♥ 7	♥ J2	♥ Q1076
♦ Q108	♦ 74	♦ A8643	♦ KQJ65	♦ K3	♦ KQJ2	♦ A62	♦ K9753
♣ AK107	♣ A6	♣ 842	♣ KJ5	♣ A3	♣ 9852	♣ J10952	♣ 64

113 N/Nil	114 E/N-S	115 S/E-W	116 W/Both	117 N/N-S	118 E/E-W	119 S/Both	120 W/Nil
♠ QJ432	♠ Q863	♠ AKQJ106	♠ 654	♠ KJ8	♠ 95	♠ A2	♠ J5
♥ QJ	♥ J1092	♥ AQ2	♥ 87	♥ AKJ1053	♥ 9862	♥ J4	♥ QJ9
♦ A43	♦ K82	♦ A2	♦ 9864	♦ 73	♦ J74	♦ QJ2	♦ KQJ3
♣ A83	♣ Q10	♣ K4	♣ KJ73	♣ 62	♣ A1097	♣ KQ10762	♣ 10943

121 N/E-W	122 E/Both	123 S/Nil	124 W/N-S	125 N/Both	126 E/Nil	127 S/N-S	128 W/E-W
♠ 64	♠ K104	♠ 8	♠ 1076	♠ 4	♠ QJ1093	♠ 843	♠ 93
♥ K952	♥ Q72	♥ Q1053	♥ J742	♥ AKQJ7	♥ 542	♥ AJ62	♥ KQJ
♦ A964	♦ A3	♦ AK96	♦ J107	♦ 1042	♦ KQ	♦ A8	♦ K763
♣ A75	♣ AK953	♣ 10864	♣ QJ9	♣ A743	♣ KQJ	♣ KJ104	♣ 9852

129 N/Nil	130 E/Nil	131 S/E-W	132 W/Nil	133 N/N-S	134 E/E-W	135 S/Both	136 W/Nil
♠ AK7	♠ K	♠ 1086	♠ 42	♠ K	♠ 2	♠ KQ	♠ - - -
♥ Q643	♥ Q763	♥ QJ1093	♥ 6543	♥ KJ10742	♥ J9632	♥ AJ432	♥ Q109742
♦ AKJ	♦ 542	♦ AK4	♦ 5432	♦ Q65	♦ Q853	♦ 843	♦ 74
♣ 752	♣ AKJ54	♣ K6	♣ A82	♣ J96	♣ QJ10	♣ QJ6	♣ 108652

137 N/E-W	138 E/Both	139 S/Nil	140 W/N-S	141 N/Both	142 E/Nil	143 S/N-S	144 W/E-W
♠ Q98	♠ A64	♠ K	♠ A84	♠ 632	♠ QJ10	♠ AQ2	♠ Q65
♥ 109	♥ A98	♥ AQ873	♥ 104	♥ K9865	♥ J1098	♥ AK754	♥ Q10
♦ 1042	♦ KQ93	♦ 10642	♦ KQ76	♦ A54	♦ Q109	♦ AK	♦ 9543
♣ A9854	♣ A53	♣ KJ5	♣ Q986	♣ AK	♣ Q107	♣ K43	♣ 9854

145 N/Nil	146 E/N-S	147 S/E-W	148 W/Nil	149 N/N-S	150 E/E-W	151 S/Both	152 W/Nil
♠ Q942	♠ AQ432	♠ 10754	♠ 752	♠ 9854	♠ AK42	♠ 2	♠ 82
♥ J65	♥ QJ	♥ 4	♥ KQ6432	♥ 10632	♥ KQJ3	♥ AJ642	♥ 10965
♦ QJ109	♦ KJ876	♦ J9654	♦ KQ	♦ J108	♦ 7	♦ AK103	♦ 10973
♣ 92	♣ A	♣ 1093	♣ 86	♣ 72	♣ AQJ4	♣ KQ7	♣ 1095

153 N/E-W	154 E/Both	155 S/Nil	156 W/N-S	157 N/Both	158 E/Nil	159 S/N-S	160 W/E-W
♠ 8542	♠ KQJ1092	♠ Q9	♠ AQ64	♠ 109862	♠ 109843	♠ A753	♠ KQJ9854
♥ K2	♥ 10	♥ J96	♥ 9764	♥ 73	♥ 7	♥ Q84	♥ K2
♦ AK53	♦ J105	♦ K1092	♦ Q9	♦ J876	♦ Q87642	♦ K72	♦ KJ
♣ AK3	♣ 983	♣ AK53	♣ J63	♣ 94	♣ 10	♣ A104	♣ 73

(After each hand number, the dealer is given, followed by the vulnerability, e.g. E/Both means Dealer East, both sides vulnerable)

1 N/Nil
♠ 84
♥ J86
♦ J10972
♣ 864

2 E/N-S
♠ KQJ107
♥ 943
♦ J4
♣ QJ7

3 S/E-W
♠ J2
♥ J109
♦ AK1093
♣ 873

4 W/Both
♠ 52
♥ AKQ75
♦ 5432
♣ AQ

5 N/N-S
♠ AKJ10874
♥ K
♦ K75
♣ J2

6 E/E-W
♠ J107
♥ 953
♦ A754
♣ 865

7 S/Both
♠ 6
♥ 108
♦ QJ1062
♣ 87652

8 W/Nil
♠ KQJ
♥ A96
♦ Q75
♣ KQ84

9 N/E-W
♠ J6542
♥ AK5
♦ 8
♣ Q754

10 E/Both
♠ K107
♥ A98
♦ AQJ5
♣ QJ5

11 S/Nil
♠ 1097
♥ 97
♦ A7652
♣ A94

12 W/N-S
♠ AK94
♥ J97
♦ 87
♣ Q963

13 N/Both
♠ AQ962
♥ 64
♦ QJ7
♣ J84

14 E/Nil
♠ AJ10873
♥ K102
♦ J9
♣ 103

15 S/N-S
♠ Q643
♥ 107
♦ AQ83
♣ 543

16 W/E-W
♠ K1032
♥ 10754
♦ 96
♣ Q74

17 N/Nil
♠ Q8762
♥ A753
♦ Q10
♣ 94

18 E/N-S
♠ 3
♥ A987543
♦ 104
♣ A63

19 S/E-W
♠ 7
♥ 1065
♦ 1098652
♣ A73

20 W/Both
♠ 52
♥ KQ6
♦ J542
♣ Q1096

21 N/N-S
♠ AKJ93
♥ Q
♦ 7542
♣ A109

22 E/Nil
♠ Q42
♥ 92
♦ AQJ6542
♣ 7

23 S/Both
♠ J765
♥ AKQJ3
♦ 853
♣ A

24 W/Nil
♠ 10732
♥ 32
♦ K9876
♣ 72

25 N/E-W
♠ 98532
♥ AKJ10
♦ 10972
♣ - - -

26 E/Both
♠ QJ9
♥ 6543
♦ J10954
♣ 7

27 S/Nil
♠ KQJ1076
♥ A86
♦ 43
♣ J2

28 W/N-S
♠ AQJ10
♥ 5432
♦ K85
♣ AQ

29 N/Both
♠ 8
♥ 1097
♦ AK842
♣ AQ83

30 E/Nil
♠ 106432
♥ K3
♦ K7
♣ AQ52

31 S/N-S
♠ 2
♥ AKQ875
♦ A72
♣ 754

32 W/E-W
♠ AK1092
♥ AKJ
♦ 842
♣ 64

33 N/Nil
♠ AJ642
♥ K108
♦ 84
♣ A53

34 E/N-S
♠ 54
♥ J975
♦ 75
♣ 108765

35 S/E-W
♠ KJ964
♥ J82
♦ 7
♣ KQJ9

36 W/Both
♠ A63
♥ AQJ1072
♦ Q7
♣ 103

37 N/N-S
♠ A3
♥ KQJ6
♦ A83
♣ AK54

38 E/E-W
♠ A93
♥ Q9
♦ A10542
♣ 1087

39 S/Both
♠ 106
♥ 10875
♦ Q8732
♣ J10

40 W/E-W
♠ AQ64
♥ 87
♦ J632
♣ Q64

41 N/E-W
♠ J9
♥ K832
♦ 10985
♣ Q109

42 E/Both
♠ A74
♥ 73
♦ 874
♣ AJ1063

43 S/Nil
♠ Q109
♥ AKQ
♦ 8632
♣ AK9

44 W/N-S
♠ KJ6
♥ J103
♦ 1086
♣ AK106

45 N/Both
♠ QJ953
♥ 7
♦ Q875
♣ KJ4

46 E/Nil
♠ AKQ1042
♥ K83
♦ 42
♣ KQ

47 S/N-S
♠ J1097
♥ QJ93
♦ 65
♣ 1094

48 W/E-W
♠ A4
♥ 965
♦ K10
♣ AJ10932

49 N/Nil
♠ 10
♥ Q95
♦ Q108532
♣ A85

50 E/N-S
♠ Q108754
♥ 6
♦ K9
♣ QJ106

51 S/E-W
♠ A762
♥ 9
♦ AKQ4
♣ A543

52 W/Both
♠ 84
♥ Q4
♦ K842
♣ K8752

53 N/N-S
♠ AK98542
♥ - - -
♦ J8
♣ AK65

54 E/E-W
♠ 654
♥ KQ7
♦ K107
♣ QJ98

55 S/Both
♠ 95
♥ A7
♦ KJ9743
♣ A42

56 W/Nil
♠ 95
♥ Q97
♦ 10876
♣ 9862

57 N/E-W
♠ Q86
♥ J107532
♦ K9
♣ KJ

58 E/Both
♠ J6
♥ 73
♦ AKQ764
♣ 1083

59 S/Nil
♠ 98
♥ K986
♦ K852
♣ QJ10

60 W/N-S
♠ AKQ5
♥ AK64
♦ K85
♣ A10

61 N/Both
♠ J73
♥ 953
♦ Q1086
♣ KQ9

62 E/Nil
♠ KQ64
♥ AQ3
♦ Q54
♣ AKQ

63 S/N-S
♠ K98
♥ QJ98
♦ 10752
♣ K9

64 W/E-W
♠ Q5
♥ K742
♦ Q6532
♣ J3

65 N/N-S
♠ K9653
♥ 3
♦ AJ105
♣ 873

66 E/Nil
♠ 9
♥ J105
♦ 9852
♣ 109652

67 S/E-W
♠ 10
♥ J105
♦ KJ109
♣ AQJ64

68 W/Both
♠ AK874
♥ 2
♦ 965
♣ K983

69 N/N-S
♠ KQJ10542
♥ 105
♦ - - -
♣ KQJ10

70 E/E-W
♠ A8
♥ QJ3
♦ KQ1097
♣ 873

71 S/Both
♠ 10954
♥ 75
♦ Q85
♣ AQ107

72 W/Nil
♠ 9
♥ 7643
♦ 10982
♣ K943

73 N/E-W
♠ K873
♥ 1062
♦ 92
♣ AJ97

74 E/Both
♠ KJ43
♥ KQ753
♦ Q7
♣ 97

75 S/Nil
♠ AQ108
♥ 73
♦ K764
♣ J107

76 W/N-S
♠ AK8
♥ KQ62
♦ A6
♣ J843

77 N/Both
♠ 9852
♥ 4
♦ AKQ8
♣ 7432

78 E/Nil
♠ Q76
♥ J43
♦ 7642
♣ KQJ

79 S/N-S
♠ A432
♥ AJ1063
♦ J6
♣ 73

80 W/E-W
♠ 98
♥ 109654
♦ AK
♣ AQ83